Catholicisms, c.1450–c.1800
Volume 2

Alfonso Salmerón on the Scriptures

Catholicisms, c.1450–c.1800

ISSN: 2754-3080 (print)
ISSN: 2754-3099 (online)

Series Editors

James E. Kelly, Durham University
Ulrich L. Lehner, University of Notre Dame
Susannah Brietz Monta, University of Notre Dame

Series Advisory Board

Simon Ditchfield (University of York, UK), Alison Forrestal (NUI Galway, Ireland), Jean-Pascal Gay (Université Catholique de Louvain, Belgium), John McCafferty (University College Dublin, Ireland), Noel O'Regan (University of Edinburgh, UK), Erin Rowe (Johns Hopkins University, USA), Stefania Tutino (UCLA, USA), Thomas Wallnig (University of Vienna, Austria)

This new interdisciplinary series focuses on Catholicism as it grew to become a global movement. Recognizing that the early modern Catholic Church was a supranational institution, the series is not limited to one particular country or geographical area but includes work on any location where there was activity relating to Catholicism, from its old heartlands in Europe to 'new' grounds of activity in both north and south America, Asia, and Africa. The timeframe is broad, covering what might be described as a period from revolution to revolution. The late fifteenth century saw the invention of the printing press and the stirring of reform movements within the Church, while the French Revolution and the height of the Enlightenment saw the experience of Catholicism change rapidly afterwards. Cognizant of the scholarly work that is being carried out across various subject areas, the series brings together work from a range of disciplines in one place, covering subjects such as history, theology, literary studies, music, art history, material and visual culture, political theory, and gender studies.

Monographs and coherent essay collections which explore the diverse ways in which Catholicism developed across the globe during the early modern period are welcome.

Other books in the series may be viewed on the Boydell & Brewer website.

Alfonso Salmerón on the Scriptures

Theological Perspectives from a Founding Jesuit (1515–1585)

Sam Zeno Conedera, SJ

© Sam Zeno Conedera, SJ 2024

All rights reserved. Except as permitted under current legislation no part of this work may be photocopied, stored in a retrieval system, published, performed in public, adapted, broadcast, transmitted, recorded or reproduced in any form or by any means, without the prior permission of the copyright owner

The right of Sam Zeno Conedera, SJ to be identified as the author of this work has been asserted in accordance with sections 77 and 78 of the Copyright, Designs and Patents Act 1988

First published 2024

A Durham University IMEMS Press publication
in association with
The Boydell Press
an imprint of Boydell & Brewer Ltd
PO Box 9, Woodbridge, Suffolk IP12 3DF, UK
and of Boydell & Brewer Inc.
668 Mt Hope Avenue, Rochester, NY 14620–2731, USA
website: www.boydellandbrewer.com
and with the
Institute of Medieval and Early Modern Studies
University of Durham

Any permissions requests, including translation requests, should be directed to Boydell & Brewer at the address above

ISBN 978-1-914967-06-1

A CIP catalogue record for this book is available from the British Library

The publisher has no responsibility for the continued existence or accuracy of URLs for external or third-party internet websites referred to in this book, and does not guarantee that any content on such websites is, or will remain, accurate or appropriate

Contents

	Acknowledgments	vi
	List of Abbreviations	vii
	Note on the Text	viii
	Introduction	1
1.	Expounding the Gospel History	15
2.	Integrating Scripture and Tradition	49
3.	Contemplating the Mysteries	85
4.	Honoring Mary	116
5.	Saving Souls	150
6.	Defending the Church	186
7.	Promoting Good Mores	223
8.	The *Commentaries* and the Jesuits	257
	Conclusion: The Wisdom of Salmerón	291
	Bibliography	295
	Index	314

Acknowledgments

I owe a debt of gratitude to many people for the completion of this book. To my family and friends, especially Bronwen McShea, who gave valuable suggestions for improving the writing. To my fellow Jesuits, especially Tony Sholander and James Duffy, without whom the book might never have been written, and Bryan Norton and Stephen Wolfe, who helped me with the Latin translations. To the Santa Clara University Jesuit community, which provided me fellowship and a quiet place to work. To my colleagues at Saint Louis University, especially Hal Parker, who read drafts and provided helpful feedback. Finally, to my mentor Teo Ruiz, whose kindness, attention, and example have made me into a historian and a Hispanist. To him I dedicate this book.

Abbreviations

AHSI	Archivum Historicum Societatis Iesu
ARSI	Archivum Romanum Societatis Iesu
CBP	Alfonso Salmerón, *Commentarii in Omnes Epistolas B.Pauli Apostoli et Canonicas*, 4 vols. (Cologne: Antonius Hierat and Johannes Gynmnicus, 1614–1615)
CEH	Alfonso Salmerón, *Commentarii in Evangelicam Historiam et in Acta Apostolorum*, 12 vols. (Cologne: Antonius Hierat and Johannes Gynmnicus, 1612–1614)
DT	*Jacobi Laínez secundi praepositi generalis Societatis Jesu Disputationes tridentinae*, 2 vols., ed. Hermann Grisar (Innsbruck: Felicianus Rauch, 1886)
DTC	Dictionnaire de théologie catholique
ES	*Epistolae P. Alphonsi Salmeronis*, 2 vols. (Madrid: Gabriel López del Horno, 1906–1907)
FN	Fontes Narrativi
IHSI	Institutum Historicum Societatis Iesu
LM	Lainii Monumenta
MHSI	Monumenta Historica Societatis Iesu
MI	Monumenta Ignatiana
PL	Patrologia Latina

Note on the Text

Salmerón's *Commentaries* exist only in their original Latin editions. Unless otherwise indicated, all translations are my own.

Introduction

When Alfonso Salmerón received instructions in 1569 to prepare his extensive notes on Scripture for publication, he replied to his superior general Francis Borgia (1510–72) in the following terms:

> Regarding what Your Paternity commands me with respect to preparing my writings for publication, I consider it most difficult, because they are a great sea, and they are undigested, and a man does not know where to begin or end. Aside from this, it is a task that requires strength and the help of neighbors, both of which I lack. As long as my health does not improve from what it is now, I don't know how I could do anything. But I trust that the Lord will grant health to me, as I desire it to serve and obey Your Paternity in all things and entirely [*en todo y por todo*]. In the end, time, which is the great discoverer of things, will show the course of action to be taken in this matter.[1]

These words proved prescient, for time would eventually open the way for the greatest achievement of this Jesuit theologian's life.

Despite his initial reluctance, Salmerón set himself to work, and by the early 1580s, he had completed a massive commentary on the New Testament.[2] Several Jesuit editors, including Robert Bellarmine (1542–1621), Diego Páez, and Francesco Fogliani, examined various parts of it during the writing process.[3] In the meantime, Salmerón began writing on the Book of Genesis,

---

[1] *Monumenta Historica Societatis Iesu* (hereafter *MHSI*). *Epistolae P. Alphonsi Salmeronis* (Madrid: Gabriel López del Horno, 1906–1907) (hereafter *ES*), vol. 2, no. 317, 187.

[2] Jean-François Gilmont, *Les écrits sprituels des premiers jésuites: Inventaire commenté* (Rome: IHSI, 1961), 156. Gilmont believed that the volumes on the Gospels were finished by 1575, and the volumes on the Epistles by 1580. It is clear from Salmerón's correspondence that already by 1575 he had completed numerous volumes. *ES*, vol. 2, Appendix II, no. 30, 803; *ES*, vol. 2, no. 497, 653.

[3] *ES*, vol. 2, xxviii; *ES*, vol. 2, Appendix II, no. 35, 807–11.

producing an incomplete commentary that is not extant.[4] When he reached his final days in 1585, the New Testament commentary, although complete, was not yet published. On his deathbed, Salmerón made his editor Bartolomé Pérez de Nueros promise to see it through, but another twelve years were to pass before the work began coming off the presses.[5]

Salmerón's *Commentaries* consists of sixteen volumes in total, running to nearly eight thousand folio pages. The first twelve volumes were published by Luis Sánchez in Madrid between 1597 and 1601, and the remaining four all appeared in 1602.[6] Matthias Colosinus and Baretius Baretius published at least the first volume at Brescia in 1601.[7] Antonius Hierat and Johannes Gymnicus produced two complete and nearly identical editions at Cologne in 1602–4 and 1612–15, the latter of which is cited throughout the present work.[8] Like the Madrid edition, the Cologne versions are divided into two main parts. The first consists of twelve volumes entitled *Commentaries on the Gospel History and the Acts of the Apostles* (hereafter *CEH*). The second part, *Commentaries on All the Letters of Saint Paul and the Catholic Epistles* (hereafter *CBP*), is a four-volume, book-by-book exegesis of the remainder of the New Testament.[9] The first volume of the *CEH* is divided into *prolegomena*, the

---

[4] Carlos Sommervogel, *Bibliothèque de la Compagnie de Jésus*, new edition, 12 vols. (Brussels: Oscar Schepens, 1896), vol. 7, col. 483.

[5] *ES*, vol. 1, xxv–xxvi. The reason for the delay is unclear, as Pérez de Nueros testifies that Salmerón left them ready for publication.

[6] Alfonso Salmerón, *Commentarii in Evangelicam Historiam et in Acta Apostolorum*, 12 vols. (Madrid: Luis Sánchez, 1597–1601); Alfonso Salmerón, *Commentarii in Omnes Epistolas B. Pauli et Canonicas*, 4 vols. (Madrid: Luis Sánchez, 1602).

[7] Alfonso Salmerón, *Commentarii in Evangelicam Historiam et in Acta Apostolorum*, vol. 1, *De Prolegomenis in Sacrosancta Evangelia* (Brescia: Matthias Colosinus and Baretius Baretius, 1601). At least the first volume was known to the publishers at Cologne. Colosinus and Baretius composed a letter to the reader, which is reproduced in the Cologne edition, but without their names.

[8] Alfonso Salmerón, *Commentarii in Evangelicam Historiam et in Acta Apostolorum*, 12 vols. (Cologne: Antonius Hierat and Johannes Gynmnicus, 1602–1604); Alfonso Salmerón, *Commentarii in Omnes Epistolas B. Pauli et Canonicas*, 4 vols. (Cologne: Antonius Hierat and Johannes Gynmnicus, 1604); Alfonso Salmerón, *Commentarii in Evangelicam Historiam et in Acta Apostolorum*, 12 vols. (Cologne: Antonius Hierat and Johannes Gynmnicus, 1612–1614); Alfonso Salmerón, *Commentarii in Omnes Epistolas B. Pauli et Canonicas*, 4 vols. (Cologne: Antonius Hierat and Johannes Gynmnicus, 1614–15).

[9] The Apocalypse is the only book for which Salmerón does not provide a verse-by-verse commentary, on the grounds that it would be "temerarious" to do so. Instead, he offers general observations and notes on some key passages. *CBP*, vol. 4, 346.

remaining volumes of the *CEH* use chapter divisions called *tractatus*, and the *CBP* is organized into *disputationes*.¹⁰

The sixteen volumes constitute one of the most ambitious works of biblical commentary from the period, and the only original work of theology intended for publication from an original founding member of the Jesuit order. Despite this, the *Commentaries* have remained largely unknown in modern times, even among specialists in historical theology, early modern Catholicism, and Jesuit Studies. The present work is the first comprehensive study of Salmerón's magnum opus to appear in any language.

The Life of Salmerón

There are two principal sources for Salmerón's life: the volumes of correspondence and other materials edited for the *Monumenta Historica Societatis Iesu*, and the short *vita* written by the Jesuit historian and hagiographer, Pedro de Ribadeneyra (1526–1611).¹¹ The latter source was written as a kind of appendix to the same author's life of Diego Laínez (1512–65), and Ribadeneyra explains his intent to honor Salmerón not only as a first companion and fellow laborer of Ignatius of Loyola (1491–1556), but also as "a son and almost a disciple" of Laínez.¹² Ribadeneyra was also motivated by Salmerón's reputation for sanctity, given the holy manner of his death in Naples and the reaction of its citizens, who delayed his burial for an entire day by taking relics from his

---

[10] Salmeron explains his choice of *disputationes* in terms of the polemical intent of the later set of volumes. *CBP*, vol. 1, Preface, 3rv. At the same time, there is little difference in the style or methods developed across these three genres. John Willis, "A Case Study in Early Jesuit Scholarship: Alfonso Salmerón, S.J., and the Study of Sacred Scripture," in *The Jesuit Tradition in Education and Missions: A 450-Year Perspective*, ed. Christopher Chapple (Scranton, PA: University of Scranton Press, 1993), 52–68, at 64.

[11] Ribadeneyra's *vita* relies largely upon a letter of Pérez de Nueros. *ES*, vol. 2, Appendix II, no. 36, 811–19. The best modern biography is William Bangert, *Claude Jay and Alfonso Salmerón: Two Early Jesuits* (Chicago, IL: Loyola University Press, 1985). A list of major events in his life is available in Ulderico Parente, "Alfonso Salmerón 1515-1585," *AHSI* 59 (1990): 279–93.

[12] Miguel Lop Sebastià, *Alfonso Salmerón, SJ (1515–1585): Una biografía epistolar* (Madrid: Comillas, 2015), Appendix, 359–72, at 359. Ribadeneyra's *vita*, which first appeared in 1594, was later translated from Spanish into Latin and included at the beginning of the *Commentaries*. It is more accessible in its modern Spanish version, which serves as the basis of the passages translated into English.

body and clothing.[13] Despite this, there was apparently never any attempt to raise him to the altars.[14]

Alfonso Salmerón was born in September 1515 in Toledo of parents from villages near the city. He had two sisters and at least one brother, Diego, who later entered the Society of Jesus, before dying young in 1545.[15] Unlike Ignatius, who came to studies late in life, Salmerón was born for the life of the mind.[16] He arrived at the University of Alcalá de Henares in 1528 to enroll at the newly established Trilingual College, where he distinguished himself for his mastery of the classical languages and his ability to recite long selections of poetry from memory.[17] Here he became friends with Diego Laínez, and the two decided to continue their studies in Paris in 1533. Upon arriving in the Latin Quarter, their first encounter was with Ignatius, who soon took them under his wing. By January 1534, Salmerón had made the Spiritual Exercises, and in 1536 he earned his Master of Arts and completed his "year and a half" of theology.[18] By the time the companions left Paris in November, his formal education was nearly complete.

Salmerón received tonsure, minor orders, subdiaconate, and diaconate during June 1537, but was too young to be ordained a priest with the other companions, so he waited until September. They journeyed to Rome the following year and undertook the deliberations that would lead to the establishment of the Society of Jesus. Together with Paschase Broët, Salmerón was

[13] Lop Sebastià, *Alfonso Salmerón*, Appendix, 366–68.

[14] By the seventeenth century, a reputation for sanctity no longer sufficed for canonization. One also needed "acolytes" to report miracles and obtain support among influential people. Paolo Parigi, *The Rationalization of Miracles* (New York: Cambridge University Press, 2012), 80–81.

[15] Lop Sebastià, *Alfonso Salmerón*, 40.

[16] For a discussion of Ignatius as a theologian, see Ignacio Ramos Riera, "¡He aquí a nuestro Padre teólogo! [*FN* II, 202]. ¿Qué es lo 'ignaciano' y lo teológico ignaciano?" in *Dogmática ignaciana: "Buscar y hallar la voluntad divina" [Ej 1]*, ed. Gabino Uríbarri Bilbao (Madrid: Comillas, 2018), 44–69.

[17] The Trilingual College, founded in 1528, gave students a rigorous instruction in Latin, Greek, and Hebrew. The course of study for each language lasted three years, during which time students were forbidden to communicate in the vernacular. It seems reasonable to hypothesize that Salmerón completed a full course of one language and two-thirds of another, most likely Latin and Greek. See Antonio Alvar Ezquerra, "El Colegio de San Jerónimo o Colegio Trilingüe," in *Historia de la Universidad de Alcalá*, ed. Antonio Alvar Ezquerra (Alcalá de Henares: University of Alcalá de Henares, 2010), 215–22.

[18] This was a technical term that indicated completion of a basic requirement, rather than the designation of an exact duration of time.

sent on a diplomatic mission to Ireland and Scotland in 1541, which bore little fruit and led to their brief imprisonment in Lyons as suspected spies on the return trip. Despite this failure, Salmerón was entrusted with further diplomatic missions. In 1555, he undertook a legation to Germany, Poland, and Lithuania on behalf of Pope Paul IV, he made numerous visits to Flanders in the company of multiple cardinals, and he served as a go-between with the pope during tense moments in the Society's relations with the Holy See.

He spent most of the 1540s preaching in various Italian cities, including Modena, Rome, Venice, and Padua. These labors built a formidable reputation for him as a sacred orator, and preaching would become a mainstay of his ministry until his health gave out years later. He was consistently in demand wherever he went, especially for the Lenten season.[19] Salmerón's correspondence shows that he took pride in his abilities, as well as in the crowds that showed up to hear him.[20] He was given the honor of preaching at St. Peter's in Rome in 1564, and he returned to preach during Lent in 1569 at the request of Pope Pius V. Much of the *Commentaries*' content was first prepared and delivered in the context of preaching.[21]

Salmerón's most significant experience on the ecclesiastical stage, however, was his participation in all three convocations of the Council of Trent as a papal theologian. Impressed with the learning and devotion of the first companions, and confident of their ecclesiology, Pope Paul III gave to Ignatius the faculty of choosing two men to send to the council in the name of the Holy See. The Jesuit general initially did not expect Laínez and Salmerón to accomplish much in the theological arena, and he manifested greater concern for their care of the poor in Trent. Events, however, would change his mind. On December 27, 1546, the feast of John the Evangelist, the thirty-one-year-old Salmerón became the first priest to preach before the council. This sermon, which expounded John's relationship to the Blessed Virgin Mary and gave a stirring call for reform, so impressed its hearers that it was

---

[19] One scholar regards preachers for Advent and Lent as among the most prized celebrities of the day. Emily Michelson, *The Pulpit and the Press in Reformation Italy* (Cambridge: Harvard University Press, 2013), 22.

[20] To take just one example, he reports in 1554 that some members of the congregation, which was three or four times larger than it had been the year before, wished that Lent would last longer so they could hear him preach more. *ES*, vol. 1, no. 46, 114–15. This is despite the fact that, by his own account, he regularly spoke for ninety minutes to two hours at a time. *ES*, vol. 1, no. 46, 115.

[21] For a brief assessment of Salmerón's preaching based on unpublished manuscript sources, see Mario Scaduto, *L'epoca di Giacomo Laínez, 1556–1565: L'azione* (Rome: Edizioni La Civiltà Cattolica, 1974), 505–14.

published the following year, making it the first original work ever published by a Jesuit author.[22]

More importantly, Laínez and Salmerón made significant contributions to the theological debates at the first convocation, and they acquired renown as men of learning and sanctity. This redounded to the Society's benefit, since the order was still largely unknown. Subsequent popes were pleased with the service they had rendered and sent them to the additional convocations. Although he became increasingly disillusioned with the council, Salmerón was one of very few participants in all three convocations. Their common labors forged a closer bond of friendship and theological mindset between Laínez and Salmerón, and played a significant role in the conciliar debates.[23]

In 1549, Salmerón received a teaching mission at the University of Ingolstadt in Bavaria. In preparation for this, he sat for doctoral exams in theology at Bologna, along with Peter Canisius (1521–97) and Claude Jay (1504–52). Salmerón later recalled without fondness their experience before the rigorous Dominican examiners, but it is a testament to his memory and learning that he earned his doctorate after a relatively brief period of formal study of theology. The teaching mission, however, was not a great success. The students were mostly dumbfounded by the Latin lectures of Salmerón, who in turn was unable to communicate in German, which left him mostly unable to exercise ministry outside the classroom. He was recalled to Rome in 1550 to discuss the draft of the Jesuit *Constitutions*, but this was only a stopping point on the way to the longest assignment of his life.

In the early 1550s, Naples was one of numerous major cities that showed interest in establishing a Jesuit college, and Salmerón was sent there to preach Lent in 1551 as a way to encourage the endeavor. Although other commitments would frequently take him away from the city, it was his primary base of operations for the remainder of his life. Assigned as superintendent of the

---

[22] The text has been published numerous times since then and translated into English. *Oratio Reverendi Patris Magistri Alphonsi Salmeronis de Societate Iesu Theologi, nuper in Concilio Tridentino habita, in qua ad exemplar Divi Ioannis Evangelistae vera Praelatorum forma describitur* (Rome: Stephanus Nicolinus, 1547); Juan Tejada y Ramiro, *Colección de cánones y de todos los concilios*, vol. 4 (Madrid, 1859), 755–62; John Hughes, "Alfonso Salmeron: His Work at the Council of Trent," (PhD dissertation: University of Kentucky, 1974), Appendix III, 236–52.

[23] For a thorough study of their contributions at Trent, especially concerning the Eucharist, see Niccolo Steiner, *Diego Laínez und Alfonso Salmerón auf dem Konzil von Trient: Ihr Beitrag zur Eucharistie-und Messopferthematik* (Stuttgart: Kohlhammer, 2019).

school in 1552, he was made the first provincial of Naples in 1558.[24] During this time, he was occupied primarily with administrative affairs, overseeing the growth of the Society in southern Italy, and maintaining close relations with the viceroys who ruled the Kingdom of Naples in the name of the Spanish King, Philip II. He briefly served as the order's vicar general while Laínez undertook a mission to France in the early 1560s. Already in 1566, Salmerón reported his declining physical condition: loss of vision, hearing, and teeth, and a lack of energy.[25] It was not until 1576, however, that he was relieved of duty as provincial and replaced by Claudio Acquaviva (1543–1615). Unlike other Spanish Jesuits whom superior general Everard Mercurian removed from positions of power in Italy and sent back home, Salmerón remained in Naples as the province's *éminence grise*, where he prayed and wrote until his death. Along with Ribadeneyra, he was one of the first Jesuits to undertake writing as a primary mission.

Although the present work is more concerned with the *Commentaries* than their author's life, it is worth recording a few assessments of Salmerón's character. In a letter to Duke William of Bavaria, Ignatius praises Canisius and Salmerón together for their integrity of life, knowledge of the Scriptures, and erudition.[26] According to Luis Gonçalves, Ignatius once said in response to the accusation that Jesuits were hypocrites, that the only hypocrites he had ever met in the Society were Salmerón and Nicholas Bobadilla (1511–90). Gonçalves adds that the remark was made in their presence, and that both men had a notably happy appearance opposed to hypocrisy.[27] Bernardino

---

[24] As Oberholzer has shown, Salmerón was one of the companions with whom Ignatius took counsel on the most important matters. He regards it as a mystery that Salmerón was made a provincial only after Ignatius's death. Paul Oberholzer, "El círculo de los primeros compañeros y las competencias en el establecimiento de la nueva Orden," in *Diego Lainez (1512–1565) and his Generalate: Jesuit with Jewish Roots, Close Confidant of Ignatius of Loyola, Preeminent Theologian of the Council of Trent*, ed. Paul Oberholzer (Rome: IHSI, 2015), 15–34.

[25] *ES*, vol. 2, no. 269, 72. He nearly died in Padua in 1547 of the plague, and was afflicted by quartan fever for the rest of his life.

[26] *MHSI. Monumenta Ignatiana* (hereafter *MI*). *Sancti Ignatii de Loyola epistolae et instructiones* (Madrid, 1903–1911), vol. 2, no. 873, 541.

[27] *MHSI. MI. Fontes Narrativi de S. Ignatio de Loyola et de Societatis Iesu initiis* (hereafter *FN*), vol. 1, *Narrationes scriptae ante annum 1557*, ed. Dionisio Fernández Zapico and Cándido de Dalmases (Rome: MHSI, 1943), 541, 730. The meaning of Ignatius's words is difficult to decipher. Although there is a slight discrepancy between the Portuguese and Spanish texts of Gonçalves's *Memoriale*, both versions connect this episode to Ignatius's rules for modesty, which give precise instructions about Jesuit manners of dress, speech, facial expressions, movement of the hands,

Realino says it was a singular grace to have entered the Society during the time of this "great pillar of Christian truth."[28] Ribadeneyra effusively praises Salmerón's virtues and holiness, integrity, courteousness, contempt for honors, diligent study, observance of the Church's rites and ceremonies, and numerous other qualities.[29] Many other contemporaries offered words of praise during his life and after his death, as the *Monumenta* volumes attest.

Less flattering portrayals may also be found. Robert Bellarmine reports that when he showed Salmerón the errors that he had found in his "immense volumes," at first the latter became angry and tried to defend his positions, but "on the following day he emended everything with a peaceful mind, and, unless I am mistaken, this acquaintance benefited him a great deal."[30] Perhaps basing his judgment partly on Bellarmine's story, Bangert describes Salmerón thus:

> Open and friendly in his youth—Ignatius used to tease him about his naïveté—he became grave and solemn, even gloomy, under the burdens as religious superior and conciliar theologian. His chief weakness was excessive sensitivity, petulance, even a tinge of hysteria, when criticized or challenged. In some ways this brilliant man never grew up.[31]

Given that the *Commentaries* were written during Salmerón's old age, the present study may help adjudicate between these conflicting assessments.

A Neglected Source

Before delving into the content of the *Commentaries*, it is important to note that they have received surprisingly little attention since they came to light at the turn of the seventeenth century. During and after his lifetime, Salmerón's work was occasionally honored. The province congregation of Upper Germany recommended that General Congregation III (1573) encourage and

---

and so forth. Did Ignatius mean that the two men in question were models of the rules of modesty, or violators of them? One scholar thinks that the meaning is that Salmerón and Bobadilla were better than they seemed. Javier Burrieza Sánchez, "Diego Laínez: La Compañía de Jesús más allá de Ignacio de Loyola," in *Diego Laínez (1512–1565): Jesuita y teólogo del Concilio*, ed. José Garcia de Castro Valdés (Madrid: Comillas, 2013), 55–99, at 79.

[28] Mario Scaduto, *L'epoca di Giacomo Laínez, 1556–1565: Il governo* (Rome: Edizioni La Civiltà Cattolica, 1964), 301.

[29] Lop Sebastià, *Alfonso Salmerón*, Appendix, 370.

[30] *The Autobiography of St. Robert Bellarmine*, trans. Ryan Grant (Post Falls, ID: Mediatrix Press, 2016), 47.

[31] Bangert, *Jay and Salmerón*, 355–56.

strengthen Jesuits preparing works for publication, mentioning Salmerón by name.[32] He also appears in the *Imago Primi Saeculi* and other commemorative volumes.[33] The Jesuits Pedro Morales (1538–1614) and Cornelius A Lapide (1567–1637) refer to him occasionally in their commentaries on Scripture.[34] The nineteenth-century German theologian Matthias Scheeben regarded the late sixteenth and early seventeenth centuries as a golden age for Catholic exegesis, and he lionized Salmerón as a representative of it.[35] None of this, however, has ever translated into a wide readership.

In the meantime, Salmerón has had several critics. Baroni says that he did not contribute to serious progress in the study of Scripture.[36] De Lanversin, while acknowledging Salmerón's learning, takes exception to his literalism and preference for the safest exegetical and theological positions.[37] John Hughes, in his study of Salmerón's work at Trent, largely follows de Lanversin, repeating some of his sentences verbatim.[38] By and large, however, Salmerón has simply been ignored. Sympathetic writers, such as Willis and Delville, have only used his writings in the context of larger historical-exegetical studies.[39] The few works focused on the *Commentaries* exclusively are brief or deal with relatively narrow topics.[40] John O'Malley, while praising Salmerón's erudition

---

[32] Bangert, *Jay and Salmerón*, 331.

[33] John Bolland, ed., *Imago Primi Saeculi Societatis Jesu* (Antwerp: Balthasar Moretus, 1640), 291–92; Matthias Tanner, ed., *Societatis Jesu Apostolorum Imitatrix* (Prague: Charles University, 1694), 41.

[34] Pedro Morales, *In Caput Primum Matthaei* (Lyons: Horatius Cardon, 1614), passim; Cornelius A Lapide, *Commentarii in quatuor Evangelia* (Antwerp: Martin Nutius, 1639), passim.

[35] Matthias Scheeben, *Handbook of Catholic Dogmatics*, bk. 1, *Theological Epistemology*, pt. 2, *Theological Knowledge Considered in Itself*, trans. Michael Miller (Steubenville, OH: Emmaus Academic, 2019), §1084–86, 247.

[36] Victor Baroni, *La Contre-Reforme devant la Bible* (Lausanne: La Concorde, 1943), 246.

[37] F. de Lanversin, "Salmerón, Alphonse," in *Dictionnaire de théologie catholique*, (Paris: Letouzey et Ané, 1898–1950) (hereafter *DTC*), vol. 14, pt. 1, cols. 1040–47. He considered the *Commentaries* inferior to the work of Juan de Maldonado.

[38] Hughes, "Alfonso Salmeron," 29–35.

[39] John Willis, "Love Your Enemies: Sixteenth Century Interpretations," (PhD dissertation: University of Chicago, 1989); Jean-Pierre Delville, *L'Europe de l'exégèse au XVIe siècle: Interprétations de la parabole des ouvriers à la vigne (Mt 20:1–16)* (Leuven: Leuven University Press, 2004), 534–48.

[40] Melquíades Andrés, "La compasión de la Virgen al pie de la cruz, deducida de su triple gracia, según Salmerón," *Estudios Marianos* 5 (1946): 359–88; Ignacio

as "outstanding," rarely cites him in *The First Jesuits*.[41] Markus Friedrich's magisterial survey of Jesuit history makes no reference to Salmerón's magnum opus.[42] Others have lamented the general neglect of the *Commentaries* and their author.[43]

This neglect needs to be remedied for three reasons. First, as already noted, the *Commentaries* are a major example of the flourishing of Catholic biblical studies in the late sixteenth and early seventeenth centuries, a phenomenon that is now receiving more scholarly attention.[44] Second, Salmerón is an important witness to the direction that Catholic theology took in the decades following Trent. The council looms large in the *Commentaries* without dominating them, and Salmerón's exegesis incorporates both what Trent actually said and what he wishes it had said. Third, the *Commentaries* are an indispensable source on the early Society of Jesus. Modern research has attempted to balance the traditional focus on Ignatius with attention to the other founding members. Among them, Salmerón alone composed a major work of theology for the educated reader, making the *Commentaries* a unique source for the theological education, mindset, and priorities of the first companions.

Riudor, "Influencia de San Bernardo en la mariología de Salmerón y Suárez," *Estudios Marianos* 14 (1954): 329–53; Igna Kramp, "Der Jesuit Alfonso Salmerón (1515–1585) als humanistischer Theologe: Ähnlichkeiten und Unterschiede zu Erasmus von Rotterdam," *Theologie und Philosophie* 90 (2015): 504–27; Santiago Madrigal Terrazas, "'Nuestra santa madre Iglesia hierárchica' [Ej 353]: La Iglesia de Jesucristo según los *Commentarii* de Salmerón" in *Dogmática ignaciana: "Buscar y hallar la voluntad divina" [Ej 1]*, ed. Gabino Uríbarri Bilbao (Madrid: Comillas, 2018), 468–502; Sam Zeno Conedera, "Forgotten Saint: The Life and Writings of Alfonso Salmerón, SJ," *Studies in the Spirituality of Jesuits* 52, vol. 4 (2020): 1–34.

[41] John O'Malley, *The First Jesuits* (Cambridge: Harvard University Press, 1993), 259.

[42] Markus Friedrich, *The Jesuits: A History*, trans. John Noël Dillon (Princeton: Princeton University Press, 2022).

[43] David Martín López, "Claroscuros de la vida de Alfonso Salmerón Díaz, un jesuita ejemplar de primera generación," *Magallánica* 2, vol. 4 (2016): 29–56; Marius Reiser, "The History of Catholic Exegesis, 1600–1800," in *The Oxford Handbook of Early Modern Theology, 1600–1800*, eds. Ulrich Lehner, Richard Muller, and A.G. Roeber (New York: Oxford University Press, 2016), 75–88, at 78.

[44] Luke Murray, *Jesuit Biblical Studies after Trent: Franciscus Toletus and Cornelius A Lapide* (Göttingen: Vandenhoeck and Ruprecht, 2019); Antonio Gerace, *Biblical Scholarship in Louvain in the 'Golden' Sixteenth Century* (Gottingen: Vandenhoeck and Ruprecht, 2019).

Division of the Present Work

With this rationale in mind, the present work aims to provide a serious exposition and critical study of the *Commentaries*. Simply put, the praise and blame of earlier writers lack adequate foundation in a coherent understanding of Salmerón's vision and project. The lack of such a study is perhaps understandable, given that his work is lengthy, repetitive, and defies easy summary or categorization. Like many exegetes of his time, Salmerón was not concerned with the New Testament narrowly conceived, for he saw it as containing, whether explicitly or implicitly, the whole of Christian revelation. As de Lanversin says, "one may not separate in Salmerón the exegete from the theologian."[45] The key for this study was finding a question that could sift and organize the work's prodigious content without losing the thread of unity.

The organizing question of the present work is the following: how does Salmerón understand the tasks of the theologian? It was chosen on the basis of two considerations. First, Salmerón unites rather than separates the labors of exegesis and theology, such that his magnum opus is both a commentary and a work of biblical and dogmatic theology. In his mind, no one rightly may be called a theologian who does not take Scripture as his point of departure; conversely, no one may be called an exegete who ignores or rejects the other ways God has revealed himself to mankind. Second, a number of major themes and areas of emphasis recur in the *Commentaries*, so much so that they emerge as Salmerón's theological priorities. Accordingly, the aforementioned question seemed like the best way to capture both the unity and internal differentiation of the *Commentaries*.

Igna Kramp, one of the few contemporary scholars who has written on the *Commentaries*, claims in a concise article that Salmerón comes very close to Erasmus of Rotterdam's (1466–1536) ideal of the theologian. She identifies just two major differences between them: the importance of outward religious practice, and the value of scholastic theology.[46] As it happens, Salmerón himself was highly critical of Erasmus, and it is not difficult to see why. His vigorous defense of the Vulgate, his attempt to integrate Scripture, tradition, and ecclesiastical authority, his strong Mariology, and his militant attitude towards heresy make for significant contrasts with the Dutch humanist. Although Kramp mentions that Salmerón, like Martin Luther (1483–1546), was exasperated with Erasmus's neutrality on confessional issues, she does

---

[45] De Lanversin, "Salmerón, Alphonse," in *DTC*, vol. 14, pt. 1, col. 1041.
[46] Kramp, "Alfonso Salmerón," 524.

not account for the Jesuit theologian's persistent, fiery polemic against him.[47] Granted that he owed more to the pioneering humanism of Erasmus than he was willing to admit, Salmerón clearly understood the tasks of the theologian in such a way that Erasmus represented a prime example of the failure to accomplish them. This is because Salmerón saw the ordering of parts within the theological whole in a different way, so that the emphases, methods, and tools of biblical humanism do not have quite the same meaning or purpose in his thought as they do in Erasmus's.

There are other authors besides Erasmus, however, who offer a better perspective on Salmerón's *Commentaries*. Although it lies beyond the scope of the present work to provide a full comparative study of early modern exegesis, several writers have been selected to place Salmerón within context. Delville cites the year 1571 as a point of departure for "Baroque exegesis," which he says was becoming an affair of great specialists.[48] This year corresponds to the publication of Cornelius Jansen the Elder's (1510–76) *Commentary on his Concordance and the Whole Gospel History*, which was likely one of the principal influences on Salmerón, as will be explained further on.[49] Juan de Maldonado (1533–83) was a famous Jesuit exegete of the late sixteenth century whose *Commentaries on the Four Gospels* was published posthumously in 1596–97.[50] Another Jesuit, the Portuguese exegete Sebastião Barradas (1543–1615) published four volumes of *Commentaries on the Gospel Concordance and History* at the turn of the seventeenth century.[51] This little-known work bears many similarities to Salmerón's.[52] Finally, the former Catholic priest and abbot turned Huguenot leader Augustin Marlorat (c. 1506–62) published *A Catholic Ecclesiastical Exposition*

---

[47] Kramp, "Alfonso Salmerón," 504.

[48] Delville, *L'Europe de l'exégèse*, 547–53.

[49] Cornelius Jansen, *Commentariorum in suam concordiam, ac totam historiam evangelicam* (Louvain: Petrus Zangrius Tiletanus, 1571).

[50] Maldonado's *Commentaries* went through numerous editions over the two decades following their first publication. The one cited in the present work is the 1602 Mainz edition. Juan de Maldonado, *Commentarii in quatuor evangelistas* (Mainz: Arnoldus Mylius, 1602). Acquaviva intended to send Maldonado to Naples to assist Salmerón with the editing of his *Commentaries* in 1583, but Maldonado's sudden death prevented that. *ES*, vol. 2, no. 524b, 720–21.

[51] Sebastião Barradas, *Commentaria in concordiam et historiam evangelicam*, 4 vols. (Mainz: Hermann Mylius, 1600–1609). Although the first volume was published at Coimbra in 1599, the Mainz edition appears to be the first complete version.

[52] Although Barradas's later volumes occasionally reference Salmeron's *Commentaries*, Barradas had substantially completed his own work before the publication of Salmerón's.

of the New Testament in 1561, a year before his execution on the charge of high treason for his seizure of the city of Rouen. As will be explained in the next chapter, Salmerón considered his *Commentaries* as a rebuttal to Marlorat.[53] All of these authors shed light on the historical and intellectual context of Salmerón's magnum opus.

Each of the first seven chapters of the present work is dedicated to one of the tasks of the theologian. "Expounding the Gospel History" accounts for the unusual organizational schema of the *Commentaries*, as well as the central role that history plays in the author's understanding of Scripture. "Integrating Scripture and Tradition" explains Salmerón's view that the Bible must be read as harmonious with other sources, such as the Church Fathers and Scholastic Doctors, the ecumenical councils, and the teachings of popes. "Contemplating the Mysteries" shows how Salmerón aimed to lead the reader into prayer, as well as how he organized the principal content of the Christian faith. "Honoring Mary" illustrates the crucial role that the Blessed Virgin plays in numerous aspects of Salmerón's theology, whereas "Saving Souls" explains his position on the key topics of justification, the theological virtues, and the Church's sacraments. "Defending the Church" explores Salmerón's ecclesiology: its mystical dimension, its theory of civil and ecclesiastical polity, and its sustained polemic against perceived enemies of the Church. "Promoting Good Mores" demonstrates Salmerón's concern for Christian praxis on several levels—liturgy, the relations between the sexes, and moral theology more generally—and illustrates his view that the faith demands coherence between belief and action. The final chapter, "The *Commentaries* and the Jesuits," departs from this schema of the tasks of the theologian to answer the crucial question of how Salmerón portrayed his own religious community, and how his thought compares with that of his close friend Diego Laínez.

Salmerón's initial reluctance to undertake the *Commentaries* should not blind the reader to the pleasure he took in leaving for posterity the fruits of his meditation upon Scripture. According to Juan de Polanco's *Chronicon*, Salmerón was known as the "Solomon of Naples" in that city on account of his surname and his prodigious learning.[54] In the general preface of the

---

[53] Augustin Marlorat, *Novi Testamenti catholica expositio ecclesiastica, id est, ex universis probatis theologis (quos Dominus diversis suis ecclesiis dedit) excerpta, a quodam verbi Dei ministro, diu multumque in theologia versato, sive bibliotheca expositionum Novi Testamenti, id est, expositio ex probatis omnibus theologis collecta, et in unum corpus singulari artificio conflate, quae instar bibliothecae multis expositrobus refertae esse possit*, 2 vols. (Geneva: Henricus Stephanus, 1561).

[54] MHSI. *Vita Ignatii Loiolae et rerum Societatis Jesu historia, auctore Joanne Alphonso de Polanco, eiusdem Societatis sacerdote* (Madrid: Agustín Avrial, 1898), vol. 6, 263.

Commentaries, he observes that it is easy to please people with preaching, but harder to give something of lasting value, and that after a lifetime of study, he has finally obtained the opportunity to write something for the good of the Church of God.⁵⁵ He describes the Gospels as the kernel and compendium of all Scripture, the key to all the mysteries, and the sea of the immense wisdom of God.⁵⁶ If the *Commentaries* are the distillation of Salmerón's lifelong engagement with Scripture, then the present work is a distillation of the *Commentaries*. Like Solomon, the Jesuit theologian wished to leave behind wisdom of lasting value.

Despite Salmerón's intent to communicate perennial truths, not all of his ideas have stood the test of time. Some of the content and tone of the *Commentaries* may shock or scandalize readers accustomed to the more irenic approach towards members of other Christian communities and other religions that the Catholic Church and the Society of Jesus have undertaken in recent times. Salmerón's polemical stance towards Protestants and Jews in particular reflects both the circumstances of his age and the sources upon which he relied. His views are communicated here as a matter of historical record, not in order to justify or perpetuate them.

While the present work aims to provide a comprehensive view of the *Commentaries*, they are so extensive that many things have been passed over. None of these omissions seem to obscure the overall significance of the work, but such a claim depends on the limitations and priorities of my own judgment. The present work is the definitive study of the *Commentaries* so long as it remains the only study. Perusing these prodigious tomes is assuredly worth the effort, for the *Commentaries* are very much the "great sea" that their author described in 1569. There I encountered tempests and doldrums, favorable winds, undiscovered shores, strange marvels, and even the occasional monster.

Finally, I should answer a question that has been posed to me numerous times: whether I "identify" with Alfonso Salmerón. The answer must be negative, for a span of several centuries separates him from the present, and in any case the historian's relationship with the departed is subject to certain limitations. At the same time, when looking at the sixteenth century through his eyes, I often perceived that it was an age at once distant and strangely familiar, as if seen *per speculum et in aenigmate* (1 Cor 13:12).

For his role in the religious reform of Naples, see Romeo de Maio, *Alfonso Carafa: Cardinale di Napoli (1540–1565)* (Vatican City: Biblioteca Apostolica Vaticana, 1961).

⁵⁵ *CEH*, vol. 1, Preface, 3v–4r.

⁵⁶ *CEH*, vol. 1, Preface, 6r.

1   Expounding the Gospel History

After explaining that historians ordinarily must wait until their subject has performed heroic deeds before they begin writing about him, Salmerón observes that

> the matter is otherwise with Christ, who before he was born had many historians who described the mysteries of the Messiah with words and writings, deeds and sufferings, and on account of their certitude, foretold in advance those things that would come to pass. They did not speak only of Christ's great and heroic deeds, but also the least little things, because all things are great and deep in Christ.[1]

This passage illustrates well Salmerón's understanding of Jesus's unique place at the center of history, as well as the central role that history plays in his theological project.

The core of Salmerón's exegetical work consists of twelve volumes on the "Gospel history" and the Acts of the Apostles. The concept of the Gospel history, as well as various other senses of *historia*, were central to his understanding of Scripture and the tasks of the theologian. The unusual structure of the *Commentaries*, which has puzzled the few scholars who have studied them, can be at least partly explained in terms of these historical ideas. Salmerón provided a definition and taxonomy of history that placed the Gospels and their authors at the top of an interlocking hierarchy of literary genres. He practiced historical inquiry himself to demonstrate the harmoniousness of the four Gospels and their agreement with other ancient writings.[2] He explained the history of the world in terms of God's action within it, with the Incarnation as the pivotal moment. Finally, Salmerón was attentive to the historical and social context, or "life setting," of the biblical world, so as to assist the

---

[1]   *CEH*, vol. 4, 569.

[2]   Although Salmerón certainly used history for polemical purposes, the *Commentaries* support the thesis that Catholics and Protestants were also interested in history for its own sake. Irena Backus, *Historical Method and Confessional Identity in the Era of the Reformation (1378–1615)* (Boston, MA: Brill, 2003), 2–3.

reader in understanding the sacred text. Even if appreciation for history was characteristic of early Jesuit theology and education, Salmerón's interest was unusually high.³

The Structure and Rationale of the *Commentaries*

One of the most perplexing aspects of Salmerón's work is its structure. Although partially dependent on existing models, the *Commentaries* blend them in a way that appears to be unique in the history of Catholic exegesis.⁴ Their author clearly borrowed from the genre of the Gospel harmony, in which all the passages from the four evangelists are rearranged according to the commentator's understanding of their chronological order, and with apparent discrepancies smoothed over. Notable examples of this approach can be found in patristic authors, such as Tatian and Augustine, and by the early seventeenth century, Catholics and Protestants alike had authored about fifty original works of this genre.⁵ Salmerón departed from a straightforward Gospel harmony in two significant ways.

First, Salmerón provided a stout volume of *Prolegomena*, which lays out his positions on a wide variety of methodological issues. Second, and more importantly, Salmerón switched his organizational schema about a third of the way through his treatment of the Gospels. Volume 2 discusses the deeds of the Eternal Word prior to the Incarnation, Volume 3 deals with the infancy of Jesus, and Volume 4 follows his life up to the final entrance into Jerusalem.

---

³ Pietro Leturia, "Il contributo della Compagnia di Gesù alla formazione delle scienze storiche," in *La Compagnia di Gesù e le scienze sacre: conferenze commemorative del quarto centenario dalla fondazione della Compagnia di Gesù tenute alla Pontificia università gregoriana, 5–11 novembre 1941* (Rome: Gregorian University, 1942), 161–202; Markus Friedrich, *The Jesuits: A History*, trans. John Noël Dillon (Princeton: Princeton University Press, 2022), 313–14.

⁴ "Alfonso Salmerón wrote biblical commentaries that have no parallel in the history of exegesis, at least up to his own day. Arguably, he produced what can be called the first interdisciplinary commentaries on the Bible in the modern era." John Willis, "A Case Study in Early Jesuit Scholarship: Alfonso Salmerón, S.J., and the Study of Sacred Scripture," in *The Jesuit Tradition in Education and Missions: A 450-Year Perspective*, ed. Christopher Chapple (Scranton, PA: University of Scranton Press, 1993), 52–68, at 65.

⁵ Arnaldo Pinto Cardoso, *Da Antiga à Nova Aliança: Relações entre o Antigo e o Novo Testamento em Sebsatião Barradas (1543–1615)* (Lisbon: Instituto Nacional de Investigação Científica, 1987), 46. For an overview of the Gospel harmony in this period, see Kirsten MacFarlane, "Gospel Harmonies and the Genres of Biblical Scholarship in Early Modern Europe," *Renaissance Quarterly* 76 (2023): 1027–67.

Much of the material of Jesus's public ministry, however, is distributed into four separate volumes. Volume 5 deals with the Sermon on the Mount, Volume 6 comments on the miracles of Jesus, Volume 7 is dedicated to his parables, and Volume 8 is given over to his public disputations. This "thematic interlude" disrupts the chronological progression of events, even though Salmerón attempted to integrate these events into the overall narrative.

The chronological arrangement of the *Commentaries on the Gospel History* resumes in Volume 9, which deals with the Last Supper, continues through the Passion and the Resurrection in Volumes 10 and 11, respectively, and concludes with the commentary on Acts of the Apostles in Volume 12. The *Commentaries on All the Letters of Saint Paul and the Catholic Epistles* treat each remaining book of the New Testament individually in the order of their appearance in the Vulgate. This means that Salmerón sought to blend several organizational schemas: a discussion of method (Volume 1), Gospel harmony (Volumes 2–4 and 9–11), thematic (Volumes 5–8), and book-by-book (Volume 12 of *CEH*, Volumes 1–4 of *CBP*).[6] On the face of it, it is a haphazard arrangement, and one that defies easy explanation. Given his insistence on conformity to tradition, it is remarkable that Salmerón chose to organize the *Commentaries* in this unprecedented way.

He offered only limited insight into his decision. In a brief secondary preface to the whole work, he explains that it is divided into twelve volumes, following a chronological progression through the life of Christ, but he does not explain the purpose of the thematic interlude.[7] In the preface to Volume 4, he says that his intent is to divide up the treatment of the Lord's public ministry into three parts to make the work more concise, and that he has extracted the Sermon on the Mount, miracles, parables, and disputations from this narration and put them in their own volumes, for the sake of greater convenience.[8] This account, unfortunately, does little to illuminate his approach, not only because it is an inexact description of the organization of the volumes, but also because it is unclear how it makes the work more concise or convenient for the reader.[9]

---

[6] The first volume of *CBP* opens with chapters that are effectively *prolegomena* to the works of Paul, even though they are labeled *disputationes*.

[7] *CEH*, vol. 1, Preface, 7r.

[8] *CEH*, vol. 4, Preface, 3rv.

[9] Willis suggests that the chronological ordering was inspired by the *Spiritual Exercises*, but Salmerón does not explain his choice in these terms. Willis, "Case Study," 63.

Even if any explanation must be conjectural in the absence of explicit evidence, it is possible to construct a plausible hypothesis. It has already been observed that Salmerón considered his writings to be "a great sea" when he received from Francis Borgia the command to publish them in 1569. He possessed a considerable body of material, but no organizational schema for it. The idea for a "Gospel history" appears to have come from Cornelius Jansen the Elder, the first bishop of Ghent, who in 1571 published his *Commentaries on the Concordance and Complete Gospel History*.[10] This was a follow-up to his *Concordance of the Gospels*, published in 1549. The latter was a brief chronological arrangement of all the Gospel passages, whereas the former included commentary on them.[11]

There are several reasons for thinking that Salmerón followed Jansen in his organization of the *Commentaries*. First, Jansen used the distinctive term "Gospel history" in the title of his work, which seems to be its earliest appearance among Catholic writers.[12] Second, Salmerón was familiar with Jansen and admired him. In a letter of 1571, Salmerón thanks Cardinal Sirleto for sending him a copy of Jansen's commentary on Ecclesiasticus, which had been published in 1569. Although he has some critical words for the difficulty of the text and the author's translation of Greek into Latin, Salmerón calls Jansen "a great man" [*un grand' uomo da bene*] whose writing is wise and orthodox.[13] Salmerón must have eventually obtained a copy of Jansen's commentary on the Gospels, for he cited it periodically, while repeating his praise of the author.[14]

In addition, Giovan Francesco Araldo, a Jesuit chronicler in Naples in the late sixteenth century, made an explicit link between Salmerón and Jansen.

---

[10] Cornelius Jansen, *Commentariorum in suam concordiam, ac totam historiam evangelicam* (Louvain: Petrus Zangrius Tiletanus, 1571).

[11] For an introduction to Jansen's exegesis, see Jean-Paul Delville, "Jansenius de Gand (1510–1576) et l'exégèse des paraboles," *Revue d'Histoire Ecclésiastique* 92, no. 1 (1997): 38–69.

[12] Calvin uses the expression *historia Evangelica* several times at the beginning of his *Gospel Harmony*. The first use appears in the letter to the leaders of Frankfurt, and the other two in the *argumentum*. John Calvin, *Harmonia ex Evangelistis tribus composita* (Geneva: Etienne Vignon, 1582), a3r, a3v, a4r. A modern translator renders it as the "Gospel story." John Calvin, *A Harmony of the Gospels: Matthew, Mark, and Luke*, trans. A.W.N. Morrison (Grand Rapids, MI: Eerdmans, 1994), vol. 1, ix. Unlike Calvin and Jansen, Salmerón consciously coordinated the term with other genres of historical writing, which seems to favor the translation "Gospel history," at least in the context of the *Commentaries*.

[13] *ES*, vol. 2, no. 338, 241.

[14] *CEH*, vol. 1, 458. Salmerón calls him "truly a man wondrously learned."

At the end of July [1569], finding himself still tired and unable to preach on account of old age, Father Salmerón began to write about the Gospels, and make a good commentary [*fare una bella catena*]. After it was finished a few years later, he discovered that Jansen had written a very beautiful work, and had brought it to light and published it. For this, or for some other reasonable cause, the work of the said Salmerón was never published during his life or after it, despite how hard he had worked on it. And in this year of 1595, when I write this, nothing is said about publishing it.[15]

There are numerous problems with this account. First, Araldo was apparently unaware that Francis Borgia had instructed Salmerón to undertake the project. Second, he seemed to think that Salmerón decided not to publish his work because Jansen's commentary made it redundant. Not only is Salmerón's text much longer than Jansen's, but the former includes numerous references to the latter. Third, Salmerón's correspondence shows that he continued to write into the final years of his life, and on his death bed he made his editor, Pérez de Nueros, promise to bring the *Commentaries* to completion.[16]

Araldo's observation that there was no plan to publish the *Commentaries* is most likely owed to the fact that Pérez de Nueros was sent to Spain in 1587 to be the rector and professor of theology at the Jesuit college at Alcalá. After attending General Congregation V, he found himself at the Jesuit college in Madrid when in 1597 he was summoned to Rome as assistant for Spain, in which capacity he served until 1608.[17] It seems likely that Pérez de Nueros took the draft of the *Commentaries* with him to Spain in 1587, completed the preparation of the volumes in the 1590s, and gave them to a publisher in Madrid before leaving for Rome.[18] There is evidence, however, that the Jesuit

---

[15] Francesco Divenuto, *Napoli, l'Europa e la Compagnia di Gesù nella "Cronica" di Giovan Francesco Araldo* (Naples: Edizioni Scientifiche Italiane, 1998), 102.

[16] *ES*, vol. 1, xxv–xxvi.

[17] F.B. Medina, "Pérez de Nueros y Maynar, Bartolomé," in *Diccionario histórico de la Compañía de Jesús*, ed. Charles O'Neill (Madrid: Comillas, 2001), vol. 3, 3092–93.

[18] This theory is supported by the fact that the *Commentaries* include a dedicatory letter from Pérez de Nueros to Claudio Acquaviva, which states that he had the work published at the latter's instruction. Boero, however, claimed that it was Fogliani who finished revisions of the *Commentaries* in Naples, then took all of Salmerón's manuscripts with him to Rome. Only later were they sent to Madrid, where they were finally published. This theory is based partly on a letter of Fogliani to Acquaviva from 1585, but clearly considerable time was to pass before the *Commentaries* actually came to light. Giuseppe Boero, *Vie du Père Jacques Lainez…suivie de la biographie du Père Alphonse Salmerón*, trans. Victor de Coppier (Paris: Descleé de Brouwer, 1894), 304; *ES*, vol. 2, Appendix II, no. 35, 807–11.

brother Cristobal López, Ribadeneyra's longtime assistant, was supervising the publication of Salmerón's works in 1602–03.[19]

Jansen may have been the proximate inspiration for Salmerón's idea of the Gospel history, but the term and the concept appear elsewhere in the exegesis of the period. Barradas's harmony has "Gospel history" in its title, and Marlorat and Maldonado use the term to mean the narration of the life of Christ.[20] In 1597, the Dutch Jesuit Francis Coster (1532–1619) published a vernacular treatment of the Passion entitled *Fifty Meditations on the Whole History of the Passion and Suffering of Our Lord Jesus Christ*, which reorganizes the Gospel accounts chronologically. The engravings of Jerome Nadal's (1507–80) famous *Annotations and Meditations on the Gospels* of 1595 were published separately in 1593 under the title *Images of the Gospel History*.[21]

If a Catholic bishop inspired the historical orientation and organization of the *Commentaries*, a non-Catholic influenced another aspect of the work's structure. In the general preface, Salmerón explains how the writings of Marlorat motivated him.

> For I confess that I was powerfully moved to undertake this work from the time that certain new commentaries on the New Testament, along with many scholia, of more recent heretics, that is, Theodore Beza and Augustin Marlorat, came into our hands, namely *Catholic Ecclesiastical Commentaries: Or, A Library of Commentaries on the New Testament*. For thus the latter [Marlorat], having abandoned the font of living water, and certainly the orthodox tradition, wrote a huge volume, which he sewed and joined together as if into one body, with great labor and expense, out of dissipated cisterns that cannot hold water, and from the stinking ditches of the heretics

---

[19] Claire Bouvier, *Être écrivain et religieux au Siècle d'or: Pedro de Ribadeneyra S.I. et le Ministère de l'écriture dans la Compagnie de Jésus* (Madrid: Casa de Velázquez, 2023), 68. This may have been the first Cologne edition or the incomplete Brescia edition.

[20] Augustin Marlorat, *Novi Testamenti catholica expositio ecclesiastica, id est, ex universis probatis theologis (quos Dominus diversis suis ecclesiis dedit) excerpta, a quodam verbi Dei ministro, diu multumque in theologia versato, sive bibliotheca expositionum Novi Testamenti, id est, expositio ex probatis omnibus theologis collecta, et in unum corpus singulari artificio conflate, quae instar bibliothecae multis expositrobus refertae esse possit*, 2nd ed. (Geneva: Henricus Stephanus, 1564), vol. 1, 1; Juan de Maldonado, *Commentarii in quatuor evangelistas* (Mainz: Arnold Mylius, 1602), vol. 1, col. 3.

[21] Franciscus Costerus, *Vyftich meditation van de gantsche historie der Passie en des lijdens Ons Heeren Jesu Christi* (Antwerp: Jan Mourentorf, 1597); Jerome Nadal, *Evangelicae Historiae Imagines ex ordine Evangeliorum, quae toto anno in Missae sacrificio recitantur, in ordine temporis vitae Christi digestae* (Antwerp: Martin Nuyts, 1593).

of our age, that is, Luther, Bucer, Zwingli, Oecolampadius, Melanchthon, Calvin, Brenz, Musculus, Bullinger, and others of this stock.[22]

It is unsurprising that this book aroused Salmerón's ire, for in addition to its constant references to the aforementioned authors, it is peppered with attacks on Catholic belief and practice. Marlorat's compendium of Protestant exegesis finds its counterpart in Salmerón's copious citations of Catholic authors, the purpose of which was to counter the allegedly false interpretations of Scripture provided by the former.[23]

History and the Gospel History

Salmerón did not content himself with the mere term "Gospel history," but rather he articulated a theory of it. He did not enter into the intricate debates about the nature of history and historical writing that emerged in the fifteenth and sixteenth centuries, particularly among Italian authors like Patrizi, Giovio, Bruni, Guicciardini, Vives, and others.[24] He did provide, however, a definition, concept, and taxonomy of history to explain and justify his choice of the term "Gospel history."[25] His approach may be seen as part of the "revolution of ecclesiastical history" of the second half of the sixteenth century, which sought to determine guidelines for the reliability of evidence, though without yet purging the criteria of confessional or political affiliation.[26]

The first major explanation of the Gospel history appears in the preface of Volume 4, which is entitled, *The History of the Life of our Lord Jesus Christ, Up Until the Lord's Supper*. It narrates the "naked history of the life of our Lord Jesus Christ."[27] History, Salmerón says, is nothing other than "the exposition

---

[22] *CEH*, vol. 1, Preface, 6rv. Salmerón's choice of language is obviously intended to ridicule the full title of Marlorat's work.

[23] Salmerón mentions Marlorat's work elsewhere as a compilation of the commentaries of heretics, which he says is neither Catholic nor ecclesiastical. *CBP*, vol. 1, 56.

[24] For an overview of these debates, see Anthony Grafton, *What Was History? The Art of History in Early Modern Europe* (New York: Cambridge, 2007).

[25] *Historia* had a wide semantic range in the period, referring to "an object of inquiry and a mode of inquiry, a specific branch of learning and a more general way of knowing." Frederic Clark, "The Varieties of *Historia* in Early Modern Europe," in *New Horizons for Early Modern European Scholarship*, ed. Ann Blair and Nicholas Popper (Baltimore, MD: Johns Hopkins University Press, 2021), 112.

[26] See Katrina Olds, *Forging the Past: Invented Histories in Counter-Reformation Spain* (New Haven, CT: Yale University Press, 2015).

[27] *CEH*, vol. 4, Preface, 2r.

or narration of things done," especially by those who witnessed them. He cites the testimony of Cicero that the first law of history is to say nothing false, along with this paean: "As to history, the witness of the ages, the illuminator of reality, the life force of memory, the teacher of our lives, and the messenger of times gone by, what other voice but the orator's invests it with immortality?"[28] Yet Salmerón says that few historical writers of antiquity lived up to such a standard, citing the words of Josephus, Quintilian, and Cicero on the unreliability of profane historians.

The failure of most writers to live up to the dignity of history sets up a contrast with the Gospel history.

> The Gospel history is without doubt unique and singular, since it is constant in the truth throughout all things, most full of usefulness and most brief: in which nothing disagrees, nothing contradicts itself, nothing resists either those who handed down the Gospel in writing or the prophets who foretold those things about to happen. Nothing is more august or more illustrious, nothing more magnificent or more solid or simpler, or more disinclined or foreign to every rhetorical trick, in the end nothing more conducive to reforming human life or carrying it towards what is better, or perfecting it.[29]

In addition, Christ had writers who told of his words and deeds beforehand with most certain prophecies, and their works are so trustworthy that no one can doubt their truth or authority. "No prince or emperor was fated to this; only Christ could give to his writers this privilege of sanctity and authority."[30]

In Salmerón's telling, Christ is not the only cosmic figure who has historians working for him. Satan sought to obscure the light of the Gospel history by inspiring his instruments to write the life of the magician Apollonius of Tyana, with the intent of showing that there was another man equal to Christ. Porphyry and Julian the Apostate likewise made weak and virulent arguments against the Gospel teaching, as did those who impudently published the spurious *Acts of Jesus with Pilate*. "All those people, nevertheless, certainly accomplished nothing, and it was hard for them to kick against the goad."[31] Although he did not use the term, Salmerón treated the genre of historical writing as an aspect of *praeparatio evangelica*, that is, of the way that events

---

[28] *CEH*, vol. 4, Preface, 2rv; Cicero, *On the Ideal Orator*, eds. James May and Jacob Wisse (New York: Oxford University Press, 2001), 133.

[29] *CEH*, vol. 4, Preface, 2v.

[30] *CEH*, vol. 4, Preface, 2v.

[31] *CEH*, vol. 4, Preface, 3r. Apollonius of Tyana was a Greek philosopher from Cappadocia born around the same time as Christ. The sophist Philostratus wrote a biography of him about a century after his death.

and developments prior and apparently extraneous to the Incarnation were in fact preparing the world for it. Historical writing is part of a larger cosmic struggle between God's plan for redemption and Satan's attempt to frustrate it, and historians *qua* historians ultimately belong to one of two transhistorical groups: those who write on God's behalf, and those who write on Satan's.[32]

Salmerón was interested in the relationship between the Gospel history and other historical genres, as demonstrated by the taxonomy he provided at the beginning of his volume on the Acts of the Apostles. He repeats his definition of history as the "narration of things done" while contrasting divine and human history. The former, which seems to be coterminous with Scripture, is superior to the latter with respect to its subject matter, its age, and its form, since truth is its criterion. Divine history does not contain fictitious creatures or false words, nor does it rely upon proofs or eloquence.[33] Yet there are also degrees of excellence within divine history. The Gospel history is superior to the history of the primitive Church in Acts, which in turn is better than the histories of the Old Testament. Salmerón claims that Luke was superior to the historians of the Old Testament because he was an eyewitness to what he wrote, his works are more concise, and they bear greater fruit. Acts of the Apostles is to be read frequently, because the Church renews herself by doing so.[34]

Salmerón was at pains to defend the historicity of the events narrated in Scripture, as illustrated by his distinction between divine history and parable. Whereas history is "the narration of something that really happened" (*narratio rei alicuius vere gestae*), parable is "the narration of some sensible thing invented for the sake of teaching spiritual things" (*narratio alicuius rei sensibilis efficta ad docendum spiritualia*). To illustrate the contrast, he notes that some Fathers thought the Book of Job was a parable, others a history, whereas still others said it was both.[35] In a similar vein, some Fathers along with Cajetan thought that the story of Lazarus (Lk 16:19–31) was a parable,

---

[32] Belief in a "demonic superconspiracy" against Western Christendom was common in the early modern period, and served as the underpinning of other, more limited conspiracy theories. François Soyer, *Antisemitic Conspiracy Theories in the Early Modern Iberian World: Narratives of Fear and Hatred* (Boston, MA: Brill, 2019), 43–48.

[33] *CEH*, vol. 12, 1–2.

[34] *CEH*, vol. 12, 8.

[35] *CEH*, vol. 4, 535. Salmerón thought it was a history, and attacked the Talmudists for making Job into a fable, a view he said was held by the most insane heretics of the age, the Anabaptists. He found confirmation of the book's historical veracity in the Church's celebration of the feast of Job on May 10. *CEH*, vol. 1, 154–55.

whereas others said it was a true story, or a mix of the two. Salmerón defended both of these passages as history, and placed his commentary on Lazarus in Volume 4 rather than Volume 7, reinforcing the criterion of history as telling things that really happened.[36]

Salmerón identified other categories of history as well, such as ecclesiastical history, which is distinct from, yet related to, divine history.

> The Holy Spirit also wanted to give a point of departure for others to continue the apostolic history that he had begun, so that we might embrace not only divine, but also ecclesiastical history, which is written by the ancient and orthodox Fathers, and is outside the canon, and so that we might feed not only on the canonical books, but also on the ecclesiastical books of the Fathers and on traditions.[37]

The *Commentaries* rely extensively on Church historians. In one place Salmerón lists some of his preferred sources: Eusebius, Rufinus, Sozomen, Socrates, Theodoritus, Evagrius, Jerome, and Prosper of Aquitaine.[38] The Church, he says, reads these histories in her temples and uses them in preaching, and the Scholastic Doctors often accept their veracity. Even so, God is not their author in the same way that he is of divine history; only Scripture is totally beyond doubt.[39]

Ecclesiastical history differs from divine according to its subject matter, since the former is not about articles of faith, but about the lives of saints, or about things that happened in the Church after the death of the apostles. Sometimes the content is not entirely true, and its style is often fancier, since it is a matter of human ingenuity. Although divine history bears greater fruit, sometimes ecclesiastical history has greater power to move someone. The example Salmerón cites is Augustine, who at first found Scripture wanting in comparison to Cicero's *Hortensius*, but then was moved to conversion by the *Life of Anthony*.[40]

Another category that Salmerón identifies is apocryphal history, which contains many uncertain and false things. Its primary author is the devil and

---

[36] *CEH*, vol. 4, 535. He also dealt with a textual issue: certain Greek codices, as well as some French missals, say that Jesus identifies the Lazarus story as a parable. Salmerón countered that these words are not found in the Vulgate, other Greek codices, the Syriac Gospel, or the revised Roman Missal [of 1570].

[37] *CEH*, vol. 12, 14–15.

[38] *CEH*, vol. 12, 15.

[39] *CEH*, vol. 12, 3; *CEH*, vol. 12, 6.

[40] *CEH*, vol. 12, 3.

its organ is the heretic, as Pope Gelasius taught.[41] According to Salmerón, the writings of this genre are worse than the fables of the Gentiles, for they contain some truths, but they are like honey mixed with poison, or the snake hiding in the grass, and few people are able to distinguish truth from error where they are concerned. These books, which are hidden in the corners of heretics rather than brought out into the light of the Church, are worse than all other kinds of histories.[42]

Salmerón's taxonomy of history, then, is as follows. Divine history, which is conterminous with Scripture, consists of three subcategories. The Gospel history, or the narration of the Lord's life, is the highest, followed by the history of the primitive Church related in Acts. The histories of the Old Testament, while inspired, are lesser in dignity and contain material that may lead astray the uninitiated. Ecclesiastical history deals with the life of the Church after the death of the apostles. Although not preserved from error like divine history, it is still of considerable value. Profane history deals with matters not pertaining directly to God's work. It often fails to live up to the standard of truth, but is not bad as such, whereas apocryphal history has the devil as its principal author and purports to deceive men about the things of God. Salmerón provided the most sustained discussion of the nature of history among all the exegetes under consideration.

The coordinating role that history plays in the *Commentaries* is also evident when compared with Salmerón's view of poetry and rhetoric. The Jesuit theologian had been trained in the classical poets and orators from his youth, and his ability to recite these sources in old age impressed Pérez de Nueros.[43] He used these sources, however, primarily for adorning his prose or providing exempla, while explicitly rejecting allegorical readings of the poets, or using them to explain the mysteries of faith. Observing that some have used Ovid's *Metamorphoses* in this way, or correlated the doctrines of creation or Christ's double birth with the figures of Prometheus and Bacchus, respectively, Salmerón asserts that this method is illegitimate, since the things of faith cannot be known by natural reason. Virgil may have prophesied of Christ in the Fourth Eclogue, but unlike the prophets of Scripture, he did not know what he was saying.[44]

As for rhetoric, Salmerón praised it as a necessary instrument for disputing the enemies of the faith. He observes that whereas no nation has done

---

[41] *CEH*, vol. 12, 6.
[42] *CEH*, vol. 12, 7. Salmerón uses the tern "Gentiles" to mean "pagans."
[43] *ES*, vol. 2, Appendix II, no. 36, 818.
[44] *CEH*, vol. 1, 355–56.

more than the Christian one to educate its youth in rhetoric and dialectic, the "Mohammedans" and others flee from disputation. Salmerón's treatment of rhetoric abounds with military language: as the Philistines tried to take away the weapons of the Israelites, so the heretics of the age attack liberal arts and schools. Public disputes concerning the faith are compared to the combat of the martyrs.[45] He gives rhetoric, therefore, a higher place in the hierarchy of disciplines than poetry, because it is more useful for the cause of true Christianity.[46]

At the same time, Salmerón subordinated rhetoric to divine power, and noted that the apostles lacked secular eloquence and used simple speech in their preaching. He censures mere verbal ornament rather sharply. "Those who are weaker in faith and authority indeed tend to take refuge in the pigments of oratory and the pimping of rhetoricians to better persuade others of their position."[47] Continuing the analogy, Salmerón compares seeking applause through such devices to the improper use of makeup. Just as pretty women or honest matrons dirty more than adorn their faces with paint, so also does rhetorical affectation render the truths of the Catholic faith contemptible to their hearers.[48] Clearly Salmerón had a strong mistrust of poetry and rhetoric, those great pillars of Renaissance education, unless they were tethered to truth. History, understood as the account of things that really happened, provided for him this link.

The author of the *Commentaries* strove to be not just a theorist of the historical discipline, but also a practitioner of it. Conscious that the chronological rearrangement of the four evangelists is a work of interpretation, Salmerón sought to demonstrate the rationale for his choices. Limitations of space prevent a complete study of his arrangement of the Gospel history, but one example should suffice to demonstrate his method. What events follow in the

---

[45] *CEH*, vol. 8, 2–3.

[46] The restrained approach to rhetoric is perhaps surprising given its importance in early Jesuit education. See Jaska Kainulainen, "Virtue and Civic Values in Early Modern Jesuit Education," *Journal of Jesuit Studies* 5 (2018): 530–48. Of course, Salmerón understands rhetoric as a discipline aimed at persuading others, which is somewhat different from O'Malley's idea of the "rhetorical dimension" as a distinctive feature of early Jesuit ministries. See Stephen Schloesser, "Accommodation as a Rhetorical Principle: Twenty Years after John O'Malley's *The First Jesuits* (1993)," *Journal of Jesuit Studies* 1 (2014): 347–72.

[47] *CEH*, vol. 12, 17.

[48] *CEH*, vol. 12, 18. Elsewhere, he lambasts histrionic preachers who employ "fake tears, loud cries, and womanish wailing and howling" while preaching on the Lord's Passion. *CEH*, vol. 10, Preface, 3v.

chronology of Christ's life after his baptism and temptation in the desert? Salmerón places the legation from Jerusalem to John the Baptist (Jn 1:19–28) as the next event, following Eusebius and Jerome.[49] Then comes the encounter between the disciples of John and Jesus on the "next day" (Jn 1:35–42), followed by the events of the day after that in the same chapter (Jn 1:43–51). The calling of Philip and Nathaniel at the end of Jn 1, Salmerón explains, takes place in the context of Jesus's first journey to Galilee.[50]

Solicitous that the reader not lose the thread of the narrative, Salmerón says that the events recounted in Jn 2 and Jn 3 come next, but that he has relegated them to the volumes on miracles and disputes, respectively. Jn 4:3 refers to a second journey of Jesus into Galilee, which is the same one mentioned in Mt 4:12 and Mk 1:14, after Herod put John the Baptist in jail. He deals with the apparent disagreement among the evangelists by noting that Luke (3:20) and John (3:24) describe the Baptist's incarceration by way of anticipation, whereas Matthew (14:3) and Mark (6:17) recount it retrospectively.[51] On this second journey, Jesus stops in Samaria and meets the woman at the well (Jn 4:4–42).[52] The narrative resumes in Mt 4:13, when Jesus goes to Capernaum. This means that, according to Salmerón, many events narrated by John occurred chronologically between Mt 4:12 and Mt 4:13.[53]

Although Salmerón's distribution of the Gospel material across volumes with different organizational schemes makes it difficult to follow his chronology, he offers at each stage of the text a rationale for his choices. His mastery of the Scriptures, as well as his knowledge of the various positions taken by other theologians, allowed Salmerón to construct his own chronological arrangement, comparing it with other accounts and defending it against objections. This is the same procedure that Jansen uses.[54]

Salmerón believed that the life of Christ was not only capable of being arranged in harmonious chronological order, but also that the precise timing and duration of its major events could be identified. He attempted to do so on the basis of historical data and calculations properly so called, while also relying on liturgical and symbolic correlations. A good example is found in *Prolegomenon XXXIX*, which is dedicated to calculating the true age of Christ

---

[49] *CEH*, vol. 4, 145.
[50] *CEH*, vol. 4, 171.
[51] *CEH*, vol. 4, 178.
[52] *CEH*, vol. 4, 184.
[53] *CEH*, vol. 4, 207.
[54] For example, see Jansen, *Commentaries*, Pars Secunda, 233.

and the dates of his conception, birth, Baptism, and so forth. Salmerón took his cue from secular historians.

> Profane historians, who have undertaken to relate the life and deeds of some illustrious and great ruler, carefully and diligently try, as far as possible, to write a full account of the entire time of his life, and what happened at what age, and the progressions of the virtues which he performed with the growth of his life.[55]

He observes that while numerous books of the Old Testament follow this same method regarding the kings and the prophets, the New Testament is not so precise about the life of Christ. With the Fathers and ecclesiastical historians as his sources, the Jesuit theologian offers his own calculations of these details of Christ's personal history. He begins with the assertion that the Lord was conceived on Friday, March 25, which rests on two main sources: the Church's celebration of the feast of the Incarnation on this date, and the testimony of Chrysostom, Augustine, and Athanasius, whose works he cites verbatim. Christ's conception would have taken place exactly nine months prior to the date of his birth, that is, December 25. In support of this date, Salmerón relies on the Church's celebration of Christmas, as well as a catena of seven theologians and ecclesiastical historians.[56]

He also seeks to correlate Christ's life with major events of Roman history: the lives and reigns of Augustus and Tiberias, the institution of the Julian Calendar, the rule of consuls, and so forth, relying on a plethora of ancient and Christian sources.[57] Several pages of calculations yield the following conclusions: Christ was conceived and born in the forty-second year of the rule of Augustus (beginning from his triumvirate), and in the forty-fifth year of the institution of the Julian Calendar. He was baptized, as Luke says, in the fifteenth year of Tiberius, at which time he was thirty years and thirteen days old. Salmerón thoroughly sifts through the testimonies of a long list of historians and theologians in support of this claim, contradicting the view of Nicholas of Lyra (1270–1349), Lefèvre d'Etaples (1450–1536), and Cajetan (1469–1534) that Christ was actually twenty-nine years and thirteen days old. Once again, he finds extraneous reasons of fittingness to support his

---

[55] *CEH*, vol. 1, 439.

[56] *CEH*, vol. 1, 439–40. He ridicules "a certain heretic" Matthew Brouart (Beroaldus) for claiming that Christ was born in September on the autumnal equinox. *CEH*, vol. 1, 441.

[57] This interest in correlating Gospel events with other historical sources was a feature of biblical studies in Paris during Salmerón's time there. See Sheila Porrer, *Jacques Lefèvre d'Étaples and the Three Maries Debate* (Geneva: Librairie Droz, 2009).

calculations: the Council of Neocaesarea prohibited the ordination of anyone who had not completed his thirtieth year, and as high priest, Jesus must have attained this age.[58] In Salmerón's view, expounding the Gospel history requires serious historical as well as exegetical work. In this respect, he was not alone, as Jansen, Maldonado, Barradas, and Marlorat also attempted to precisely calculate the birth and other events of Christ's life.[59]

The Evangelists as Historians

The excellence of the Gospel history, as explained above, concerns not only the greatness of its subject matter, i.e., the Lord's life, but also the authority and sanctity of its authors, for a true history is written by true historians. Salmerón dealt with a number of questions pertaining to Jesus's choice of the four evangelists as the authors of his life, their qualities as historians, and the specific times and circumstances of their writing. Once again, he relied on their analogical relationship to other kinds of historians.

Why did Jesus write nothing himself? One reason, according to Salmerón, is that he preferred to have "living paper," that is, hearts of flesh, upon which to write his teachings. There was also the danger that if Christ himself had written, the other books of Scripture might have been lost or vilified as inferior.[60] Why did he choose the disciples rather than illustrious historians of his own time? As the authors of the Old Testament were holy men, it was fitting that the authors of the New Testament be even holier, rather than unbelievers and sinners. The Jews, who have a hard time believing in Christ's Gospel anyway, would have rejected him even more thoroughly if testimony of his life had come from Gentile authors.[61]

But Salmerón's explanation was not merely a moralistic one, for he also found fault with the ancient historians' aptitude and judgment. Numerous Roman historians, he says, wrongly mocked the Christians. Homer saw Achilles as the very image of a prince or emperor, and Ulysses as a most prudent man. In reality, Achilles was savage, bloodthirsty, and monstrous, and Ulysses was crafty, treacherous, and a liar. Xenophon made a similar error in his positive

---

[58] *CEH*, vol. 1, 441–46.
[59] Jansen, *Commentaries*, Pars Prima, 56; Maldonado, *Commentaries*, vol. 2, cols. 85–88; Barradas, *Commentaries*, vol. 1, 388–90; Marlorat, *Expositio*, vol. 1, 327.
[60] *CEH*, vol. 1, 393–95.
[61] *CEH*, vol. 1, 396.

assessment of Cyrus.⁶² Salmerón saves his heaviest fusillade, however, for his foremost ancient authority on historical writing.

> Cicero said he would dedicate himself assiduously to the memory of his daughter, and that he would bring it about through testimonies of all the most distinguished men of genius both Greek and Latin, that his daughter be regarded as a goddess. With such care, he wrote to Atticus to buy a field in a renowned place, where the shrine of Tullia could be built. But what did he really accomplish? He wrote two books on his daughter's death, in which he likely tried, by an outpouring of his immense innate ability and by all the oratorical resources, arguments, devices, polish, and embellishments he had learned, to persuade posterity that Tullia was a goddess. But his contemporaries as well as posterity mocked the old-lady tears of the silly father and his failed scheme.⁶³

In Salmerón's eyes, not even the finest writer of pagan Rome was suitable qua historian for the task of writing the Gospels.

By contrast, the evangelists were historians, even if they were not all eyewitnesses. Although in the preface of Volume 4 he emphasizes the importance of eyewitness testimony, elsewhere he mitigates this point when dealing with the question of why some Gospels were written by those who never saw the Lord.

> It must thus be said that the Evangelists wrote as historians, which does not require being present for all the things they describe while they were happening. For if this were necessary, hardly anyone could be a historian, except for a short time, that is, only of his own age, and not even of the whole of it, since he would have to exclude infancy, and childhood, and the whole part of his life that he describes but did not see.⁶⁴

According to such an absurd standard, he says, Moses could not have written the history of more than two thousand years, nor would Berossus, Josephus, or Livy be counted as historians. "It must be said that it is enough to be a historian to know that the things that one is writing are true, even if one did not see them, and that one is trustworthy to recount them."⁶⁵ Divine history may be immeasurably greater than its profane counterpart, but the former still shares natural standards with the latter.

---

[62] *CEH*, vol. 1, 396–97.
[63] *CEH*, vol. 1, 397.
[64] *CEH*, vol. 1, 412.
[65] *CEH*, vol. 1, 412.

Viewed in this light, the sacred authors are rightly considered historians, an idea to which Salmerón often returned. As Luke explains in his prologue (Lk 1:1–4), he wrote his Gospel rightly and perfectly, relying on the fact that he had been instructed by those who saw the Lord's deeds and who were ministers of his word.[66] Salmerón claims that the Virgin Mary was the eyewitness source for the accounts of her son's infancy.[67] John writes "like a good historian" when he identifies the time and place of the Jewish legation to John the Baptist.[68] Salmerón observes that Luke explains who the Ethiopian eunuch is (Act 8:27–28) like a historian would, giving his nation, sex, office, and religion.[69] This work of writing history, even in the case of the Gospels, includes the exercise of literary skill on the author's part. Salmerón explains what a historian does: "diligently and in a satisfactory way bring together the truth from all over, and then go through each part, and lastly relate it in the order and by the method that is more pleasing."[70] Although other exegetes under consideration, especially Maldonado, treated the evangelists as historians, Salmerón was more emphatic about it.

The final criterion for the Evangelists' reliability as historians is an external one: the testimony and judgment of the Church, which Salmerón considered stronger than seeing the Lord with one's own eyes, or than having the autographs of the Gospels.[71] This sort of argument may appear circular, but the Jesuit theologian needed to explain why the four canonical Gospels alone are trustworthy. He names a total of fifteen ancient documents, including the Gospels of Judas and Thomas, that claimed to be authentic but that were rejected by the Church. Salmerón says these documents were composed by heretics to spuriously trace their teachings back to Christ. He is even critical of the *Protoevangelion of James*, which narrates the Virgin Mary's life from birth until the coming of the Magi. He calls it a "mere fable" for the many uncertain things it contains. Despite his dim view of these sources, Salmerón acknowledges that they contain truths, and that the Fathers sometimes cited them.[72]

---

[66] *CEH*, vol. 1, 413.
[67] *CEH*, vol. 2, 241.
[68] *CEH*, vol. 4, 146.
[69] *CEH*, vol. 12, 184.
[70] *CEH*, vol. 2, 240.
[71] *CEH*, vol. 1, 413.
[72] *CEH*, vol. 1, 400–2. In addition, Salmerón himself relies on the *Protoevangelium*, whether directly or indirectly, for much information about the youth of the Blessed Virgin.

The aforementioned point underscores an important aspect of Salmerón's understanding of history and historians: theological data and concepts are not excluded from their purview. Although Salmerón distinguished between what is accessible to the senses and natural reason from what is accessible only by divine revelation, he did not limit the historian's scope to the former. Theological and historical labor and insight merge and become effectively indistinguishable. Salmerón did not share the modern aim of separating historical inquiry from theological commitments.

Although his aim was to compose a single, harmonious Gospel history, Salmerón was conscious of the different perspectives that the four evangelists provided. Ezekiel's vision of the four living creatures (Ez 1), which since the second century has been associated with the four Gospel writers, was Salmerón's interpretative key for explaining how each Gospel emphasizes a different mystery of Christ's life. Matthew, symbolized by the man, points to the weakness of the Mediator's flesh as well as to the Incarnation. Mark, the lion, indicates the strength of his spirit and stands for the Resurrection. Luke, the bull, illustrates that Jesus is both priest and victim, which corresponds to the Passion. John, the eagle, signifies the Lord's divinity and his Ascension.[73] Salmerón adds that the multiplicity of accounts does not undermine the unity of the Gospel, as shown by the fact that Ezekiel speaks of four animals in the first chapter of his book, but of only one in the tenth chapter.[74] The four accounts agree in doctrine, and four is also a perfect number, as manifest in the four rivers of Paradise, the four extremities of Jacob's ladder, the four Latin Doctors, and so forth.[75]

Although Salmerón was more interested in the evangelists' message than in their personal biographies, he did not neglect the latter altogether. He distinguishes Mark from John Mark (Acts 12:12), and identifies this evangelist as the companion of Peter.[76] Salmerón follows the ancient tradition that says Luke was a painter and a physician, identifying him as Paul's companion.[77] John's identity receives the most attention of all. Appealing to the tradition of the Church, Salmerón claims that the author of the fourth Gospel was the Apostle John, who was one and the same person as the "Beloved Disciple," and who was also the author of three New Testament epistles and the

---

[73] *CEH*, vol. 1, 407–8.
[74] *CEH*, vol. 1, 408.
[75] *CEH*, vol. 1, 404–5.
[76] *CEH*, vol. 1, 128; *CEH*, vol. 1, 413.
[77] *CEH*, vol. 12, 8; *CEH*, vol. 1, 413.

Apocalypse.[78] As the one who most clearly revealed the Lord's divinity, John occupies pride of place among the evangelists, and his Gospel has primacy among the four.[79] Salmerón emphasizes his closeness to the Blessed Virgin, calling John the first of Mary's spiritual children after Jesus.[80]

The harmoniousness of the four Gospel accounts is essential to Salmerón's characterization of the evangelists as reliable historians. This harmoniousness means not only that the events narrated within may be arranged in chronological order, but also that their content is consistent, despite apparent disagreements. Salmerón sought to demonstrate this in multiple ways. On the negative side, he challenged the idea that non-Christian authors agree among themselves more so than the four evangelists did. He points to disagreement among the followers of Mohammed, since men like Averroes and Avicenna ridiculed the Qur'an. The heretics did not agree with each other, as the many examples of discord among Lutherans, Anabaptists, Sacramentarians, and Swenfeldians shows.[81] On the positive side, Salmerón confronted concrete cases of apparent disagreement among the evangelists to demonstrate their consistency. One example in particular brought out his understanding of the evangelists as historians: the comparison of the genealogies of Christ offered by Matthew and Luke.

Salmerón did not begin with the discrepancies between the two genealogies, but rather with the aims of the evangelists in recounting them. One of Matthew's goals was to show that Jesus was the true Messiah, that is, the one promised in the Old Testament, and thereby convince both Jews and infidels.[82] Salmerón adds that formerly the Hebrews studied genealogy for three reasons: assigning priestly office, determining marriage and inheritance, and figuring out from which family the Messiah would come. This makes the genealogies important, and Salmerón rebukes those who would dismiss careful examination of them. "'They are just names, and have no use.' What are you saying? God speaks, and you dare to say his words have no use?"[83]

Salmerón undertook a lengthy textual, historical, and theological exegesis of all the names in each of Matthew's lists of fourteen, offering interpretations

---

[78] *CEH*, vol. 1, 92; *CBP*, vol. 4, 327. Citing Jerome, Salmerón mentions that some think that 2 Jn and 3 Jn were written by another John, known as the "theologian" and the "presbyter."
[79] *CEH*, vol. 1, 433–34.
[80] *CEH*, vol. 3, 264.
[81] *CEH*, vol. 1, 414.
[82] *CEH*, vol. 3, 177; *CEH*, vol. 3, 216.
[83] *CEH*, vol. 3, 184.

at both the literal and spiritual levels. For example, he rejects the editorial decision of Santes Pagninus to remove Rahab's name (Mt 1:5), and dismisses Erasmus's concern about whether the text should read *de Rahab* or *ex Rahab*. The presence of sinful women in the genealogy shows that Christ came to take away sins. Rahab is an image of the Church of the Gentiles, because after being a fornicator, she united herself to Christ as represented by the scouts (Josh 2).[84] Salmerón quarrels with Josephus about the timeline of Boaz begetting Obed, and defends the ability of old men to sire children.[85] He also displays his penchant for numerology: the fourteen generations correspond to the number of years that Joseph spent in Egypt, as well as to the Ten Commandments plus the four Gospels.[86]

Salmerón begins to deal with discrepancies when he arrives at the third set of fourteen generations. According to him, Matthew obtained the names he used from annals kept in the Jerusalem temple, whereas Luke relied on commentaries, like Philo's *Breviarium*, for the names that do not appear in Scripture.[87] Salmerón then offers a list of all the differences between their genealogies, and considers various solutions to the problem. One theory, attributed to Nazianzen, is that different names are used for the same people. Another is that Matthew provides a genealogy according to the flesh, whereas Luke's is according to the spirit. A more respectable theory, held by Cajetan and Nicholas of Lyra, is that Matthew gives Joseph's lineage, whereas Luke gives Mary's. Salmerón rejects all of these explanations, offering in each case numerous reasons why they are unlikely.[88]

His preferred theory accounts for the fact that the two genealogies have real differences only in the third part. Eusebius attributed to an unnamed African historian the idea that there were two different lines of descent: one legal, the other natural. According to this account, Mathan had two sons: Eli and Jacob. When the former died without children, Jacob took his wife and sired Joseph, which made him the son of Eli according to the Law. Authorities supporting this theory include Justin Martyr, Eusebius, John Damascene, Ambrose, and others.[89] By way of conclusion, Salmerón offers the contrasting priorities of the two evangelists to explain the differences in their lists. The root cause is that Matthew was supposed to show the face of the man, that is,

---

[84] *CEH*, vol. 3, 193–94.
[85] *CEH*, vol. 3, 194–95.
[86] *CEH*, vol. 3, 198.
[87] *CEH*, vol. 3, 204–5.
[88] *CEH*, vol. 3, 206–9.
[89] *CEH*, vol. 3, 209.

the weakness of Christ according to the flesh, whereas Luke, the face of the bull, was supposed to show the priestly or spiritual descent, that is, according to the Law.[90]

Although the foregoing is only a summary of Salmerón's longer and much more detailed treatment of the genealogies, it suffices to demonstrate his conviction of the ultimate harmony of the different Gospel accounts, despite appearances to the contrary, as well as his ability to compare and integrate prodigious source materials into his own solution.

Christ, the Center of History

If Salmerón's primary interest was the Gospel history, that is, the narration of the life of Jesus, he also placed it within the larger framework of the history of the world, with two principal aims in mind. First, he sought to demonstrate that Christ was the center of history: everything before him was preparation for him, and everything after pertains to the proclamation of his teaching until he returns in glory. Second, he wanted to show that neither Jews nor Gentiles ever lacked God's providential care throughout history. As will be explained in Chapter 5, this point is crucial to his soteriology, which emphasizes the role of human freedom, and therefore also human culpability. For Salmerón, world history was theodicy on a grand scale.

In his commentary on the Prologue of John's Gospel, Salmerón explains that Christ was the light of both Jews and Gentiles prior to his Incarnation. Drawing on the allegory of the cave, he says that the Mosaic Law was like the light of dawn that allows eyes to adjust and prepare for the full light of day, which shone in all the major figures of the Old Testament.

> The patriarchs, prophets, and all the just went before Christ, the King of Kings, like forerunners and ministers, testifying of his coming, teaching, and life not only by their words, but also by the example of a most holy life, and laying out and prefiguring by their illustrious and heroic deeds Christ's sacred mysteries, and singular and plainly divine works.[91]

Salmerón follows this claim with a catena of examples illustrating the point, making extensive use of typology to show how God sought to forestall Jewish unbelief in Christ. He spoke to Moses out of a bush and a cloud, that is, inanimate things, to show that it would not be impossible for him to speak through the human nature that he was to assume. He made the rod of Aaron grow

---

[90] *CEH*, vol. 3, 210.
[91] *CEH*, vol. 2, 146.

without any liquid, to show that the Word was to be conceived without any seed. He showed the closed door of Ezekiel's prophecy as a sign of the mystery of Mary's perpetual virginity. He showed that Christ was to attain salvation for all through the cross by sending Noah to save the world with the ark. All told, Salmerón lists in this passage seventeen events of the Old Testament that prefigured a particular mystery of the life of Christ.[92]

Christ's status as light to the Gentiles before the Incarnation was a less straightforward matter, since Salmerón could not rely so extensively upon the Bible. Appealing to Thomas, Salmerón says that faith was infused into the Gentiles before the Incarnation.[93] More controversially, he says that propositions accessible to natural reason, namely, that God exists and that he rewards the good, implicitly contain the mysteries of the Trinity and the Incarnation. He thinks the pagans had a notion of eternal life and death, as seen in the belief in the Elysian fields and the waters of the underworld, or in Book X of Plato's *Republic*.[94] As Ambrose and Prosper of Aquitaine said, God was generous to the Gentiles in both spiritual and temporal things.[95] The dispersion of the Jews spread the expectation of the Messiah's coming, and Scripture gives instances of the worship of the true God by certain Gentiles. God communicated philosophy to them so that they could learn to live rightly as a preparation for the gift of faith.[96]

One manifestation of God's providence to the Gentiles was his assigning of angels to them, for which the following verse is a key locus: "When the Most High divided the nations: when he separated the sons of Adam, he appointed the bounds of people according to the number of the children of Israel" (Deut 32:8). When dealing with the textual variants between the Hebrew Old Testament and the Septuagint, Salmerón expresses his preference for the latter's "the number of the angels" to "the number of the sons of God" or "the number of the sons of Israel" found in the Hebrew versions. After a lengthy discussion of the arguments for each, as well as possible interpretations found in the Fathers, Salmerón claims that the true meaning of the verse is that "God has established angels for all the nations, so that they might protect the peoples from the hostile demons, and lead them to the worship of the true God and their salvation."[97]

---

[92] *CEH*, vol. 2, 146–47.
[93] *CEH*, vol. 2, 149; *ST*, II–IIae, q. 2, a. 7, ad. 3.
[94] *CEH*, vol. 2, 149.
[95] *CEH*, vol. 2, 152–53.
[96] *CEH*, vol. 2, 155.
[97] *CEH*, vol. 1, 59.

The most important figures for Salmerón's argument about God's providence to the Gentiles, however, were the Sibyls. The sources attributed to them have a long, complicated, and fragmentary history. In brief, the *Sibylline Books* were a collection of Greek hexameters supposedly written by female priests endowed with the gift of prophecy. According to Roman legend, a collection of these came into the hands of Tarquinius Superbus, who entrusted them to the Senate, which periodically consulted them for predictions of future events. They were supposedly lost when the Temple of Jupiter burned in 83 BC. A new collection was procured, which the general Flavius Stilicho burned around AD 405. Another collection of prophecies in Greek hexameter, the *Sibylline Oracles*, is quoted by Josephus and patristic authors like Lactantius, who saw in them an elevated conception of divinity that harmonized with Christianity.[98] Scholars believe that this collection took its final form sometime in the fifth century, and that it contains Jewish and Christian interpolations. The Sibyls entered a new phase of their history during the fifteenth century, after relative neglect during the Middle Ages. Their number and names were standardized, and their function changed from predicting apocalyptic disaster to foretelling aspects of the life of Christ.[99] Editions of the *Oracles* appeared in the 1540s, which Salmerón consulted along with the fragments found in ancient Christian sources.[100]

Whatever their origin and authenticity, the writings of the Sibyls played a crucial role in Salmerón's understanding of divine providence toward the Gentiles.

> The Sibyls therefore are as if conscious of divine counsel, preaching of Christ among the nations, like the prophets among the Jews, so that beforehand they would await him, receive him in the present, and afterwards believe in him. Whence Diodorus of Sicily says in his *Historical Library*: "The Sibyls are women prophets, full of God."[101]

---

[98] Peter Dronke, *Hermes and the Sibyls: Continuations and Creations* (New York: Cambridge University Press, 1990), 8.

[99] Robin Raybould, *The Sibyl Series of the Fifteenth Century* (Boston, MA: Brill, 2017), 2.

[100] Xystus Betuleius, *Sibyllinorum Oraculorum* (Basel: Johannes Oporin, 1545); Sebastian Castellio, *Sibyllina Oracula: De Graeco in Latinum conversa, et in eadem annotationes* (Basel: Johannes Oporin, 1546). Unlike Salmerón, Castellio thought that new data from pagan sources could alter the history contained in the Bible. Backus, *Historical Method*, 129.

[101] *CEH*, vol. 2, 156.

Salmerón explains that God chose men to prophesy among the Jews and women among the Gentiles, so as to honor both sexes with this gift. He adds that, even if by nature men are wiser, God chose women also for this task so that they might be more greatly admired.[102] Although he denied that the Sibylline prophecies were of equal authority as the Scriptures, they certainly had a parallel function, as well as certain features in common. Salmerón says it is fitting, for example, that the books of the prophets were burned by King Joachim (Jer 36:22–32), just as the Sibylline books were burned at the command of the emperors. He also notes that both prophets and Sibyls were sometimes regarded by others as insane.[103]

After consulting numerous pagan and Christian sources on the number and location of the Sibyls, Salmerón explains that the world could only attribute their prophecies to God (who had in fact inspired them), on account of their virginity, holiness of life, and use of heroic verse.[104] He claims that these prophecies have been accepted by the Church, as shown in the opening verses of the sequence *Dies irae* in the Mass of the Dead.[105] Salmerón cites numerous representatives of a long tradition of Christian writers who made these claims: Clement of Rome, Justin Martyr, Lactantius, Augustine, Eusebius, and Katherine of Alexandria.

As for the content of the Sibylline prophecies, Salmerón says they testify widely to Christian revelation: the unity of God and the Trinity of persons, the creation of the world, the resurrection of the dead, future beatitude, and the particulars of the life of Christ and his mother.[106] To show that this is the case, he cites numerous excerpts from the edition and Latin translation of Betuleius:

> Then great God's son will come to humankind
> Clothed in the flesh, in human form on earth.
> His name will have four vowels, and consonant
> Twofold. I shall expound its total sum:
> Eight units, and as many tens as well,

---

[102] *CEH*, vol. 2, 159.

[103] *CEH*, vol. 2, 164.

[104] *CEH*, vol. 2, 157. He qualifies this claim by acknowledging that some of the Sibyls worshipped idols, but he does not think this robbed them of their prophetic gift, any more than it did Balaam (Num 24). *CEH*, vol. 2, 164.

[105] *CEH*, vol. 2, 158.

[106] *CEH*, vol. 2, 159.

And eight hundreds to disbelieving men
Shall make it manifest.[107]

These lines make for a riddle, the solution to which is the name of Jesus in Greek (Ἰησοῦς), which has four vowels and a single repeated consonant. The numerical value of each line in the original Greek text is equivalent to each of the letters of his name, and the total value is 888. Following Bede's *Commentary on Luke*, Salmerón further observes that the numerical value of each of the six letters adds up to 888, which is a figure of the Resurrection.[108]

All told, Salmerón cites verbatim more than twenty excerpts from these poems in Latin translation, and he identifies the teachings and mysteries of Christ that each one communicates. He correlates these not only to the prophecies of the Old Testament, but also to the testimonies of other pagan authors. Cicero wrongly saw the fulfillment of the Sibylline prophecy of a future ruler in Julius Caesar, whereas the reports of Tacitus and Suetonius about expectations of a ruler to come from the East were certainly fulfilled in Christ.[109] Salmerón says that the Sibylline texts had to be more obscure than the writings of the prophets, for the Gentiles, unlike the Jews, did not have hope of the Messiah. "But certainly, just as the prophets are able to refute the Jews, who deny Christ and his mysteries, so also the Sibyls confound the pagans."[110] In other words, the Sibyls served not only to prepare the Gentiles for the coming of Christ, but also to confirm their guilt in rejecting him.

The essential point, however, is that "the providence of God for procuring the salvation of the Gentiles was never lacking at any time."[111] Salmerón confirms this with lengthy citations from Chrysostom, Justin Martyr, and John Damascene, and he cites Clement of Alexandria's view that those who lived rightly before the coming of Christ, whether by the Law or by philosophy, were made righteous. If the "Gospel history" in the strict sense is the narration of the life of Christ, in a secondary sense it is the account of his manifestation, whether openly or obscurely, to the whole human race from its beginning. And while Salmerón characterizes the human race's response to these overtures primarily in terms of rejection, he looks at the brighter side as well.

---

[107] J.L. Lightfoot, *The Sibylline Oracles: With Introduction, Translation, and Commentary on the First and Second Books* (New York: Oxford University Press, 2007), 311–12. The English translation is Lightfoot's.

[108] *CEH*, vol. 2, 160.

[109] *CEH*, vol. 2, 164.

[110] *CEH*, vol. 2, 163.

[111] *CEH*, vol. 2, 165.

> There was never a nation so savage, so barbarous and uncouth, into which no knowledge of God, or notion of worshiping his majesty, was placed, especially since nature teaches those two principles, namely, "that God exists and that he rewards those who seek him" (Heb 11:6).[112]

Although Salmerón displayed an unusual level of interest in the Sibyls, they are by no means absent from the work of other exegetes in the period, who also treated them as prophets of Christ among the Gentiles. Jansen and Maldonado refer to them in passing, whereas Barradas explains their importance more fully, contending that "God wanted the Sibyls and Hystaspes to shine with divine light among the Gentiles, so that the way of Christ's coming might be strengthened with teaching and prophecies."[113]

The History of the Church

The *Commentaries* do not undertake a systematic treatment of Church history, or even lay out a general schema of it. Salmerón sometimes distinguished broadly among different periods, claiming that each has different needs for which Scripture provides the resources.

> Thus out of Scripture did the Church in the time of the martyrs draw out her constancy and fortitude; in the time of the Doctors, wisdom and the light of understanding; in the time of the heretics, the destruction of error; in the time of prosperity, humility and temperance; in the time of negligence and tepidity, fervor and diligence; in the time of the Church's deformity and of creeping abuses, the reform of lost mores, and the return to her pristine dignity and estate.[114]

Salmerón did not consistently favor any particular period of Church history. In one place, he says that the Church was stronger in the time of Arius because the blood of the Lamb had recently been shed, but in the context of his argument against utraquism, he disagrees with those who think that the primitive Church had greater wisdom.[115] Elsewhere he says that the early

---

[112] *CEH*, vol. 2, 183.

[113] Jansen, *Commentaries*, Pars Prima, 66; Maldonado, *Commentaries*, vol. 1, col. 94; Barradas, *Commentaries*, vol. 1, 139. Hystaspes, also known as Vishtaspa, was a quasi-mythical early follower of Zoroaster to whom a set of prophecies has been attributed.

[114] *CEH*, vol. 1, 10.

[115] *CBP*, vol. 4, 305; *CEH*, vol. 9, 320. He says, however, that charity was greater in the primitive Church.

Church was more constant in faith than now because at that time the interior and exterior voice of God was greater.[116] As a general rule, Salmerón did not dwell on periodization, nor did he treat each historical period as discrete or markedly different from any other. He emphasized the continuity and clarity of Church history.

Church history, especially the earliest centuries, became a hotly contested field in the sixteenth century. Protestants often claimed that they were returning to the teaching and praxis of the apostles and the primitive Church. The greatest achievement in this field during Salmerón's lifetime was the publication of the *Centuries of Magdeburg* by Matthias Flaccus Illyricus, which purported to show the ancient pedigree of Lutheran doctrine, and how the papacy in particular had increasingly corrupted it from the fifth century onward.[117] This was a key line of defense against the Catholic charge of novelty and disregard of tradition. Ecclesiastical authorities were sufficiently concerned about the *Centuries* that a Roman commission was established in the 1560s to refute them. Although Salmerón was recruited for the commission, in the end he was unable to contribute directly to its work.[118] It seems likely, however, that his growing awareness of the historical question during these years influenced his organization of the *Commentaries*. They were not, strictly speaking, a work of Church history like the *Ecclesiastical Annals* of Caesar Baronius (which appeared shortly after Salmerón's death), but they shared the common aim of claiming the early Church for the Catholic cause.[119]

Salmerón portrays Acts of the Apostles, which he calls "the annals of the Christian republic," in unmistakably Catholic terms.[120] According to his calculations, it covers twenty-eight years of history, and he seeks to show how already during this period Catholic teaching and practice on numerous

---

[116] *CEH*, vol. 12, 90.

[117] Matthias Flacius Illyricus, *Ecclesiastica historia congesta per aliquot iuros in urbe Magdeburgica*, 13 vols. (Basel: Johannes Oporin, 1559–74).

[118] José L. de Orella y Unzue, *Respuestas católicas a las Centurias de Magdeburgo (1559–1588)* (Madrid: Fundación Universitaria Española, 1976), 228–30. Salmerón did, however, strongly encourage Peter Canisius's writings against the *Centuries*, as shown in an effusive letter of 1572. *ES*, vol. 2, no. 366, 312–13. Canisius envisioned a team of historical writers working together against the Protestants. Orella y Unzue, *Respuestas católicas*, 207.

[119] Caesar Baronius, *Annales Ecclesiastici*, 10 vols. (Rome: Congregation of the Oratory, 1593). See Simon Ditchfield, *Liturgy, Sanctity and History in Tridentine Italy: Pietro Maria Campi and the Preservation of the Particular* (New York: Cambridge University Press, 1995), 272–327.

[120] *CEH*, vol. 12, 13.

contested issues was taking root: the celebration of the sacraments, especially holy orders, the exercise of ecclesiastical jurisdiction, liturgical ceremonies, and the like.[121] Although he acknowledged later historical events and development, he thought the Church had already acquired her full form in the apostolic age, as well as her period of greatest sanctity. Since Acts of the Apostles belongs to the genre of divine history, it provided Salmerón's most important and reliable source for the history of the Church.

Although Salmerón had a strong interest in Roman history, he was fairly restrained about the idea of the empire's providential status and its place in the history of the Church. He acknowledges that the consolidation of power under Augustus was a sign of the messianic times insofar as it took away rule from Judah, in fulfillment of Gen 49:10.[122] Luke's identification of the princes and priests at the time of Jesus's birth is meant to show that Christ is king and priest, and the single ruler of the Gentiles is a sign of the single God they will come to worship.[123] Salmerón did not dwell, however, on the conversion of the empire to Christianity, nor was he in thrall to subsequent revivals of the imperial office under Christian auspices. He praised Constantine, but he had no discernible concept of a "post-Constantinian" Church.[124] Salmerón understood Christian Rome primarily in connection with the papacy, and he had much to say about its history, as will be explained in Chapter 6.

Salmerón sometimes briefly mentioned moments in Church history in the context of some larger argument. He refers, for example, to the period when the popes dwelt at Avignon, identifying eight of them by their names and regnal years. His point here is not that the papacy fell into a low estate during this period, but rather that the Avignon popes remained the bishops of Rome, even though they were not resident there.[125] Amidst his attack on Elizabeth I for usurping primacy over the Church, Salmerón notes in passing that some think Pope John VIII from the English nation was actually a woman, known as Pope Joan. Her election, he says, would have been an error of fact rather than law, although he thinks that the story is probably false.[126] He makes pass-

---

[121] *CEH*, vol. 12, 15.

[122] *CEH*, vol. 4, 9.

[123] *CEH*, vol. 4, 11–12.

[124] Salmerón says that "Constantine the Great" fulfilled the duty of kings to divine worship when he endowed the Church with basilicas. *CEH*, vol. 3, 372 (Hh5v).

[125] *CEH*, vol. 12, 537.

[126] *CBP*, vol. 2, 149. Salmerón's identification of "Pope Joan" with John VIII and the English nation matches Bartolomeo Platina's account.

ing reference to the wars fought in Bohemia (that is, the Hussite wars) for the upholding of Church traditions.[127]

Just as Salmerón relied mainly on Cicero for his concept and standard of history, but criticized Cicero's own errors in the field, he also used one of his most frequently cited ecclesiastical historians to showcase the potential for error. According to Jerome, there was no Church historian who surpassed Eusebius in antiquity, diligence, or judgment, but Salmerón offered a litany of his errors, whether of a historical or a theological character. For example, Eusebius said that the Cephas corrected by the Apostle Paul (Gal 2:9–14) was one of the seventy-two disciples, whereas Paul lists him together with John and James as pillars, that is, apostles. Another error is the claim that Paul had a wife, which goes against all the Latin and Greek Fathers, as well as Paul's own words (1 Cor 7:7). Eusebius followed Irenaeus and Dionysius of Alexandria in ascribing the Apocalypse to a disciple of John rather than to the evangelist himself, attributed the first preaching at Rome to Peter instead of Barnabas, and confused the succession of bishops at Rome. In total, Salmerón lists twenty-four errors of Eusebius, and assures the reader that he could add more of them.[128] He says his purpose is not to incite ill-will or hatred against Eusebius, but rather to show that the works of the ancient Fathers have to be read with care.

Although the Gospel history was the primary concern of the *Commentaries*, the history of the Church played an ancillary role, particularly the apostolic period recounted in the Acts of the Apostles. Salmerón believed that God's providence was at work in particular ways in particular times and circumstances of the Church's history, and that ecclesiastical historians were an important, though not infallible, resource. Salmerón did not offer anything like a complete ecclesiastical history on the model of Baronius, but he was no less committed to claiming the centuries after Christ for the Catholic Church.

Sitz im Leben

Another aspect of Salmerón's use of history is captured by the German expression *Sitz im Leben*, or "life setting," that became commonplace in twentieth-century biblical criticism. He provided the reader with copious background information and context for Jesus's world. To some extent, interest in the "life setting" of the Bible was always a feature of exegesis, and Salmerón relied considerably on patristic authors and ancient historians for his

---

[127] *CEH*, vol. 12, 93.
[128] *CEH*, vol. 12, 3–6.

information. Yet the sixteenth century witnessed a deepening of this interest, above all from the 1570s, when the research of antiquarians and Christian Hebraists was increasingly incorporated into biblical commentaries.[129] Benito Arias Montano, the famous editor of the *Biblia Regia*, writes confidently in one of his prefaces that "there is no history that does not openly show how necessary is knowledge of the places that are mentioned in the various passages of Holy Scripture."[130] Montano and his team helped provide maps and detailed geographical descriptions, an example that other exegetes would follow in subsequent decades.

Since Salmerón wrote during the 1570s, he ought to be regarded as one of the pioneers of this increasing interest in the geography, history, and culture of the biblical world. As usual, he weaved together history and theology into a single account. At the beginning of *Prologomenon XL*, Salmerón explains his purpose thus:

> Because the Gospel history, written by the four Evangelists, and the Acts of the Apostles encompass many histories, whether of the kings of Judaea, or of the Roman emperors and governors sent to Judaea, I determined that it would not be useless to bring forth certain things taken from Josephus, and Hegesippus, and Eusebius of Caesarea, and other proven authors, whether foreign or domestic, that shed light on the Gospel, so that no one would be found ignorant of foreign and profane history, or deterred from reading and enjoying the Gospel.[131]

The Jesuit theologian wanted his reader to have a wealth of context and background information for understanding the life of Jesus.

He provides a catalog of Roman emperors from Augustus to Vespasian and Titus, and of the governors from the same period, along with accounts of their main duties and records of periodic Jewish uprisings. The client kings of Judaea, especially Herod the Great, receive similar treatment. Salmerón offers a panoramic vision of the geography of the region, describing its major features, calculating distances, and comparing the accounts of ancient and medieval authors. He then deals with the history of its conquest and occupation by the

---

[129] Adam Beaver, "Scholarly Pilgrims: Antiquarian Visions of the Holy Land," in *Sacred History: Uses of the Christian Past in the Renaissance World*, ed. Katherine van Liere, Simon Ditchfield, and Howard Louthan (New York: Oxford University Press, 2012), 267–84.

[130] Benito Arias Montano, *Prefacios de Benito Arias Montano a la Biblia Regia de Felipe II*, ed. and trans. María Asunción Sánchez Manzano (León: University of León, 2006), 190.

[131] *CEH*, vol. 1, 461.

Israelites, the distribution of the tribes, and subsequent divisions of the land at various times in their history.[132]

Salmerón dedicates a chapter of fifteen pages to the description of Jerusalem and its temple. He offers numerous possible etymologies of the city's name, and then provides a description of its topographical features, important buildings, arrangement of its gates and walls, and so forth. His treatment is diachronic as well as synchronic, as he discusses the building stages of the two different Jewish temples, as well as the excavations undertaken by Helena. Salmerón descends to details that one might only expect from someone who had actually visited the city. When describing the interior of the Holy Sepulcher, he says:

> All around are elevated places and oratories, in which those who profess the Christian name were accustomed to pray, and in which praises, psalms, and hymns are sung according to the custom of each by Greeks, Latins, Ethiopians, Syrians, Georgians, and others.[133]

His description of life in Jerusalem is vivid, despite being dependent upon secondary sources, and perhaps echoes the aspiration of the first Jesuit companions to establish themselves in the Holy Land. Barradas surpassed Salmerón in this regard, dedicating over thirty distinct treatises to the Jerusalem temple, its parts and furnishings, and the duties and vestiture of its priestly divisions.[134]

Sometimes Salmerón explains puzzling Gospel passages by considering the particular objects and customs of everyday life. Some ask how the penitent woman (Lk 7:37–50) could have washed Christ's feet with her tears, but they do not understand how the use of elevated couches facilitates this.[135] Rooftops in Palestine were flat and used as gathering places, meaning that "shouting from the rooftops" was an equivalent for speaking in public places.[136] When Jesus warns of the punishment that will befall those who scandalize the little ones (Mt 18:6), he is referring to the practice whereby especially wicked criminals were tied to stones and thrown into the depths.[137] Salmerón spends several pages discussing alabaster and nard in connection with the anointing

---

[132] *CEH*, vol. 1, 471–505.
[133] *CEH*, vol. 1, 514.
[134] Barradas, *Commentaries*, vol. 2, 166–219.
[135] *CEH*, vol. 4, 298.
[136] *CEH*, vol. 4, 366.
[137] *CEH*, vol. 4, 444.

of Jesus (Mt 26:7), citing a host of ancient authors who explain their nature and function.[138]

Perhaps the most fascinating instance of Salmerón's interest in the life setting of the Scriptures was his treatment of meals and banquets. Here he relied not only on the Bible, but also on profane sources, especially the ancient poets, to explain dining customs that shed light on particular Gospel passages. "Formerly when men ate and drank, or celebrated banquets, they were accustomed to sit at table, each one in his own seat, as we also are accustomed to doing."[139] He cites multiple verses from the Old Testament that describe people sitting down to eat, before observing that at some point this custom went into decline throughout the world, and that for the sake of delicate living, people began to recline on couches (*triclinia*) at meals. After describing these couches and their arrangement, with citations from Cicero, Macrobius, and other Roman poets, he notes that men and women sat at separate tables. This custom is evident, for example, when the daughter of Herodias has to go out to dance before the men and return to the women's dining area to speak to her mother (Mk 6:24).[140]

It was likewise customary to eat only after washing and anointing oneself. Cicero and Plautus testified to this, as did Jesus when he chastised the Pharisee for offering him no water or oil before the meal (Lk 7:44–46). The practice of taking off one's shoes before dining is evident in Christ's washing of the apostles' feet (Jn 13:5–10), which was done to avoid getting the couches dirty, and Salmerón cites four different poets to confirm this practice. People used to be seated according to rank rather than randomly, which is why the Pharisees are criticized for their ambition for the places of honor (Mt 23:6), and why Jesus tells his hearers not to seek the highest position at meals (Lk 14:10).[141] As he discusses various customs, Salmerón occasionally refers to his own times.

> They also brought out songs and musical instruments at banquets to arouse merriment, and they played praises of illustrious men on the flute, as Cicero says in the fourth *Tusculan Disputation*, which even now is done among our countrymen, that is, the Spaniards.[142]

---

[138] *CEH*, vol. 4, 590–94.

[139] *CEH*, vol. 1, 217.

[140] *CEH*, vol. 1, 217. Salmerón cites Mt 14, but the point he wishes to illustrate is much clearer in Mark.

[141] *CEH*, vol. 1, 218–19. Salmerón remarks that it was considered indecent to seat more than four people on a single couch.

[142] *CEH*, vol. 1, 219.

While explaining that those whom God calls to a higher state are wont to celebrate a banquet, as Elisha did when Elijah summoned him (1 Kgs 19:21), Salmerón says that this is also true of priests and religious in his time when they are ordained or make their profession, as well as of those who enter marriage or assume political office.[143]

In similar fashion, Salmerón provides a wealth of information on the celebration of weddings, burial customs, and even the method of crucifixion in the time of Jesus, mining and comparing the sources available to him so that the reader might better understand the context of the Gospel history.

Conclusion

Salmerón's choice of the "Gospel history" as an organizing principle for the *Commentaries* indicates the crucial role that history played in his understanding of the theologian's tasks. He understood the Gospels as history, and their authors as true historians; indeed, they are the most perfect historical works ever written, on account of the dignity of their subject matter, and because God guarantees the veracity of their testimony. They harmonize with each other, and harmonize also with other true histories of whatever sort. The exegete is responsible for demonstrating the chronological sequence of the Gospel history and for corroborating its testimony with any and all historical material that is available to him.

According to Salmerón, all of human history finds its fulfillment in the Gospel history, as demonstrated by the signs and prophecies that God communicated to Jews and Gentiles alike across the ages. A theologian must be able to show how the coming of Christ was foretold not only in Scripture, but also in extrabiblical sources like the *Sibylline Oracles*, a task that amounts to a kind of theodicy: ignorance of God's works and teaching is man's fault, not God's. Church history plays an important ancillary role in the *Commentaries*, not only as part of the struggle with Protestantism, but also as a locus for communicating Salmerón's theological views. Finally, the theologian must use all his resources to provide the *Sitz im Leben* of the biblical world for the reader, so that the historical distance between the past and the present may be partly overcome.

Salmerón's "historical consciousness" certainly had its limits. He had a much stronger sense of "the past as past" with respect to biblical times than he did of Church history more broadly, which he treated as more of a continuous unity. Since his most important commitments were theological, and since he

---

[143] *CEH*, vol. 1, 211.

believed in the unity of truth, Salmerón presented his historical data in such a way as to smooth over any possible discrepancies with the Catholic faith. In other words, he generally presupposed the harmony he sought to demonstrate.[144] It is nevertheless clear that he thought that a good theologian must be a good historian as well.

---

[144] Grafton and Olds observe that historians of this period, Catholic and Protestant alike, were not above fudging evidence for their confessional purposes. Grafton, "Church History," 7; Olds, *Forging the Past*, 16.

2 Integrating Scripture and Tradition

In the course of a jeremiad against hypocrites who wish to turn the thoughts of men toward merely human prudence, Salmerón counsels his reader to listen instead to angelic words. "The angels are sacred scripture, and the ecclesiastical traditions, and the examples and teachings of the saints, all of which we acknowledge as angels and messengers of God and his divine will."[1] This statement captures well his understanding of the harmonious relationship among the various aspects of the Church's teaching and life, the demonstration of which is one of the theologian's tasks. Salmerón's magnum opus is not only a commentary on the New Testament, but also a biblical theology, that is, one that takes scripture as its inspiration, source, and point of departure. His method was quite the reverse of *sola Scriptura*, insofar as he sought to integrate the Bible with the Fathers, Doctors, councils, and other witnesses to Christian doctrine.

The work of integration, however, demanded not just an assertion of harmony, but also an explanation of how these sources related to each other and testified to the Catholic faith as a coherent whole. Although Salmerón's attempt was not entirely coherent, the *Commentaries* stand out for their sustained attention to method. Throughout the work, he followed the lead of other sixteenth-century theologians, such as John Driedo, Melchor Cano, and Martín Pérez de Ayala, in attempting to explain the relationship between scripture, the other witnesses to Christian doctrine, and the profane disciplines.

This chapter begins with Salmerón's discussion of scripture: its rationale, greatness, inerrancy and inspiration, senses and interpretation, and so forth. The Jesuit theologian spent considerable effort developing lists of rules and canons for the interpretation of scripture, and dealt with technical issues like the study of biblical languages, textual problems, and translations. This is followed by the question of tradition and its relationship to scripture in the faith and life of the Church. Although Salmerón used tradition as a category, he was more apt to employ the expression "the Fathers and the Doctors" as witnesses to tradition. This touched upon a major issue of his day: the relationship

---

[1] *CEH*, vol. 3, 407.

between the Church Fathers and the Scholastic Doctors. He sought to steer a middle course between extreme positions, while showing a preference for the philosophy of Thomas Aquinas, in keeping with broad trends of the early Jesuits. Finally, Salmerón had to deal with works written during his own times. Neither rejecting nor embracing everything that was new, he evaluated contemporary theologians for their conformity to the Catholic tradition and their ability to bring forth new insights.

The Greatness of Scripture

Salmerón wrote during a time of immense productivity and creativity in Catholic exegesis that some have called a "Golden Age."[2] Its fecundity can be traced to numerous factors: the reforming impulse evident after the final convocation of the Council of Trent; the legitimation of exegetical methods and skills that had been previously under suspicion; the theological debates within the Catholic fold. Delville takes 1571, when Cornelius Jansen the Elder published his Gospel harmony and commentary, as a point of departure for this flowering, and he places Salmerón in a line of Spanish exegetes who were active in the late sixteenth and early seventeenth centuries.[3]

Salmerón opens the *Commentaries* with an explanation of scripture's rationale and greatness.

> We accept as indubitable, and acknowledged by all, that sacred scripture was dictated and administered to us through men inspired by the Holy Spirit and endowed with extraordinary sanctity, and received into a canon and approved by the Catholic Church. Scripture passes on and teaches our ultimate end, as well as opportune aid and assistance for attaining it.[4]

Scripture reveals what human reason alone could not know about God, without subjecting the learner to great difficulty or long study. Salmerón enumerates the reasons why divine teaching was put into writing: writing aids the weakness of the memory; a written source is easier to trust than what is

---

[2] Matthias Scheeben's description of this period as a *Blütezeit* was followed by numerous German Jesuits of the nineteenth century. Antonio Gerace, *Biblical Scholarship in Louvain in the 'Golden' Sixteenth Century* (Gottingen: Vandenhoeck and Ruprecht, 2019), 12.

[3] Jean-Pierre Delville, *L'Europe de l'exégèse au XVIe siècle: Interprétations de la parabole des ouvriers à la vigne (Mt 20:1–16)* (Leuven: Leuven University Press, 2004), 437, 582–86.

[4] *CEH*, vol. 1, 1.

handed down; accepting an external source involves the exercise of humility and charity; and a written work cannot be obscured by self-love, the senses, or the deceit of demons.[5] "Rightly therefore a single scripture was entrusted to us, which we use like a Lydian stone for testing the spirits and all doctrine, according to the understanding of the Catholic and Orthodox Church."[6] Christ, who established the New Testament, is also the key to understanding the Old, as the texts of the latter refer to him. Salmerón says that some only study the exterior letter of scripture without the divine light of understanding, but knowing the Bible without embracing Christ is like embracing a cadaver.[7]

Salmerón defends the mysteriousness and difficulty of scripture from "new and recent teachers" who claim that the Bible is open [*aperta*] and transparent [*perspicua*].[8] The "perspicuity" of scripture, or the idea that it is readily intelligible to every individual reader and therefore does not need authoritative interpretation, was a major source of controversy in the sixteenth century.[9] Salmerón appeals to scripture itself and its images of sealed books (Apoc 5:9, Dan 12:4), as well as to Fathers like Jerome and Chrysostom to support his view. The difficulty of scripture is manifest in the profundity of its mysteries, the multiplicity of its senses, and its prediction of the future. Apparent contradictions, such as the different accounts of creation in Gen 1 and 2, or the creation of light before the sun, or the different accounts of the crucifixion and the Resurrection, add to the difficulty.[10] Other challenges include the variety of languages and use of figures, the breadth of topics, the lack of punctuation and diacritical marks, and the rapid change of speakers.[11] Salmerón asks rhetorically why, if all scripture is clear, was there need for Timothy to learn it from his infancy (2 Tim 3:15), or for Paul to study at the feet of Gamaliel (Act 22:3)?

This mysteriousness of scripture, the Jesuit theologian says, points to God's greatness and wisdom, which exceed the grasp of human intellect, and to his desire to humble human pride. Men must ask him to open the "seven seals" and make their manifold contents known, and the obscurity of scripture

---

[5] *CEH*, vol. 1, 1–3.
[6] *CEH*, vol. 1, 3.
[7] *CEH*, vol. 1, Preface, 3r; *CEH*, vol. 1, 5.
[8] *CEH*, vol. 1, 10.
[9] For a recent, if polemical, treatment of the subject, see Casey Chalk, *The Obscurity of Scripture: Disputing Sola Scriptura and the Protestant Notion of Biblical Perspicuity* (Steubenville, OH: Emmaus Road Publishing, 2023).
[10] *CEH*, vol. 1, 14.
[11] *CEH*, vol. 1, 14–15.

helps God to hide its meaning from the unworthy.[12] Allowing everyone to make their own judgments about scripture "would be like allowing the blind to make judgments about color."[13] Salmerón repeats the common view of Catholic theologians that the Church and her teachers establish the norm for interpreting scripture. No one, he says, is allowed to interpret apart from her; even if stars and signs were to appear outside the Church, they would be for naught.[14]

This does not mean, however, that Salmerón wished to restrict access to the scriptures to the clergy and the learned alone, for he distinguished different roles or levels of participation with respect to scripture. The primary teacher of scripture is Christ, and the hearers are those who listen to scripture with faith, which takes away all desire of the flesh [*affectum carnis*]. Thus Jews, pagans, and heretics, as well as Christians who follow after flesh and blood, are not included among the hearers. Reading scripture illuminates the mind, purging it of errors and filling it with divine truth; men inflamed with evil desires cannot burn with divine love. Salmerón observes that prayer often does more to aid the understanding of scripture than reading or studying.[15]

The *Commentaries* deal with the issue of biblical inspiration and establishment of the canon, although not in such a way as to easily locate Salmerón's position within the debates of the age. He asserts the roles of both the Holy Spirit and the human authors.

> Even if all the sacred and canonical books have none other than the Holy Spirit, who spoke through the prophets and apostles, as their authors, it is not to be understood that this excludes assistants [*administros*] as their proximate and immediate authors.[16]

Salmerón was aware that the formation of the biblical canon had a long history behind it, and he appealed to the Tridentine decree that intended to settle the matter.[17] He observes that the books of Job, Tobias, Judith, Esther, and

---

[12] *CEH*, vol. 1, 16–18.

[13] *CEH*, vol. 1, 12.

[14] *CEH*, vol. 3, 356.

[15] *CEH*, vol. 1, 7–9.

[16] *CEH*, vol. 1, 92.

[17] *CBP*, vol. 3, 77. As for the patristic debate, he thinks that when a greater part of the churches retains a book as canonical, the doubters should concede. His concrete case of this is the Apocalypse, which took longer to be universally accepted than most other books. *CBP*, vol. 4, 347; Council of Trent, Session 4, *Decretum primum: recipuntur libri sacri et traditiones apostolorum*.

the Maccabees are uncertain as to the amanuensis or stylus that the Holy Spirit used to dictate them. His vocabulary may suggest a "dictation" theory of scriptural authorship, but he did not give a detailed treatment of the matter.[18] At the very least, he thought that the sacred authors were in their right mind while they wrote; prophets understand their own prophecies, contrary to the claim of the Montanists that they wrote in ecstasy, and their content is coherent, unlike what Mohammed wrote in the Qur'an.[19] Scripture must be free from error, for otherwise it collapses, resulting in the destruction of the Catholic faith, as well as all heresies that claim biblical foundation.[20]

The Senses of Scripture

Salmerón undertook a thorough explanation of the various senses of scripture. The history of exegesis bears witness to several different schemas, but at the most basic level, there is a distinction between the literal and the spiritual senses, which has deep roots in the Church Fathers. It was common to subdivide the spiritual sense into three additional categories: allegorical, anagogical, and moral, although other terms (e.g. tropological) were also used. The sixteenth century gave rise to a host of new issues concerning the interpretation of the Bible, and some Protestants objected strongly to the use of the allegorical sense. The *Commentaries* often take a defensive tone about the senses of scripture in the face of these challenges.

Salmerón's discussion of the senses of scripture is notably dependent upon Nicholas of Lyra, the widely read medieval exegete who was an important source for biblical scholarship in the sixteenth century. Perhaps his most significant achievements were the popularizing of certain Jewish authors, and increasing reverence for the literal sense of the text.[21] Salmerón begins his discussion of the literal and spiritual senses with the image of scripture as

---

[18] For a discussion of "dictation" theory, see Aidan Nichols, *The Shape of Catholic Theology: An Introduction to Its Sources, Principles, and History* (Collegeville, MN: Liturgical Press, 1991), 116–19.

[19] *CEH*, vol. 1, 169.

[20] *CEH*, vol. 1, 417–18; *CEH*, vol. 3, 361.

[21] Deanna Klepper, *The Insight of Unbelievers: Nicholas of Lyra and the Christian Reading of Jewish Text in the Later Middle Ages* (Philadelphia, PA: University of Pennsylvania Press, 2007), 32; Wai-Shing Chau, *The Letter and the Spirit: A History of Interpretation from Origen to Luther* (New York: Peter Lang, 1995), 149, 157; Ian Christopher Levy, *Introducing Medieval Biblical Interpretation: The Senses of Scripture in Premodern Exegesis* (Grand Rapids, MI: Baker Academic, 2018), 229.

the book "written within and without" (Apoc 5:1), with the literal sense corresponding to the exterior and the spiritual to the interior. This idea is taken from the opening of two of Lyra's works: the second general prologue and the prologue *in moralitates Bibliorum*.[22] This does not mean, however, that Salmerón agreed with Lyra on all points, as will be demonstrated.

Salmerón acknowledged the fundamental distinction between literal and spiritual senses, which he also called historical and mystical.[23] The literal sense is concerned primarily with the words of scripture, whereas the spiritual is concerned with the things of scripture.[24] Even if the spiritual sense is of greater value, the literal is the "principal" [*praecipuus*] sense, because without it the spiritual sense cannot be established.[25] There is no text of scripture that lacks a literal sense, even when there is a transfer from literal to spiritual; whenever an allegory from the Old Testament is produced in the New Testament, it becomes literal. The spiritual or mystical sense, by contrast, is not found everywhere in scripture.[26]

While acknowledging traditional schema of the literal and spiritual senses and the subcategories of the latter, Salmerón dismissed several other senses that some writers identified, such as elementary, physical, and prophetic. The last, which occupied most of his attention, consists of using scripture to predict the outcome of battles or please princes. Joachim of Fiore, Girolamo Savonarola, Guillaume Postel, and the Flagellants are named as the practitioners of this erroneous manner of interpreting the Bible.[27] Salmerón also rejected the teaching of Nicholas of Cusa, who said that the Church can propose different meanings of scripture in different periods of history. He says this would eliminate the ancient interpretations and introduce new ones, which is dangerous and destroys the authority of scripture.[28]

---

[22] *PL*, vol. 113, col. 29, 33.

[23] There appears to be a subtle distinction between the "literal" and "historical" senses, even though he often uses the terms synonymously. When discussing the interpretation of Is 9:1–7, Salmerón says that the prophecy refers to Christ literally, but not historically, since the latter would mean that Isaiah was talking about someone of his own time. *CEH*, vol. 4, 211–12.

[24] *CEH*, vol. 1, 68–69.

[25] *CEH*, vol. 1, 68; *CEH*, vol. 1, 71.

[26] *CEH*, vol. 1, 344.

[27] *CBP*, vol. 3, 378; *CEH*, vol. 1, 437.

[28] *CEH*, vol. 8, 193.

The Literal Sense

Salmerón's treatment of the literal sense is subtle and complex, as well as prolix; he provides three sets of fifty canons to explain it. A key aspect of Salmerón's understanding of the literal sense concerns its use in the Old Testament with reference to Christ. Against certain exegetes, he maintains that Christ is spoken of in the Old Testament at the literal level, not merely the spiritual, citing Fathers who hold this opinion.[29] Anytime the sacred text attributes something to a person that exceeds his dignity, Salmerón argues, it is referring to the Messiah at the literal level. For example, Ps 44 is about Christ and the Church at the literal level, because it would be excessive to speak thus of the marriage of Solomon and the daughter of Pharaoh.[30] The Pentateuch, however, has few literal references to Christ, and speaks of him mostly in spiritual types, such as Noah's Ark, Isaac going up the mountain to be offered in sacrifice, the serpent lifted up in the desert, and many others.[31]

Although he says that the literal sense is not divided into subcategories, Salmerón accepts the idea that there can be multiple literal senses of a scriptural text, following Nicholas of Lyra, who was a great advocate for this idea.[32] The citation of "Thou art my son, this day I have begotten thee" (Ps 2:7) in the Letter to the Hebrews (5:5) refers, at a literal level, to the eternal generation of the Son from the Father, the glorious resurrection of Christ from the dead, the Father's bestowal of priesthood on the Son, and the Son's natural generation by the Virgin Mary. All these senses are different, Salmerón insists, and all are literal rather than spiritual, as Thomas, Augustine, and Jerome said.[33]

Part of his motivation was saving the exegesis of the Fathers, who provided various literal senses for any given passage.[34] Although Salmerón did not say so explicitly, the multiplication of literal readings was clearly a strategy to bind together the plurality of texts and interpretations accepted in the tradition of Catholic exegesis. Literal senses cannot be assigned haphazardly, however; they must be both true and literal, in conformity with the Church's tradition, and not contradictory to each other. The primary literal sense, according to

---

[29] *CEH*, vol. 1, 68.
[30] *CBP*, vol. 3, 670.
[31] *CEH*, vol. 1, 342.
[32] See Philip Krey and Lesley Smith, eds., *Nicholas of Lyra: The Senses of Scripture* (Boston, MA: Brill, 2000).
[33] *CEH*, vol. 1, 80–81; *CEH*, vol. 1, 83–84.
[34] *CEH*, vol. 1, 85.

Salmerón, is the one that conforms best to reason and to what precedes and follows it in the text.[35]

The literal sense of scripture includes the use of tropes or figures, which allow the sacred author to communicate more elegantly and facilitate the reader's understanding. Salmerón contrasts these figures or tropes at the literal level with the "proper" sense, which is also literal, and he provides rules for distinguishing them. For example, anyone who interprets "This is my body" from the Last Supper narratives in a figurative sense follows John Calvin's (1509–64) condemned and heretical teaching. There are other verses, by contrast, that must be taken in a figurative rather than a proper sense, lest they lead to grave wickedness. No one should read the Lord's instructions about eunuchs (Mt 19:12) in a literal sense and castrate himself. In a similar vein, Salmerón remembers hearing a Lutheran in Germany argue for clerical marriage on the grounds that Paul says that he gave birth to Philemon in chains (Philem 1:10), which is an unwarranted use of the non-figurative literal sense.[36]

Some books of the Old Testament provide special challenges for determining the literal sense, an issue that brings out greater nuance in Salmerón's thought. Although elsewhere he asserts the Davidic authorship of the Psalter, he admits that it is divided into multiple books of an uncertain number of authors, which do not preserve composition in the order of time.[37] The Canticle of Canticles is another difficult case for the literal sense. The first erroneous interpretation comes from the Jews and their "blind rabbis," who follow the superficial meaning of the text and claim that the book is about Solomon and his wife, the daughter of Pharaoh. This opinion was followed by "a certain heretic of our age" who took the pseudonym "Zerchinta."[38] Salmerón calls this interpretation "sordid," "vile," and "dangerous," for the Holy Spirit would not inspire something that breathed of mere lasciviousness and immodesty. Nicholas of Lyra's interpretation, that the Canticle speaks of God's rule over his people, as of a wife subject to her husband, has nothing profound about it, according to Salmerón.

> It must be said with the Fathers of the Catholic Church, that the true and proper sense must be taken not from the words according to their grammatical meaning, but from the things themselves immediately signified by the words (as we do with parables). That book describes and celebrates with

---

[35] *CEH*, vol. 1, 89.

[36] *CEH*, vol. 1, 227.

[37] *CEH*, vol. 1, 161–63.

[38] The man in question was Nikolaus Zurkinden (1506–88), a Reformed member of the city council in Bern, active during the middle of the sixteenth century.

praise the union of the Word with human nature, or of the bridegroom Christ with the Church, or with its greatest member the God-bearing Virgin, who is the primary spouse, or with any given soul made a spouse of God through faith and charity.[39]

Salmerón goes on to explain that the Canticle of Canticles' references to body parts, such as mouth, lips, breasts, and so forth are not to be understood in a carnal sense, but rather to sweet and tender things of the mind, as Origen and Jerome testified.

Salmerón varied as to how literally he took the literal sense. On the one hand, he cites Jerome for the view that many things are said in scripture according to the opinion of the time, rather than the truth of things.[40] On the other hand, there are numerous instances when Salmerón might have been expected to apply this principle but did not. For example, he says that the six days of creation were twenty-four-hour periods rather than metaphorical days, because the latter interpretation risks falling into the error of the Gnostics.[41] The serpent in the Garden of Eden, he claims, does not just stand for the devil by way of metaphor, but actually is the devil in the guise of a serpent. His general principle is that there is no need to seek a figurative or tropic sense when the words admit of a literal sense.[42]

Although Salmerón was not satisfied with appeal to authority alone, he often used it as a kind of backstop. Near the end of a list of canons for the literal sense, he says that if they are insufficient, recourse must be had to the Church. By this he means a descending set of authoritative sources or statements, in the following order: the ecclesiastical traditions and the apostolic canons, followed by the ecumenical councils, then the interventions [*sanctiones*] and decretal letters of the Roman Pontiffs, the Fathers and orthodox Doctors, and finally, the praxis of the Church, by which he means the lives of the saints.[43] Here again, his desire for the integration of scripture and tradition is manifest.

---

[39] *CEH*, vol. 1, 167.

[40] *CEH*, vol. 1, 123.

[41] *CEH*, vol. 1, 139.

[42] *CEH*, vol. 1, 233. This may have been a response to a longstanding exegetical issue in the Fathers, which Luther also discusses, about the literal meaning of the text. Following some earlier theologians, Luther held that it was a serpent possessed by the devil. See Jussi Koivisto, "Martin Luther's Conception of the Serpent Possessed by the Devil (Gen 3) and the Antecedent Tradition," in *"Wading Lambs and Swimming Elephants:" The Bible for the Laity and Theologians in the Late Medieval and Early Modern Era*, ed. Wim François and August den Hollander (Walpole, MA: Peeters, 2012), 111–51.

[43] *CEH*, vol. 1, 131–33.

While the other exegetes under consideration agreed with Salmerón on the priority of the literal sense, they did not always apply it in the same way. Maldonado focused almost exclusively on the literal sense to the exclusion of the spiritual, often dismissing an interpretation as "allegory." Although he accepted spiritual interpretations in principle, he showed little enthusiasm for them, preferring to remain on the literal plane.[44]

The Spiritual Sense

Establishing a definition of the spiritual sense was no straightforward matter, requiring Salmerón to sift through a variety of opinions. He rejected as inadequate the view of Alonso Tostado that the mystical sense is the one intended by the Holy Spirit, since this applies to the literal as well. He also rejected the view that the literal sense is what the proximate and immediate (human) author intended, but not necessarily what the Spirit intended. The advocates of this explanation thought they were preserving the Spirit from false utterances, such as the fool's statement "there is no God" (Ps 13:1), or the serpent's words in Gen 3. Relying on Augustine, Salmerón says that the Spirit may well be implicated in words that the human author does not understand. For example, Moses was not present at creation, but the Spirit taught him to say "in the beginning God created heaven, and the earth" (Gen 1:1). In a like manner, Caiaphas did not know or understand the prophetic meaning of his words, "it is expedient for you that one man should die for the people" (Jn 11:50).[45]

The Jesuit theologian considers the view of Nicholas of Lyra, that "the literal sense is that which is expressed in words and letters immediately from the intention of the Holy Spirit," from which it follows that the use of metaphors and figures belongs to the spiritual rather than the literal sense.[46] An example of this would be the Lord's words "I am the vine: you are the branches" (Jn 15:5). According to Lyra's explanation, the literal sense refers to a natural vine,

---

[44] Maldonado, *Commentaries*, vol. 1, col. 720; Maldonado, *Commentaries*, vol. 2, col. 167.

[45] *CEH*, vol. 1, 339.

[46] *CEH*, vol. 1, 339. There may be some confusion here owing to Lyra's shifting vocabulary. In the Prologue of his *Postilla moralis*, Lyra seems to have taught that whatever sense is present first in a passage is designated as the literal sense. If only a spiritual sense is present (that is, where the things signified by words in turn signify other things), then that becomes the literal sense. However he understood Lyra, Salmerón's intent was defending the view that all of scripture has a genuine literal sense, and that metaphor belongs to it. See James Kiecker, *The* Postilla *of Nicholas of Lyra on the Song of Songs* (Milwaukee, WI: Marquette University Press, 1998), 17.

whereas the spiritual sense is that Christ is the true vine insofar as he is the principle of men's good works and merits. Salmerón rejects this theory as well, on the grounds that it would mean that many passages of scripture lack a literal sense.[47]

After reviewing these and other opinions, Salmerón offers his own definition of the spiritual sense.

> The spiritual sense moreover is that which is designated from the very things that truly happened [*ex rebus ipsis vere gestis*] which are expressed by words from the intention of the Holy Spirit. I said, "from the very things that truly happened," because things that are imaginary and made up do not pertain to the spiritual sense, but to the literal, as Thomas says.[48]

He goes on to explain that the visions of the prophets, or the dreams of Pharaoh and Nebuchadnezzar, remain within the literal sense, because they were only imaginary and the signs of things that were really to happen. Daniel's vision of the stone cut from the mountain (Dan 2:34–35) refers to Christ at the literal level, not the spiritual. It is significant that, just as the concept of "things that truly happened" is central to Salmerón's understanding of the Gospel history, and of its authors as historians, so also it is central to his definition of the spiritual sense of Scripture. When the Holy Spirit communicates through things rather than words, they must be things that really happened.

Having put forth a definition, Salmerón proceeded to lay down rules about the spiritual sense and its application. The spiritual sense can only be grasped with the aid of the Spirit of God, for "animal man" (which Salmerón contended includes Jews and heretics) cannot receive it. According to Salmerón, the Lord himself loved allegories and parables, and the spiritual senses placed in Scripture by Christ or the apostles are not for the hearer to take or leave according to his fancy, but rather they encourage him to ponder their meaning.[49] The spiritual senses are uncertain and obscure, which is one reason why the demonstration of dogmas can only come from the literal sense. This does not mean, however, that the spiritual senses are totally lacking in probative force. When Paul or other sacred authors offer spiritual interpretations, as in the allegory of the two women (Gal 4:22–31), their claims are certain, because these authors had the right [*ius*] to interpret scripture. The same is true of the interpretations of the Fathers that have been confirmed by the Church.[50]

---

[47] *CEH*, vol. 1, 339–40.
[48] *CEH*, vol. 1, 340; cf. Thomas Aquinas, *Quaestiones Quodlibetales*, 7, q. 6, a. 1–3.
[49] *CEH*, vol. 4, 202; *CEH*, vol. 4, 279 (Aa2r); *CEH*, vol. 1, 355.
[50] *CEH*, vol. 1, 343–44.

Although he dealt with all the subcategories of the spiritual sense, Salmerón gave proportionally more attention to the allegorical, perhaps because it was most disputed in his time. All wars in scripture, he says, speak allegorically of Christ's battle with Satan, or of the human spirit's battle with the flesh, and all conflicts which witness the defeat of those who are confident in their own powers teach the importance of placing one's hope in God. The liberation from captivity in Egypt and Babylon signify freedom from original sin and personal sin, respectively.[51] Praise of wisdom and the Church are directed toward the Blessed Virgin, notably in the Psalms and the Canticle of Canticles.[52]

Against the opinion of Tostado, Salmerón says that the allegorical sense can be applied to the New Testament, especially the words and deeds of Christ. When he commanded that Lazarus be unbound from his burial cloths (Jn 11:44), this refers allegorically to the power of Catholic priests to bind and loose sin. Caesarea Philippi (Mt 16:13) stands for Rome, which is the supreme tribunal for opinions about who Christ is, which are uttered by the mouth of Peter.[53] Illegitimate and adulterous unions signify Christ's union with the Gentiles, whereas the Virgin Mary's standing outside asking to speak to Jesus (Mt 12:46) signifies the rejection of the synagogue.[54] Nicodemus came to Christ at night because he was far from the knowledge of him, and Judas went out at night, signifying that he was not going to return to the light of faith, or to Christ for forgiveness.[55]

While he defended such spiritual readings, Salmerón still counseled caution. Nothing is to be attributed to the spiritual sense that is manifestly literal, and it is absurd to bypass the literal sense of a given passage to go straight for the mystical one.[56] Since the spiritual sense cannot demonstrate dogmas by itself, it is not very effective for fighting against heretics or other Catholics.[57] The prudent exegete does not try to bring out all four spiritual senses when interpreting a given passage, but limits himself to one or two.[58]

Other exegetes of the period took different approaches to the spiritual sense. Maldonado's reserve has already been mentioned, whereas Marlorat, in keeping

---

[51] *CEH*, vol. 1, 346; *CEH*, vol. 1, 353.
[52] *CEH*, vol. 1, 348.
[53] *CEH*, vol. 1, 345.
[54] *CEH*, vol. 1, 346.
[55] *CEH*, vol. 1, 354.
[56] *CEH*, vol. 1, 345; *CEH*, vol. 1, 343.
[57] *CEH*, vol. 3, 399; *CEH*, vol. 8, 7–8.
[58] *CEH*, vol. 1, 344.

with a common Protestant trend, completely rejected the traditional taxonomy of literal and spiritual senses.[59] Barradas gave even more space to the spiritual sense than Salmerón by frequently including entire sections of commentary under the heading "moral exegesis" (*morale*), a designation that included all the traditional spiritual senses. Pinto Cardoso rightly says that despite his insistence on the priority of the literal sense, Barradas's work was not a modern, Erasmian commentary, but largely spiritual in the medieval tradition.[60]

Languages, Texts, and Translations

Salmerón's educational background put him in a good position to appreciate the importance of languages for biblical study, specifically Latin, Greek, and Hebrew. His words on this subject, along with the scholarship of this "Golden Age" more generally, show that Trent's defense of the Vulgate did not have a chilling effect on language study among Catholic exegetes.[61] Jansen, Maldonado, Barradas, and Marlorat all demonstrate their command of Greek and Hebrew throughout their works. Salmerón begins with a short historical defense of the study of languages, citing Jerome, the Council of Vienne, and the promotion of languages at universities, particularly the trilingual colleges.[62] The many Greek and Hebrew or Aramaic words used in the Gospels are another reason for study of these languages, and one needs to know the meaning of particular phrases that do not translate well into Latin, a language that suffers from a lack of articles.[63] Salmerón explicitly rejects the claim that there is an inherent link between the study of languages and heresy; many of the Church's great men knew languages without becoming heretics, and there were plenty of heretics, like Berengar, Wycliff, and Hus, who knew only Latin.[64]

---

[59] Marlorat, *Expositio*, vol. 1, 211.

[60] Arnaldo Pinto Cardoso, *Da Antiga à Nova Aliança: Relações entre o Antigo e o Novo Testamento em Sebsatião Barradas (1543–1615)* (Lisbon: Instituto Nacional de Investigação Científica, 1987), 59.

[61] Salmerón explicitly rejects the view that Trent's decree rendered Hebrew and Greek useless. *CEH*, vol. 1, 421. Post-Tridentine Catholic exegetes were interested in the Hebrew and Greek languages and biblical texts. Luke Murray, "Jesuit Hebrew Studies after Trent: Cornelius a Lapide (1567–1637)," *Journal of Jesuit Studies* 4 (2017): 76–97.

[62] *CEH*, vol. 1, 243–44.

[63] *CEH*, vol. 1, 250; *CEH*, vol. 1, 244–48.

[64] *CEH*, vol. 1, 254–55.

The biblical languages were not mere tools for Salmerón, but sources of historical interest, theological reflection, and delight. He says that God infused the Hebrew language into the minds of Adam and Eve so that they could name all the creatures of the earth. It was spoken by all the first human generations, and it is the ancestor of all the languages of the east, such as Ethiopian, Aramaic, Arabic, and so forth, just as Latin is of French and Spanish. Hebrew was the first language in which God expressed the divine mysteries, especially the Holy Trinity and the Incarnation. Salmerón says that Hebrew is likely the language of heaven, for the angels chant *qadosh qadosh qadosh* (Is 6:3), and in the Apocalypse, the blessed sing "alleluia." Another reason for Hebrew's dignity is its brevity: it does not inflect by case, it does not have a neuter gender, it lacks comparatives or superlatives, it often uses abstract nouns in place of concrete ones, and so forth.[65]

The *Commentaries* show much more than a passing interest in these linguistic matters. Salmerón observes that translations from Hebrew vary so greatly because a single noun may mean many things, and he provides a long list of formulas.[66] Continuing in the same fashion, he provides thirty-three rules concerning Hebrew verbs and participles.[67] Some verbs have a particular idiomatic meaning: "giving a hand" means promising obedience or confirming a pact, "building a house" means giving powers and faculties to inferiors, and "knowing" a woman means copulating with her.[68] His praise of Hebrew does not prevent Salmerón from issuing cautionary counsel: "shoemaker, not beyond the shoe" [*sutor, ne ultra crepidam*]. Students should learn Hebrew grammar and the meaning of words, but all else should be left to the tradition of the Fathers. He advises them to look to the works of François Vatable and Santes Pagninus for instruction. In particular, he warns against studying scripture with Jews. Salmerón avers that the Christian Doctors who did so, like Origen, Eusebius, and Jerome, only did so with great care, and that they extirpated all Jewish perfidy and venom from their works.[69]

Although his treatment of Greek was somewhat less extensive, Salmerón still dealt at length with some of its idiomatic expressions, adverbs, and prepositions, offering comparisons with the Hebrew, and giving examples of the implications for understanding and translating the New Testament. All told,

[65] *CEH*, vol. 1, 256–58. Salmerón does not reject, however, the probable and pious opinion that in heaven all languages will sing God's praise.
[66] *CEH*, vol. 1, 258–80.
[67] *CEH*, vol. 1, 281–301.
[68] *CEH*, vol. 1, 297–98.
[69] *CEH*, vol. 1, 68.

nearly a hundred pages are dedicated to these linguistic issues, and Salmerón refers his readers to Augustine's *Locutionum in Heptateuchum*, Jerome's commentary on Genesis, and the contemporary authors John Driedo, Pagninus, and Benito Arias Montano for further instruction.[70] He clearly endorsed the "return to the sources" characteristic of biblical humanism, while rejecting the positions and excesses of some of its advocates.

The controversy over languages was closely related to the controversy over biblical texts and translations. The sixteenth century witnessed an explosion of new editions of the Hebrew and Greek texts of both testaments, Latin versions (whether corrections of the Vulgate or fresh translations), the Aramaic Targum and Gospels, and translations into European vernacular languages. There was, in addition, a major dispute over the relationship of philology and textual criticism to theology, as well as the respect owed to the Catholic Church's longstanding use of the Latin Vulgate for worship and public disputation. Some believed that theological disputes could ultimately be resolved by establishing an authoritative text, which would give philology the status of a master discipline, and effectively exclude those who had not learned Greek and Hebrew. Others, while not denying the usefulness of language studies, relied more on the tradition of scholastic thought, and viewed with suspicion any attempt to replace the Vulgate with some new text or translation.[71] For Salmerón, directives from the Society of Jesus were also relevant.[72] Although he defended the Vulgate, his position on these matters was subtle and incorporated his characteristic interest in God's providence in history.

One of the questions posed early on in the *Commentaries* is which version of scripture should be accepted as true and genuine: the Vulgate, the Septuagint, the Hebrew text, or one of the new translations that appeared in the sixteenth century.[73] After a complaint about the confusion that new versions

---

[70] *CEH*, vol. 1, 329.

[71] See Allan Jenkins and Patrick Preston, *Biblical Scholarship and the Church: A Sixteenth-Century Crisis of Authority* (Aldershot: Ashgate, 2007), 3–80.

[72] Ignatius wanted his fellow Jesuits to study the original languages so that they could defend the Vulgate on every single point, an instruction that Laínez and Salmerón mitigated with the codicil, "everything that with reason and honesty can be defended." Benedict Fischer, Wim François, Antonio Gerace, and Luke Murray, "The 'Golden Age' of Catholic Biblical Scholarship (1550–1650) and its Relation to Biblical Humanism," in *Renaissance und Bibelhumanismus*, ed. J. Marius J. Lange van Ravenswaay and Herman Selderhuis (Göttingen: Vandenhoeck & Ruprecht, 2020), 217–74, at 245.

[73] This issue was controversial among Protestants as well as among Catholics. See Jennifer Powell McNutt and David Lauber, eds., *The People's Book: The Reformation*

and translations have caused, Salmerón says that if the Hebrew autograph of the Old Testament were extant, it would be the authoritative text, but since it is not, recourse must be had to other criteria.[74] After reviewing the history of controversy and various manuscript traditions of the Greek Bible that led Jerome to undertake his own Latin translation, he builds a case for the Vulgate (as well as the Septuagint) that rests on several pillars: ecclesiastical authority, God's providence in history, the inspiration of the Holy Spirit, and the subterfuge of the Jews.[75]

In the sixteenth century, the origin of the Septuagint was known principally from the *Letter of Aristaeas* (third or second century BC), which is quoted extensively in Josephus. Unlike most modern scholars, Salmerón took this account as historically reliable.[76] More importantly, it played a key role in his understanding of God's work in history, for he thought that the Septuagint was the work of the Holy Spirit, as numerous Fathers had said. He compares the translation of the Septuagint to the giving of the Mosaic Law, and says that both events were attended by signs and miracles.[77] Its use in the synagogues for centuries before and after Christ gave the Septuagint the force of tradition, and Salmerón criticizes the ancient editors Aquila, Theodotion, and Symmachus for writing alternative Greek texts.[78] This parallels his complaint against the proliferation of alternative versions during the sixteenth century.[79]

Salmerón saw the Septuagint as improving upon certain shortcomings of the Hebrew language. He observes that, contrary to the claims of contemporary rabbis, the diacritical marks [*dictiones*] were not revealed to Moses, but were invented at the time of the Massoretes, as the Talmud and the Kabbalists show. This feature of the text was a source of confusion, which the Septuagint

---

    and the Bible (Downer's Grove, IL: IVP Academic, 2016); Orlaith O'Sullivan, ed., *The Bible as Book: The Reformation* (London: British Library, 2000).

[74] *CEH*, vol. 1, 23.

[75] *CEH*, vol. 1, 23–24. As to the first of these, Salmerón says that the Catholic Church has accepted the Vulgate, the work of a holy man hated by heretics, as authentic for thirteen centuries, and that it has been approved by Trent.

[76] For the text, commentary, and reception history, see Benjamin Wright, *The Letter of Aristeas* (Boston, MA: De Gruyter, 2015); L. Michael White and G. Anthony Keddie, *Jewish Fictional Letters from Hellenistic Egypt: The Epistle of Aristeas and Related Literature* (Atlanta, GA: SBL Press, 2018).

[77] *CEH*, vol. 1, 47.

[78] *CEH*, vol. 1, 48.

[79] In a letter to Cardinal Antonio Caraffa, Salmerón defends the authority of the Septuagint against the new "hebraizanti e rabbinizanti" that were born in the sixteenth century. *ES*, vol. 2, no. 504, 669.

helped to correct.[80] The loss of the Hebrew autograph, as well as the original knowledge that would have rendered it unambiguous, created a situation for which God, in the course of time, provided a remedy.

The Vulgate, according to Salmerón, came about in a similar way: under the inspiration of the Holy Spirit in response to particular needs in history.

> If someone were yet to insist that we bring forth our judgment on such an important matter, I would hardly hesitate to assert that its author translated the Hebrew into Latin with the guidance and assistance of the Holy Spirit, and that I was convinced of this for the following reasons.[81]

He goes on to explain that just as the prophets, apostles, and evangelists bequeathed the scriptures to the faithful with the assistance of the Holy Spirit, so also the Spirit elected to oversee their translation into other languages. The gist of Salmerón's argument is that since the Spirit foresaw that the Vulgate would be approved by the Church, he arranged in advance to guide Jerome to a correct understanding and translation. This explanation was not foreign to the theological discourse of the sixteenth century. The Parisian theologian Pierre Couturier of the College Ste. Barbe made a similar argument, and he may even have been Salmerón's source for the idea.[82]

The final element of Salmerón's case for the Septuagint and the Vulgate is the charge of Jewish subterfuge. Although the Jews had long used the former text and were the original witnesses to its providential origin, in the times of Justin Martyr and Tertullian they began to criticize it, because these early Christian apologists were claiming that Christ had fulfilled its prophecies.[83] Basing himself largely on the accounts of early patristic authors, Salmerón gives examples of the ways that Jews have corrupted or contested the text of the Old Testament, whether in Greek or Hebrew, for the sake of denying that Jesus is truly the Messiah.

To take one example, the verse "let us put wood on his bread" (Jer 11:19), which Christians interpret as a prophecy of the crucifixion, is missing from some Hebrew codices, but present in others. According to Justin Martyr's *Dialogue with Trypho*, this demonstrates that Jews maliciously sought to remove the verse, but that they were not entirely successful.[84] This partial cor-

---

[80] *CEH*, vol. 1, 38–39.
[81] *CEH*, vol. 1, 26.
[82] Erika Rummel, *Erasmus and his Catholic Critics* (Nieuwkoop: De Graaf, 1989), vol. 1, 64.
[83] *CEH*, vol. 1, 49.
[84] *CEH*, vol. 1, 34.

ruption of the Hebrew text, which was taught not only by the Fathers, but also erudite men of recent times, is the final reason for upholding the Septuagint and Vulgate against the Hebraizing tendencies of the sixteenth century.[85] The new translations of the Old Testament made directly from the Hebrew are accommodated to Jewish "perfidy." Salmerón rejects as absurd the idea that for centuries the Church was bereft of a true and genuine edition of scripture, which can only be remedied by turning to the synagogue. Why, he asks, would we seek to learn from our capital enemies?[86]

If the Septuagint and Vulgate are not to be replaced, this does not mean that other versions are useless. The Hebrew text of the Old Testament may be accepted insofar as it does not contradict the other two. In a like manner, the Greek text of the New Testament may be consulted, but it is not a more reliable source than the Vulgate, because the former has been corrupted.[87] These rules do not conform to what he says elsewhere, namely, that the Hebrew and Greek texts are needed to correct the Vulgate. Since he attributed the errors of the Vulgate to the passage of time and the wickedness of copyists, however, perhaps he thought that the internal resources of the Vulgate textual tradition were sufficient. Yet he also says that when the Hebrew, Greek, and Aramaic texts of the Old Testament agree, their authority is superior to the Vulgate's.[88] It may be that Salmerón never entirely resolved the question in his own mind.[89]

His interest in the issue notwithstanding, Salmerón never said which edition of the Vulgate he was using. The period of his writing coincided with major efforts to implement the Tridentine decree about correcting Jerome's venerable translation. The first edition that emerged was John Henten's Louvain text of 1547, which was printed in multiple places and revised again by Francis Lucas in 1574 and 1583.[90] In a letter of 1572, Salmerón reports having obtained an unbound copy of the Antwerp Bible, a multivolume polyglot edition published under royal auspices by Christopher Plantin.[91] By this

---

[85] *CEH*, vol. 1, 39. Salmerón mentions Paul of Burgos, Francisco de Vitoria, Jacob of Valencia, Melchor Cano, and John Driedo as authorities.

[86] *CEH*, vol. 1, 65–66.

[87] *CEH*, vol. 1, 94.

[88] *CEH*, vol. 1, 248.

[89] His main ideas, however, are in line with the thought of John Driedo. Gerace, *Biblical Scholarship*, 41.

[90] Gerace, *Biblical Scholarship*, 25.

[91] *ES*, vol. 2, no. 362, 302–3. Since the Antwerp Bible was printed between 1568 and 1573, it seems unlikely that Salmerón obtained all the volumes in 1572.

time however, he had already written a significant part of the *Commentaries*, and in all likelihood he was often recalling the scriptural text from memory, meaning that his work may not reflect a single standard edition.[92] Sometimes he refers to the text of a specific edition, such as the Complutensian Polyglot.[93] Although he says that vernacular translations are not in themselves bad and that they had never been altogether forbidden, he never used them himself.[94] Salmerón effectively sidestepped an issue that elicited considerable discussion in the sixteenth century among Catholics and Protestants alike.[95]

Salmerón's case for the Vulgate illustrates his desire to integrate scripture and tradition, for the longstanding usage of the Church and the testimony of the Fathers were crucial to his case. He regarded this usage, however, not as a mere accident of history, but rather as the result of God's providential action in history. According to Salmerón, God did not allow the Church to be bereft of a genuine scriptural text, and so he arranged for versions to be composed in Greek and Latin, under the inspiration of the Holy Spirit, once the Hebrew autograph had been lost.

Tradition

Although scripture and tradition are inseparable in the *Commentaries*, it is not easy to pin down how their author understood the relationship between the two, as his several discussions of tradition are not entirely consistent with each other. Although Salmerón employed the term "tradition," he was more apt to speak of "the Fathers and the Doctors" and "the custom of the Church," meaning that these concepts and their function in his thought have to be explained.

Salmerón's discussion of tradition took place against the background of sixteenth-century debates. Numerous Catholic writers, including John Fisher, John Driedo, Johann Eck, and Melchor Cano, wrote on the relationship of scripture and tradition, particularly in response to Protestant challenges.[96]

---

[92] Bernardino Realino, one of Salmerón's friends and fellow Jesuits in Naples, said that he knew all of scripture by heart. *ES*, vol. 2, Appendix II, no. 37, 820.

[93] *CEH*, vol. 3, 382–83. He observes, for instance, that Cardinal Cisneros only included the Targum of the Pentateuch in the Complutensian Bible because of the false interpretations of the Aramaic sources.

[94] *CBP*, vol. 2, 257.

[95] Sergio Fernández López, *Lectura y prohibición de la Biblia en lengua vulgar: Defensores y detractores* (León: Universidad de León, 2003).

[96] For a survey of their thought on this issue, see Mathias Mütel, *Mit den Kirchenvatern gegen Martin Luther? Die Debatten um Tradition und auctoritas patrum auf*

Major issues included the material sufficiency of scripture for Christian faith, the logical or temporal priority of scripture versus tradition, and the taxonomy and content of tradition(s).[97] One likely explanation for the difficulties surrounding Salmerón's understanding of tradition is that he appeared to follow different authors at different places in the *Commentaries*, and made no apparent attempt to reconcile the discrepancies.

The first discussion of tradition appears in the *Prolegomena*, where Salmerón gives a definition and taxonomy of it. "The name of tradition is usually given in the scriptures to all divine laws, whether imparted in writing or without it, whether in the Old or the New Testament."[98] A second level of meaning applies to all things that the apostles established by their own authority, or that the Fathers in general councils, or the Roman Pontiffs as the shepherds of the Church, instituted. Thirdly, there are the traditions, which can be called ecclesiastical, canonical, synodal, conciliar, or pontifical, that do not properly pertain to divine law, even if they bind on the faithful as if they were divine. There are, finally, human traditions that Christ and Paul both criticize (Mt 15:2–6; Col 2:8).[99]

Salmerón was careful to distinguish the things in the fourth category from the things in the second and third. Precepts of ecclesiastical tradition are determinations of the divine law, and include such things as the laws governing the observance of the Lord's day, the obligation to confess once a year, the laws of fasting, and so forth.[100] He adds that ecclesiastical traditions are not to be kept if they offend against charity, without specifying how this is to be determined.[101] Here he does not distinguish clearly between scripture and tradition, since the latter seems to include the content of the former. This reflects the view of John Driedo, whose *On Ecclesiastical Writings and Teachings* was the most important influence on the Tridentine discussions of tradition. Both authors integrated scripture and tradition in similar ways, and they showed an

---

dem Konzil von Trient (Paderborn: Ferdinand Schöningh, 2017).

[97] According to Bangert, the medieval theological legacy and terminological obscurity regarding tradition "filled the halls of Trent with a thick theological haze." William Bangert, *Claude Jay and Alfonso Salmerón: Two Early Jesuits* (Chicago, IL: Loyola University Press, 1985), 69.

[98] *CEH*, vol. 1, 208.

[99] *CEH*, vol. 1, 208.

[100] *CEH*, vol. 1, 208.

[101] *CEH*, vol. 1, 209.

appreciation for historical development, attempting to balance the merits of the Fathers and the Scholastic Doctors.[102]

The second treatment of tradition appears near the beginning of Volume 8, where Salmerón discusses the *loci*, or sources, of theology. He cites Melchor Cano's *On Theological Sources*, which is widely regarded as the foremost work on method of the sixteenth century.[103] Salmerón says that the *loci* can be reduced to three headings. First, "divine authority expressed in sacred letters," which is a synonym for scripture. Second, divine authority as expressed in the traditions of Christ and the apostles that were not written down, but transmitted *viva voce*, or by the authority of the Catholic Church, or general councils, or the uniform testimony of the Fathers, or even the Scholastic Doctors. Third, natural reason as applied in all the human disciplines, including philosophy and history.[104] This taxonomy gives clear priority to scripture, followed by a broad range of sources lumped together as tradition. This list is nearly identical to Cano's, except that Salmerón grouped the items under three headings, whereas the Dominican theologian assigned each one its own number.[105] Here Salmerón gives scripture a clear priority over tradition, the latter of which is not internally differentiated, unlike in his first account.

Cano's account of the *loci* does not match the vision of the *Commentaries* where history is concerned. Cano and Salmerón agreed on the importance of human history for the study of theology, and the former gave a lengthy and robust treatment of this topic.[106] Yet Cano did not seek to incorporate history into his understanding of scripture, as Salmerón did with the "Gospel history." This point confirms the impression that in his accounts of tradition, Salmerón was repeating the ideas of his contemporaries, without trying to work out their discrepancies.

In his first volume on Paul, Salmerón gives his third and most robust account of tradition, beginning with a close reading and a definition. *Paradosis/traditio* is the "doctrine of salvation handed on *viva voce* by the Church,"

---

[102] John Driedo, *De ecclesiasticis scripturis et dogmatibus* (Louvain: Bartholomaeus Gravius, 1535); Wim François, "John Driedo's *De ecclesiasticis scripturis et dogmatibus* (1533): A Controversy on the Sources of the Truth," in *Orthodoxy, Process, and Product*, eds. Mathijs Lamberigts, Lieven Boeve, and Terrence Merrigan (Walpole, MA: Uitgeverij Peeters, 2009), 85–118.

[103] In the absence of a modern critical edition or availability of the first edition (1563), another early edition is cited here. Melchor Cano, *De locis theologicis* (Louvain: Servatius Saffenus, 1569).

[104] *CEH*, vol. 8, 7.

[105] Cano, *De locis theologicis*, bk. 1, 4–5.

[106] Cano, *De locis theologicis*, bk. 11, 552–669.

which includes things that are written down in scripture as well as things that are not.[107] While this appears to match his first definition, here he is more specific about tradition's priority over scripture. He compares the live, apostolic preaching of the Gospel favorably to the written word, claiming that the former is more persuasive. He observes that Christ taught precepts and doctrine from his own mouth to the apostles, but that he commanded nothing about writing Gospels. Tradition is older than scripture, not only in the New Testament, but going all the way back to Abraham, who had the faculty of teaching long before anything was written down. Salmerón also claims for tradition the features of clarity [*claritas*] and perspicuity [*perspicuitas*] that he denies to scripture, which cannot be the judge of its own interpretative problems [*dubia*].[108]

According to Salmerón, the heretics can bend Scripture to their mind, but what the common people know is tradition, not scripture.[109] He even claims that the truth of scripture is proven by its conformity with tradition, and that errors against the latter were the motive for writing the canonical letters of the New Testament.[110] For these reasons, Salmerón says that the live preaching of the Gospel, rather than scripture, is the principle and origin of the Church.[111] According to him, tradition is so reliable that the Church could turn to it as a living source even if the Bible were hidden or lost. Scripture commends tradition more than tradition commends scripture, and tradition is indispensable for showing that the Septuagint and the Vulgate are without error in things necessary for salvation.[112] As in Volume 1, here Salmerón distinguishes between numerous levels of tradition: divine, apostolic, and ecclesiastical. Examples of the first include the meaning of scripture and the number of the sacraments; of the second, the Lenten fast, abstaining from meat, and not transferring bishops from see to see; of the third, the custom of praying toward the east. Salmerón points out that some things handed down are only for the sake of piety rather than salvation, such as the account of the Lord's appearance to Peter on the Appian Way, when he said, "I go to Rome to be crucified again."[113]

---

[107] *CBP*, vol. 1, 212.
[108] *CBP*, vol. 1, 217.
[109] *CBP*, vol. 1, 217.
[110] *CBP*, vol. 1, 218.
[111] *CBP*, vol. 1, 207.
[112] *CBP*, vol. 1, 215–16.
[113] *CBP*, vol. 1, 213.

How can the discrepancies between Salmerón's accounts of tradition be explained? One possibility is that his views developed over time, and that the view expressed in the volume on Paul represents his mature position. If this is the case, then his esteem for tradition increased over time, for in the third account, he identified tradition with the Gospel message itself, rather than as secondary content. In modern theological terms, his later view might be described as *sola traditio*, or an understanding of tradition as the life and consciousness of the Church, which is theologically prior to the Bible, and of which scripture forms an essential part.[114]

Even if this account is the correct one, the question still remains of how this shift in perspective came about. Salmerón did not betray any awareness that his various accounts stood in tension with each other, so some conjecture is inevitable. One possible explanation is that while writing the *Commentaries* he came across Martín Pérez de Ayala's *On Divine, Apostolic, and Ecclesiastical Traditions*.[115] Published in 1549, this was the only major treatise from the period specifically dedicated to the concept of tradition.[116] Salmerón's third explanation echoes Pérez de Ayala's, including the detail about the transmission of tradition during the age of the patriarchs.[117] Another possibility is that the shift of perspective was the result of Salmerón's own reflection and reasoning. The temporal gap between the Resurrection and the writing down of the Gospels and Epistles may have led him to see the sacred texts as secondary to the apostolic preaching. This is consistent with his apparent rejection of the material sufficiency of scripture. He says that if a teaching is not found in the Bible, then it is found in tradition or in solid arguments deduced from both. He appears to think that the Marian doctrines of the Immaculate Conception and the Assumption are examples of this.[118] Whatever the explanation, Salmerón's understanding of tradition reflected the influence of the principal Catholic thinkers of his time, but without ironing out the differences between them.

---

[114] Nichols, *Shape of Catholic Theology*, 176–77.

[115] Pérez de Ayala was a member of the Order of Santiago who later became a bishop of several sees in Spain, and participated in two convocations of the Council of Trent.

[116] Martín Pérez de Ayala, *De divinis, apostolicis, et ecclsiasticis traditionibus* (Cologne: Jaspar Gennepaeus, 1549). See Antonio Miralles, *El concepto de tradición en Martín Pérez de Ayala* (Pamplona: University of Navarre, 1980); Mütel, *Mit den Kirchenvatern*, 108–35.

[117] Pérez de Ayala, *De divinis*, 14r. Yet Salmerón never cites Pérez de Ayala or his work directly.

[118] *CEH*, vol. 3, 401. At the same time, he said that no teachings could be contrary to scripture, and that it regulates all doctrines. *CEH*, vol. 1, 4.

He nevertheless exerted himself more strenuously than the other exegetes under consideration, who dealt with the question rather tersely, if at all. Jansen remarks that heretics reject the Church's norms regarding external things as "human traditions," while asserting that she places divine precepts before human ones.[119] Maldonado identifies three categories of tradition: things established by God and always observed by the Church, like the baptism of infants; things established by the Church, like the Lenten fast; things established by the civil power or private individuals that are not contrary to the laws of God.[120] Marlorat mocks the "puerile traditions" regarding the dress, food, and ceremonies of the "courtiers of tyrants, that is, the priests and the monks."[121]

The Fathers and the Doctors

Although Salmerón dealt directly with the concept of tradition, he was more apt to speak of "the Fathers and the Doctors" as the counterpart to scripture. There seem to be two reasons for this: first, authoritative interpretations of scripture are more commonly found in their works than anywhere else; second, Salmerón had encyclopedic knowledge of these sources. He not only used them, but he also sought to integrate them at a theoretical level in an age when some were seeking to separate them.

The sixteenth century witnessed significant controversy over the use of patristic and scholastic resources. Erasmus and others introduced a polemic between the Bible and the Fathers, on the one hand, and the Scholastic Doctors, on the other, to the detriment of the latter. The principle of *sola scriptura* raised the stakes considerably, although leading Protestants often appealed to the authority of the Fathers, especially Augustine, in support of their positions.[122] In other words, it was not an issue of whether but how the Fathers were to be used, and numerous authors wrote guides explaining which patristic authors and works should be read, and in what order.[123] Among Catholic

---

[119] Jansen, *Commentaries*, Pars Tertia, 6.

[120] Maldonado, *Commentaries*, vol. 1, cols. 316–17.

[121] Marlorat, *Expositio*, vol. 2, 5.

[122] "The Protestant reformers had a general respect for the fathers and summoned them particularly as a defensive strategy." Esther Chung-Kim, *Inventing Authority: The Use of the Church Fathers in Reformation Debates over the Eucharist* (Waco, TX: Baylor University Press, 2011), 31.

[123] Irena Backus, *Historical Method and Confessional Identity in the Era of the Reformation (1378–1615)* (Boston, MA: Brill, 2003), 196–252.

authors, lines were not usually drawn so sharply between biblical-patristic and scholastic approaches, as Lu Ann Homza has demonstrated in the case of Renaissance Spain.[124]

The sheer number of authors and amount of material cited in the *Commentaries* is impressive. Hardly any name from Christian antiquity is missing, famous or obscure, Eastern or Western. Ambrose, Augustine, Jerome, Gregory the Great, Basil, John Chrysostom, Athanasius, and Gregory Nazianzen are present in abundance, but so are Theophylact, Vincent of Lérins, Cyprian of Carthage, Cyril of Alexandria and Cyril of Jerusalem. On any given page, Salmerón can easily offer a dozen citations from the Fathers, and he often cites the original source verbatim.[125] Salmerón never provided an explicit taxonomy of what makes a Father or a Doctor, and sometimes he used these terms interchangeably. Roughly speaking, the "Fathers" are important Christian writers of recognized sanctity and orthodoxy until the time of John Damascene, with the inclusion of a few later figures like Rupert of Deutz and Bernard of Clairvaux. Salmerón also cited the works of Origen and Tertullian, while recognizing that the Church condemned some of their teachings.

Salmerón's copious citations of the Fathers and Doctors reflects a common feature of Catholic exegesis in the period. Jansen and especially Barradas filled their pages with the witness of the tradition, whereas Maldonado used them more selectively. Marlorat's approach was different. He references scripture constantly, along with the commentary of other Protestants (and occasionally Catholic textual editors like Erasmus), but only rarely the Church Fathers. He did not make, in other words, a concerted effort to claim Augustine or other patristic authors for the Calvinist cause, even though this was a fairly common feature of Reformed theology and apologetics.

Salmerón's deployment of patristic and scholastic authors offers important insight into his method. Just as using scripture to interpret scripture is a way of demonstrating the unity, divine authorship, and Christocentrism of the whole Bible, providing the exegesis of the Fathers and Doctors shows that scripture cannot be understood apart from the authority and witness of the Church's saints and teachers. This "thick" presentation of scripture aimed to bring out its richness, texture, and spiritual depth. The polemical motivation

---

[124] Lu Ann Homza, *Religious Authority in the Spanish Renaissance* (Baltimore, MD: Johns Hopkins University Press, 2000).

[125] Salmeron is just one example of the many Jesuits who contributed to a revival of the Fathers in the sixteenth and seventeenth centuries. See Dominique Bertrand, "The Society of Jesus and the Church Fathers," in *The Reception of the Church Fathers in the West: From the Carolingians to the Maurists*, ed. Irena Backus (New York: Brill, 1997), vol. 2, 889–950.

was also important, as Salmerón understood his approach as the diametrical opposite of his opponents'. He saw the *Commentaries* as a compendium of the wisdom of past ages, in contrast with the impudent disregard of it by Protestants.[126] Rightly or wrongly, he thought they had abandoned the Fathers rather than reconceived the use of them.[127] The comparison of sources, however, has another function: providing the reader with the opportunity to arrive at his own conclusions on matters of legitimate debate.[128]

Scholastic thought was a more complex issue, as it had been widely criticized from at least the late fifteenth century. During his studies at Alcalá and Paris, Salmerón would have been exposed to vigorous debates about method between advocates of humanism and scholasticism.[129] The *Commentaries* raise the issue when dealing with the use of the human disciplines for the study of scripture. Salmerón lists a number of common objections to scholasticism: one has to spend one's whole life in such studies before getting to scripture; it is contentious and seems to be condemned by the Bible itself; Aristotle committed many errors; the *Apostolic Constitutions* enjoin believers to stay away from pagan books.[130] The Jesuit theologian was not convinced by these arguments, however, and he put forth a moderate defense of this theological method.

---

[126] In one place, Salmerón says that the heretics refuse to receive and pass along the teaching of the Fathers. *CEH*, vol. 4, 215.

[127] In the words of one scholar, this view was "a single indisputable point of agreement in the diverse uses and explorations given to the Church Fathers by the theologians of the Roman obedience in the seventeenth century." Jean-Louis Quantin, "The Fathers in Seventeenth Century Roman Catholic Theology," in *The Reception of the Church Fathers in the West: From the Carolingians to the Maurists*, ed. Irena Backus (New York: Brill, 1997), vol. 2, 951–86, at 951.

[128] This feature of the *Commentaries* may owe to Salmerón's experience as a teacher. John Driedo, who was highly influential in the sixteenth century, also taught students to think for themselves. John Murphy, *The Notion of Tradition in John Driedo* (Milwaukee, WI, 1959), 32.

[129] Philippe Lécrivain, *Paris in the Time of Ignatius of Loyola (1528–1535)*, trans. Ralph Renner (St. Louis, MO: Institute of Jesuit Sources, 2011), 141–46. See also Rummel, *Erasmus and his Catholic Critics*; Katherine van Liere, "Humanism and Scholasticism in Sixteenth-Century Academe: Five Student Orations from the University of Salamanca," *Renaissance Quarterly* 53, no. 1 (2000): 57–107; Paul Grendler, "The Universities of the Renaissance and Reformation," *Renaissance Quarterly* 57, no. 1 (2004), 1–42; Grantley McDonald, *Biblical Criticism in Early Modern Europe: Erasmus, the Johannine Comma, and Trinitarian Debate* (New York: Cambridge University Press, 2016).

[130] *CEH*, vol. 1, 329.

He sought to take a middle way between two extreme views.[131] The first was Luther's, which consisted of a complete rejection of humane studies, especially scholasticism. The second view said that such studies were not only useful, but also necessary, for understanding scripture. Against excessive reliance on scholasticism, Salmerón says that only Christ is necessary for receiving the faith and attaining eternal life, not Plato, Aristotle, or any other philosopher. Anyone who thinks he can get to heaven by philosophy or the Mosaic Law builds a tower of Babel. At the same time, he says that these studies are the greatest asset to the Church for both understanding and explaining scripture and refuting errors. Here Salmerón invokes the principle that grace does not destroy but perfects nature. Just as Moses, Daniel, and others learned the wisdom of the Egyptians and the Babylonians, so also have the Church's saints learned the wisdom of the ancients. This helps explain why the Church has always supported learning with the establishment of schools and academies.[132]

Salmerón's case for scholastic theology relied on history, although he tried to argue simultaneously for its newness and its antiquity. The authors he identifies as scholastics are all from the second millennium, and he admits their relative newness when he says, "later medicines tend to be better, as the Greek proverb has it."[133] Desirous of establishing an older pedigree, Salmerón locates scholasticism's origin in the life of Christ, who first disputed with the doctors in the temple (Lk 2:46), and then continued to do so with the Pharisees during his public ministry. Paul and Stephen carried on this tradition of debating when they spoke of "the Messiah, the Law, predestination, grace and free will, faith and works, marriage, the resurrection, and many other mysteries."[134] In Salmerón's portrayal, these biblical figures were strikingly preoccupied with the debates of the sixteenth century. What defines scholasticism, according to

---

[131] This search for a middle way likely owed something to the thought of Vitoria and Cano, although Salmerón did not follow them in sharply criticizing common scholasticism. See Fernando Domínguez Reboiras, "Biblical Criticism," in *A Companion to the Spanish Scholastics*, eds. Harald Braun, Erik de Bom and Paolo Astorri (Boston, MA: Brill, 2022), 165–98, at 176–77.

[132] *CEH*, vol. 1, 330–32. For a fuller treatment of Salmerón's defense of profane disciplines, see Christoph Sander, "Alfonso Salmerón über weltliche Wissenschaften im Dienste der Bibelexegese," *Freiburger Zeitschrift für Philosophie und Theologie* 64, no. 2 (2017): 344–60.

[133] *CEH*, vol. 1, 335. Elsewhere he rejects the argument of heretics that the Church has erred during the four hundred years of scholasticism. *CBP*, vol. 1, 198.

[134] *CEH*, vol. 1, 335.

Salmerón, is not its immediate historical origin and context, but its "debating" [*disputatrix*] method.¹³⁵

The great advantage of scholasticism, according to Salmerón, is its ability to explain things briefly, so that students may learn the mysteries in a short time. Scholastics make distinctions that the Fathers did not, because such distinctions became necessary for the sake of refuting heretics. Salmerón appeals to ecclesiastical authority as well. Lateran IV approved scholastic studies and the works of Peter Lombard, and the works of Thomas received approval from Urban VI and Innocent V. The Church has also approved the conferral of academic degrees, and Trent decreed that no one without a laureate in theology or canon law may be made a bishop.¹³⁶

Not only did he defend and encourage scholastic studies, but Salmerón also proposed a concrete plan for pursuing them. One need not spend one's whole life in scholastic studies, he says, which would be like looking down at someone's feet forever without ever lifting up the gaze to contemplate the beauty of the head. Instead, one should begin with five or six years of logic and philosophy around the age of twelve or fifteen before moving on to another five or six years of scholastic theology, at which point one can move on to "higher theology" around the age of twenty-five.¹³⁷ The higher theology seems to be commentary on scripture.¹³⁸

Salmerón finishes his treatment of scholastic theology with the following comparison:

> And therefore there are two kinds of theology. One is armored or helmeted theology, bearing shield and spear. The shield is for catching the enemy's darts, that they may not inflict harm, while the spear is for slaughtering and overcoming their errors. For which reason the poets used to depict Minerva, whom they called the light of wisdom and Pallas, armed with helmet, and breastplate, and javelin. The other kind of theology is unarmed, and meeker.

---

¹³⁵ *CEH*, vol. 1, 336.

¹³⁶ *CEH*, vol. 1, 336.

¹³⁷ *CEH*, vol. 1, 333. Early Jesuits were generally more interested in philosophy for its connection to theology than for its own sake. Paolo Galtier, "La compagnia di Gesù e la teologia dommatica," in *La Compagnia di Gesù e le scienze sacre: conferenze commemorative del quarto centenario dalla fondazione della Compagnia di Gesù tenute alla Pontificia università gregoriana, 5–11 novembre 1941* (Rome: Gregorian University, 1942), 45–81, at 65.

¹³⁸ This sense of balance is reflected in Salmerón's suggestion in 1575 that Jesuit scholastics in Naples attend one lecture on scripture and one lecture on scholastic theology each day, rather than one on the former and two on the latter. *ES*, vol. 2, no. 461, 566.

It is not strong enough to go forth onto the battlefield to meet the enemy, but is suitable for all the faithful, even the little ones, to whom it is not given to dispute the mysteries of faith or Christian theology.[139]

It should be clear that although he distinguished between the Fathers and the Scholastic Doctors, he wanted to highlight what they had in common. Any theology that engages in disputation or makes systematic use of reason merits the name "scholastic," and this sort of theology is indispensable for the Church, especially for fighting against heretics. In other words, the Jesuit theologian sought not only to integrate scripture with tradition, but also to integrate the most important witnesses of the latter, the Fathers and the Doctors, with each other.

It is commonly observed that the Society of Jesus has a historical tendency toward "loose Thomism," and that at least through the generalate of Acquaviva, the order was marked by debates about how loose it should be.[140] The *Commentaries* were completed before figures like Bellarmine and Suárez had articulated a distinctive version of Jesuit Thomism, which makes Salmerón one of the best witnesses to an earlier theological mindset.[141] Did he prefer one of the schoolmen in particular?

While his theology was obviously disputatious, Salmerón did not use the distinctive literary forms of scholastic thought, and he used distinctly scholastic terminology rather sparingly. He nevertheless evinced a clear preference for the thought of Thomas Aquinas, the schoolman he cited most frequently and almost always approvingly. His explanation of the relationship between faith and reason is basically Thomistic.[142] Salmerón says that God is not the formal cause of all things, but the ideal or exemplar cause, as Thomas teaches.[143] The gift of faith, according to Aquinas, concerns both the interior persuasion of belief and the ability to propose and explain things exteriorly.[144] The Jesuit theologian uses Thomas's argument from the *Commentary on the Sentences* to

---

[139] *CEH*, vol. 1, 338.

[140] See Franco Motta, "Jesuit Theology, Politics, and Identity: The Generalate of Acquaviva and the Years of Formation," in *The Acquaviva Project: Claudio Acquaviva's Generalate (1581–1615) and the Emergence of Modern Catholicism* (Boston, MA: Institute of Jesuit Sources, 2017), 353–74.

[141] Stefania Tutino, *Uncertainty in Post-Reformation Catholicism: A History of Probabilism* (Oxford: Oxford University Press, 2018), 53.

[142] *CEH*, vol. 1, 338.

[143] *CEH*, vol. 2, 139.

[144] *CEH*, vol. 1, 20.

show that the Incarnation does not undermine divine simplicity.[145] Salmerón agrees with Thomas and numerous other Doctors that Mary and Joseph were both virgins.[146] In the *Summa Theologiae*, Thomas explains that martyrdom can be attained not only by the confession of faith, but by any virtue by which faith is shown.[147]

If Salmerón's basic intellectual framework, and most of his theological positions, were Thomistic, he rarely used the term "Thomist," and he never applied it to himself.[148] One possible explanation is that Salmerón appears to have had a strict understanding of the category. One of the many sources of turmoil during Acquaviva's generalate was the protracted dispute concerning intellectual conformity within the order. When Salmerón's opinion was solicited in 1582, around the time that the *Commentaries* were being completed, he replied with a letter opposing uniformity. Although he acknowledges that it would be good and useful to attain it, "it is exceedingly rare to find agreement of doctrine and the same consensus of minds and wills, even in men endowed with great sanctity, as I can easily show from experience and illustrious examples." Salmerón cites the quarrels between Paul and Barnabus, Peter and Paul, Cyprian and Pope Cornelius, and numerous others in support of this point.[149]

Salmerón did not think it was expedient for the Society to choose any Doctor or scholastic theologian as its leader, so that everyone would be compelled to swear to his words and opinions, and fight for them as for home and hearth. He says that no Doctor up to his time has been correct in all his writings and opinions, and that no one will be in the future. Of all the Church's holy men who have expounded theology, Thomas Aquinas stands out for his perspicacity, his ability to explain and find supporting evidence in the ancient Fathers, and his ability to defend the faith from the cunning and deceits of the heretics. That is why "our Father Ignatius of happy memory" wanted Jesuits to study him particularly among the scholastics.[150] At the same time, the founder did not think it necessary to bind Jesuits to all his opinions. Not even the Dominicans, he adds, are required to follow Thomas in everything.

---

[145] *CEH*, vol. 3, 10.

[146] *CEH*, vol. 4, 325.

[147] *CEH*, vol. 5, 132.

[148] He refers to the opinion of *Thomistae* on simony. *CEH*, vol. 10, 168. In his commentary on 1 Cor 1:11–13, he draws an analogy with contemporary intellectual schools or factions: Thomists, Scotists, and nominalists. *CBP*, vol. 2, 5; *CBP*, vol. 2, 9.

[149] *ES*, vol. 2, no. 522, 710–11.

[150] *ES*, vol. 2, no. 522, 711–12.

The Jesuit theologian identifies three views of Thomas to which he cannot reconcile himself: the pope's power to dissolve a ratified but unconsummated marriage, the validity of clandestine marriages, and opposition to the Immaculate Conception. He adds that there are other views of Thomas's, including those taken from philosophical principles, that lack solid and firm foundation. If the Jesuits bound themselves to any particular theologian, he says, they would seem to love a man more than the truth itself.[151]

> And so, I fear that, while trying to heal the illness of divergent theological opinions, we might inflict a greater wound, such that they would say that, by a wondrous metamorphosis, we have been transformed from Jesuits into Thomists or Dominicans.[152]

His esteem for Aquinas and other Dominicans notwithstanding, Salmerón clearly did not wish to be identified as one of them. A "Thomist," in his view, was someone who followed Thomas in all things, not merely in most.

Nova et Vetera

The heart of Salmerón's theological work is commentary on the Vulgate text of scripture, aided by knowledge of Greek and Hebrew, according to the mind of the Fathers and Doctors of the Church. This does not mean, however, that he looked only to the past. He regularly referred to "recent" authors, that is, those who lived in the fifteenth and sixteenth centuries, and he used them in two ways. First, he cited them as sources for his own exegetical labors and theological positions. Second, he sometimes offered his own evaluation of recent authors. Salmerón sought to take the best of what his age produced and incorporate it into the *Commentaries*.

Volume 7, which treats Jesus's parables, offers a good illustration of how Salmerón made eclectic use of sixteenth-century methods. He interprets the parables according to an agricultural analogy: the root [*radix*], shell [*cortex*], and the marrow or fruit [*medulla sive fructu*]. These correspond respectively to the parable's aim [*scopus*], the sensible similitude it employs, and the spiritual sense. Salmerón acknowledges that there are numerous difficulties involved in explaining each aspect. Not only is the Lord's aim not always clear, but the sensible similitude may be hard to understand on account of the difference in times and mores between the reader and the biblical world. Grasping the spiritual sense is a challenge because the comparison between sensible and

---

[151] *ES*, vol. 2, no. 522, 712.
[152] *ES*, vol. 2, no. 522, 713.

spiritual things cannot be exact.[153] These difficulties, however, did not prevent him from applying this method of exegesis to each of the Gospel parables.

Delville explains that Salmerón's approach here involves a creative arrangement of the method of other exegetes of the period. Luther and Bucer, followed by Cornelius Jansen the Elder and Juan de Maldonado, prioritized the search for the *scopus*, whereas the interest in the *cortex* follows the philological investigations of figures like Erasmus, Beza, and Jansen. Salmerón's personal contribution was twofold: first, he arranged his treatment of the parables in terms of a progression through the three different parts of his analogy; second, he provided the copious florilegia that are characteristic of the *Commentaries* as a whole. On top of that, he was the first author in centuries to offer a complete treatise on the parables; only Irenaeus and Simon of Cassia were his predecessors in this respect.[154] In other words, this part of the *Commentaries* was traditional, synthetic, and innovative all at once.

Salmerón also had more direct ways of using contemporary authors. Prominent names of Catholic theology from the fifteenth and sixteenth centuries are peppered throughout the work: Alonso Tostado, Nicholas of Cusa, John Eck, Richard Tapper, John Fisher, Johann Faber, Lefèvre d'Étaples, Melchor Cano, Albert Pigge, and John Driedo, to name several. In general, he treated them as interlocutors rather than as allies or opponents, meaning that he dealt with their positions on a case-by-case basis, agreeing or disagreeing according to his own convictions.[155]

To take a random sampling, Alonso Tostado is cited with considerable frequency on exegetical questions. Salmerón thought he was right about Mary and Joseph being of the same tribe, but wrong about the significance of Christ's first temptation in the desert.[156] He praises Eck for defending the "reverence" theory of Joseph's desire to dismiss Mary, and for defending the Eucharist against heretics.[157] Ruard Tapper was wrong to advocate utraquism, but Salmerón agreed with him that sacrifice consists in consecration alone.[158] Juan de Torquemada, Tostado, Eck, and Domingo de Soto are cited as examples of the consensus of Catholic Doctors that the pope cannot be the head

---

[153] *CEH*, vol. 7, 15.

[154] Delville, *L'europe de l'exegese*, 534–43. Juan de Granada published his treatise on the parables in 1585, the year of Salmerón's death.

[155] The two Catholic theologians he treats as enemies (Erasmus and Cajetan) are discussed in Chapter 6.

[156] *CEH*, vol. 3, 214; *CEH*, vol. 4, 122.

[157] *CEH*, vol. 3, 238; *CEH*, vol. 8, 214.

[158] *CEH*, vol. 8, 184; *CEH*, vol. 9, 223.

of the Church Militant if his jurisdiction is received from others.¹⁵⁹ Salmerón usually disagreed with Lefèvre d'Étaples, as when the latter said that the rich man (Lk 16:22) was in Purgatory rather than Hell, or that Christians are forbidden to go to court against each other as a matter of precept, or the that Lord may have despaired on the cross.¹⁶⁰ He thought Melchor Cano was correct to say that even a council convened by a pope needs the pope to confirm its decrees, but that he was probably mistaken to claim that the Eucharistic sacrifice consists of all four major aspects of the Mass, rather than just the consecration.¹⁶¹ Salmerón treated Cano as another orthodox theologian, rather than as an inveterate enemy of the Society of Jesus.¹⁶²

Salmerón's most extensive and fascinating discussion of contemporary authors is found in his first volume on the works of Paul, where he offers his assessments of contemporary theologians, eighteen in all, who have commented on the apostle's writings. Lefèvre d'Étaples was too critical of the Vulgate, following Valla and Erasmus, and he advanced certain novelties, which is why his works were placed on the Index produced by the council fathers at Trent. Cardinal Marco Grimani inclined too much toward the teaching of Pelagius in his works on Romans and Galatians. Salmerón praised the outstanding commentaries on all of Paul's letters by Ambrogio Catarino, who was effective at refuting the errors of heretics, and he had good things to say about the "pious" Francis Titelmans, who rendered the apostle's meaning clearer and plainer in his *Paraphrases* on Paul and the Catholic epistles. Domingo de Soto sought to resolve a number of scholastic questions in his commentary on Romans, whereas Adam Sasbout surpassed others in analyzing the Greek of Paul's works.¹⁶³ Salmerón was evidently well read in contemporary theology and did not shy away from offering his judgments of it.

---

[159] *CEH*, vol. 12, 452.

[160] *CEH*, vol. 4, 545; *CEH*, vol. 5, 250; *CEH*, vol. 10, 357.

[161] *CEH*, vol. 12, 615; *CEH*, vol. 9, 222.

[162] For Cano's hostility toward the Society, see Santiago Madrigal Terrazas, *Eclesialidad, reforma, y misión: El legado teológico de Ignacio de Loyola, Pedro Fabro y Francisco de Javier* (Madrid: San Pablo, 2008), 25–54.

[163] *CBP*, vol. 1, 57–58. The work of Titelmans that Salmerón has in mind is almost certainly the *Elucidatio in omnes epistolas apostolicas* (Antwerp: Johannes Steelsius, 1540). Some of the works published under Sasbout's name were actually the work of Hasselius, so Salmerón's praise may really fall upon him. Wim François, "Augustine and the Golden Age of Biblical Scholarship in Louvain (1550–1650)," in *Shaping the Bible in the Reformation: Books, Scholars, and Their Readers in the Sixteenth Century*, eds. Bruce Gordon and Matthew McLean (Boston, MA: Brill, 2012), 235–89, at 247.

One trend in this theology looked to what was very old and even outside Christianity proper: not the classical world, but the Jewish mystical tradition. The latter was being revived in the sixteenth century as the field of Christian Hebraism. The controversy over the Kabbalistic inquiries of Johann Reuchlin in the early sixteenth century, which included charges of "Judaizing," did not stop the development of Christian Hebraism, and by the 1570s it had entered the mainstream of biblical scholarship.[164] This field went beyond the Hebrew language itself to include rabbinical and Kabbalistic materials, as well as Jewish liturgical tradition. Salmerón mentions the work of Reuchlin and the German Hebraist Sebastian Münster, and he also relied on the work of Benito Arias Montano, the editor of the Antwerp Polyglot Bible.[165] Montano's denunciation to the Spanish Inquisition in 1574, however, may have discouraged the Jesuit theologian from mentioning him very often in the *Commentaries*.[166] On the one hand, Salmerón used a good deal of this material for his own theological purposes, but on the other hand, he rejected what he regarded as its dangerous elements.

Although Salmerón used rabbinical sources to identify the characteristics of the Messiah, and he took an interest in Jewish ritual and priesthood, he rejected and ridiculed the Kabbalah. He sees Kabbalah as part of a deplorable interest in the occult among his contemporaries.[167] He singles out Pico della Mirandola for wrongly saying that magic and Kabbalah were the greatest knowledge that confirmed the divinity of Christ.[168] In his exegesis of the story

---

[164] See William Horbury, "Petrus Galatinus and Jean Thenaud on the Talmud and the *Toledot Yeshu*," in *Jewish Books and their Readers: Aspects of the Intellectual Life of Christians and Jews in Early Modern Europe*, eds. Scott Mandelbrote and Joanna Weinberg (Boston, MA: Brill, 2016), 125–50; Robert Wilkinson, *The Kabbalistic Scholars of the Antwerp Polyglot Bible* (Boston, MA: Brill, 2007); Brian Copenhaver and Daniel Stein Kokin, "Egidio da Viterbo's *Book on Hebrew Letters*: Christian Kabbalah in Papal Rome," *Renaissance Quarterly* 67, no. 1 (2014):1–42.

[165] *CEH*, vol. 6, 18. In a letter of 1576, he thanks Mercurian for sending him one of Arias Montano's books. *ES*, vol. 2, no. 491, 641.

[166] Anthony Grafton, "Church History in Early Modern Europe: Tradition and Innovation," in *Sacred History: Uses of the Christian Past in the Renaissance World*, eds. Katherine van Liere, Simon Ditchfield, and Howard Louthan (New York: Oxford University Press, 2012), 3–26, at 22.

[167] *CEH*, vol. 6, 18–20. In a letter to Cardinal Guglielmo Sirleto, he praises the theologian León de Castro for being the "enemy of the rabbis and everything Kabbalistic and Talmudical." *ES*, vol. 2, no. 508, 678.

[168] *CBP*, vol. 3, 573.

of the prodigal son, he compares the husks that the pigs feed on to the "figments" of the Talmud and Kabbalah (Lk 15:16).[169]

The rejection of Kabbalah sheds light on a significant aspect of Salmerón's training. Some scholars have claimed that Salmerón had already distinguished himself in Hebrew and Syriac at the Trilingual College at Alcalá, but Salmerón's own words indicate otherwise.[170] He says that he received his introduction to Hebrew grammar from a learned man who "twisted all the scriptures with such vehemence in favor of the King of France, who at that time was making war against the Emperor Charles V, so that [one knew not] if he spoke of present affairs, or of something already accomplished and completed."[171] The context of the passage is Salmerón's criticism of those who prophesy about future events on the basis of scripture, and it strongly suggests a French rather than a Spanish origin of his Hebrew studies.

There is a likely match among the known associates of the first companions in Paris: Guillaume Postel, who studied at the College Ste. Barbe in the 1530s. Showing a gift for languages, especially Semitic ones, Postel taught himself Hebrew and came to know Ignatius and his friends during those years. Later he journeyed to the Ottoman Empire and became a prominent orientalist and Christian Kabbalist, and he oversaw the publication of the Syriac New Testament. He joined the Society of Jesus in 1544, but he left just over a year later. Among his eccentric views was the belief that the King of France was destined to be the Last World Emperor who would carry out a universal restoration of Christendom.[172]

His consistent advocacy of the "Fathers and Doctors" against novelty and heresy did not prevent Salmerón from cautiously opening to the new methods and sources that the sixteenth century had to offer. This includes the exegetical approaches even of suspect people, as well as opinions on disputed dogmatic questions from the most important Catholic theologians of the period. He thought rabbinical material had limited usefulness, but that Kabbalah led down the dark path of the occult.

---

[169] *CEH*, vol. 8, 332.

[170] Stewart Rose, *St. Ignatius and the Early Jesuits* (London: Burns and Oates, 1891), 172; Igna Kramp, "Der Jesuit Alfonso Salmerón (1515–1585) als humanistischer Theologe: Ähnlichkeiten und Unterschiede zu Erasmus von Rotterdam," *Theologie und Philosophie* 90 (2015): 504–27, at 508.

[171] *CEH*, vol. 1, 79.

[172] Robert Wilkinson, *Orientalism, Aramaic and Kabbalah in the Catholic Reformation: The First Printing of the Syriac New Testament* (Leiden: Brill, 2007), 96–110.

Conclusion

The *Commentaries* are more than a running exegesis of the New Testament; they are a biblical theology that seeks to integrate scripture with tradition in its various aspects. Fully convinced of the greatness of scripture, Salmerón provided a thorough study of the inspiration, senses, texts, and translations of the Bible, which incorporated his characteristic concern for history into the defense of the Vulgate as a common edition. His account of tradition, although detailed, contains unresolved tensions and ambiguities, most likely because Salmerón did not entirely reconcile the authors upon whom he relied. His encyclopedic knowledge of the Fathers and Doctors gives a preeminent place to Aquinas, in keeping with the "loose Thomism" characteristic of early Jesuit thought, while simultaneously demonstrating affinity for Franciscan theologians. For Salmerón, theology was not frozen in time, and the contributions of newer authors and methods could be valuable, provided no harm was done to the orthodox faith. The theologian's task of integrating scripture and tradition, in Salmerón's view, demanded mastery of the sources, a love of tradition, a speculative framework, and an openness to new insights found only among men of distinguished learning and sanctity.

3   Contemplating the Mysteries

In his life of Salmerón, Pedro de Ribadeneyra describes how his subject responded to the mention of Jesus during meals.

> Sometimes it happened, while he was eating, that someone present would touch this key of Christ, and the good father, forgetting about his food, would embark upon and immerse himself so much in this infinite sea of our Lord, speaking of his excellence and wonders, that it seemed he had the Lord present before him, and was giving himself away and offering himself to him.[1]

According to this depiction, the author of the *Commentaries* was entirely taken up into the spiritual significance of his work. If one of the aims of Salmerón's magnum opus was the integration of scripture and tradition into a coherent whole, then there remains the question of how he wanted the reader to receive it. Like his forbears in the theological enterprise, Salmerón saw Christian teaching not merely as a body of propositional truths to be professed and understood intellectually, but also as a mystery into which one may enter only by way of sustained prayer. Accordingly, one of the theologian's tasks is contemplating the mysteries and aiding others to do likewise.

What is a Mystery?

Although Salmerón frequently used the term "mystery," he did not provide an extensive theoretical discussion of it. This was not unusual, for it was the common property of theology and exegesis, as the works of Jansen, Maldonado, Barradas, and even Marlorat demonstrate. The Vulgate uses *sacramentum* in numerous places to translate the Greek *mysterion*, and Salmerón took them as synonymous. He distinguishes between the broad use of these terms, found throughout the Fathers, which refers to secret holy things, and the strict use,

---

[1] Miguel Lop Sebastià, *Alfonso Salmerón, SJ (1515–1585): Una biografía epistolar* (Madrid: Comillas, 2015), Appendix, 359–372, at 371. Ribadeneyra has in mind a musical key (*tecla*).

which refers to the Church's seven sacraments that confer grace.[2] He defines a mystery in the broad sense as "a concealed or secret and hidden thing, that is, one which escapes all perception [*sensum*] and human reason."[3] Although this definition is vaguer than one would expect given his penchant for word studies, Salmerón's commentary on certain passages from Paul, notably from the Letter to the Ephesians, clarifies his meaning. When Paul writes "that he might make known unto us the mystery of his will" (Eph 1:9), Salmerón explains that this mystery is the highest wisdom.[4]

> The Incarnation, and the coming, and the saving death of the Son of God is called the 'mystery of his will.' Never would men have dared to conceive of such a hidden thing, nor having conceived of and considered it, desired and sought it, nor the apostles preached it to the world, without God's desiring to give it by a particular revelation…The cause of such a gift was God's grace and love toward us, of which the Son said: "God so loved the world, that he gave his only-begotten Son" (Jn 3:16). The work is thus said to be of the Holy Spirit, for in the Law it was only tenuously and hiddenly insinuated to a few people, whence the Lord says of Moses, "for he wrote of me" (Jn 5:46).[5]

Principally, then, "mystery" refers to Christ's entrance into the world and his endeavor to save the human race, revealing God's hidden love.

The counterpart of this mystery, however, is the effort of God's enemy to undermine it in the hearts of men.

> But Satan with his artifices and stratagems tries to obscure so great a mystery, and prevent it from being taken up in faith by men. He pretends to be zealous for God's glory, the more he corrupts our minds, saying that it befits not the divine purity and majesty of the Son of God to unite itself to your vile and putrid man-flesh, which has the likeness of sin.[6]

Just as Salmerón understood history as a struggle between these two powers, so also he understood mystery in the same terms. The implication is that the communication of the mystery is not really complete until it is received in faith. Satan cannot stop God from speaking, but he can interfere with the entrance of the message into man's heart.

---

[2] *CBP*, vol. 3, 262.
[3] *CEH*, vol. 9, 101.
[4] *CBP*, vol. 3, 177.
[5] *CBP*, vol. 3, 177.
[6] *CBP*, vol. 3, 177.

For this reason, Salmerón thought that the theologian must not only articulate what God has revealed, but also do so in a way that facilitates a genuine reception of it on the part of the reader. This is only possible if the author himself has already received and contemplated the mystery. Elaborating on this point, Salmerón says that even the wise men of India and Persia, as well as the Greek philosophers, did not undertake their intellectual labors before offering prayers, even though they lacked both the Law of Moses and the splendor of the Gospel. How much more, he says, does someone commenting on the Gospel doctrine need to offer prayer first to overcome human ignorance and weakness. The more ancient Fathers "used no greater defenses or aids to attain to true and solid understanding of scripture, than prayers, invocations, and sighs, by which they won the Holy Spirit, the interpreter of the divine Word."[7]

This emphasis on prayer and contemplation appears throughout the *Commentaries*. Salmerón directly invites the reader to contemplate a given mystery, whether the Trinity, the Nativity, or even the beauty of justice, on numerous occasions.[8] He defends the superiority of the contemplative life over the active; the former is nobler *in se*, more fruitful in act, and has more merit in itself, whereas the latter is a symbol of greater love for one's neighbor. He says that the rich, peasants, soldiers, merchants and all others who deal with affairs of the world will be happy if they work to support contemplatives and thereby share in their fruits.[9] The Blessed Virgin Mary is regularly described as a model of contemplation.[10]

Ribadeneyra's description of Salmerón's daily schedule in his waning years indicates that the Jesuit theologian put his own counsel into practice.

> During this time, his occupations [*ejercicios*] were his prayer [*oración*] in the morning, praying his Office and the litany, and saying his Mass with all devotion and recollection, which he never failed to do, regardless of whatever task or hindrance there might be. The afternoons and evenings, until the hour of dinner, he used to write, which he did with much study and attention and at great length.[11]

---

[7] *CEH*, vol. 2, Preface, 2r.
[8] *CEH*, vol. 3, 68; *CEH*, vol. 3, 294; *CEH*, vol. 5, 78.
[9] *CEH*, vol. 4, 516.
[10] *CEH*, vol. 3, 34; *CEH*, vol. 3, 85; *CEH*, vol. 3, 116; *CEH*, vol. 4, 519.
[11] Lop Sebastià, *Alfonso Salmerón*, Appendix, 365. Ribadeneyra may be dependent on a similar account by Bartolomé Pérez de Nueros, Salmerón's editor. *ES*, vol. 2, Appendix II, no. 36, 811.

The reference to Salmerón's "prayer" in all likelihood means a morning meditation, which would have lasted about an hour.[12] The old Roman Office, the structure and content of which was left practically intact in Pius V's *Breviarium Romanum* (1568) was considerably longer than the current usages in the Roman Church, and would have taken about two hours to recite each day, with the bulk of it coming at the morning hours of Matins, Lauds, Prime, and Terce.[13] It seems likely, however, that the hours of Matins and Lauds were anticipated the previous evening, for Pérez de Nueros says that Salmerón prayed the minor hours in the morning.[14] The Litany of the Saints, whether recited privately or communally, may have taken an additional twenty to thirty minutes, and the private Mass a minimum of half an hour.

Ribadeneyra offers a picture of a man who spent the bulk of his morning every day in prayer before moving on to his exegetical work in the afternoon. "The whole of his recreation and contentment was in sacred scripture, and he valued understanding a difficult passage of it more than all the goods of the world, and he spent the final fifteen years of his life writing about it."[15] In a letter to Ribadeneyra from 1583, Salmerón says that he is "in Naples living in leisure and contemplation the life of Mary."[16] The *Commentaries* were the result not only of a lifetime of study and preaching, but also of the contemplative prayer that preceded their composition on a daily basis for no less than a decade.

Salmerón did not offer anything like a definition or explanation of contemplation, or what methods of prayer ought to be used to attain it. This omission is crucial, not only because it was a disputed question in the sixteenth century, but also because it had special relevance for the Society of Jesus until at least the turn of the seventeenth century. Some Jesuits were attracted to various kinds of "mystical" prayer, such as "recollection" (*recogimiento*) that aimed at

---

[12] It took several decades to settle the issue of how long, and in what manner, members of the Society were to pray. By the end of Salmerón's life, an hour of prayer in the morning, two examinations of conscience, and Mass were commonly practiced as well as stipulated by legislation. His retirement would have left him free for more than this. See Pedro de Leturia, "La hora matutina de meditación en la Compañía naciente," in *Estudios Ignacianos*, vol. 2, *Estudios espirituales*, ed. Ignacio Iparraguirre (Rome: IHSI, 1957), 189–268.

[13] To put the matter into perspective, the Office of Salmerón's time required the praying of twelve psalms at Matins on ferial days, and eighteen on Sundays, and it did not divide individual psalms (with the exception of Ps 118) into multiple parts.

[14] *ES*, vol. 2, Appendix II, no. 36, 818.

[15] Lop Sebastià, *Alfonso Salmerón*, Appendix, 369.

[16] *ES*, vol. 2, no. 526, 723.

attaining infused contemplation. For a variety of reasons, General Mercurian took action against some of the proponents of these practices, limiting the time spent in mental prayer, and promoting the *Exercises* as the sole reliable guide.[17] Salmerón apparently wished to skirt such debates.[18]

The priority that Salmerón gave to contemplating the mysteries offers a partial explanation of the prolixity of the *Commentaries*. He evidently had no intention of composing a convenient commentary for those who wanted simple and straightforward answers or information. Instead, his aim was inviting the reader into contemplation understood as the end of the theological enterprise. He preferred to linger over the biblical texts, to savor their meaning, and to offer to his reader something of this same experience.[19] His occasional use of direct address (*candide lector* and similar formulas) may be seen as an attempt to engage in this way.

The role that the mysteries played in the layout of the work supports this hypothesis. As explained already, the *Commentaries* have an unusual organizational structure that combines chronological, thematic, and book-sequential elements. There are three principal mysteries that Salmerón returns to time and again: the Trinity, the Incarnation, and the Eucharist. The capital importance of these three is communicated in several ways. First, Salmerón sometimes groups them together, emphasizing that they are the highest mysteries. He says that natural similitudes fall short of divine things, "especially concerning the mysteries of the Trinity, Incarnation, and Eucharist," and calls the Incarnation and the Eucharist the highest mysteries of the faith.[20] Elsewhere he asserts that it is enough to have the rudiments of faith, whereas the subtle

---

[17] J. Michelle Molina, *To Overcome Oneself: The Jesuit Ethic and Spirit of Global Expansion, 1520–1767* (Berkeley, CA: University of California Press, 2013), 28–29; Philip Endean, "'The Strange Style of Prayer: Mercurian, Cordeses, and Álvarez," in *The Mercurian Project: Forming Jesuit Culture 1573–1580*, ed. Thomas McCoog (St. Louis, MO: Institute of Jesuit Sources, 2004), 351–97.

[18] He says that because it is hard to pay attention for a long time, prayer should be brief and ejaculatory. It is not clear, however, what exactly he means by "brief," as he says that praying for an hour may seem like a very short time. *CEH*, vol. 10, 123.

[19] Salmerón makes a rare reference to his own prayer in his commentary on Jn 3:16, where he says that as often as he hears, says, or meditates upon these words, he sees shining lights that expel all the shadows, scruples, and anguish of his soul, and feels fires and flames warm his frigid heart, so that he can also inflame others. *CEH*, vol. 8, 56.

[20] *CBP*, vol. 2, 244; *CEH*, vol. 8, 223.

points of the mysteries of the Trinity, Incarnation, and the Eucharist are for the mature.[21]

Second, each of these mysteries has more than one long treatise dedicated to it, for which a relevant biblical text serves as the point of departure. Third, some of these treatises are placed within the overall organizational schema of the *Commentaries* in a way that underscores their importance. Most of Volume 2 is given over to the Prologue of John's Gospel, and this text is the point of departure for Salmerón's main discussion of the Trinity. Volume 3, which contains the infancy narratives of Matthew and Luke, is largely concerned with the Incarnation. Most of Volume 9, which resumes the chronological progression through the Gospels after four volumes of thematic interlude, is given over to the Eucharist, followed by another major discussion of the Trinity. In other words, the discussions of the three principal mysteries occur at the points of "beginning" within the overall narrative structure of Salmerón's work. Fourth, the *Commentaries* are peppered with asides and references to these three mysteries even when something else is being discussed, indicating that, in Salmerón's estimation, the Christian faith always returns to them.

Aside from these three principal mysteries, Salmerón provides a list of ten main mysteries of the Lord's life: the Incarnation, the Nativity, the Adoration of the Magi, the Presentation in the Temple, the Baptism, the Entrance into Jerusalem, the Passion (*mors*), the Resurrection, the Ascension, and the Sending of the Holy Spirit.[22] It is noteworthy that the first six of these are contained in Volumes 2–4, and that Volume 4 ends with the Entrance into Jerusalem. The thematic caesura of Volumes 5–8 contains none of the major mysteries of this list, the treatment of which resumes in Volume 10, after the Last Supper. One explanation for the unusual arrangement of the middle volumes is that they lack these major mysteries, and thus are better suited to a thematic principle of organization.

Even if this explanation must remain somewhat conjectural, it is nevertheless unmistakably clear that the *Commentaries* aim at leading the reader into the mysteries of the Christian faith. What follows is a summary of Salmerón's treatment of them according to the aforementioned taxonomies. It is important to note that he brought to bear the various resources at his disposal, without separating exegesis from dogmatics, or doctrinal questions from historical ones, or patristic from scholastic methods and styles. Each of these approaches contributed to the understanding of the mysteries, and Salmerón employed each to the degree that it served this purpose. Linguistic skill and

---

[21] *CBP*, vol. 4, 66.
[22] *CEH*, vol. 3, 98.

conceptual clarity were necessary but not sufficient for Salmerón's mystagogical approach, for which the Fathers and the Doctors provided the model.

The Trinity

Salmerón discusses the Trinity at length in two places: his commentary on the Prologue of John's Gospel (Volume 2), and his treatment of Jesus's "farewell discourse" (Jn 15) in Volume 9. Taken together, these sections treat the internal life of the Trinity, the relationship of the Trinity to creation, and the particular way that man participates in this mystery. Although the *Commentaries* are not laid out like a scholastic treatise, it is noteworthy that Salmerón placed the discussion of the Triune God prior to the discussion of the One God. The latter theme, which is discussed in terms of what can be known about God by reason alone, appears only briefly in Volume 3. The emphasis is on knowledge of God from scripture rather than nature.

Salmerón begins with the assertion that the Prologue of John's Gospel does not merely imply the mystery of the Trinity, but states it openly. According to the Jesuit theologian, John says that the Word is with the Father from all eternity, such that the Father cannot exist or be conceived without him, and that by loving each other, they produce the Holy Spirit.[23] Salmerón's aim was to show that, contrary to the assertions of some sixteenth-century exegetes, the mystery of the Trinity is explicitly taught in scripture and, while certainly above reason, is not contrary to it. This does not mean that all the Church's terms for articulating this mystery are found there, so Salmerón introduces and defends basic terminology of Trinitarian theology, like substance, person, procession, and so forth, saying that such language makes clearer the teaching of the New Testament.[24]

Salmerón undertook a careful commentary on the Prologue. His method was to first explain the words, then establish their true meaning for the sake of the intellect and the affect, and finally explain how to build up Christian life and mores.[25] There is much in the way of philological analysis, as when he discusses the meaning of the "Word" (*logos*) and justifies its translation as *verbum*. *Verbum* denotes an internal word, which he compares to Hannah's speaking to herself (1 Sam 1:13), Mary's keeping all things in her heart (Lk 2:19), and Paul's hearing "secret words" (2 Cor 12:4). It best expresses a number of ideas

---

[23] *CEH*, vol. 2, 5.

[24] *CEH*, vol. 2, 6–15; *CEH*, vol. 2, 103.

[25] *CEH*, vol. 2, 16.

associated with the second person of the Trinity: his role in the production of creatures, the pure and immaterial mode of that production, his perfect imaging of the Father with whom he is consubstantial, and several others.[26] Salmerón even appeals to the teaching of philosophers like Zeno the Stoic, who says that the *logos* is the maker and governor of all things.[27] Trinitarian doctrine instructs Christians in multiple ways. The presence of the Word in the beginning shows that God is not alone, and that the solitary life is not the happiest, since it is lacking in the good of friendship and perfect charity.[28]

The close-reading of the Prologue aims to establish the divinity of the Word, the real distinction between the persons, and the difference between the processions. Salmerón claims that the first four sentences from John's Gospel articulate four dogmas concerning the Word: his eternity, his distinction from the Father, his consubstantiality and divinity, and his coeternity.[29] He adds that if the Word is not God, the people of Israel are guilty of idolatry, since they use plural names for God.[30] Salmerón sees the distinction between the divine persons in the use of the preposition *pros/apud* as well as in the lack of an article before "God" in "the Word was God" [*theos ēn ho logos*].[31] Relying on a long tradition of theological commentary in the West, he explains that the Son proceeds from the Father according to the mode of the intellect, and the Holy Spirit from the Father and the Son according to the mode of the will. These processions show that God is always in act and communicating the divine goodness even before creation began.[32]

The relationship between the Father and the Son with the Spirit receives more extensive treatment in Salmerón's commentary on Jn 15. He thinks that the very name "Paraclete" is a sign of the Spirit's divinity, since no one but God can perfectly console the rational creature.[33] Without the Spirit, Salmerón says, the apostles could have objected that the Lord had sent them to preach the Gospel in vain. "For this reason, the Lord promises them the coming of the Holy Spirit, who would both inflame their tongues and confirm their

---

[26] *CEH*, vol. 2, 20.
[27] *CEH*, vol. 2, 21.
[28] *CEH*, vol. 2, 29.
[29] *CEH*, vol. 2, 46.
[30] *CEH*, vol. 2, 31.
[31] *CEH*, vol. 2, 34.
[32] *CEH*, vol. 2, 12–13.
[33] *CEH*, vol. 9, 412.

teaching with miracles."³⁴ Thereafter Salmerón treats a number of doctrinal points about the Spirit. From the fact that the Spirit is sent by the Father in the name of Christ, the Jesuit theologian deduces that the Spirit is a living and distinct person, and that he has the faculty and freedom to come *sponte sua*. Against the "error of the Greeks," he maintains that the Spirit proceeds from the Father and the Son, saying that there is no opposition of relation between the Father and the Son with respect to the production of the Spirit.³⁵ Clearly one of Salmerón's main aims is establishing a firm biblical foundation for the Roman Church's teaching on the immanent Trinity.

Aware that the Scholastic Doctors disagreed amongst themselves on the more technical aspects of the relations between the persons, Salmerón cautiously follows Thomas.

> Being the Father therefore constitutes the person, for all other absolutes are common to the Son, and the Fathers say together that all things in the Trinity are one, except for the opposition of relations. There is therefore no distinction in absolutes, and this has been received as the common opinion, which Blessed Thomas also follows.³⁶

He observes, however, that other Scholastic Doctors said that the persons are not constituted by their relations. Since the Church has not defined the matter, he regards the position of Thomas as a theological opinion rather than an article of faith.³⁷ At the same time, Salmerón is favorable to the concept of *circumincessio*, present in the works of Scotus, Durandus, and Ockham, but absent from Aquinas's.³⁸ As with so many other questions, Salmerón generally followed Thomas, but he remained open to alternative positions, especially on matters of free debate.

Salmerón did not treat the difficult and technical language of Trinitarian theology as an obstacle to contemplation, but rather saw it as safeguarding the mystery so that it could be properly received. Citing Rupert of Deutz, Salmerón invites the reader to meditate on the "delights and enjoyment" of the Trinity, which are also suggested in the verse, "I was with him forming all things, and was delighted every day, playing before him at all times" (Prov

---

[34] *CEH*, vol. 9, 469.

[35] *CEH*, vol. 9, 470–71.

[36] *CEH*, vol. 2, 119.

[37] *CEH*, vol. 2, 121–22. For a discussion of these issues, see Russell Friedman, *Medieval Trinitarian Thought from Aquinas to Ockham* (New York: Cambridge University Press, 2010), 5–49.

[38] *CEH*, vol. 2, 110.

8:30). This playing, he explains, is nothing other than the ineffable delight of the divine goodness by which the Creator delighted in his Word before he made anything.[39] This passage shows Salmerón's appreciation for the affective dimension of the Trinitarian mystery.

The creation of the world is the first aspect of the Trinity's relationship to creation that Salmerón addresses, beginning from the words "all things were made by him" (Jn 1:3). He sees a connection between the Prologue and Gen 1, saying that John supplies what was missing from the words of the "stammering shepherd" Moses.[40] He establishes a number of doctrinal points concerning creation: the world is not eternal, it is not the result of necessary emanation, as certain Platonists and Peripatetics said, and it has God as its exemplary cause but not its formal cause.[41]

The other aspect of the Trinity is its dwelling in man. The verse "and we will come to him and will make our abode with him" (Jn 14:23) elicits the following words:

> This is another greater and more excellent promise. "We will come," he says in the plural, the Father, I, and the Paraclete, not in a visible but in a spiritual inhabitation through internal consolation, and grace, and other gifts, and the increase of charity. It is no obstacle that his presence is not always felt, for not on this account is the Trinity to be believed to be absent... The person who believes in and loves God is therefore a temple of the Most Holy Trinity, and this abiding of the Trinity in the heart of the believer was foreshadowed when Abraham received the angels as guests, seeing three and adoring one [Gen 18:1–16]. Happy is the faithful one who is worthy to receive this guest.[42]

In Salmerón's view, the mystery of the Trinity culminates for man not merely in the intellectual understanding of it, but also in its indwelling and sharing of divine life.

Other exegetes of the age used scripture as an opportunity to reflect on the mystery of the Trinity. Jansen's and Maldonado's treatments of John's Prologue are heavily laden with Trinitarian dogmatics, especially the relationship between the Father and the Son, and Maldonado is notably aggressive towards

---

[39] *CEH*, vol. 2, 140.
[40] *CEH*, vol. 2, 46.
[41] *CEH*, vol. 2, 138–39.
[42] *CEH*, vol. 9, 418.

the Arians.⁴³ Barradas saves his discussion of the Trinity for the very end of his *Commentaries*, where a substantial dogmatic treatise serves as an addendum to the preaching of the apostles.⁴⁴ Although Marlorat does not offer lengthy doctrinal excursus, he says that John's Prologue teaches the divinity of Christ as well as the distinction of the persons of the Father and the Son.⁴⁵

Although his primary aim was leading the reader into the mystery, Salmerón was aware that some denied the doctrine of the Trinity, including those who accept the authority of scripture. He rails against those who reject it, including Mohammed, Jews, pagans, and the heretic Arius.⁴⁶ Anti-Trinitarianism was not merely a historical issue, as it experienced a resurgence in the sixteenth century among figures like Michael Servetus, who was famously executed in Calvin's Geneva.⁴⁷ Significant space is given to refuting Arius's arguments, with copious citations from the Fathers, Doctors, and councils, followed by a similar treatment of the "new sectarians" and "new Tritheists and Sabellians" who held the same view.⁴⁸ Salmerón displays some knowledge of the history of the new Arians, distinguishing various nuances in their teaching, and observing that Servetus and "Scheg Kius Brentianus" spread the heresy in Poland, Transylvania, and Hungary.⁴⁹

Salmerón sought to bolster his biblical evidence for the Trinity by citing the classic verses used in support of it, and by rejecting Arian exegesis of verses that seem to oppose it, such as "the Father is greater than I" (Jn 14:28). One of the most controverted verses in the sixteenth century was the so-called "Johannine comma," which in the standard Vulgate reckoning is 1 Jn 5:7. The text reads, "and there are three who give testimony in heaven, the Father, the Word, and the Holy Spirit. And these three are one." This interpolated text owes its origin to Spanish Vulgate manuscripts from the ninth century, and

---

⁴³ Jansen, *Commentaries*, Prima Pars, 2–17; Maldonado, *Commentaries*, vol. 2, col. 380–438.

⁴⁴ Barradas, *Commentaries*, vol. 4, 433–47.

⁴⁵ Marlorat, *Expositio*, vol. 1, 421–22.

⁴⁶ *CEH*, vol. 2, 42.

⁴⁷ Salmerón comments that in Calvin's kingdom, they burn those, like Servetus, who do not agree with their teachings. *CBP*, vol. 1, 258–59.

⁴⁸ *CEH*, vol. 2, 65–84; *CEH*, vol. 2, 84–102.

⁴⁹ *CEH*, vol. 2, 100. Salmerón is referring to the Lutheran polymath Jakob Degen (1511–87), who as an adult adopted the surname Schegk or Schegkius. He distinguished himself in languages, Aristotelian philosophy, and medicine. In response to critics who accused him of Arian teaching, he wrote a treatise refuting the teaching of Michael Servetus.

it was eventually taken into the textual tradition at Paris, whence it spread to the rest of Western Christendom. Erasmus was the first to challenge the authenticity of the verse, claiming that it could not be found in ancient Greek manuscripts, although he did not take a consistent position across the various editions of his New Testament.

The "comma" became a flashpoint among Catholics and Protestants alike on both textual and doctrinal grounds.[50] Salmerón vigorously defended the verse, appealing to its presence in numerous Greek codices (which in fact had been interpolated), as well as its use as a locus for authoritative teaching, such as in the documents of Lateran IV. In his view, the rejection of the comma was a danger to the mystery itself, as well as to the Church's authority to interpret scripture.[51] This discussion provides a good showcase of his conservative disposition on disputed exegetical and doctrinal questions.

There is, finally, a significant liturgical dimension to Salmerón's discussion of the Trinity. He sometimes makes direct use of liturgical sources, as when he cites the preface of the Most Holy Trinity, or when he complains that Luther's *Enchiridion* (1543) expunged "Holy Trinity, one God, have mercy on us," from the litanies.[52] Most strikingly, however, he ends each *tractatus* of the volumes on the Gospels and Acts with a doxology. The verbal formulas vary somewhat, but invariably he ends his thoughts on a given topic with words glorifying the Father, the Son, and the Holy Spirit. They are reminiscent of the liturgical formulas used at the end of orations in the Roman Rite.

The Incarnation

The primary discussion of the Incarnation appears in Volumes 2 and 3. "The Incarnation is nothing other than the supreme and ineffable favor by which the Word, who is the only-begotten and natural Son of God, and with whom he is also one God with the Father, became flesh, that is, became man."[53] The key to understanding Salmerón's treatment of this mystery is that it was not necessary, but most fitting (*convenientissima et maxime accommodata*) for God to become man, a case that he articulates at length.[54]

---

[50] See Grantley McDonald, *Biblical Criticism in Early Modern Europe: Erasmus, the Johannine Comma, and Trinitarian Debate* (New York: Cambridge University Press, 2016).

[51] *CEH*, vol. 2, 49–52.

[52] *CEH*, vol. 2, 111; *CEH*, vol. 2, 113.

[53] *CEH*, vol. 2, 197.

[54] *CEH*, vol. 2, 207; *CEH*, vol. 3, 8–16.

The idea that man occupies an axial position within creation, and that Christ occupies an axial position between God and man, was crucial to Salmerón's understanding of the Incarnation.

> For God wished to honor and exalt the whole world by this mystery of the Incarnation. All creatures are divided between the purely corporeal, the purely spiritual, and those in the middle, which are made of both. If the Word had assumed the purely corporeal, the greater and spiritual creatures would not have been honored. Again, if he had assumed a pure spirit or an angel, he would have deprived corporeal creatures of such honor and dignity. Since man is a certain intermediate creature, and made out of body and spirit, and is like a certain compendium of the world, the Word willed to assume him, so that in him all creatures together would seem to be honored and exalted.[55]

Far from being a source of scandal, as it is for pagans, Jews, and Muslims, the Incarnation entirely befits God's nature, without being a necessary consequence of it.

Salmerón was more effusive than usual concerning this mystery, and he grasped for human analogies to capture its greatness. One of these appears in his treatment of the appearance of the Angel Gabriel to Mary.

> This sweetest and most beautiful Gospel of the Annunciation contains the extraordinary and in all respects illustrious legation that God sent to the Blessed Virgin Mary through the Angel Gabriel about the business of the Incarnation...But this legation, which we have before us, surpasses the others that take place by human initiative as much as God is greater than man, and as much as the business of the Incarnation of the Son (in whom alone the salvation of the whole world was born) is known to surpass all the world's business. For from it that golden and saving peace and concord of the human race with God followed, and the marriage of human nature with the divine person of the Word for the sake of establishing perpetual peace was procured.[56]

The choice of the legation analogy should be viewed in light of the enormous investment in the reception of embassies and persons of rank during the sixteenth century, something with which Salmerón would have been familiar given his own diplomatic activities.[57] The implication is clear: if such

---

[55] *CEH*, vol. 2, 198.

[56] *CEH*, vol. 3, 1.

[57] See Teofilo Ruiz, *A King Travels: Festive Traditions in Late Medieval and Early Modern Spain* (Princeton, NJ: Princeton University Press, 2012); Braden Frieder,

wonder and spectacle is spent on merely human affairs, this divine "business" is infinitely worthier of it.

The mystery of the Incarnation, in Salmerón's view, reveals who God really is, both in terms of his power and his great love for mankind. David's wife marveled to see him dancing and jumping before the ark (2 Sam 6:15), but the Word made a much greater leap into the Virgin's womb, and from there to the manger, to the cross, into death and hell, and then back up to heaven.[58] This show of power is all for the sake of love.

> If you wished to show the greatest love toward your friend, you could not unite yourself more to him, or make yourself more intimate to him, than if you gave him such a hug that you penetrated him completely and became him, and further, that he became most lovable to you, and you to him.[59]

Salmerón uses the verb *deificare*, which has a long pedigree in Christian theology, to express the communication of divine life to mankind.[60]

> But he could not have poured out and communicated himself outside himself more greatly, than by thus inundating the creature, so that he makes himself the creature. Nor again could he have made the creature run back and return more to himself, than by making it God. From this it follows that God does not look upon you, creature, as a slave, but as a relative and a neighbor, loving you with the highest love, so that he could say, "I am human, I think nothing human is alien to me" [Terence, *The Self-Tormentor*, 1.1.77].[61]

In putting this theological twist on Terence's adage, Salmerón was following certain Fathers who had made the same observation about the significance of the Incarnation.

In his commentary on 1 Tim 1:15, Salmerón deals with the thorny question of whether God would have become incarnate if there had been no sin. He notes the positions of various theologians, placing Thomas and Bonaventure in the negative camp, and Alexander of Hales, Scotus, and Ambrogio Catarino on the opposite side. Limits of space prevent a thorough discussion

---

Chivalry and the Perfect Prince. Tournaments, Art, and Armor at the Spanish Habsburg Court (Kirksville, MO: Truman State University Press, 2008).

[58] *CEH*, vol. 2, 210.
[59] *CEH*, vol. 2, 209–10.
[60] *CEH*, vol. 3, 9. See David Meconi and Carl Olson, eds., *Called to Be the Children of God: The Catholic Theology of Human Deification* (San Francisco, CA: Ignatius Press, 2016).
[61] *CEH*, vol. 2, 209.

of Salmerón's position, but he favored the idea that the Incarnation would not have taken place apart from sin. He relies, first of all, on the testimony of scripture, which gives deliverance from sin as the main reason for Christ's coming.[62] Aside from scripture, Salmerón also makes use of councils, the Fathers, and even the blessing of the Paschal candle at the Easter Vigil in support of this view.[63]

The Eucharist

Salmerón typically identified the Eucharist as the third of the principal mysteries, not as a sign of its lesser importance, but because it extends and, in some sense, completes the other two. He dedicates more total space in the *Commentaries* to this mystery than to any other, and frequently refers to it in passing when talking about other subjects. The Eucharist is evidently on Salmerón's mind very often, so much so that only basic coverage of his views is possible here. Since it is both a *mystery* in the broader sense of the term and one of the seven *sacraments*, the Eucharist will be treated here and in Chapter 5.

The Eucharist's connection to the Trinity and the Incarnation is not discussed in any systematic way, but the associations are clear. Salmerón says that the two highest mysteries of the faith are the Word hidden in the flesh, and the Word made flesh, hidden in the Eucharist.[64] He calls the Eucharist the sacrament of the unity of the Father and the Son, and he says that the Incarnation and the Eucharist are the two occasions when Jesus puts his divinity in the midst of men.[65] The Eucharist's status as a "higher mystery" is indicated by the fact that John, who deals with the more profound mysteries more than the other Evangelists, writes about it in the sixth chapter of his Gospel.[66] The meaning of the name "Emmanuel," Salmerón says, is fulfilled in the Eucharist, for God is with us every day in its celebration.[67]

One way that Salmerón highlights the status of the Eucharist as a mystery is by explaining how it recapitulates the whole life of Christ. The relevant passage cannot be reproduced in its entirety, but a few excerpts illustrate his method.

---

[62] *CBP*, vol. 3, 418–19.
[63] *CBP*, vol. 3, 420–21.
[64] *CEH*, vol. 8, 223.
[65] *CEH*, vol. 2, 111; *CEH*, vol. 2, 38 (Dr).
[66] *CEH*, vol. 8, 186.
[67] *CEH*, vol. 3, 259.

He fled into Egypt to escape the sinners planning to kill him. So also does the Lord depart from these who unworthily eat and drink judgment upon themselves, because no fruit is bestowed upon them, while he goes to others who received grace with the fruit of receiving the sacrament.[68]

Here Christ is sold by Judas, that is, by priests avariciously selling Masses and the ministry of the sacraments. He is cursed by Caiaphas and the attending priests, that is, the heretics who deny that Christ is present in the sacrament. He is laughed at and mocked by the Jews, that is, by false Christians who confess and say with their mouths, "Hail, King of the Jews." He is spit on by those who blaspheme the sacred host.[69]

Not only is the entire mystery of the Lord's life contained in the Eucharist, but it is also re-enacted each time the Eucharist is celebrated in the life of the Church.

Salmerón saw the Eucharist's status as a mystery reflected in the uttering of the words "mystery of faith" [*mysterium fidei*] at Mass, during the institution narrative of the Roman Canon. "Mystery" in this context refers not just to an image or figure, but to the reality of body and blood. Salmerón says that although the Eucharist is the "mystery of love," the expression "mystery of faith" is used to show that it is also the sacrament of progress in faith, as well as the sacrament of unity and charity as to its fruits. It is said over the chalice rather than the host to recall the blood of the lambs in Egypt at the time of the exodus. He cites the commentaries on the Canon of the Mass of Odo of Cambrai and Innocent III in support of his views.[70]

Another aspect of the Eucharistic mystery that Salmerón vigorously upheld was the Real Presence, and the closely related teaching of "transubstantiation." People who love each other, he says, often leave behind an image of themselves when they go away, but the Lord left his very presence.[71] The Real Presence, in fact, elicited what is surely one of Salmerón's most impressive catenas, which goes on uninterrupted for nine pages. He begins with the teachings of the ecumenical councils, especially Trent, and proceeds to the teaching of the popes. Next come the "Doctors" (by which he actually means the Fathers from the earliest times up to Bernard), "who more highly and more openly

---

[68] *CEH*, vol. 9, 193.
[69] *CEH*, vol. 9, 195.
[70] *CEH*, vol. 9, 101–2.
[71] *CEH*, vol. 9, 146.

philosophized on this mystery in their writings and commentaries."[72] He easily cites a hundred sources, often verbatim, in defense of the Real Presence.[73]

The nuptial dimension of the Eucharist also appears in the *Commentaries*. One particularly striking passage speaks of it as the culmination of Christ's courtship with the human race.

> Christ, while planning to unite himself to the Church, drove forth the negotiations of the marriage that was to take place in the Incarnation by sending angels and prophets, first to the patriarchs and priests, and then to the elders of Abraham's family, as if to the parents of the human race. When he had obtained consent, he sent to her most magnificent and precious gifts, by which he could effectively win her love and incline her heart toward him. Among these, the most divine gift of the Holy Eucharist has the first place, as a sign that he has already given himself by the taking on of flesh, and then by the suffering of death, and as a most certain pledge, that he will give himself to his bride to enjoy fully in glory.[74]

The Eucharist is central to Salmerón's exposition and defense of the Catholic faith, as will be shown more clearly in Chapter 5, where its role as a sacrament is discussed.

Mysteries of the Lord's Life

As explained above, Salmerón spoke of particular episodes of the life of Jesus as mysteries, and sought to lead the reader into them. Given that here he was concerned with events, he gave proportionately more attention to historical context than to dogmatic definitions and technical language. Although Salmerón did not explain why he considered these particular events as the main mysteries, it seems that he thought they revealed the deeper truths of Christ's life, often in ways that explicitly connect with the three principal mysteries. What follows is a sampling of these ten principal mysteries.

The Nativity

Salmerón explains that the Lord was born into the world in human flesh "so that he might more sweetly and gently draw and attract us to himself, for infancy has a wondrous power and efficacy of winning over the hearts

---

[72] *CEH*, vol. 9, 154.

[73] *CEH*, vol. 9, 153–61.

[74] *CEH*, vol. 9, 116.

of men."[75] After an inquiry into the historical circumstances of Joseph's and Mary's return to Bethlehem in accordance with the census reported in Luke's Gospel, Salmerón identifies numerous allegorical and moral meanings of the location of Christ's birth. As Christ underwent his passion outside the camp (Heb 13:13) and ascended from the Mount of Olives outside Jerusalem (Acts 1:12), so he was born outside Bethlehem. The fact that there was no room for him at the inn, which is often a place of corrupt morals, shows that public places should be kept in a dignified state, so that Christ may be received in them. His presence in the stable among the beasts is a sign that by following their passions, men before his coming were leading an animalistic life, as the psalmist says: "man when he was in honor did not understand, he is compared to senseless beasts, and is become like to them" (Ps 48:13). The manger shows that he became the food of men, by which irrational and beastly men become rational, spiritual, and holy.[76]

Although the Gospels make no mention of the presence of ox and ass at the Nativity, Salmerón treats this detail as historical, not least because it fulfils the prophecies of Habakkuk 3:2 and Isaiah 1:3: "in the midst of two animals you will be recognized, and the ox knoweth his owner, and the ass his master's crib: but Israel hath not known me, and my people hath not understood."[77] The latter prophecy in its original context, as Basil and Jerome explained, reproves the Jews for not recognizing their lord, creator, and shepherd. Salmerón, however, thinks that it can be extended to the birth of Christ, since Herod, the priests, the scribes, and the Pharisees did not recognize him, but the animals did.

Salmerón draws lessons from the poverty of Christ's birth. He did not come to take away men's money, but his poverty was not so extreme that he was without swaddling cloths, garments that are a sign of his likeness to Adam, who covered himself in animal skins and enjoyed some goods of the earth.[78] These cloths are also a sign of his sharing in man's infirmity and a foreshadowing of the Passion.[79] Salmerón challenges the reader directly to recognize Christ's presence in poverty more generally.

---

[75] *CEH*, vol. 3, 300.

[76] *CEH*, vol. 3, 289–90.

[77] *CEH*, vol. 3, 293. Salmerón cites the Septuagint version of Habakkuk, as opposed to the text of Jerome's Vulgate, which reads, *in the midst of the years thou shalt make it known.*

[78] *CEH*, vol. 3, 290.

[79] *CEH*, vol. 3, 292; *CEH*, vol. 3, 294.

> But you will say: "if I had been there with Christ, I would certainly have shown him great honor." I believe you, assuming you had recognized him, for otherwise you would have done the same as others. This is why, if now you believe, Christ has been shown to you in the poor and sick; exert yourself there. If you do not believe this, your unbelief has been revealed, for holy men are commonly found in dirty places. For God chose the contemptible and humble things of this world to confound the things that are great in the eyes of the world. Accuse yourself therefore of infidelity, and ask for faith.[80]

Such exhortations are typical of Salmerón's intent to sting the reader's conscience so that the mystery might penetrate more deeply into him.

Poor and hidden though the Nativity may have been, Salmerón cites numerous ancient and medieval sources for events that took place throughout the world on the same day, thus indicating the significance of Christ's birth for the whole of human history. According to Eusebius, oil flowed from the earth in Trastevere on the day of Christ's birth, and other sources claim that Augustus, after receiving from Pythian Apollo the prophecy of the birth of a Hebrew God-child, erected an altar on the Capitoline dedicated to the "firstborn god." According to another account, Augustus consulted the Sibyl, who told him that she saw at Rome a halo, inside of which was a beautiful virgin with her infant son, indicating the birth of a king more powerful than he. Salmerón rejects, however, the claim made by Innocent III and the *Historia scholastica* that the building of the Temple of Peace coincided with the birth of Christ, for Suetonius and Pliny attributed the work to Vespasian.[81]

He sees multiple levels of meaning in the choir of angels that descend from heaven to adore and sing "glory to God in the highest" (Lk 2:14). Angels come to express their joy and to show men how to praise God, since they do not know how. As an angel once stood with a flaming sword at the door of paradise to keep men out, so now angels invite them in through the door that is Christ.[82] The words "peace on earth" lead Salmerón to reflect on the peace that Christ brought with his birth, in response to the objection that the world is still full of wars. He says that Christ restored the principal peace between God and men, and between angels and God, and that the other kinds of peace are possible if men do not put up obstacles. He notes, however, that the peace of Christ dwelling in hearts makes war with the world, the flesh, and the devil,

---

[80] *CEH*, vol. 3, 292.
[81] *CEH*, vol. 3, 291.
[82] *CEH*, vol. 3, 305.

and that peace with sin aids the devil's war against God. In other words, he regarded spiritual conflict as endemic to man's condition.[83]

The Presentation in the Temple

The Presentation in the Temple took place forty days after Christ's birth together with the Purification of the Blessed Virgin. Salmerón finds symbolic meaning in the offering of the sacrificial birds, identifying the turtle-dove [*turtur*] with the contemplative life and the pigeon [*columba*] with the active life, both of which Jesus and Mary practiced to the highest degree.[84] More importantly, this redemption of Jesus before the Law points to the redemption of the Israelites from Egypt and to the redemption he was to accomplish on the cross. This teaches Christians that they too must offer to God their "firstborn," that is, whatever is dearest to them, as well as mortifications of their bodies as sacrifice.[85]

The appearance of Simeon in the temple at the Presentation (Lk 2:25) shifts Salmerón's focus to the theme of prophecy.

> When a son is born to a king, everyone is accustomed to freely consult the judgment of astrologers to understand what will happen to him. In a like manner, the Holy Spirit wished to preach through the prophet Simeon the things that could not be known about the Son of God from the heavens and the stars.[86]

Salmerón explains that this "righteous man" was one of the twenty-four priests who ministered in the temple, which is why the Church customarily portrays him as a priest or a bishop. He thinks that Simeon was one of the few Jews who expected a spiritual Messiah rather than a carnal, worldly leader.[87] He has high words of praise for his canticle *Nunc dimittis*. "And Simeon exults wondrously, after the manner of the swan, of which someone said, 'the swan is the singer of his own funeral.'"[88]

---

[83] *CEH*, vol. 3, 309.

[84] *CEH*, vol. 3, 379. Salmerón has much to say on the supposed differences between these two kinds of animals, despite the fact that modern biologists consider them identical.

[85] *CEH*, vol. 3, 380.

[86] *CEH*, vol. 3, 382.

[87] *CEH*, vol. 3, 383–84.

[88] *CEH*, vol. 3, 386. The line, as noted in the margins, comes from the Roman poet Martial. *Epigrams*, 13.77.1.

Simeon's words about the child as "a sign which shall be contradicted" (Lk 2:34) allow Salmerón to comment, following Bernard, on how Christ was contradicted not only throughout his life, but even before he entered into human history. The Incarnation was revealed to Lucifer and his allies before the creation of the world, and they contradicted it, because the Son of God was not to take on an angelic nature, but the seed of Abraham. "In his malice the devil contradicted so great a mystery," and from there he and his allies were cast into hell. Beginning with the contradiction of the serpent in Paradise, Salmerón goes on to recount the devil's attempts to contradict God, destroy man, and persecute the Jews throughout all the ages of history. After the resurrection, he persecuted Christ's ministers and raised up Jews, tyrants, Saracens, heretics, bad Christians, and hypocrites, such that the Jews at Rome could say to Paul "for as concerning this sect, we know that it is everywhere contradicted" (Act 28:22).[89] Today, Salmerón adds, the devil tries to take away from Christ the souls for which he shed his blood through the works of the heretics. "Do you see, prudent reader, how many tentacles and nets the devil sets for trapping souls, and leading them away from the Church of Christ?"[90] This passage illustrates well how Salmerón is able to connect a single verse from scripture with other mysteries.

The Entrance into Jerusalem

Although Salmerón does not pinpoint the beginning of this mystery, it seems that a good place to begin is *Tractatus XXXI* of Volume 4, where Jesus sees the city and begins to weep over it, before he goes into the temple to drive out the sellers (Lk 19:41–46). The entrance into Jerusalem, according to Salmerón, confirms Christ's three offices, for the children proclaimed him as king, he purified the temple as priest, and he foretold the destruction of the city as prophet. The passage also shows that there are two emotional responses (*affectus*) necessary for the Christian life: tears of commiseration from the heart, and zeal to punish the violators of the Lord's temple. Salmerón thinks that Luke is the only one who tells of Jesus's tears over Jerusalem because he intends to portray him as a priest, whose task is to weep over the sins of the people. Jesus begins to cry over Jerusalem, he explains, because it preferred the false and carnal peace of the devil over his own messianic peace, in imitation of Sodom and Egypt. It was not because he feared his own passion and death, but their destruction, that Jesus wept.[91]

---

[89] *CEH*, vol. 3, 392–93.

[90] *CEH*, vol. 3, 393.

[91] *CEH*, vol. 4, 602.

Salmerón considers the objection that this behavior pertains more to "little women" and children than to strong men and magnanimous princes, and that it was especially unfitting for Christ to cry on the day of his glory and triumph, while the crowds proclaimed his praises.

> It is a rare and memorable thing that, although the Lord Jesus was not unaware of the ignominious slaughter prepared for him, he was more afflicted by another's calamity than by his own, especially since the latter was imminent, indeed five days away, whereas the former was a long way off, that is, forty-two years away. In addition, so that the mystery of so much weeping may be more fully acknowledged, he laments the destruction of the Jews which was justly inflicted by God, whereas he does not lament that he was made to bear the cross unjustly and by the greatest iniquity.[92]

Salmerón regards his weeping as a sign that "the Lord Jesus was a true man, not a stone man or a Stoic."[93] His words anticipate the devotion to the Sacred Heart: "These indeed are the four rivers going forth from the paradise of the heart of Christ, watering the whole earth of the Church, and cleansing her from the filth of sin, then refreshing her against the ardor of inner concupiscence."[94] At least in certain circumstances, Salmerón thought it was appropriate for men to cry.

The expulsion of the sellers from the temple demonstrated the second necessary emotional response of the Christian life. According to Salmerón, Jesus did this to show that "they" (presumably Jews collectively) were to be punished, and cast out of the temple and Jerusalem, and despoiled of all their goods. He intended, furthermore, to show that the elders and priests, whose task it was to guard religion and the people, were the cause of the whole people's ruin. In a similar vein, Jesus wished to show how bad ministers are thrown out of the temple of the Church: first by losing the grace of God, then the obedience and reverence of the people, then by suffering a sudden and violent death, and finally by the second death of Gehenna, where they will pay for their impiety and negligence.[95] These commentaries on Christ's emotional states show the true humanity that he assumed in

---

[92] *CEH*, vol. 4, 602.

[93] *CEH*, vol. 4, 603.

[94] *CEH*, vol. 4, 603. Devotion to the Heart of Christ is not uncommon in the writings of sixteenth-century Jesuits, especially Peter Canisius. Henry Shea, "The Beloved Disciple and the *Spiritual Exercises*," *Studies in the Spirituality of Jesuits* 49, no. 2 (2017): 1–35, at 30–32.

[95] *CEH*, vol. 4, 606–7.

the Incarnation. Jesus's sinless and rightly ordered soul was capable of a dramatic swing between two intense emotional responses.

The Passion

Since he dedicated an entire volume to the mystery of the Passion, it is impossible to do more than summarize Salmerón's commentary. One notable feature is the lengthy preface he provides on the importance of contemplating the Passion frequently and seriously, showing once more his mystagogical approach.[96]

Following his usual method, Salmerón sought to illuminate the meaning of scripture with scripture. For example, he provides a lengthy exegesis of Ps 21 to show that it foretells the Passion. Salmerón breaks down the psalm text into three sections: the first deals with the miseries of the Passion, the second is Jesus's prayer to the Father, and the third predicts the Resurrection and the building up of the Church.[97] Rejecting all efforts at using "O God my God, look upon me: why hast thou forsaken me?" (Ps 21:2) as a denial of Christ's divinity, Salmerón explains that the "forsaking" in question refers to the separation of body and soul.[98] He proceeds line-by-line, comparing versions of the text, considering the teachings of various theologians, and taking positions of his own. The "dogs" that surround Christ (Ps 21:17) are the Gentiles who crucified him, whereas the lion's mouth and the "unicorns" (Ps 21:22) refer either to the power of the demons, or to the Jews and Gentiles acting as their instruments.[99]

Salmerón's commentary on the events of the Passion is replete with references to other biblical figures and types, as well as the moral lessons they communicate to Christians. In the time of Samuel, the Jews asked for a king against the will of God (1 Sam 8), and in the Passion they denied the king sent them by the will of God.[100] When David had grown old and cold, he received the Sunamite woman (1 Kgs 1:1–3). In a like manner, when the human race had grown old and cold, it was given the humanity of Christ, fervent with

---

[96] *CEH*, vol. 10, 1–9.

[97] *CEH*, vol. 10, 74.

[98] *CEH*, vol. 10, 75. He rejects as "heretical" and "insane" the view of Melanchthon that Christ cried out in desperation because he had lost God's help.

[99] *CEH*, vol. 10, 81; Salmerón adds that the unicorn or "monocerot," which is the enemy of the elephant, is distinct from a rhinoceros, and that a monocerot was often seen in Rome. *CEH*, vol. 10, 83.

[100] *CEH*, vol. 10, 271.

divine blood, to warm it with love.[101] The seven times that Christ shed his blood – at the circumcision, in Gethsemane, at the flagellation, with the crown of thorns, from his hand, from his feet, and from his side – stand for the fact that he died to take away the seven deadly sins.[102]

Salmerón emphasized the priestly character of the Passion with specific liturgical associations. He observes that the subterranean places under the temple brought the blood of the sacrifices to the Kidron, so that Christ's passing over the Kidron on his way to Gethsemane shows that his blood far surpasses all other sacrifices.[103] The Jesuit theologian says that in his death, Christ was a true priest who put on all the pontifical vestments: the amice veiling his head in the house of Caiaphas, the alb in the house of Herod, the cincture in the garden when he was bound, the purple garment in the house of Pilate, and the stole when he was bound by the neck to the cross he carried.[104] The Lord's tunic remains whole as a sign of the permanence of his eternal priesthood, whereas the rending of the high priest's garments signifies the end of the Jewish priesthood.[105] Salmerón thinks that when Pilate showed Jesus to the crowd and said "Behold the Man" (Jn 19:5), his ministers lifted his garment, as is done with the priest's chasuble when he elevates the host or offers incense.[106] He compares the two thieves crucified with Jesus to the deacon and subdeacon who assist the priest at Solemn Mass.[107]

Salmerón dramatized the Passion more so than any of the other mysteries. Although he never mentions the *Spiritual Exercises*, his vivid descriptions bear some similarity to the "composition of place" used in this source. For example, he describes at length the movement and positioning of the various figures in the courtyard outside the high priest's house at the time of Peter's denial, so as to better prepare the reader to imagine the scene.[108] Elsewhere he lingers over a word for emphasis, as when Pilate shows Jesus to the crowd and says "Behold the Man" (Jn 19:5).

> Behold, contemplate him, because he is your flesh and your brother, not stone, not iron, or a beast of burden, so that you do not degenerate further

---

[101] *CEH*, vol. 10, 57.
[102] *CEH*, vol. 10, 59.
[103] *CEH*, vol. 10, 100.
[104] *CEH*, vol. 10, 61 (Fr).
[105] *CEH*, vol. 10, 186.
[106] *CEH*, vol. 10, 258.
[107] *CEH*, vol. 10, 297.
[108] *CEH*, vol. 10, 198.

from human nature... Behold the man, who is put before you for imitation, you who asked to be like God, like that first man Adam... Behold the man, who is the man of sorrows and infirmity, and tempted in all things like us, but without sin, so that he could wipe away and oppose himself to the just wrath of God for us.[109]

Along with this goes an interest in the sensory data of the Passion, as when Salmerón offers a list of all the things Christ suffered in his five senses.[110] Here again is a possible indication of the influence of the *Spiritual Exercises* and its "application of the senses."[111]

The Jesuit theologian raised the question of who was to blame for the execution of Christ. On the one hand, Salmerón wants to implicate everyone, saying that both the Jews and the Gentiles condemned and killed Jesus, which means that neither people is allowed to be puffed up against the other.[112] He says of Pilate's washing of his hands (Mt 27:24) that not all the water of the Jordan could have cleansed his conscience of guilt.[113] On the other hand, he lays the heaviest responsibility on the Jewish leaders, saying that their sin was greater than Pilate's or even Judas's.[114] Salmerón also includes a mini-treatise on the continuing punishment of the Jews across the ages, which will be dealt with in more detail in Chapter 6.

Toward the end of Volume 10, Salmerón organizes his discussion of the Passion around Christ's "seven last words." It was not uncommon in his time to listen to preaching on this theme on Good Friday. To take one example, Salmerón provides a rich and varied commentary on the words "I thirst" (Jn 19:28). First, he uses a natural analogy: when deer are hunted and tired out, they go to the waters to save their life, as Ps 41 says: "as the hart panteth after

---

[109] *CEH*, vol. 10, 258.

[110] *CEH*, vol. 10, 7.

[111] This method is explained in *MHSI. MI. Series Secunda: Exercitia Spiritualia S. Ignatii de Loyola et eorum directoria*, vol. 1, *Exercitia Spiritualia* (hereafter *SpEx*), eds. Joseph Calaveras and Cándido de Dalmases (Rome: IHSI, 1969), §121–26, 336–38. For more on the application of the senses, including its connection to the Carthusian tradition, see Joseph Maréchal, "Application des sens," in *Dictionnaire de spiritualité ascétique et mystique* (Paris: Beauchesne, 1937–75), vol. 1, 810–28; Emily Ransom, "St. Ignatius in the Affective School of Ludolph of Saxony," *Studies in the Spirituality of Jesuits* 53, no. 3 (2021): 1–41.

[112] *CEH*, vol. 10, 209.

[113] *CEH*, vol. 10, 272.

[114] *CEH*, vol. 10, 264.

the fountains of water, so my soul panteth after thee, O God."¹¹⁵ The hart, as a generous and free animal, represents Christ, and the hunters and their dogs represent Gentiles and Jews. According to Salmerón, Christ experienced both corporeal and spiritual thirst on the cross, the former on account of the loss of water from his torments. Spiritually, he was thirsty for suffering on behalf of God's honor and the salvation of souls.¹¹⁶

One idea that Salmerón advances with particular zeal is that the death of Christ should be remembered with sorrow and tears. He says that in his time, some people began to claim, based on the words "weep not over me, but weep for yourselves" (Lk 23:28) that Christians should be joyful and happy about the death of Jesus. According to Salmerón, Erasmus was the first to advance this view, which despite a warning from the Sorbonne he continued to defend. The Jesuit theologian claims that Luther and his disciples picked up this idea, and that during Holy Week, and especially on Good Friday, they celebrate with banquets, meat, and drinks.¹¹⁷ This same error spread in many Catholic places; Salmerón says that when was in Paris for studies, the people of Morins (*Morinenses*) began to teach it publicly.¹¹⁸ It has proved impossible to find any historical documentation corroborating this charge against Lutherans, or the people of Morins. Against these practices, Salmerón appeals to the mournful behavior of the men and women at the cross, but even more so to the Church's liturgical ceremonies during Holy Week: the altars are stripped, the images are covered, the bells are not rung, the Alleluia and the Gloria are omitted, and so forth.¹¹⁹

The final aspect of the Passion and Death that Salmerón deals with is the descent into the underworld, which he divides into several regions. Lower hell is the place of the damned, whereas upper hell has three subdivisions: the limbo of the Fathers, Purgatory, and the place of children who died without circumcision or Baptism.¹²⁰ Salmerón insists that Christ's soul descended into upper hell, against the teaching of Bucer and Calvin that the Creed's

---

[115] His choice of this verse may have been inspired by its use during the blessing of the font at the Easter Vigil.

[116] *CEH*, vol. 10, 360–66.

[117] Erasmus's words against mourning Christ's death were censured by the Paris theological faculty, prompting him to offer further defenses of his position. Desiderius Erasmus, *Collected Works of Erasmus: Paraphrase on Luke 11–24*, trans. Jane Phillips (Toronto: University of Toronto Press, 2003), 215–16.

[118] *CEH*, vol. 10, 284.

[119] *CEH*, vol. 10, 286–89.

[120] *CEH*, vol. 10, 408.

words "he descended into hell" refer to the punishment of the damned that Christ suffered in his Passion. Salmerón rails against this view as blasphemy and heresy.[121] He notes that Lefèvre d'Étaples, Nicholas of Cusa (1401–64), and Girolamo Seripando (1493–1563) took a similar position: the motive for Christ's descent was suffering the pains of hell on behalf of mankind. Salmerón counters that this position is a novelty and unknown to the Church of God for all centuries.[122] The real motive for the descent, he says, was freeing the souls in the limbo of the Fathers, which includes those who had implicit faith, good works, or repentance for their sins. Salmerón did not think that infants who only had original sin were freed, since they did not have faith or the saving sacrament. He sides with numerous Franciscans against Thomas and Durandus in favor of the view that Christ also completely emptied Purgatory.[123]

The Resurrection

Salmerón opens Volume 11 of the *Commentaries* by posing the question of whether life is a tragedy, a comedy, or both. He replies that for the wicked, life begins with joy, honor, and happiness, but ends in pain, weeping, and misery, as in the case of the rich man (Lk 16:20–31). By contrast, the just and pious begin in humility, pain, and mourning, but end in joy and glory, as in the case of Lazarus from the same Gospel passage.[124] The Resurrection is the great moment of joy and triumph that brings to an end the pain and sorrow of Jesus's earthly life and passion. As Salmerón explains, "therefore the lamb immolated on the cross has changed into the lion, who is the strongest of animals, and therefore their king. This is the lion of the tribe of Judah."[125]

Salmerón communicates the notion of the Resurrection as victory by using an analogy from Roman history. He says that Roman law only allowed a triumph when the commander had fought against more than five thousand enemy troops in a single array, saved the better part of his own army, and conquered a significant province. According to Plutarch, Julius Caesar was granted a triumph on five occasions for victories in foreign wars, but none for

---

[121] *CEH*, vol. 10, 412–14.

[122] *CEH*, vol. 10, 415–16.

[123] *CEH*, vol. 10, 420–21.

[124] *CEH*, vol. 11, 1. Although Salmerón portrays the Resurrection as sorting out the wicked from the just, he does not treat it as a confessional issue. See Erin Lambert, "The Reformation and the Resurrection of the Dead," *Sixteenth Century Journal* 47, no. 2 (2016): 351–70.

[125] *CEH*, vol. 11, 10.

his civil wars, since this feat was not considered worthy. Salmerón then makes a direct comparison to Jesus:

> And Christ our extraordinary commander [*imperator*] had wars against the most warlike enemies, first the demons, second the world, third the flesh, fourth the Jews, and lastly against death itself, and each of these was worth a thousand enemies. Indeed, he was able to kill a thousand, if Saul conquered a thousand, and David ten thousand [1 Sam 18:7–8]. Nor did he only save the greater part of his army, but what is greater, even the whole of it. For indeed his divinity was whole, his soul whole, his body whole on the third day, and finally the heroic virtues that adorned his mind were whole. In addition, Jesus did not subject just one province to God's true rule, and he did so by means of an extraordinary kind of victory, truly without slaughter or blood.[126]

This victory is meant to be shared by all the just, for in the resurrection, the Church will be all white, just as those who celebrated triumphs in ancient Rome wore this color.[127]

Salmerón's characteristic interest in history is manifest in numerous ways. He wanted to show that the Old Testament foretold the Resurrection through types and prophecies, and thus was made known to Jews and Gentiles alike long before it happened. The centerpiece of this claim is an exegesis of Ps 117, which speaks of Christ's victory over his enemies, both Jewish and Gentile: "all nations compassed me about, and in the name of the Lord I have been revenged on them" (Ps 117:10).[128] The Resurrection also hearkens back to Genesis, since it took place on the "eighth day" as a sign of the new creation; just as light was made on the first day, Jesus is the light of the world.[129] Not only did the Sibyls predict the Resurrection, but so did "Job the Gentile," who according to Salmerón lived before the time of Moses. The passage that begins "I know that my redeemer liveth, and in the last day I shall rise" (Job 19:25–27) was God's way of publicizing the Resurrection for Jews and Gentiles on "sheets of lead" for eternal memory, just as Marcus Agrippa placed his name on the Pantheon in Rome.[130]

---

[126] *CEH*, vol. 11, 7.

[127] *CEH*, vol. 11, 75.

[128] *CEH*, vol. 11, 3–4. Ps 117 features prominently in the Divine Office of the Octave of Easter.

[129] *CEH*, vol. 11, 5–6.

[130] *CEH*, vol. 11, 26.

In addition, much of this volume is given over to placing in chronological order the various appearances of the risen Lord and reconciling their apparent inconsistencies. This is, of course, a characteristic feature of the *Commentaries*, but Salmerón also finds types and spiritual meanings in the historical details. Mystically, the rolling back of the stone (Mt 28:2) means the revelation of mysteries.[131] Jesus left his linens behind in the tomb, like Elijah leaving his mantle, for two reasons. First, there is no need for clothing in heaven, and second, he wanted to leave testimony against the Jews who lied about the Apostles stealing his body.[132] John's arrival at the tomb before Peter shows that there are those in the Church holier than the Vicar of Christ, but John may have let him enter the tomb first out of fear or deference to his office (Jn 20:4–8).[133]

Salmerón had much to say about the Lord's encounter with Mary Magdalene, especially John's account of it (Jn 20:11–17). He credits her with being the first to announce the Resurrection, just as a woman was the first to sin and the first to hear the announcement of the Incarnation.[134] He speaks of the reciprocal, vehement love between her and Jesus. When Jesus finally speaks to her, it is because he can no longer contain himself, like Joseph before his brothers (Gen 45:1). Salmerón notes the perplexity of commentators over the words "do not touch me" (Jn 20:17), and rejects the explanation of Cajetan that Mary had tried to hug him, on the grounds that "his authority and majesty was so great among everyone, but especially among women, that while he lived, they never dared to rush into his embrace."[135] After reviewing the opinions of the Fathers, Salmerón concludes that Jesus was telling her not to lose the merit of faith by touching.[136]

As with the Passion, there is an emphasis on sensory data, especially how Christ's appearance to the disciples was confirmed through their senses. In Lk 24, Jesus shows that it is really he through the three principal senses of sight, hearing, and touch.[137] Salmerón also thinks that Christ's smell drew the disciples near, as hungry whales emit a smell that attracts fish.[138] He was aware

---

[131] *CEH*, vol. 11, 70.
[132] *CEH*, vol. 11, 83.
[133] *CEH*, vol. 11, 82.
[134] *CEH*, vol. 11, 72.
[135] *CEH*, vol. 11, 94–95.
[136] *CEH*, vol. 11, 96.
[137] *CEH*, vol. 11, 128.
[138] *CEH*, vol. 11, 129.

of the problems that the Resurrection presents at the level of the senses and corporeal reality. He says that Jesus did not eat after the Resurrection out of bodily necessity, citing the opinion of Thomas that the food he ate was not turned into the substance of Christ, but was consumed like fire consumes water, or like the sun consumes vapor.[139] Salmerón also asks if Christ went to the bathroom during this period. While he does not resolve the question, he leaves open the possibility that Christ did not.[140]

The historicity, harmony, and coherence of the Resurrection accounts was a major concern of the other exegetes under consideration. Maldonado treats the matter at length, whereas Barradas does so more succinctly.[141] Jansen's exegesis of the relevant passages begins with a kind of prologue defending the historicity and harmony of the different Gospel accounts, which he then seeks to demonstrate in each case.[142] Marlorat observes certain discrepancies in the details and seeks to harmonize them, but he does not thematize the historicity issue in the same way as the Catholic authors, nor does he address the canonical or textual issues of Mk 16.[143] Although all writers deal with the theological and spiritual significance of the Resurrection, only Barradas dramatizes it after the fashion of Salmerón, especially in the numerous *morale* sections he provides.

Conclusion

The task of integrating scripture and tradition finds its practical application in teaching the reader to contemplate the mysteries of the Christian faith. Throughout a lifetime of prayer and study, Salmerón sought to interiorize these mysteries at intellectual and affective levels, and in his magnum opus, he wanted to initiate the reader into the same experience. The mysteries, like scripture and tradition, form part of a coherent whole, so that touching upon one touches upon all of them. The Trinity, the Incarnation, and the Eucharist play a coordinating role in Salmerón's thought, and he selects ten principal mysteries from the life of Jesus for his exegesis of the Gospels. These mysteries offered Salmerón the additional opportunity to demonstrate his understanding

---

[139] *CEH*, vol. 12, 27.

[140] *CEH*, vol. 11, 128.

[141] Maldonado, *Commentaries*, vol. 1, cols. 661–88; Barradas, *Commentaries*, vol. 4, 336–38.

[142] Jansen, *Commentaries*, Quarta Pars, 611–14.

[143] Marlorat, *Expositio*, vol. 1, 267; Marlorat, *Expositio*, vol. 1, 303.

of the unity of scripture, as well as the teaching of the Fathers and Doctors. The prodigious learning Salmerón brought to bear, as well as the Church's dogmatic definitions and technical language did not, in his view, obscure the simplicity of the Gospel or burden the intellect. Instead, they safeguarded the mysteries and brought forth their hidden content for the sake of prayer and contemplation.

4 Honoring Mary

Salmerón's reluctance to divulge personal information is briefly set aside with these words directed to the Virgin Mary:

> And therefore I, as far as it pertains to me, with the whole fullness of my faith regard this as pleasing and firmly established, and so I bring forth from the bottom of my heart these words: Behold your servant, my Lady; let it be done to me according to your faith and your will.[1]

Despite her relative obscurity in the canonical Gospels, no other biblical figure besides Jesus captured Salmerón's mind and heart quite like Mary.[2] Mother and son are intricately intertwined in his writing, so that Mariology is an extension of Christology according to the Jesuit theologian's method of contemplating the mysteries. Mary is both directly implicated in these mysteries as they unfold in the Gospels and the first one to contemplate them, according to the words of Luke: "Mary kept all these words, pondering them in her heart" (Lk 2:19).

Mary was crucial to both Salmerón's piety and the architectonics of his theological project.[3] Her condition as "full of grace" gives her a unique status within the divine plan, which Salmerón explained using his preferred resources: Old Testament typology, literal and spiritual reflection upon her role in the New Testament, patristic and scholastic doctrinal excursus, and historical and biographical information from extrabiblical sources. Liturgical material, already evident in his discussion of the mysteries of faith, carried

---

[1] *CEH*, vol. 3, 83.

[2] Ribadeneyra confirms that Salmerón was especially devoted to Mary, saying that she was one of his favorite topics of conversation. Miguel Lop Sebastià, *Alfonso Salmerón, SJ (1515–1585): Una biografía epistolar* (Madrid: Comillas, 2015), Appendix, 359–372, at 371.

[3] The best study of Salmerón's Mariology is still Melquíades Andrés, "La compasión de la Virgen al pie de la cruz, deducida de su triple gracia, según Salmerón," *Estudios Marianos* 5 (1946): 359–88. It is based on the relatively obscure Madrid edition of the *Commentaries*, the pagination of which is different from the Cologne editions.

even more weight in his presentation of Mary. For Salmerón, a truly biblical theology required a defense of the Blessed Virgin, for her position and prerogatives in Catholic teaching was the primary target of the Protestant attack on the veneration of the saints.[4] Yet his Mariology went above and beyond this in lavishing accolades upon her. Salmerón was a vigorous apologist for the Immaculate Conception, and more notably still, an early advocate of the title *coredemptrix*, which flows from her status as the "New Eve."

At the same time, Salmerón's Marian maximalism pushed him to be more adventurous than usual on issues of method. Aware that many of the Fathers and Doctors did not agree with his positions, Salmerón explicitly sided with later theologians over earlier ones. What is more, he acknowledged a subordinate, but apparently authentic and authoritative, role for the universities and even the ordinary faithful in settling theological questions, nuancing the predominantly top-down cast of his thought. Although Peter Canisius and Francisco Suárez are more famous as early modern Mariologists, Salmerón was no less committed to honoring Mary, which he regarded as a principal task of the theologian.[5]

Mary in the Old Testament

In Salmerón's view, the Old Testament speaks of Mary in the literal sense just as genuinely, if less frequently, as it does of Christ. His exegesis of one particular prophecy illustrates the point: Is 7:14, with its famous debate about the proper translation of the Hebrew word *'almah*. Jewish commentators claimed that the rendering of *'almah* as *parthenos* [virgin] in the Septuagint and the New Testament was incorrect, and therefore that the Christian claim about the prophecy's fulfillment in Jesus was false. This was a common issue for Christian exegetes, as Maldonado, Jansen, and Barradas all attempted to answer this challenge as well.[6] Salmerón begins his close-reading in an unusual way by noting the resonance between two etymologically unrelated terms:

---

[4] This conflict played out in various ways across Europe during the sixteenth century. Robert Miola, "Stabat Mater Dolorosa: Mary at the Foot of the Cross," *Sixteenth Century Journal* 48, vol. 3 (2017): 653–79.

[5] Ignacio Riudor, "Influencia de San Bernardo en la mariología de Salmerón y Suárez," *Estudios Marianos* 14 (1954): 329–53, at 329. Salmeron wrote Canisius a letter in the early 1570s encouraging him to complete his treatise on the Blessed Virgin, and assuring him of the great reward he would receive for doing so. *ES*, vol. 2, no. 366, 313–18.

[6] Maldonado, *Commentaries*, vol. 1, cols. 37–39; Jansen, *Commentaries*, Prima Pars, 54–55; Barradas, *Commentaries*, vol. 1, 378–80.

'*almah* and the Latin *alma* (kind, benevolent), an adjective that the Church applies to Mary in the liturgical text *Alma Redemptoris Mater*.[7]

As for the Hebrew term itself, he cites Jerome for the view that '*almah* comes from the verb *halam*, meaning "to hide," and that in the Punic language '*almah* means "virgin." He then cites instances of the word's use in the Old Testament, where most often it refers to a young woman who has had no sexual relations. Salmerón identifies several alternative Hebrew words, such as *bethulah* and *nahara*, that would have been better choices had the author been speaking of a non-virgin.[8] Again following Jerome, he claims the meaning of '*almah* in Is 7:14 is "hidden virgin." This designation applies well to Mary, he says, who is "an enclosed garden and a sealed fountain" (Cant. 4:12).[9] Salmerón does not offer a "purely" philological analysis, but instead adorns it with spiritual resonances taken from other parts of scripture as applied to Mary in the Church's liturgy.

The translation of '*almah* as "virgin," and the connection of the verse with the prophecy of Christ's birth, was also linked to Salmerón's defense of Mary's perpetual virginity, and of the dignity of virginity more generally. In his exegesis of the Lord's status as first-born, Salmerón says that Mary always remained a virgin. "Since according to the divine nature he is the only-begotten of the Father as the perfect son, it was also fitting that he be the only-begotten of the mother according to the human nature."[10] Salmerón offers a number of reasons why Mary could not have had other children after Jesus, including that the desire to do so would have been a sign of incontinence, something she did not experience on account of her freedom from sin.[11] Even Marlorat left open the possibility of Mary's perpetual virginity. He says that scripture does not provide enough data to determine what happened after the birth of Jesus, and he discourages inquiry into the issue because it is rooted in the vice of curiosity.[12]

---

[7] *CEH*, vol. 3, 252–53.

[8] *CEH*, vol. 3, 253–54. A contemporary Mariologist explains that the related verb is actually '*alam*, "to be strong," although he agrees that the Old Testament usage of the noun is always for a young girl presumed to be a virgin. Juan Luis Bastero, *Mary, Mother of the Redeemer*, trans. Michael Adams and Philip Griffin (Dublin: Four Courts Press, 2006), 71–72.

[9] *CEH*, vol. 3, 253.

[10] *CEH*, vol. 3, 263.

[11] *CEH*, vol. 3, 263.

[12] Marlorat, *Expositio*, vol. 1, 7.

In his exegesis of Mt 1:25, Salmerón enters into a lengthy discussion of the meaning of the word "until," seeking to demonstrate, on the basis of comparison with other verses of scripture, that it does not mean that Joseph had conjugal relations with Mary after she had borne Jesus.[13] He is indignant at those who deny Mary's virginity, for he equates the idea of her having sexual relations with the violation of the holy places. When explaining Joseph's regard for Mary's particular condition, he asks, "Would he have dared touch her, when he knew that she was the sanctuary [*sacrarium*] of the Holy Spirit, and the mother of the Messiah?"[14] In a similar vein, he applies Paul's words to Mary, "if any man violate the temple of God, him shall God destroy" (1 Cor 3:17).[15] The "brothers" of the Lord mentioned in the Gospels, he says, are not Jesus's biological brothers, nor even Joseph's children from a previous marriage, but more likely the children of Mary's sisters.[16]

Salmerón made historical as well as theological arguments on behalf of virginity. Aware of the Protestant argument that Jewish women did not take vows of virginity, Salmerón produces evidence from scripture in support of the idea. Jeremiah, Elijah, and Elisha all lived celibate lives.[17] The prophetess Anna (Lk 2:36–38) lived in a state of continence in the temple for many years after her widowhood. In addition to separating women from men during worship, the temple authorities also supported women who chose to live their lives in a permanent state of virginity. Salmerón also sees evidence for the practice of virginity in the common life of the Essenes, as described by Pliny and Josephus.[18] He says this state of virginity is certainly superior, as shown by the fact that Jesus, Mary, John the Baptist, and John the Evangelist all chose it.[19]

Salmerón did not limit himself to the Marian prophecies of the Old Testament according to the literal sense, but he also made ample use of typology and other spiritual meanings. His preferred designation for Mary in this regard was the "New Eve," an idea already evident in second-century authors like Irenaeus and Justin Martyr. They and many subsequent Fathers saw parallels between Mary's relationship to Eve and Jesus's relationship to Adam in the salvation of mankind, insofar as each reversed the choices made by the

---

[13] *CEH*, vol. 3, 228.
[14] *CEH*, vol. 3, 228.
[15] *CEH*, vol. 3, 263.
[16] *CEH*, vol. 3, 265.
[17] *CEH*, vol. 3, 30.
[18] *CEH*, vol. 3, 60; *CEH*, vol. 3, 114.
[19] *CEH*, vol. 8, 392.

first parents.[20] The principal scriptural locus of this parallel is found in the Angel Gabriel's visit to Mary (Lk 1:26–38) and the serpent's visit to Eve (Gen 3:1–6). Salmerón cites the words of Peter Chrysologus, "The angel treats of salvation with Mary, because an angel had treated of ruin with Eve."[21] Eve fell because she had no fear of God, so it was fitting that Mary was frightened by the appearance of the angel and his greeting.[22] The Eve-Mary parallel has significance for the whole human race and the cosmos, for the latter's *fiat* was made on behalf of all the elect, past, present, and future, so that she is rightly called the mother of all the living.[23]

The Eve-Mary parallel, according to Salmerón, is why Jesus always refers to her as "woman," never as "mother." In his exegesis of the wedding at Cana (Jn 2:1–11), he says that God's first miracle was bringing forth Eve from Adam's side. Just as the first Adam brought perdition upon the human race through his excessive indulgence toward her, so the second Adam gave the human race the opportunity to return to God through marriage when he said to the second Eve, "what is that to me and to you, woman?"[24] Aware that Chrysostom, Theophylact, and Euthymius thought that Christ rebuked his mother with these words, Salmerón cites the contrary testimony of Justin, Augustine, and Cyril.[25] "Woman" was also a designation of Mary's status as her son's helper; as Gen 2:18 says, "it is not good for man to be alone," and her request at Cana is an instance of her exercising this role. Salmerón even calls her "Christ's instigator and cooperator" [*instigatrix et cooperatrix Christi*].[26] "But Mary did not have this dignity of working together with Christ because she had given him flesh, but more because she received of his spirit, as if she had been made from his rib."[27] Salmerón even claims that Paul's description of Christ as being "made of a woman" (Gal 4:4) is a reference to Mary's status as the new Eve.[28] Maldonado, by contrast, was much cooler

---

[20] See Luigi Gambero, *Mary and the Fathers of the Church: The Blessed Virgin Mary in Patristic Thought*, trans. Thomas Buffer (San Francisco, CA: Ignatius Press, 1999), 52–58.

[21] *CEH*, vol. 3, 22; cf. Peter Chrysologus, *Sermo* 142, *PL*, vol. 52, col. 0579b.

[22] *CEH*, vol. 3, 47.

[23] *CEH*, vol. 2, 150.

[24] *CEH*, vol. 6, 33.

[25] *CEH*, vol. 6, 35.

[26] *CEH*, vol. 6, 39.

[27] *CEH*, vol. 6, 39.

[28] *CBP*, vol. 3, 136–37. He took this position against Luther, who contended that Paul was insulting Mary here by only calling her a woman. Instead, Salmerón says, it was

towards the Eve-Mary parallel, denying that it was the reason Jesus called his mother "woman."[29]

Eve was not the only Old Testament type of Mary that Salmerón identified. Miriam, the sister of Moses, was like Mary, not only because she was a celibate virgin, but also because she was the sister of the high priest.[30] Mary's reception of the leaven of Christ was prefigured by Sarah, who brought out leaven to make cakes for the three guests (Gen 18:6).[31] Salmerón produces a catena of biblical women whose virtues Mary possesses to a pre-eminent degree: she is more lovable than Rebekah, more fertile than Leah, more beautiful than Rachel, greater than the Queen of Sheba, stronger than Judith, and so forth.[32] The woman of Proverbs (31:10–31) refers mystically to Mary, for she sewed the net of her son's humanity that is used for catching souls.[33] Salmerón even produces a mnemonic device for remembering her five singular graces using the letters of the name *MARIA*, and also assigns to each of the letters the names of Old Testament women who are types of her: Miriam, Abigail, Rebekah and Rachel, Judith, and Anna.[34]

Mary is also compared to men or even inanimate objects of the Old Testament. Abraham, like the Blessed Virgin, did not doubt that he would be able to generate a child, even though he was old.[35] As he became the father of a multitude, she became the mother of all the faithful.[36] Her face shone at the Incarnation like the face of Moses when he came down from the mountain (Ex 34:29–35).[37] She shows herself to be a daughter of David by following Ps 102, blessing God and contemplating his mercy.[38] Surely the strangest com-

---

Luther who insulted Paul.

[29] Maldonado, *Commentaries*, vol. 2, cols. 465–66. He says that Jesus did not call himself the "son of man" on account of Adam either.

[30] *CEH*, vol. 3, 24.

[31] *CEH*, vol. 7, 47.

[32] *CEH*, vol. 3, 39.

[33] *CEH*, vol. 7, 63.

[34] *CEH*, vol. 3, 26. The five graces are *Mater misericordiae, Advocata afflictorum, Refugium redeuntium, Inventrix iustitiae* and *Innocentia et indulgentia*, and *Amica Angelorum*. Salmerón admits that this little exercise is more pious than sound.

[35] *CBP*, vol. 1, 401.

[36] *CEH*, vol. 3, 93.

[37] *CEH*, vol. 3, 261. Salmerón says that only Joseph was permitted to see this, lest the princes of the world or the devil become aware of what was happening, or ordinary people think it was magic.

[38] *CEH*, vol. 3, 116.

parison is to Araunah the Jebusite (2 Sam 24:16–18), who sold his threshing floor to King David so that he could build an altar there. Salmerón says that Mary is a suitable foundation for Christ because she has no elevation [*mons*] of pride.[39] Her perpetual virginity was prophesied by the burning bush, Aaron's rod, Gideon's dry fleece, Isaiah's shoot of Jesse, and Ezekiel's closed door.[40]

Mary in the New Testament

The relative brevity of the Blessed Virgin's appearance in the Gospels did not prevent Salmerón from saying a great deal about her. She provided another point of entry into the mysteries of the Lord's life, especially as the one who is described as keeping things in her heart. Salmerón also wished to resolve particular disputed questions about her life, which led him to compare the opinions of the Fathers and the Doctors. Above all, his exegetical strategy was tying Mary closely to Jesus, such that her life became a mimesis of his. He thus combined two major aspects of the retrieval of Marian devotion after Trent: demonstrating its pedigree in scripture and tradition against the charges of Erasmus and Protestants, and adapting the Marian biblical passages to the same methods of "visualization" described in the previous chapter.[41]

The Annunciation

Salmerón finds great significance in the *mise en scène* of the Annunciation, insisting that Mary was in an inner secret place when the angel came for her, like Sarah in the tent (Gen 18:6).[42] Ecclesiastical artists are wrong to depict Gabriel flying through the air and landing on the roof, which is not at all consistent with the angel's appearance or behavior. Instead, he came to Mary in her enclosed garden, where, like the widow Judith enclosed in her chamber (Jdth 8:5), she was at prayer.[43]

---

[39] *CEH*, vol. 2, 167.

[40] *CEH*, vol. 3, 26.

[41] Nathan Mitchell, *The Mystery of the Rosary: Marian Devotion and the Reinvention of Catholicism* (New York: New York University Press, 2009), 16–19, 79–80.

[42] *CEH*, vol. 3, 33. Here he mocks Luther's musings about whether she was in a secret place, or in her family's home, or, as the *Protoevangelium of James* has it, outside carrying jars of water. Salmerón thinks, along with numerous Fathers, that carrying water was a task beneath the Blessed Virgin.

[43] *CEH*, vol. 3, 34.

When Gabriel arrived, she was praying about the matter that he was to announce to her: that she would become the mother of the Savior. Salmerón regards it as perfectly natural that young Jewish girls, who lived with the expectation of the Messiah's coming, would have hoped to be his mother, especially since she was from the line of David. By way of analogy, he says that if the King of Spain announced that he was seeking a wife from Rome or Naples, all the young noble ladies of those places would hope to be the one chosen.[44] Yet he adds that there was no ambition in the Blessed Virgin, for she waited to be summoned to a higher calling, like King Saul and Pope Gregory.[45]

Salmerón offers a grammatical analysis of the angel's words to Mary, noting the double meaning of *xaīre* as a greeting and a call for rejoicing. The analysis of *kexaritōmenē* leads to polemical engagement with Erasmus and the Protestants. The scholar from Rotterdam dared to attack Jerome's translation "full of grace" [*gratia plena*] and substitute in its place "gracious" [*gratiosa*]. Salmerón defends the Vulgate reading with appeals to the Fathers and the Syriac version of the Gospels. As to the heretics' objection that "full of grace" would make Mary equal to Jesus, Salmerón responds that Stephen was said to be full of grace and fortitude (Act 6:8), and that the apostles, martyrs, confessors, and other saints were also full of grace.[46]

Since Erasmus had used this same point to argue that "full of grace" was not something particular to Mary, Salmerón had to explain how her condition was different. Even if Christ, Mary, and Stephen are all said to be full of the Spirit or full of grace, their respective modes are different. As Bernard says, Jesus is the font of life, but Mary is the aqueduct. She is, in Salmerón's words, "proximately and uniquely bound" to Christ.[47] Salmerón explains her role as pure mother to all of her sons and how this is distinct from the role of the other saints. Luther, he says, put forth a "Jovinian and paradoxical theology" when he denied the order and various ranks [*gradus*] of the just. "Hence this is the fable a certain disciple of Luther puts forth,

---

[44] *CEH*, vol. 3, 47–48. One wonders if Salmerón was thinking of the interactions Charles V had with the throngs of women who came out to greet him in the ceremonial entries and balls held in the cities under his rule. The emperor, of course, never married again after the death of Isabella in 1539. Geoffrey Parker, *Emperor: A New Life of Charles V* (New Haven, CT: Yale University Press, 2019), 399–400.

[45] *CEH*, vol. 3, 35.

[46] *CEH*, vol. 3, 37–38. Another prominent Jesuit of the period also rails against the use of *gratiosa*. Peter Canisius, *De Maria Virgine Incomparabili, et Dei Genitrice Sacrosancta* (Ingolstadt: David Sartorius, 1573), 250.

[47] *CEH*, vol. 3, 37.

'Any Christian is full of grace, and God equally favors us, when he has us for his sons, and does not impute our sins to us.' Thus speaks that disciple of the devil."[48] Salmerón defends the Vulgate and the theological truth that he thinks it accurately expresses. He explains that "full of grace" means not only that the Blessed Virgin is full of uncreated grace, but also that she shares in Christ's capital grace. This means it is her task to communicate grace to the rest of the mystical body of the Church.[49]

Mary and Joseph

Matthew's words about Joseph's intent to put Mary away quietly (Mt 1:19) leads to a discussion of the relationship between the two of them. Salmerón is remarkably thorough in explaining Joseph's state of mind and motivation for the proposed course of action. The Fathers offered three explanations, which in modern theology are called "suspicion," "perplexity," and "reverence."[50] Without using this terminology, Salmerón examined all three theories and the patristic and scholastic witnesses behind them. Although he often left disputed questions open to the reader's judgment, in this case he argued vehemently in favor of one theory over the others. The first view [suspicion], which Salmerón says was more common among the Fathers and has the prima facie support of the Gospel text, is that Joseph doubted Mary's chastity and was distressed to see her pregnant.[51] The second explanation [perplexity] is that Joseph, while not doubting Mary's testimony, did not understand the mystery of the Incarnation. The third theory is that while Joseph did understand the mystery, out of reverence for it he counted himself unworthy to be Mary's consort.[52]

Salmerón attacks the suspicion theory with a series of rhetorical questions. If Joseph knew that Mary was bound by a vow of virginity, he asks, would he have believed that she had violated it so quickly? If he had seen nothing but holy behavior from her, how could such a thought have come into his mind? If he were really a just man, would he have wanted her to escape punishment for such a serious crime? Citing "the jurists," Salmerón

---

[48] *CEH*, vol. 3, 38.

[49] *CEH*, vol. 3, 40.

[50] *Ignatius Catholic Study Bible: The New Testament* (San Francisco, CA: Ignatius Press, 2010), 8.

[51] *CEH*, vol. 3, 235.

[52] *CEH*, vol. 3, 236–37.

says there is no piety or mercy when it conflicts with prudence and justice. He argues moreover that Joseph could not have demonstrated before the law that Mary ought to have been stoned, even if he had wanted to, because he would not have been able to establish the time of her pregnancy. Salmerón brings forth numerous additional arguments and answers to objections in favor of the third theory, namely, that Joseph thought himself unworthy to be Mary's husband. He thinks that their relationship was characterized by love and trust from the beginning.[53]

This relationship culminated in a real marriage, a point that Salmerón, following the Franciscan school, was at pains to demonstrate. It was arranged by God, like the unions of Adam and Eve, and Hosea and the prostitute.[54] Their consent made them true spouses, even if one ought to refrain from calling Joseph and Mary "man and wife," since this designation is reserved for those who consummate their union.[55] In their case, consummation was not necessary, not only because they had given their consent, but also because their marriage truly had the three goods of marriage identified by Augustine: "offspring, fidelity, and the permanent bond" [*proles, fides, sacramentum*].[56] Salmerón even goes so far as to say that Mary and Joseph truly became one flesh.[57]

The Jesuit theologian finds types of Joseph in Noah and Joseph the son of Jacob, and applies to him the verse "faithful and wise servant" (Mt 24:45). Salmerón says that Joseph was privileged to receive the sanctifying effect of Mary and Jesus, and singles out for praise his practice of blind obedience.[58] He objects to ecclesiastical artwork that depicts Joseph as an old man at the time of his marriage, for it was God, not old age, who extinguished concupiscence in him. Salmerón approves of the custom observed in Germany of showing him as robust and relatively young, and says that the "old man" iconography is acceptable only as symbolically signifying his virtue and chastity of mind.[59]

---

[53] *CEH*, vol. 3, 239–41.
[54] *CEH*, vol. 3, 233.
[55] *CEH*, vol. 3, 224.
[56] *CEH*, vol. 3, 225.
[57] *CBP*, vol. 3, 260.
[58] *CEH*, vol. 3, 235.
[59] *CEH*, vol. 3, 227. His words about Germany notwithstanding, Salmerón's portrayal of Joseph is consistent with the emerging patterns of devotional texts and imagery concerning Joseph in Spain and its empire. Charlene Villaseñor Black, "Love and Marriage in the Spanish Empire: Depictions of Holy Matrimony and Gender

The Visitation

According to Salmerón, Mary's motivation for visiting Elizabeth was confirming the truth of the angel's words and rejoicing in them, as well as carrying out her religious duty to her kin. Yet there was a still more important reason: her presence enabled the sanctification of John the Baptist in the womb and fulfilled the prophecy that he would be filled with the Holy Spirit. Like her son, Mary came not to be served, but to serve.[60] When she arrived, Salmerón says, she filled the house with the scent of her ointments (Cant 1:4), and was like the moon illuminated with the rays of Christ the Sun, or like the woman clothed with the sun (Apoc 12:1).[61]

The Visitation provides Salmerón with the opportunity to comment on Mary's canticle, the *Magnificat*, in which she set aside her usual reticence for the sake of praising the Trinity.[62] The Blessed Virgin, he says, has multiple causes for rejoicing in God. She is the one who crushes the serpent's head, that is, original sin. Her joy is like that of someone in the presence of her spouse, a joy of heavenly things, which are the opposite of carnal delights.[63] Salmerón is fond of the image of Mary's singing the canticle, to which he returns periodically throughout the *Commentaries*.[64] As an aside, Salmerón laments that heretics reject the Feast of the Visitation, despite the fact that the event is narrated in scripture.[65]

The Purification of Mary

The presentation in the temple is paired with Mary's purification, and Salmerón treated both aspects of the mystery. He maintains that Mary was not defiled even in a ritual way by giving birth, meaning that there was no real cause for her purification. Like her son, however, she kept the Law.[66] The miraculous nature of her giving birth meant that she did not need a long

---

Discourses in the Seventeenth Century," *Sixteenth Century Journal* 32, no. 3 (2001): 637–67.

[60] *CEH*, vol. 3, 84.
[61] *CEH*, vol. 3, 86.
[62] *CEH*, vol. 3, 99.
[63] *CEH*, vol. 3, 103.
[64] *CEH*, vol. 3, 161; *CEH*, vol. 5, 296; *CEH*, vol. 10, 52; *CBP*, vol. 2, 144.
[65] *CEH*, vol. 3, 96.
[66] *CEH*, vol. 3, 376.

convalescence, having been freed from the experience of pain. He therefore calls for the destruction of ecclesiastical art that depicts her reclining in bed for the entire period leading up to her purification.[67]

One of the Marian verses that gives Salmerón the greatest difficulty is "thy own soul a sword shall pierce" (Lk 2:35). Acknowledging that theologians are free to propose their views on matters the Church has not defined, he rejects Augustine's explanation that the verse speaks of the sword of doubt that passed quickly through her mind, on the grounds that one cannot attribute doubt to the Blessed Virgin. Chrysostom, followed by Hugh of St-Cher and Peter Comestor, thought that the verse referred to the soul of her son, but Salmerón objects that the grammar clearly refers to Mary's soul. Others propose that the verse signifies that Mary participates in the grace of martyrdom, which according to Thomas is the highest gift.[68] Salmerón sees a problem, however, with this explanation: if martyrdom is the highest gift, then women like Agnes, Lucy, and Katherine could be seen as superior to Mary. Salmerón says that Mary did participate in the gift of martyrdom, on the grounds that there is no gift present in the saints that is not also present in Mary in a more eminent way. She was more than a martyr, because her love was stronger than death.[69] Salmerón rejects the theory that the sword refers to the death of Mary while her son was on the cross, saying that she was constant and faithful beneath the cross, and did not actually die.[70] The Church, he says, knows nothing of the supposed mystery of the Virgin's death and return to life.[71]

The Finding in the Temple

The finding of Jesus in the temple was an occasion for Salmerón to defend the harmoniousness of the Holy Family in the face of Jesus's apparent harshness toward his parents. He says that the Lord spoke to Mary and Joseph as a superior to an inferior because he wanted to temper their love for their offspring [*affectum carnis*], so as to teach them that divine love is prior to parental love,

---

[67] *CEH*, vol. 3, 377.

[68] *CEH*, vol. 3, 393.

[69] *CEH*, vol. 3, 393–97.

[70] Although he emphasizes Mary's sharing in her son's suffering, he explicitly rejects the motifs of spasm, swooning, and crucifixion that appear in other devotional works of the sixteenth century. Jessica Boon, "The Agony of the Virgin: The Swoons and Crucifixion of Mary in Sixteenth Century Castilian Passion Treatises," *Sixteenth Century Journal* 38, no. 1 (2007): 3–25.

[71] *CEH*, vol. 3, 398–99.

and help them understand that his divine mission would take him away from them.[72] Here Salmerón walked a careful line between allowing that Mary could be ignorant of something for a time and defending her from the charge of misunderstanding. His explanation is that she was a prophetess who kept things in her heart, and that even great prophets may not know certain things until they investigate them more thoroughly.[73]

Despite the fact that Mary and Joseph needed this instruction, Salmerón was insistent that they had theological faith, and that they were not ignorant of the principal Christian mysteries. They already knew from Jesus's infancy, for example, that he was God. Here Salmerón rejects the "impious" exegesis of Erasmus, who said that Mary's misunderstanding of her son's words showed that she doubted his divinity.[74] When Joseph and Mary "wondered" at his reply, it was because his presence in the temple disputing with the doctors of the Law was a new mystery to them, not because they doubted him.[75] Salmerón also finds in Mary an example of parenting. Although only men were obliged to go the temple for the feasts, she made the journey anyway, which shows that Christians should take their children to church and teach them to pray and worship.[76]

The Passion

The longest and richest commentaries on Mary in the Gospels are reserved for the Passion, which dwell on two themes: her sharing in the sufferings of Jesus, and her being received by John. The former allows Salmerón to articulate his view of Mary's personal perfection and her cooperation in Jesus's work of redemption, bringing out its cosmic significance, whereas the latter is an important locus of his understanding of the relationship between Mary and the faithful.

Salmerón confronts the problem that only John among the evangelists put Mary beneath the cross. He favors the explanation of Ambrose (that John was more attentive to the mystical reality of the Blessed Virgin's maternal devotion) over that of Euthymius (that it was actually a different Mary). The

---

[72] *CEH*, vol. 3, 435–36. Salmerón adds that Jesus's words were primarily meant for other parents, since Mary and Joseph already had a strong grasp of this point.
[73] *CEH*, vol. 3, 437–38.
[74] *CEH*, vol. 3, 436.
[75] *CEH*, vol. 3, 433.
[76] *CEH*, vol. 3, 429.

reason Christ wanted her to be near the cross was so that her faith, praised by Elizabeth, would shine forth, and demonstrate that she believed the message of Gabriel: her son was to save the people from their sins and sit on the throne of David in the house of Jacob.[77]

For the Jesuit theologian, the fullness of grace and the fullness of suffering go hand in hand, for Mary received both.[78] Jesus wished that he and his mother would experience not only their own suffering, but also each other's, like two mirrors facing each other. This, Salmerón says, is the fulfilment of the prophecy of the sword that would pierce her soul.[79] Salmerón uses scripture, the Fathers, and the Doctors to extend Jesus's suffering to his mother. The oppression of Christ the just man by the wicked Jews (Wis 2) also refers to the oppression of Mary.[80] According to Bonaventure, Christ's words "Father, forgive them, for they know not what they do" (Lk 23:34) were also directed to his mother.[81] Salmerón contends that the Virgin's pain and sorrow flowing from her charity were greater than the pain and sorrow of any martyr. Whereas for the martyrs, charity tempers suffering, for Mary charity increased it, and compounded the suffering she experienced on account of natural affection.[82]

Salmerón's treatment of Mary's presence beneath the cross witnesses his articulation of the Eve-Mary parallel in terms of "co-redemption." Salmerón uses the title *coredemptrix* in the *Commentaries*, and he has been credited with being one of the pioneers of this usage.[83]

> For as ruin followed upon the fact that a woman approaching the tree of the knowledge of good and evil ate from it, and then died and brought her man to eat unto his death, so here in a contrary way (since indeed things are healed by their contraries) a man first tasted the bitter wood of the cross, and offered it to a woman to taste. And just as there [in Eden] the world's fall was accomplished by two people, but especially by the man, so

---

[77] *CEH*, vol. 10, 338–39.
[78] *CEH*, vol. 10, 428.
[79] *CEH*, vol. 10, 339.
[80] *CEH*, vol. 10, 34.
[81] *CEH*, vol. 10, 324.
[82] *CEH*, vol. 10, 426–27.
[83] *CEH*, vol. 3, 38. Robert Fastiggi, "Mary in the Work of Redemption," in *The Oxford Handbook of Mary*, ed. Chris Maunder (New York: Oxford University Press, 2019), 303–19, at 309. Bastero observes that the first documented appearance of *coredemptrix* is in a Latin hymn from two fifteenth-century Salzburg manuscripts. Bastero, *Mary*, 236.

also salvation and redemption came forth from two people, but principally from Christ.[84]

Salmerón produces a catena of biblical references that tie Mary's work closely to Christ's. Mary offered the sacrifice of her Son to the Father for the whole world, like Abraham and Isaac. She was like the mother of the Maccabees witnessing their martyrdom (2 Macc 7), or Hannah offering Samuel in the temple (1 Sam 1:24–28).[85] The pain of the wife of Phineas, who died when she heard that the ark had been taken and her husband killed (1 Sam 4:19), was less than the pain of Mary, who saw the true ark of God held captive with thorns and nails.[86] Salmerón even engages in a bit of wordplay when he says that the rod [*virga*] of Ps 22:4 should be understood as the virgin [*virgo*] paired with Christ the staff [*baculus*].[87]

Taking his cue from earlier theologians, Salmerón sees Mary beneath the cross in cosmic terms. From the power of the cross, she participated in the grace of perseverance from all sin, and she became an advocate for all her children. Her virginal lantern lights up the Church Militant and the Church Triumphant. Salmerón cites Irenaeus, who said that two great loves fought in her heart: the life of Christ and the salvation of mankind. She did not display excessive signs of mourning, but she did weep, for the death of Jesus touched no one more than her.[88] As Bridget says, the angels and all creation, and even the souls in the bosom of Abraham and the demons lamented the Lord's death in the person of Mary.[89]

Now Salmerón arrives at the moment to which he gave so much attention in his homily at Trent in 1546: Christ's entrusting of Mary to John, the beloved disciple.[90] Whereas at the council he used this verse as an analogy for the relationship of bishops to the Church, here he is more interested in

---

[84] *CEH*, vol. 10, 339.

[85] *CEH*, vol. 10, 339.

[86] *CEH*, vol. 10, 427.

[87] *CEH*, vol. 10, 339. His source for this idea was probably Bernard. Eva De Visscher, "Marian Devotion in the Latin West in the Later Middle Ages," in *Mary: The Complete Resource*, ed. Sarah Jane Boss (New York: Oxford University Press, 2007), 177–201, at 178.

[88] *CEH*, vol. 10, 340.

[89] *CEH*, vol. 10, 428.

[90] *Oratio Reverendi Patris Magistri Alphonsi Salmeronis de Societate Iesu Theologi, nuper in Concilio Tridentino habita, in qua ad exemplar Divi Ioannis Evangelistae vera Praelatorum forma describitur* (Rome: Stephanus Nicolinus, 1547); Juan Tejada y Ramiro, *Colección de cánones y de todos los concilios*, vol. 4 (Madrid: 1859), 755–62;

John's status as Mary's son. He explains John's presence beneath the cross in the following way: at first, he ran away with the other disciples, but then he repented and returned in tears to witness the Passion.[91] Although Cyprian said that Joseph was still alive at this time and accepted his displacement by John, Salmerón considered it more probable that he was already dead. As only a Roman emperor could give a widow who had lost her only son in battle to someone else, so Christ the Emperor, while dying in battle against his enemies from Tartarus, gave Mary to someone else.[92]

John's taking Mary "into his own," according to Salmerón, means that he lived with her on Mount Zion in some buildings he had purchased, perhaps at the Lord's suggestion, a hypothesis he attributes to Nicephorus Kallistos and Gregory Nazianzen. Why, he asks, does scripture say that John received Mary, rather than that she received him? He explains that Christ is the shepherd and Mary the sheep, so she obeyed his command from the cross. Still, John had greater need of her than she had of him, and she extended her virtues and precious merits to him in a singular way.[93] In explaining how Mary becomes John's mother and she his son, Salmerón references an unusual theological dispute on this point from the pontificate of Pius II (1458–64). A certain Baurinon claimed that John was made a natural son of Mary, which the Bishop of Brescia, Domenico de Domenici, publicly opposed. More recently, he says, a preacher in Tarragona was promoting the same idea.[94] Salmerón cites some of the arguments for this thesis and proceeds to refute them. He thinks it is metaphysically impossible to transfer one subject to another, and nonsensical to say that a man can have two mothers. John became a son of Mary by grace and charity, not by nature.[95]

John Hughes, "Alfonso Salmeron: His Work at the Council of Trent," (PhD dissertation: University of Kentucky, 1974), Appendix III, 236–52.

[91] *CEH*, vol. 10, 342.

[92] *CEH*, vol. 10, 343.

[93] *CEH*, vol. 10, 346–47.

[94] The Mariologist Jean-Baptiste Terrien cites only Salmerón's account for this debate between Baurinon and the bishop, while observing that the thesis of John's natural sonship was taught by the Franciscan Nicholas de Orbellis. Jean-Baptiste Terrien, *La Mère de Dieu et la mère des hommes: D'après les pères et la théologie* (Paris: P. Lethielleux, 1900–2), vol. 3, 307–8.

[95] *CEH*, vol. 10, 343–45.

The Resurrection

Although there is no direct scriptural evidence for the claim, Salmerón believed that the risen Christ appeared to his mother prior to the other post-Resurrection appearances recounted in the Gospels.[96] One might reasonably assume that Salmerón's proximate source for this idea was the *Spiritual Exercises*, which instructs the retreatant to contemplate this scene at the beginning of the Fourth Week of the retreat. Yet he makes no mention of the *Exercises*, but only the Fathers and Doctors. Ambrose noted that the two Marys saw the Resurrection before the Apostles in his work on virgins. "Mary therefore saw the resurrection of the Lord, and saw him first and believed. Mary Magdalene saw him too, even though she doubted until then."[97] Salmerón cites the *Opus Paschale* of the poet Sedulius, which references the Lord's appearance to his mother. "Bernard" too says that Mary "first saw the Lord in glorious form, not to overcome her doubt, but to console her with joy."[98] Salmerón cites numerous other authorities, including Rupert of Deutz and Bridget. The event is not narrated in the Gospels, he says, because it would have been impossible for the Evangelists to describe.[99]

Aside from the Fathers and Doctors, Salmerón also appealed to liturgical practice and the use of reason in support of the event. The fact that the Roman Church celebrates the first Mass of Easter at the Basilica of Mary Major testifies that the Blessed Virgin was the first to see the resurrected Lord.[100] The antiphon text "she adored the one she brought forth" [*ipsum quem genuit, adoravit*] expresses the truth that since Mary was the one who suffered the greatest pains on account of him, she should also be the first to adore him risen from the dead. Salmerón even suggests that the demands of the Fourth Commandment may have motivated Jesus, since it was an excellent way for him to honor his mother.[101] It is natural for a man returning home from a long

---

[96] He first mentions this as an aside in Volume 3, but saves his full treatment of the matter until Volume 11. *CEH*, vol. 3, 365.

[97] *CEH*, vol. 11, 86; Ambrose, *De virginibus*, PL, vol. 16, col. 0270a.

[98] *CEH*, vol. 11, 87. This appears to be taken from an apocryphal work that Salmerón attributes to Bernard.

[99] *CEH*, vol. 11, 90.

[100] *CEH*, vol. 11, 88.

[101] *CEH*, vol. 11, 88. The antiphon comes from the Magnificat at First Vespers on the Feast of the Purification.

journey or from war to first go to his mother or his wife to gladden her before he visits anyone else.[102]

Despite the scarcity of her presence in the sacred text, honoring Mary alongside Jesus was one of the tasks Salmerón identified as belonging to the theologian. She was the first to witness and contemplate the Christian mysteries, and thereby reveals both the cooperation of the sexes in the order of redemption and mankind's capacity to be truly sanctified by the reception of grace. Yet Salmerón's Mariology, although it begins with scripture, has additional dimensions. The Jesuit theologian had much to say about her place in the Church's public prayer, the two special doctrines of the Immaculate Conception and the Assumption, and numerous themes, titles, and images that appear in the Fathers and Doctors.

Mary in the Liturgy

Liturgical sources are prominent in Salmerón's teaching on Mary. In the first place, this material compensates in some measure for the relative paucity of direct biblical references to her. In the second place, public prayers to the Blessed Virgin are both points of departure for Salmerón's theologizing and sources of spiritual delight. He likes the idea, taken from the text of the *Regina pacis* [*Funda nos in pace/Mutans Evae nomen*], that the name "Eve" [*Eva*] has been made into the greeting "Hail" [*Ave*] for the Blessed Virgin, which shows how she reversed the course of events that the first woman had set in motion.[103] There is a parallel, he says, between the angel's greeting to Mary and the priest's greeting to the people at Mass.[104] The Liturgy of St. Basil includes a prayer to Mary after the offering of the sacrifice, as does the Syrian liturgy, which shows that this custom of greeting her is very ancient.[105]

In a similar vein, Salmerón correlated the words of the Hail Mary with her feasts. *Ave* corresponds to her Immaculate Conception, *Maria* to her Nativity, *gratia plena* to her Presentation, *Dominus tecum* to the Annunciation, *benedicta tu in mulieribus* to the Visitation, *et benedictus fructus ventris tui* to her giving birth in Bethlehem, *sancta Maria virgo Mater Dei* to the Purification, *ora pro nobis peccatoribus* to her Assumption, and *nunc et in hora mortis nostrae* to

---

[102] *CEH*, vol. 11, 89.
[103] *CEH*, vol. 3, 36.
[104] *CEH*, vol. 3, 40.
[105] *CEH*, vol. 3, 43.

Christ's passion.[106] There is something almost childlike in this otherwise grave and learned man's delight in making these associations. He exhorts the reader to frequently say the angel's words, which are like letters from a friend, since this pleases her. The Church's custom of praying in this fashion fulfils Mary's own prophecy: "all generations shall call me blessed" (Lk 1:48).[107]

Salmerón occasionally derived additional theological meaning from Marian liturgical sources. The *responsorium breve* for the Feast of the Assumption, *Exaltata est sancta Dei Genetrix super choros angelorum*, was one of Salmerón's favorite texts, given the frequency with which he cited it. He explains that Mary, representing the whole human race by herself, is added to the nine choirs of angels to make the number ten, which signifies all Christians.[108] His teaching on Mary's merit appeals to the antiphon *Regina coeli* because it contains the words "for he whom you did merit to bear" [*quia quem meruisti portare*].[109] When the Church does not have a proper Epistle or Gospel for a Mass, she applies a reading from some other feast, but she understands its meaning in spiritual rather than literal terms. Following this principle, the Church reads the Gospel of Mary and Martha (Lk 10:38–42) on the Feast of the Assumption, for Mary combines the virtues of both women, and she is able to contemplate and act at once.[110]

Salmerón ends his volume on the Passion with a chapter on why Saturday is liturgically dedicated to the Blessed Virgin and her lamentation at the death of her Son.[111] As Friday is given over to the memory of the cross, he says, so Saturday is given to the martyrdom of Jesus's mother, like two mirrors facing each other. Mary was the only one who maintained certain and complete faith in the Lord's Resurrection.[112] The seventh day is chosen for this remembrance because it is a day of rest, and the rest that the Lord sought and found in the Blessed Virgin surpassed his rest in the tomb.[113] Saturday also permits Christians to recall the triple grace of Mary, which corresponds to the triple grace of Christ. As the Lord had the grace of the hypostatic union, the capital

---

[106] *CEH*, vol. 3, 44–45.

[107] *CEH*, vol. 3, 43. Curiously, however, he mentions the recitation of the Rosary only once. *CEH*, vol. 10, 125.

[108] *CEH*, vol. 7, 255.

[109] *CEH*, vol. 3, 49.

[110] *CEH*, vol. 8, 185; *CEH*, vol. 3, 39; *CEH*, vol. 3, 85.

[111] Salmerón customarily preached about Mary on Saturdays, even during Lent. Andrés, "La compasión," 371.

[112] *CEH*, vol. 10, 423.

[113] *CEH*, vol. 10, 424.

grace, and the grace of being a unique person, so his Mother had the grace of maternal union, the "grace of the neck," and the grace of being a unique person.[114] The Christological cast of Salmerón's Mariology is evident here.

For Salmerón, as for other Jesuits of his time, the Church's public prayer and the biblical text were harmonious witnesses to the true understanding of Mary.[115] Not only did he draw on the former as a source of orthodox teaching, but he also took great delight in meditating on their content. His fervent devotion to her is evident in this prayer of his own composition: "O most holy Virgin, I beseech you, by the pain you suffered at that time, that I may find your Son, my Lord and my God, to whom I commend my soul, and that he may no longer permit me to wander among vanities."[116]

The Immaculate Conception

The most significant Marian controversy discussed in the *Commentaries* is the Immaculate Conception, and Salmerón's treatment of it is significant for several reasons. First, it was a major controversy not only among professional theologians, but also in the broader Catholic world.[117] While Salmerón was finishing the *Commentaries*, Diego Pérez de Valdivia completed the first work in Spanish on the subject; while the second Cologne edition of the *Commentaries* was coming off the presses, a bitter quarrel over the Immaculate Conception exploded in the city of Seville in 1613, in which Dominicans and Jesuits were the primary antagonists, and in which racial epithets played a critical role.[118] The piety of both the Spanish and the Austrian Habsburgs had the

---

[114] *CEH*, vol. 10, 426. A more systematic study of this "triple grace," and its connection to Mary's status as *coredemptrix*, may be found in Andrés, "La compasión," 375–88. The "grace of the neck" is explained below.

[115] A key aspect of Peter Canisius's strategy in Augsburg was the reintroduction of the cycle of Marian feast days. Bridget Heal, *The Cult of the Virgin Mary in Early Modern Germany: Protestant and Catholic Piety, 1500–1648* (New York: Cambridge University Press, 2007), 151.

[116] *CEH*, vol. 3, 434.

[117] See Leslie Twomey, *The Serpent and the Rose: The Immaculate Conception and Hispanic Poetry in the Late Medieval Period* (Boston, MA: Brill, 2008).

[118] Diego Pérez de Valdivia, *Tratado de la Inmaculada Concepción de nuestra Señora* (1582), ed. Juan Cruz Cruz (Pamplona: University of Navarre, 2004); Felipe Pereda, "*Vox Populi*: Carnal Blood, Spiritual Milk, and the Debate Surrounding the Immaculate Conception, ca. 1600," in *Interreligious Encounters in Polemics Between Christians, Jews, and Muslims in Iberia and Beyond*, ed. Mercedes García-Arenal, Gerard Wiegers, and Ryan Szpiech (Boston, MA: Brill, 2019), 286–334.

Immaculate Conception at its core, which affected Spanish social life as well as diplomatic relations, especially with the papacy, long into the seventeenth century.[119] Shortly after the final edition of Salmerón's *Commentaries* was published, the Spanish and Austrian Habsburgs launched a new effort in Rome to have the Immaculate Conception defined as an article of faith.[120] As a general rule, early Jesuits inside and outside of Spain were also staunch defenders of the Immaculate Conception.[121] Although modern research has made plausible connections between Marian devotion, especially the Immaculate Conception, and a host of other issues—purity of blood, wars of conquest, political and dynastic interests, and so forth—Salmerón's concerns were, by all appearances, exclusively theological.[122]

Second, his position created distinct methodological problems for Salmerón, because his general preference for more ancient Fathers and Doctors ran into the problem that many of them had opposed the Immaculate Conception. He made creative efforts to justify the opinion of later theologians on this issue, and even more surprisingly attributed to the universities and the ordinary faithful a limited share in the Church's teaching authority. These moves ought not to be regarded merely as instances of special pleading on behalf of a preferred position, but as revealing latent possibilities in Salmerón's theological method.

The main treatment of the Immaculate Conception is found in connection with Salmerón's exegesis of Rom 5:12, where he offers a series of treatises on

---

[119] See Thomas Izbicki, "The Immaculate Conception and Ecclesiastical Politics from the Council of Basel to the Council of Trent: The Dominicans and Their Foes," *Archiv für Reformationgeschichte* 96 (2005): 145–70; Rosilie Hernández, *Immaculate Conceptions: The Power of the Religious Imagination in Early Modern Spain* (Toronto: University of Toronto Press, 2019), 31–40; Cristina Bravo Lozano, "La Concepción Inmaculada de María en el contexto de la *pietas hispánica*," in *Intacta María: Política y religiosidad en la España barroca*, ed. Pablo González Tornel (Valencia: Generalitat Valenciana, 2017), 109–19.

[120] Luc Duerloo, *Dynasty and Piety: Archduke Albert (1598–1621) and Habsburg Political Culture in an Age of Religious Wars* (New York: Routledge, 2016), 465–66.

[121] Bernardino Llorca, "Los escritores jesuitas españoles y la Inmaculada Concepción en el primer período de la Compañía de Jesús," *Estudios Marianos* 16 (1955): 233–44.

[122] Amy Remensnyder, *La Conquistadora: The Virgin Mary at War and Peace in the Old and New Worlds* (New York: Oxford University Press, 2014), 127; Linda Hall, *Mary, Mother and Warrior: The Virgin in Spain and the Americas* (Austin, TX: University of Texas, 2004); Magdalena Sánchez, *The Empress, the Queen, and the Nun: Women and Power at the Court of Philip III of Spain* (Baltimore, MD: Johns Hopkins University Press, 1998), 23.

original sin and its consequences. The treatise on the Immaculate Conception opens with the observation that many people forego discussion of the topic, whereas others deny that God could have granted her this privilege at all. Salmerón counters that there are two good reasons to deal with the controversy: first, it sheds light on scripture, and second, it is not good to be silent where the truths of faith are concerned.[123] In other words, he signals immediately that the Immaculate Conception is important as a matter of biblical theology.

In keeping with his typical approach in the final four volumes of the *Commentaries*, Salmerón began with the *dubia* or objections to his own position, rather than the positive case he intended to make. The first objection is that the Immaculate Conception makes Mary equal to God. In reply, he distinguishes four levels of immortality and impeccability. Only Christ in his divine nature cannot die at all or sin; only God is subject to no law. At the second level, someone may be called immortal when he is free of death on account of being by nature indissoluble, as in the case of the good angels. Third, one is immune from death if the principles of his nature allow that he can die, but by a privilege is allowed to avoid this, like Adam before the Fall. To Mary belongs the fourth degree of immortality, which consists of the preservation from all sin.[124]

Salmerón brought forth arguments from scripture, the Fathers, and Reason, against the Immaculate Conception. The central argument is that Christ alone is portrayed as completely innocent in scripture, and that Paul, followed by many Fathers and Doctors, says that all have sinned (Rom 3:5). Salmerón singles out the mature position of Thomas, which is that Mary lacked original justice, experienced the "tinder of sin" and died a natural death, meaning that she had original sin.[125] Salmerón was likewise aware that a number of Mary's most important devotees, including Bernard and Bonaventure, did not believe in the Immaculate Conception.[126] His strategy for answering them amounts to a complex argument from authority.

Salmerón's first argument from authority involves bringing forth a multitude of theologians in favor of the Immaculate Conception against the multitude opposing it, with the aim of neutralizing the latter. He says that "some" count two hundred opponents of the Immaculate Conception; Vincenzo Bandello (d. 1507), the former Master General of the Dominican Order

---

[123] *CBP*, vol. 1, 457.
[124] *CBP*, vol. 1, 458–59.
[125] *CBP*, vol. 1, 466.
[126] *CBP*, vol. 1, 468.

and the author of a major work against the teaching, counted nearly three hundred; Cajetan identified fifteen "irrefutable" authorities.[127] Yet Salmerón says that they have falsely claimed many of those authorities, and that nearly all the teachers of theology, kings and princes, peoples, popes, and religious support the Immaculate Conception, so that he can say, "there are more with us than with them" (2 Kgs 6:16). He offers a list of the most important authorities, totaling twenty. Duns Scotus is credited with being the first to fight for the Virgin's glory on this point, followed by Richard of St. Victor, Denis the Carthusian, Robert Grosseteste, Jean Gerson, John Fisher, Johann Eck, and others.[128] Salmerón adds the observation that no one at the University of Paris is considered worthy of the master's degree unless he swears to defend and fight for this privilege of the Blessed Virgin, and that almost everyone in the Christian world outside the Dominican Order upholds it.[129] He even deals with the problem of dueling mystics, noting that Bridget of Sweden offered revelations in favor of the teaching, whereas some say that Catherine of Siena opposed it.[130]

Even if Salmerón's claim that more authorities support the Immaculate Conception than oppose it was true, he still had to account for the disagreement. He says that Augustine went to excesses in his opposition to the Pelagians, but that even he refrained from discussing the possibility of Mary's sin for the sake of the Lord's honor.[131] Genuine devotion to Mary is not based solely on the teachings of Bernard, Thomas, and Bonaventure, who in fact erred on certain issues. On this question, he says, the more recent Doctors have been more perspicacious than the ancient ones.[132] It should not be surprising that men like Chrysostom, Alexander of Hales, Albert the Great, William Durandus, and Giles of Rome did not embrace the Immaculate Conception, "whether because they were only men, or because new mysteries are revealed with the passage of time."[133]

Salmerón gave particular attention to Thomas and his commentators, since they were the principal opponents of the Immaculate Conception. He says

---

[127] *CBP*, vol. 1, 467.

[128] *CBP*, vol. 1, 476–77.

[129] *CBP*, vol. 1, 467.

[130] *CBP*, vol. 1, 478.

[131] *CBP*, vol. 1, 470–72.

[132] *CBP*, vol. 1, 468.

[133] *CBP*, vol. 1, 474. This statement about "new mysteries" is something of an outlier in the *Commentaries*, and it is highly unlikely that Salmerón intended the implication that additions can be made to the deposit of faith.

explicitly that Thomas erred in this matter.[134] At the same time, Salmerón claims that Aquinas changed his mind on the issue, saying that "many ancient codices" of the *Summa Theologiae* contain the reading "for she was most pure with respect to guilt, because she incurred neither original, nor mortal, nor venial sin."[135] He takes a "divide and conquer" strategy toward the Order of Preachers, highlighting Dominicans who either defended the Immaculate Conception, like Torquemada, or who provided an intellectual opening toward it, like Durandus and Capreolus.[136]

Having attempted to neutralize the authorities arrayed against the Immaculate Conception, Salmerón turned to the Magisterium (the Church's teaching office) and the learned authority of selected popes, bishops, and ecumenical councils to argue in favor of it. This was a difficult argument for him to make, since in his time no definition had been put forth. He cites Session 36 of the Council of Basel, which said that the Immaculate Conception is more probable and consonant with faith, reason, and the teachings of the saints, and he observes that Eugenius IV and Nicholas V approved these particular acts of the controversial council.[137] Sixtus IV instituted the Feast of the Conception with *Grave nimis*, which the Council of Trent renewed. The councils therefore provided soft support for the position that Salmerón sought to defend.

At this point, Salmerón identified an authority that scarcely appears elsewhere in the *Commentaries*: the universities. At the turn of the sixteenth century, several of them made corporate decisions to defend the Immaculate Conception. Paris did so in 1497, followed by Cologne, Mainz, and Vienna in 1499, 1500, and 1501, respectively.[138] Salmerón identifies the universities, especially in France and Spain, as theological authorities in a qualified sense.

---

[134] *CBP*, vol. 1, 427.

[135] *CBP*, vol. 1, 475. Salmerón observes that Juan de Torquemada, who upheld the Immaculate Conception, cites this version of Thomas's text. The relevant article is *ST*, III, q. 27, a. 4.

[136] *CBP*, vol. 1, 461–62. His friend Ambrogio Catarino became embroiled in controversy over this question within the Dominican Order. Giorgio Caravale, *Beyond the Inquisition: Ambrogio Catarino and the Origins of the Counter-Reformation*, trans. Don Weinstein (Notre Dame, IN: University of Notre Dame Press, 2017), 24–32.

[137] This qualification is important because by the time the council had issued the decree in 1439, Eugenius IV had already departed Basel, which led papalists to regard it as no longer a legitimate council.

[138] Bastero, *Mary*, 191. Ignatius of Loyola did not think the Jesuit students at the University of Gandía should swear to defend the Immaculate Conception, since the Church did not condemn the opposite opinion. Although he said that every Jesuit he knew upheld the teaching, condemning the opposite opinion could be

> There is no need to say that the universities usurped for themselves a duty that does not pertain to them. For we acknowledge that defining matters of faith with authority that compels and obliges everyone to accept belongs only to the Roman Pontiff and the ecumenical council. The universities nevertheless sometimes can, like teachers and Doctors, decide [*determinare*] things for the sake of settling schisms and scandals of kingdoms, especially when the pontiffs not only do not protest, but even more by their silence approve their definitions.[139]

This amounts to a limited participation in ecclesiastical authority for the universities, especially in the resolution of disputed questions. Although elsewhere Salmerón acknowledged the importance of learned men in the Church, this seems to be the only place where the universities as institutions are granted such a role.

Salmerón's appeal to "the agreement of the peoples, and the consensus of pious men" in favor of the Immaculate Conception is surprising given the overall cast of his thought, but this argument became increasingly common in Spain during the period.[140] He seemed to accept Cajetan's principle that the consensus of the people did not prevail against the teaching of the learned, but he says it is beside the point, since many of the learned also support the Immaculate Conception. Immediately he adds a word in favor of the simple against learned men. "And I fear to hear that Gospel verse: "Hath any one of the rulers believed in him, or of the Pharisees? But this multitude, that knoweth not the law, are accursed" (Jn 7:48–49).[141] Although he passes over it quickly, this passage contains *in nuce* the idea of the *sensus fidelium*. Salmerón certainly took a top-down approach most of the time, but this special case indicates that he thought that sometimes intermediate bodies, and even the ordinary faithful, recognize theological truths that others do not.

Salmerón's key appeal to ecclesiastical authority, however, was liturgical. Aware that the Roman Church had made no dogmatic declaration on the issue, he thought that her celebration of a feast under the name "Holy Conception" [*Sanctae Conceptionis*] showed that the teaching cannot be false. This feast, as well as the many altars and confraternities that bear the name of

---

  interpreted by some as taking a "spirit of manifest contradiction." *MHSI. MI. Sancti Ignatii de Loyola Epistolae et Instructiones* (Madrid: Gabriel López del Horno, 1903–11), vol. 2, no. 889, 549.

[139] *CBP*, vol. 1, 477.

[140] Hernández, *Immaculate Conceptions*, 3–4.

[141] *CBP*, vol. 1, 477. The implication is that the learned opponents of the Immaculate Conception are akin to the learned opponents of Jesus in during his lifetime.

the Immaculate Conception, would otherwise be a kind of idolatry.[142] This claim runs up against a difficulty: the Holy Conception was not celebrated everywhere, and in some places, the alternative feast of Mary's "sanctification" was observed. This referred to the idea that she was cleansed of all sin at some point during gestation, and was therefore not conceived without sin, a position taught by numerous Fathers and Doctors.[143] Salmerón rejects the argument of some opponents of the Immaculate Conception that their view is also upheld by Church authority on account of its liturgical celebration.

> It must be said that the name "conception" indicates more openly the privilege of preservation, and teaches that the conception was holy. Let no one therefore think he is celebrating the contrary of what others are celebrating concerning the sanctification, or what the Roman Church celebrates; otherwise there would be a horrendous and intolerable schism.[144]

The unified belief and practice of the Roman Church, according to the Jesuit theologian, must be the controlling one. "It does not matter if someone from the family of Blessed Dominic says, 'I believe and understand in my heart a sanctification that takes away sin.' But your internal opinion means nothing, so long as you do not protest with words."[145] Liturgical diversity, in other words, cannot be grounds for dogmatic diversity. In fact, Salmerón was exaggerating somewhat the Roman Church's support for the feast, as popes after Trent wavered on the matter. Pius V kept the feast on the calendar while suppressing the word "Immaculate."[146] Salmerón also looks East for liturgical corroboration: "Basil agrees [with Mary's sinlessness] in his liturgy, frequently calling her the most holy and inviolate Virgin, and Chrysostom in his liturgy often calls her most holy, undefiled, and blessed above all."[147]

The other exegetes under consideration showed less interest in the Immaculate Conception than Salmerón. Jansen and Maldonado offer considerable praise for Mary in their commentaries on the relevant biblical passages, but the former says nothing about this particular teaching, and the latter only

---

[142] *CBP*, vol. 1, 477.

[143] Sarah Jane Boss, "The Development of the Doctrine of Mary's Immaculate Conception," in *Mary: The Complete Resource*, ed. Sarah Jane Boss (New York: Oxford University Press, 2007), 207–35, at 218.

[144] *CBP*, vol. 1, 477–78.

[145] *CBP*, vol. 1, 478.

[146] Hernández, *Immaculate Conceptions*, 38.

[147] *CBP*, vol. 1, 476.

mentions in passing that "we" believe in the Virgin's conception without sin.[148] Barradas dealt with the matter less extensively and controversially than Salmerón. Taking the analogy of the heavenly city as his point of departure (Apoc 21), Barradas expounds upon the numerous "jewels" of Mary's privileges that adorned the "foundation" of her Immaculate Conception.[149]

The Assumption

Salmerón dedicates the last twenty-five pages of his volume on the Lord's Resurrection and Ascension to Mary's Assumption. He begins with a discussion of the celebration of the feast, which is he says is called the Dormition among the Greeks, and the Assumption among the Latins. It commemorates the truth that Mary's body and soul were taken up into heaven "after a short sleep of death," which goes against the general rule that the soul is taken up into heaven at death, while the body awaits the general resurrection.[150] This special privilege corresponds to her preservation from original sin.

As with the Immaculate Conception, Salmerón has to field the fundamental objection, voiced by both Protestants and Catholics, that scripture does not speak of the Assumption. On the grounds that Mary and Christ share the same flesh, he says that "nor wilt [thou] give thy holy one to see corruption" (Ps 15:10) applies to her, and that the Lord's words about the prince of the world having nothing on him (Jn 14:30) pertain to Mary as well.[151] In addition, there are certain passages that speak of the Assumption in a spiritual sense, and even if these do not convince the heretics, they can edify the faithful. The ark that rises to its resting place (Ps 131:8) is none other than the Blessed Virgin, as is the queen standing at the king's side (Ps 44) and the woman clothed with the sun (Apoc 12:1).[152] Following his usual method, Salmerón produces catenas of the Fathers and Doctors in support of the Assumption. He adds the celebration of the feast in numerous liturgical rites and their texts, appealing once again to the notion that the Church cannot be mistaken in her worship.[153]

What stands out in Salmerón's discussion of the Assumption, however, is his appeal to history. The opponents of the teaching claimed that history only

---

[148] Maldonado, *Commentaries*, vol. 1, 204.
[149] Barradas, *Commentaries*, vol. 1, 260–66.
[150] *CEH*, vol. 11, 298.
[151] *CEH*, vol. 11, 299–300.
[152] *CEH*, vol. 11, 304–5.
[153] *CEH*, vol. 11, 298; *CEH*, vol. 11, 300.

tells of Mary's death and burial, not her resurrection or assumption. Salmerón countered that her tomb was later found empty, just as in the case of Jesus, and he produced a sketch of Mary's life after Pentecost until the time of her death from the accounts of Greek Christian historians. He says the reason for her remaining on earth during that time was so that she could share the mysteries she had kept in her heart and help her daughter-in-law, the Church.[154] Salmerón offers numerous calculations of the duration of this period, with various authorities offering a range of Mary's age at death between sixty-three and seventy-two. He pieces together an account of the events surrounding her death and Assumption from numerous Fathers and ecclesiastical historians, including Nicephorus Kallistos and John Damascene.

When the Blessed Virgin heard the angel tell her that she was going to die, she was filled with the desire to see her son's friends, the apostles. Angels instantly transported them all into her presence, as once had happened to Habakkuk, Elijah, and Philip the deacon. Salmerón says that besides the apostles, the seventy elders were also present, who all sang a hymn in her honor. John the Evangelist commanded that two poor widows be given the two garments that she had worn her whole life, which centuries later were brought to Constantinople and placed in the Church of Mary of Blachernae.[155] Once she had received Communion and given blessings to each of the apostles, Mary predicted what would happen to each of them: Peter, that he would glorify the Lord on the cross at Rome; Thomas, that he would baptize India; Ignatius [of Antioch], that he would have the name of Jesus ever fixed in his heart, written in golden letters. Salmerón comments that he sees no harm in believing these details related by ancient writers, since they contain nothing against the faith and are consonant with piety.[156]

> When all these things had taken place, she mounted the funeral bier, all burning and aflame with the love of God and of Christ her son, which is strong as death, and without any pain sent forth her spirit into the hands of her son, she who had suffered in her heart at his martyrdom on the cross. As Augustine testifies, she was as free of pain of body as she had been free of corruption. And her son said to her first: "Arise, make haste, my love, my dove, my beautiful one, and come, for winter is now past, the rain is over and gone" (Cant 2:10–11). And the Virgin replied, "my heart is ready, O God,

---

[154] *CEH*, vol. 11, 313.

[155] *CEH*, vol. 11, 317.

[156] *CEH*, vol. 11, 317–18.

my heart is ready: I will sing, and will give praise, with my glory. Arise, O my glory, arise psaltery and harp, I will arise early" (Ps 107:2; Ps 56:9).[157]

This passage illustrates once again the way that Salmerón, and the sources he relied on, understood biblical theology. The lack of direct scriptural evidence for the Assumption did not lead him to the conclusion that it was an unbiblical teaching. Instead, the accounts of the end of Mary's life, which he took as historical sources, placed into her mouth the words of scripture that articulate themes, like the nuptial analogy, found in the Fathers and Doctors and in the liturgy.

Marian Miscellany

Besides direct commentary on the New Testament, the liturgy, and the special Marian doctrines, the *Commentaries* contain numerous digressions and passing remarks that bring out the author's devotion and interests. Salmerón found considerable riches of meaning in the spelling and etymology of Mary's name. He offers variant spellings in Hebrew, Greek, Latin, and Syriac, while complaining against Lorenzo Valla's attempt to replace the Latin spelling with the Hebrew one.[158] He says that the primary meaning of her name is "illuminated one," for just as light is the first thing God created, Mary is first in God's predestination (Prov 8:23).[159]

By contrast with Erasmus and the Protestants, who objected to alleged excesses in this regard, Salmerón lavishly bestowed encomia and honorific titles and images on Mary. Many of these were taken from tradition, but others seem to have been the fruit of his own imagination. Mary is the fourth person in dignity after the three persons of the Trinity, and mankind's third advocate before the Father after the Son and Holy Spirit. She is the first in faith (since Christ did not have this virtue), and the second in the order of predestination.[160] As noted already, he attributes to Mary a strong role in the work of redemption, and uses the titles "co-redemptrix, mediator, and cooperator in the salvation of the human race."[161] Mary is a "sweet-smelling flower," whereas

---

[157] *CEH*, vol. 11, 318.

[158] *CEH*, vol. 3, 24; *CBP*, vol. 3, 573. Salmerón regards this as an instance of what he calls "affecting Judaism" that goes against the common practice of the Church.

[159] *CEH*, vol. 3, 25.

[160] *CEH*, vol. 3, 109–10.

[161] *CEH*, vol. 3, 38. Some hint of what Salmerón means by *mediatrix* is evident in his claim that the soul of Christ in heaven is immediately illuminated by God and

all other people are spiny sinners. She is like the "exotic tree" which yields both flower and fruit at once, since she has the flower of virginity together with the fruit of her womb. Her son is the holy of holies, whereas she is the tabernacle.[162] Mystically, the field in which a treasure is buried (Mt 13:44) refers to the Blessed Virgin, as does the pearl of great price.[163] Not content with these titles and descriptions, Salmerón adds mother of mercy, life, sweetness, and our hope, advocate, queen, lady, spouse, sister, friend, and daughter.[164]

The Jesuit theologian also assigned the Blessed Virgin a specific role within the Church using corporeal imagery. In the mystical body, Christ is the head, whereas Mary is the neck. Just as all the sensory power of the head, its commands of movement, and food for nourishment go to the rest of the body by means of the neck, so also God makes all the good things he wishes to give the human race pass through Mary. Christ has adorned Mary with all the virtues, as one adorns the neck with cloth and precious stones. Whatever belongs to Christ, Salmerón says, the Church shares in by participation, and this is maximally true of Mary. He assimilates her title "Tower of David" to her role as the neck of the Church.[165] Numerous other passages of the *Commentaries* refer to Mary's singular intercessory role in communicating grace to the faithful.[166]

Salmerón was deeply concerned with proper preparation for receiving the Eucharist, for which the Blessed Virgin provides the principal model. Curiously, however, he did not refer to her reception of the Eucharist after the Ascension, but rather to her display of virtues at the Annunciation. As the Blessed Virgin had living faith that permitted her to conceive the eternal Word in her mind, so Catholics should approach the Eucharist with pure faith

---

illuminates the whole celestial hierarchy, and then the soul of the Blessed Virgin illuminates the other spiritual creatures. *CEH*, vol. 12, 455.

[162] *CEH*, vol. 3, 31. Along these same lines, he applies to her the words of Ps 45:4: *the Most High hath sanctified his own tabernacle*. *CEH*, vol. 9, 577.

[163] *CEH*, vol. 7, 53; *CEH*, vol. 7, 59. The field and pearl analogies are also made at *CEH*, vol. 3, 288.

[164] *CEH*, vol. 3, 39.

[165] *CEH*, vol. 3, 39. The motif of Mary as the neck originated with Herman of Tournai and other writers of the twelfth century, and was perpetuated by San Bernardino and other preachers. Donna Spivey Ellington, *From Sacred Body to Angelic Soul: Understanding Mary in Late Medieval and Early Modern Europe* (Washington, DC: Catholic University of America Press, 2001), 129.

[166] One scholar places particular emphasis on this aspect of Salmerón's Mariology. Severiano del Páramo, "María, Madre de la Iglesia y su influjo en el Cuerpo místico de Cristo, según el P. Alfonso Salmerón, S.J.," in *Temas Bíblicos*, vol. 3, *Temas mariológicos y josefinos* (Santander: Comillas, 1967), 115–35.

to participate in its fruits. The Virgin showed prudence when she answered the angel, "how shall this be done, because I know not man" (Lk 1:34), and likewise Christians should set aside the scruples that arise from what the senses perceive about the Real Presence, for nothing is impossible for the power of the Most High. Mary's heroic humility, expressed in the words "behold the handmaid of the Lord" (Lk 1:38), is likewise necessary for Communion. Finally, her magnanimity, which does not conflict with her humility, led her to contemplate the higher things.[167]

Enemies of Mary

Although Salmerón's opposition to all heresy is evident throughout the *Commentaries*, he had a special hatred for those who rejected Catholic teaching on Mary, people he calls "the Virgin's capital enemies, and the haters and despisers of her prerogatives."[168] This disdain is manifest in his consistent use of abusive language against them, as when he says that "they glory in being her open enemies and the offspring of the ancient serpent."[169] He thinks that the disregard or even contempt for Gabriel's greeting to her in Protestant catechisms gives the lie to their professed love of scripture. Salmerón characterizes their teachings as a reprise of Nestorianism and its denial of the title "Mother of God" [*Theotokos*].[170]

Reformation teaching on Mary was by no means a straightforward matter. Luther held to some traditional Catholic positions for a time even after his break with Rome, and others presented the mother of Jesus as a model of faith.[171] Yet there were two predominant features of Protestant treatment of Mary. The first was the rejection of figural representation, liturgical celebration, and intercessory prayer under the heading of "idolatry," and the bouts of iconoclasm that followed from it. The second was interpreting scripture in a way that showed the error of Catholic teaching, especially concerning her

---

[167] *CEH*, vol. 9, 337–39.
[168] *CEH*, vol. 3, 40.
[169] *CEH*, vol. 3, 42.
[170] *CEH*, vol. 3, 40.
[171] See Hilda Graef, *Mary: A History of Doctrine and Devotion* (Notre Dame, IN: Ave Maria Press, 2009); Beth Kreitzer, *Reforming Mary: Changing Images of the Virgin Mary in Lutheran Sermons of the Sixteenth Century* (New York: Oxford, 2004).

alleged sinlessness.[172] Salmerón attempted to refute what he regarded as false exegesis of key Marian passages of scripture.

The words "hail, full of grace" were a locus of controversy. Salmerón observes that Protestants object to using these words as prayer to Mary, and that Calvin dismisses Catholic use of them as a kind of magic exorcism. He retorts, "but who is so audacious and impudent as to call the Gospel words a magical oath?" The words of Gabriel and Elizabeth to Mary are less a prayer of petition than an act of thanksgiving.[173] As to Calvin's claim in his *Gospel Harmony* that the words were Gabriel's alone and that it makes no sense for Christians to use them to address someone who is absent, Salmerón replies that this "imposter" would do well to recall Paul's words "for what things soever were written, were written for our learning" (Rom 15:4). Mary, Salmerón says, is never absent from Christians; even if one went to the Garamantes or the Isles of the Blessed, she would hear their prayers.[174]

Salmerón also sought to defend Mary's own words and deeds from what he regarded as heretical distortions. John Calvin erroneously claimed that Mary's motivation for visiting Elizabeth was faith alone, Johannes Brenz (1499–1570) said she was obedient to God's command, and Luther claimed she was fulfilling her duty toward her pregnant relative. All three of these views, Salmerón says, are false, for "faith alone," is a false principle, the angel did not command her to go, and visiting Elizabeth was an insufficient reason for being out of the house for such a long time.[175] The Centuriators, along with Brenz, Philip Melanchthon (1497–1560), and Luther, used the finding of the boy Jesus in the temple to accuse Mary of negligence, and thus call her sinlessness into doubt. Salmerón regarded as blasphemous their attempt to draw a parallel here between the sin of Eve and the sin of Mary, replying that Mary did not know where Jesus was and lost track of him unwillingly, whereas Eve knew what she was doing and did it willfully. Salmerón cites Augustine, Ambrose, and Theophylact against them, saying that none of the Fathers ever dared to speak against Mary as do these "impious triflers."[176]

The *Commentaries* are peppered with anti-Protestant darts concerning various points of Mariology. Salmerón defends Mary's faith from Luther's charge

---

[172] Heal, *The Cult*, 63.
[173] *CEH*, vol. 3, 43.
[174] *CEH*, vol. 3, 44. The Garamantes are a region in North Africa referenced by Herodotus.
[175] *CEH*, vol. 3, 84.
[176] *CEH*, vol. 3, 428.

that the centurion's faith was greater than hers.[177] He excoriates Luther and Melanchthon for claiming that Jesus calls Mary "woman" out of disrespect, and he accuses the Calvinist Charles Doumoulin (*Molinaeus*) (1500–66) of blasphemy against the virgin birth.[178] Luther demonstrates the absurdity of the egalitarian principle when he claims that all Christians are equal to the Blessed Virgin.[179] Heinrich Bullinger (1504–75) is a "scoundrel" for writing against Catholic devotional works on Mary's lamentation during the Passion, which he claims have no warrant in scripture. In so doing, Bullinger opposes the whole Church and the teaching of the ancient Fathers.[180] If Paul calls the Thessalonians his hope, joy, and crown (1 Thess 2:19), Salmerón asks, how do the heretics object that Mary is called life, sweetness, and hope?[181]

The Jesuit theologian had strong words not only for Protestants, but also Catholics who, in his mind, dishonored Mary. Erasmus was his primary target. Salmerón cites the *Ecclesiaste* for the Dutch theologian's norms concerning her veneration: Christians should honor Christ more than Mary, nothing should be asked of her in prayer, and all customs to the contrary are inventions that depart from scripture. According to Salmerón, Erasmus even says that Marian intercession was introduced for the sake of flattering women.[182] For this, Salmerón designates him as first among the "dogmatizers and would-be teachers" [*dogmatistae et magistelli*] who attack Mary's honor by opposing praise, prayer, and preaching directed to her. He says that even if one were to set aside the universal custom and practice of the Church, which was instituted for confounding heretics and Jews, the example of the Angel Gabriel would be enough to justify honoring Mary.[183]

Salmerón contrasts this dishonor from heretics and bad Catholics by comparing it to the beliefs and behavior of Muslims, who regard Mary as the purest of all women. He supports this claim with four verses of the Qur'an in Latin translation. Muslims are not allowed to blaspheme her name, and they give greater honor to her tomb in the Valley of Josaphat than they do to the tomb of

---

[177] *CEH*, vol. 6, 145; *CEH*, vol. 6, 322.
[178] *CEH*, vol. 6, 35; *CEH*, vol. 9, 175.
[179] *CBP*, vol. 1, 224.
[180] *CEH*, vol. 10, 424.
[181] *CBP*, vol. 3, 365.
[182] *CEH*, vol. 3, 64–65.
[183] *CEH*, vol. 3, 63–64. Salmerón says, however, that Luther is worse than Erasmus for denying Mary's merit.

Christ.[184] Salmerón's strategy here is to shame Christians for showing less reverence toward Mary than nonbelievers, a point that is immediately underscored with the following observation: "nor do only the infidels, but even the demons tremble, if unwillingly, at the name of the Virgin Mary, and they are compelled to come out of bodies [when it is spoken]."[185] Just as no one is ultimately able to escape the power of Christ, no one escapes the power of his mother.

Conclusion

For Salmerón, honoring Mary was one of the keys tasks of a theologian. She appears throughout the *Commentaries* as the New Eve aiding the New Adam in bringing about the work of redemption, of whom both testaments of scripture speak both literally and spiritually. Her primary association with Christ makes her into the first recipient of his grace and the exemplar of the Christian life, especially its contemplative dimension. Salmerón expresses this by giving the mother of Jesus a parallel position in his commentary on the major mysteries of her son's life. Mary's place in the liturgy, and the special doctrines of the Immaculate Conception and the Assumption associated with her, receive extensive and passionate treatment. The attempt to justify his positions pushes the limits of Salmerón's theological method and understanding of ecclesiastical authority, opening a place for the teaching authority of the universities and the witness of the ordinary faithful. He vehemently championed the Blessed Virgin against the attacks of Protestants and the insufficient devotion of certain Catholics, wishing to demonstrate that the theologian must be her servant, just as she was the Lord's.

---

[184] *CEH*, vol. 3, 108. Salmerón does not deploy Mary either for combating Muslims or for enticing them to conversion. See Rita Tvrtković, "Our Lady of Victory or Our Lady of Beauty?: The Virgin Mary in Early Modern Dominican and Jesuit Approaches to Islam," *Journal of Jesuit Studies* 7 (2020): 403–16.

[185] *CEH*, vol. 3, 108. The view that demons can give testimony to the teachings of the Catholic Church, especially against heretics, through the people they possess, was commonly held in the sixteenth century. Euan Cameron, "Angels, Demons, and Everything in Between: Spiritual Beings in Early Modern Europe," in *Angels of Light? Sanctity and the Discernment of Spirits in the Early Modern Period*, eds. Clare Copeland and Jan Machielsen (Boston, MA: Brill, 2013), 17–52, at 39–41.

5 Saving Souls

When commenting on the verse "his name was called Jesus" (Lk 2:21), Salmerón offers the following observation: "we are more indebted to Christ, insofar as he is Jesus, than insofar as he was creator... The name Jesus, therefore, was rightly given to the Christ, for he alone is able, knows how, and wishes to save."[1] Salmerón regarded saving souls as one of the theologian's tasks in two main respects. First, the *Commentaries* were intended to initiate the reader into the Christian mysteries, so that he might avoid damnation and attain heaven. Second, he believed that the theologian must understand and teach rightly about the process and means by which man becomes righteous and attains salvation, otherwise known as justification.

This was a burning issue in the confessional polemics of the sixteenth century. Protestants made "salvation by faith alone" a rallying cry, while Catholics argued with them and with each other about how souls are justified before God. Salmerón was a key participant in the debates on this subject at the Council of Trent, and his treatment of it reads like a commentary on the conciliar decrees. His overriding concern was demonstrating God's offer of mercy to each and every person, as well as their corresponding need for this mercy. He wrote forcefully on the necessity of grace against Pelagianism, and just as forcefully on the reality of human free will. Whoever receives eternal damnation does so on account of his own choices, he thought, rather than because God withholds grace. Careful use of terminology is key to Salmerón's explanation of how these two claims cohere.

The challenge of "justification by faith alone," in turn, required an explanation of faith's relationship to the theological virtue of charity. In keeping with mainstream Catholic thought of his time, as well as the teaching of the Council of Trent, Salmerón believed that the justified man must possess both faith and charity, or more specifically, faith formed by, and working through, charity. The *Commentaries* also explain and defend the role of the Church's sacramental system in the salvation of souls. Although he acknowledged that the sacraments are "mysteries" in the broader sense of sacred, secret things,

---

[1] *CEH*, vol. 3, 331.

Salmerón's preferred approach was to treat them as instruments which confer grace upon believers. He gave greater attention to particular sacraments according to two criteria: their intrinsic importance, and the amount of controversy they generated in the disputes of the age.

God's Mercy

Before entering into the discussion of justification proper, it is important to note once again that Salmerón took a wide view of God's mercy. One of his most basic convictions was that salvation had been offered to all in Christ, and that anyone's failure to attain it owed not to the limits of God's grace or mercy, but to man's wickedness. Salmerón's understanding of the salvation of mankind is nicely captured with the following image:

> A bridge indeed is built over a swift river, so that anyone may freely cross it. If anyone throws himself off it, it is his fault, not the bridge's. In the same way, Christ is per se the cause of salvation for all, but not the cause of ruin. Ruin is rather imputed to the man who withdraws from Christ through infidelity or sin.[2]

Salmerón defines mercy as "pain and sorrow at the evil that, in our eyes, seems to befall someone undeservedly and unworthily." The seat of mercy is the *viscera*, which refers to internal organs near the heart, like the lungs, the spleen, and the liver. Although God lacks such organs and does not experience mercy properly speaking, he is said metaphorically to do so when he has mercy on someone. The use of *viscera* with respect to God expresses the depth and tenderness of his love.[3]

Mercy is not bestowed in a general way, but rather is directed toward each and every person who has a desire for salvation.[4] Salmerón insists that God wants to save each and every member of the human race, and that everyone needs to be saved. Left to itself, corrupt human nature can only incline toward wickedness, as Augustine teaches.[5] In his commentary on Jesus's words "my meat is to do the will of him that sent me" (Jn 4:34), Salmerón offers the following explanation of the Father's will:

---

[2] *CEH*, vol. 3, 391.

[3] *CEH*, vol. 3, 169–70.

[4] *CEH*, vol. 3, 116–17. Salmerón thinks there is no mercy, however, for demons, Jews, or Gentiles, whom he groups together as beings who do not fear God or humble themselves.

[5] *CBP*, vol. 1, 575.

If only Adam had spoken thus, "my food and my knowledge is to do the will of God…" His will is nothing other than that he wills all men to be saved, and come to knowledge of the truth [1 Tim 2:4]. Christ was sent for this purpose, to seek and to save what was lost, and to pursue the duty of evangelizing enjoined on him by the Father.[6]

The Jesuit theologian rejected interpretations of 1 Tim 2:4 that restricted God's desire to save all, such as the idea that he wished to save some people from all nations, or that "all" really meant "some."

Salmerón offers cautionary words about the false mercy which violates prudence and justice, since justice and mercy are the same in God.[7] He complains that some wrongly distribute their goods to pimps, parasites, and prostitutes, while neglecting the poor.[8] The Jesuit theologian objects to the custom whereby princes who come to venerate the cross on Good Friday throw down pardons of those who rightly have been convicted of crimes. He calls this a mockery of Christ rather than veneration.[9] One cannot show mercy to others and remain in sin, as some falsely conclude from the verse "give alms; and behold, all things are clean unto you" (Lk 11:41).[10] By the same token, Salmerón says, Cajetan is wrong to say that a man who forgives his neighbor, but remains in fornication, will receive mercy.[11]

Justification

The issue of justification assumed a primary place in the theological disputes of the sixteenth century, thanks in large measure to Martin Luther. As McGrath observes, the Council of Trent helped prioritize the issue among Catholics

---

[6] *CEH*, vol. 4, 202.

[7] *CEH*, vol. 3, 117.

[8] *CEH*, vol. 5, 86.

[9] *CEH*, vol. 10, 236. The Crown of Castile issued a limited number of these Good Friday pardons annually (between twenty and forty), usually for serious crimes that merited the death penalty or galley service. The ceremony was normally held in the royal chapel, with the king pronouncing his pardon over the court records at the moment when he went up to adore the cross. Scott Taylor, *Honor and Violence in Golden Age Spain* (New Haven, CT: Yale University Press, 2008), 14–15; José Luis de las Heras, "Indultos concedidos por la Cámara de Castilla en tiempos de los Austria," *Studia Histórica: Historia moderna* 103 (1983): 115–40, at 129–30.

[10] *CEH*, vol. 5, 95.

[11] *CEH*, vol. 5, 336.

as well, and Salmerón made significant contributions to its debates.[12] In the *Commentaries*, he lays out a Catholic understanding of justification, with a special emphasis on charity, relying principally on scripture and the Fathers, while refuting the teachings of Protestants.[13] Although here and there Salmerón used scholastic terminology, he followed the Tridentine decrees in mostly avoiding the disputed questions among the various Catholic schools of the sixteenth century.

Incidentally, Salmerón displayed a somewhat different attitude toward justification than the one found in Ignatius's "Rules for Thinking with the Church," which manifests a greater spirit of caution about discussing such issues. "We should not make it a habit of speaking much of predestination. If somehow at times it comes to be spoken of, it must be done in such a way that the people are not led into any error."[14] Salmerón notes that some wish to silence the debate on justification altogether. He replies that one should search scripture to try to understand it, and that there is nothing scandalous about it.[15] His apostolic endeavors reflected this mindset. In the early 1540s, Cardinal Morone expelled Salmerón from Modena because he freely preached on justification against the Lutheran position.[16]

Salmerón's main treatments of justification appear in his commentaries on Romans and Galatians, and in both places, he begins with a definition of terms. He observes that the verb *iustificandi* was unknown to the profane

---

[12] Alister McGrath, *Iustitia Dei: A History of the Christian Doctrine of Justification*, 4th ed. (New York: Cambridge University Press, 2020), 307; John Hughes, "Alfonso Salmeron: His Work at the Council of Trent," (PhD dissertation: University of Kentucky, 1974), 83–87; Niccolo Steiner, *Diego Laínez und Alfonso Salmerón auf dem Konzil von Trient: Ihr Beitrag zur Eucharistie-und Messopferthematik* (Stuttgart: Kohlhammer, 2019), 100–05.

[13] His stated aim is expounding the consensus of the Church and showing how the heretics have wickedly opposed it. *CBP*, vol. 3, 3.

[14] *MHSI. MI. Series Secunda: Exercitia Spiritualia S. Ignatii de Loyola et eorum directoria*, vol. 1, *Exercitia Spiritualia*, ed. Joseph Calaveras and Cándido de Dalmases (Rome: IHSI, 1969), 556–58; English trans. Louis Puhl, *The Spiritual Exercises of St. Ignatius: Based on Studies in the Language of the Autograph* (Chicago, IL: Loyola Press, 1952), §366–67, 160. Context may well explain the difference, since Ignatius seems to have been concerned with avoiding free discussion of this topic among ordinary people, rather than in learned theological discourse.

[15] *CBP*, vol. 1, 571.

[16] Salmerón's testimony may be found in Massimo Firpo and Dario Marcatto, *Il processo inquisitoriale del Cardinal Giovanni Morone: Edizione critica*, (Rome: Istituto Storico Italiano per L'età Moderna e Contemporanea, 1981–1995), vol. 2, pt. 1, 335–46.

authors and has many meanings in scripture and the ecclesiastical authors. In the proper theological sense, *iustitia Dei* is that which makes men righteous before God, and is called justice or righteousness *simpliciter*.[17] Elsewhere, he defines justification as "the making of a just man, or what is the same thing, the attaining of justice."[18] Salmerón further distinguishes between active and passive justification. The one who justifies makes someone just by his action, whereas the one who receives justification is made just. God justifies someone when he remits his sins, reconciles the sinner to himself, and gives him the gift of justice, by which he can keep the law and strive toward the eternal reward.[19] Salmerón mentions the forensic sense of justification, whereby God pronounces someone just without actually making him so. This concept was a major source of controversy in the period, but Salmerón swiftly dismisses it as contrary to scripture.[20]

Like the Council of Trent, Salmerón offers a list of the causes of justification in an Aristotelian sense, although here he makes no reference to the council or to the discrepancies between its list and his.[21] Despite his intent to steer clear of scholastic disputes, he takes a distinct position concerning justification's formal cause.[22] Trent calls it simply the "righteousness of God," but Salmerón observes that the Doctors disagreed about its nature. Some said it was all three theological virtues, whereas Thomas proposed Aristotle's notion of metaphorical justice, which means a rectitude of order within the interior disposition. Others said that it was simply grace, citing Paul's use of the term in this context. Salmerón parted company with all of them, however, taking the view of Augustine that the formal cause is charity. He cites a catena of biblical verses, several texts of Augustine, and the authority of Alexander of

---

[17] *CBP*, vol. 1, 96–95 (H5v–H6r).

[18] "Iusti effectio, sive quod idem est, iustitiae adeptio." *CBP*, vol. 3, 3.

[19] *CBP*, vol. 3, 3. It is worth observing that in his opinion given before the Council of Trent, Salmerón included sharing in the divine nature and being adopted as a son among the gifts of justification, whereas these are not mentioned at this point in the commentary on Galatians. Hughes, "Alfonso Salmeron," Appendix II, 221–35; *Concilium Tridentinum: Diariorum, actorum, epistularum, tractatuum nova collectio*, ed. Societas Goerresiana (Freiburg im Breisgau: Herder, 1901–2001), vol. 5, 265–72.

[20] *CEH*, vol. 3, 4.

[21] Council of Trent, Session 6, *Decretum de justificatione*, Ch. 7.

[22] The formal cause refers to a gift that God infuses into the soul by which, through the remission of sins, believers are reconciled to God and become his adopted sons.

Hales, Bonaventure, and Scotus in support of this position. It is a significant instance of him taking the Franciscan position over the Thomistic view.[23]

Just as he enumerates the causes of justification, Salmerón also enumerates its various stages. He follows Trent's explanation of "first" justification, which is the transfer of man from the state into which he is born as a son of Adam to the state of grace and adoption as a son through the second Adam.[24] Ordinarily this happens through the administration of Baptism.[25] "Second" justification occurs after a justified person falls into sin and needs to be reconciled. Biblical examples of this include the repentance of King David, the Apostle Peter, and the prodigal son. Lapsed men can be restored through faith and the sacrament of Penance.[26] Salmerón also speaks of "third" and "fourth" justification, which entail maintaining the righteousness one already has and increasing it, respectively. This is his way of expressing, in different words, Trent's notion that the justified are able to increase in virtue and righteousness.[27]

Like most Catholic theologians of his time, Salmerón adhered to a "factitive" understanding of justification, meaning that the grace of God actually transforms a person and empowers him to do things of which he would otherwise be incapable. The just man, he says, can keep the whole law, which means observing the worship of God with its rites and ceremonies, and keeping the commandments. It does not mean that one can live entirely without sin in this life, as some wrongly interpret Augustine.[28] Salmerón believed that even some Catholics had strayed from the correct teaching under Protestant influence.[29] He laments that Albert Pigge (1490–1542), otherwise a great defender of the faith, was deceived by Bucer into thinking that salvation is possible only with the addition of imputed righteousness, a position Salmerón also attributes to the professors of the University of Cologne.[30]

---

[23] *CBP*, vol. 3, 8–9.

[24] *CBP*, vol. 3, 44; Council of Trent, Session 6, *Decretum de justificatione*, Ch. 4.

[25] *CBP*, vol. 3, 6.

[26] *CBP*, vol. 3, 42.

[27] *CBP*, vol. 3, 44–45; Council of Trent, Session 6, *Decretum de justificatione*, Ch. 10.

[28] *CEH*, vol. 2, 250.

[29] McGrath singles out Salmerón as someone who misunderstood Melanchthon's distinction between justification and regeneration, and who erroneously concluded that Protestants excluded transformation altogether. McGrath, *Iustitia Dei*, 311.

[30] *CBP*, vol. 3, 19.

Predestination and Election

Predestination was another issue intertwined with justification. Many Protestants attacked as "Pelagian" the idea that man could play any role in his salvation, since it is entirely dependent upon the action of God, who chooses in advance who is saved and who is not. The Council of Trent asserted the real role that human free will plays in salvation and condemned the denial thereof, but without resolving all of the problems associated with the issue. The apparent conundrum in fact runs deep: if man can only be saved because God has predestined him, how can free will play a real role in salvation? If it requires divine action to actually bring any given person to heaven, does it follow that some souls go to hell because God does not provide them with the grace they need?

It must be acknowledged that Salmerón's treatment of predestination appears rather dated from the standpoint of the turn of the seventeenth century, when the *Commentaries* were published. He died three years before the publication of Molina's *Concordia* and therefore was unaware of the ensuing *De auxiliis* controversy, which pitted Jesuits and Dominicans against each other in an extremely subtle and difficult dispute that ended inconclusively, when the pope simply forbade further discussion and instructed the antagonists to stop accusing each other of heresy.[31] Salmerón's treatment of the issue lacked the subtlety and sophistication of this debate, but he articulated some of the positions and priorities that would become characteristic of the Society of Jesus, especially the emphasis on human freedom. In his explanation, "to predestine" means ordering something to its end, like a father who before his children are born decides to send one to study, another to court, and the third to the military. Then, when the time comes, he actually sends them. "Predestination is therefore nothing other than God's design and good favor towards some, whom he has decided to direct and raise up to surely attain eternal salvation."[32]

However straightforward this definition may appear, there is a crucial distinction between the "predestined" and the "elect" in Salmerón's vocabulary. The former are not all the people to whom God has given efficacious grace unto salvation, but rather those few, like the Blessed Virgin and John the Baptist, who are infallibly preserved in grace on account of their special role

---

[31] See Kirk MacGregor, *Luis de Molina: The Life and Theology of the Founder of Middle Knowledge* (Grand Rapids, MI: Zondervan, 2015).

[32] *CBP*, vol. 1, 572. "Est igitur Praedestinatio nihil aliud, quam propositum, ac beneplacitum Dei erga quosdam, quos et dirigere, et erigere in aternam salutem certo assequendam determinavit."

in God's plan. Everyone else has the possibility of being saved, since that is God's universal will for the human race; only a man's own free choices lead to his damnation. The elect, therefore, are all the predestined plus everyone who perseveres in God's grace and does not, through their own fault, forfeit it.[33] Anyone can persevere by means of "common grace," but the predestined are given more grace so that they can persevere without fail [*omnino*].[34] In response to the objection that the predestined no longer have free will, Salmerón counters that their free will is actually made stronger. This is because, contrary to the opinion of the "rabble," the ability to sin is not true freedom.[35]

One of the ways Salmerón articulated his own position on predestination was by rejecting the theses of others. He says election does not depend on man's merits, but on God's goodness and grace.[36] He rejects the theory that God chooses some for damnation from all eternity.[37] He acknowledges his disagreement with Augustine and certain Scholastic Doctors, who say that the "foreknown" [*praesciti*] are predestined to eternal death.[38] According to Salmerón, the true meaning of "foreknowledge" [*praescientia*] in scripture is "fore-love" [*praediligere*]. This is the cause of predestination, not a consequence of it.[39] Other theologians say that, while God does not predestine anyone to eternal death, he does want to punish many people for the disobedience of Adam and Eve, a thesis that Salmerón rejects as detracting from God's mercy.[40]

Another view that Salmerón refutes is that men are elected in view of their foreseen merits [*post praevisa merita*], a position held by Irenaeus, Tertullian, Ambrose, and other Fathers. Augustine, however, rejected this view as Pelagian, and Thomas agreed with him that election precedes all sanctification and good works.[41] If man's works were the reason or cause of election, Salmerón

---

[33] *CBP*, vol. 1, 191; *CBP*, vol. 4, 250. Salmerón is careful to say that the truth of who is predestined escapes man's knowledge, and that men do not have experiential knowledge of grace.

[34] *CBP*, vol. 1, 575.

[35] *CBP*, vol. 1, 574.

[36] *CBP*, vol. 3, 168.

[37] *CBP*, vol. 3, 169. He does not refer to this view by the name "double predestination."

[38] *CBP*, vol. 1, 73.

[39] *CBP*, vol. 1, 570–71.

[40] *CBP*, vol. 3, 169.

[41] *CBP*, vol. 3, 169.

says, it would rightly be called "post-destination" [*postdestinatio*].⁴² The Epistle to the Galatians shows that predestination is not on account of foreseen merits, but it is rather the cause of those merits.⁴³ This rejection of election in view of foreseen merits is almost a mantra for Salmerón that demonstrates his anti-Pelagian credentials.⁴⁴ In terms of the *De auxiliis* controversy, his position may be identified with the "Congruism" of Bellarmine and Suárez, as opposed to the view of Lessius, Molina, and Francisco de Toledo.⁴⁵

Salmerón's use of the vocabulary of "predestined" and "elect" does not quite resolve the basic problem of explaining why some people are given the gift of perseverance, and others are not. According to him, the gift of perseverance is manifest mainly in four things: hearing the word of God, giving alms, receiving the Eucharist, and constant prayer.⁴⁶ He cites Augustine's statement in *De correptione et gratia* that he does not know why perseverance is not given to all. Salmerón remarks, "But it is a wonder that such a great man as Augustine was in the Church of God could have been ignorant on this point, for he thought that no one could be saved who was not predestined."⁴⁷ Salmerón observes that elsewhere in the same work, Augustine says that men can persevere if they wish and have no excuse for failing to do so.

Not satisfied with the explanation of the Bishop of Hippo, the Jesuit theologian thought he could provide a better answer to the question. "Perseverance is not given to all, in the sense that they are to persevere in such a way that they cannot fall away. This is not owed to all, since everyone is given sufficient grace to be able to persevere."⁴⁸ He defends this state of affairs by saying that it would not be fitting [*pulchrum*] for everyone to be given the same grace, and continues with a brief discourse defending the principle of inequality. "It is just like in a commonwealth, where not everyone is equal, rich, strong, or equally noble in the city."⁴⁹ Whether this explanation was entirely satisfactory or not,

---

⁴² *CBP*, vol. 1, 568.

⁴³ *CBP*, vol. 3, 173.

⁴⁴ *CBP*, vol. 1, 72; *CBP*, vol. 1, 571; *CBP*, vol. 3, 596.

⁴⁵ Robert Matava, *Divine Causality and Human Free Choice: Domingo Báñez, Physical Premotion, and the Controversy* De Auxiliis *Revisited* (Boston, MA: Brill, 2016), 28. In context, Salmerón may have wished to distance himself from the position of his friend Ambrogio Catarino, who came under suspicion of the Spanish Dominicans and eventually of some Jesuits as well. Caravale, *Beyond the Inquisition*, 208.

⁴⁶ *CBP*, vol. 1, 112.

⁴⁷ *CBP*, vol. 1, 114.

⁴⁸ *CBP*, vol. 1, 114.

⁴⁹ *CBP*, vol. 1, 114.

Salmerón unmistakably highlighted God's generosity toward everyone and man's culpability in failing to receive it.

Since he took the damnation of Judas as an established fact, Salmerón did not believe that God's universal salvific will resulted in the actual salvation of all.[50] How optimistic was he about the rest of the human race? One passage suggests that he thought few would be saved: the fact that only two of John's disciples were present when Jesus was passing by (Jn 1:35) shows that few persevere in the ways of God.[51] Another passage, by contrast, is less bleak. While commenting on the disagreement between Augustine and Thomas on the predestination of the angels, Salmerón opines that less than half of them rebelled against God. He then asks rhetorically why the same cannot be true of men, suggesting that he sees a salvation rate of more than fifty percent as reasonable.[52] Commenting on the opinion that the number of the saved is greater than that of the damned, at least among Christians, Salmerón says that he does not see a good reason to believe either position, and that he prefers to treat it as God's secret.[53]

If the total number of the saved remains a mystery, Salmerón still leaves the door open for those who die without hearing the Gospel, relying on the thought of Aquinas. In his commentary on the words "if I had not come, and spoken to them, they would not have sin" (Jn 15:22), Salmerón distinguishes between privative infidelity and negative infidelity. The former entails active resistance to the divine light, whereas the latter is simply being in a state of original sin without the knowledge of Christ. Salmerón says that the latter condition does not entail any new sin of unbelief, or any punishment beyond what is already owed for original sin. If people in this condition live according to the natural law (which he says is impossible anyway without some faith in God and his grace), then they are saved through implicit faith in Christ. This implicit faith means believing that God exists, and that he rewards those who seek him, as Thomas teaches in his commentary on the Letter to the Hebrews.[54] Acknowledging that many Fathers and Scholastic Doctors disagree with this view, Salmerón says, "We nevertheless believe and assert without any pertinacity what seems to us more probable, and more consonant

---

[50] *CEH*, vol. 4, 176; *CEH*, vol. 3, 333.

[51] *CEH*, vol. 4, 164.

[52] *CBP*, vol. 3, 172.

[53] *CEH*, vol. 8, 356.

[54] *CEH*, vol. 9, 467; Thomas Aquinas, *Commentary on Hebrews*, Ch. 11, lect. 2. Salmerón says elsewhere that no one is condemned for ignorance of Christ or Baptism, but for other sins. *CEH*, vol. 12, 259.

with the mercy of God, and the blood of Christ, and the benevolence of the Holy Spirit, submitting all to the judgment of the Church."[55]

Other exegetes vary in their treatment of predestination. Maldonado says relatively little on the subject. While acknowledging the reality of predestination in several places, he says that he prefers the interpretation of the Greeks, which is that those who are not illuminated do not wish to be.[56] He explicitly rejects the Calvinist position as well.[57] Barradas surprisingly steered clear of Molina's work, but he nevertheless expressed his own views in numerous places. Like Salmerón, he defends the reality of free choice of the will, rejects predestination *post praevisa merita*, and emphasizes God's personal, providential care for each and every man.[58] Jansen echoes the rejection of predestination *post praevisa merita*.[59] Marlorat discusses predestination in connection with a wide array of scriptural passages, expounding the Calvinist position.[60]

Merit

The doctrine of merit was another crucial piece of Salmerón's understanding of justification and the salvation of souls. The issue of "works righteousness" preoccupied Protestant and Catholic thinkers of the sixteenth century. In brief, Luther and others accused Catholics of seeking to attain salvation by their own efforts and the observance of ecclesiastical law, thus falling back into both Pelagianism and Judaism. Salmerón's defense of the doctrine of merit and the role of works was strongly anti-Pelagian as well as anti-Jewish, an approach that was consistent with his prejudices as well as an attempt to meet the Protestant attack on its own terms.

His key idea is that there is a difference between works performed prior to faith and grace, which do not obtain merit, and works performed from faith and grace, which do. He identifies three kinds of good works. The first are those that are performed according to the light of nature without faith, which do not justify or dispose to justification except very remotely, insofar as doing

---

[55] *CEH*, vol. 9, 468.

[56] Maldonado, *Commentaries*, vol. 1, cols. 515–17; Maldonado, *Commentaries*, vol. 2, col. 411.

[57] Maldonado, *Commentaries*, vol. 2, col. 503.

[58] Barradas, *Commentaries*, vol. 3, 301–03; Barradas, *Commentaries*, vol. 3, 101.

[59] Jansen, *Commentaries*, Part 2, 371.

[60] See Marlorat, *Expositio*, vol. 2, 223; Marlorat, *Expositio*, vol. 2, 170; Marlorat, *Expositio*, vol. 2, 260.

such moral works makes someone less indisposed to divine grace. The second kind are performed according to the light of faith, but prior to the reception of charity and grace, and these are accepted by God as sufficient dispositions for justification, even though they do not properly have the merit of it. As an example, Salmerón offers the fasting of the men of Nineveh (Jon 3). The third kind of works are those that come from faith through charity by a person already justified, which have the foundation [*ratio*] of merit.[61]

The question of merit is closely related to the question of what being justified "freely" [*gratis*] means. The heretics, Salmerón says, have wrongly understood Paul's use of this term. According to Melanchthon, it means that one is justified by faith alone, without any works preceding, following, or accompanying. Salmerón counters with a close-reading based on scripture and profane authors alike, which yields the conclusion that *gratis* (and its Greek and Hebrew equivalents), "is an adverb signifying what someone does without any debt or merit of another, or if someone does owe a debt, there is nevertheless nothing owed by the receiver."[62] He finds confirmation of this position in the Council of Trent as well as the Fathers. "We are said to receive justification as a free gift [*gratis*] because nothing that precedes justification, neither faith nor works, would merit the grace of justification."[63]

This anti-Pelagian explanation of works was directed at the first prong of the Protestant criticism, for Salmerón agreed with leading Protestants that nothing that man does can earn salvation. He mounted a defense against the second prong of the Protestant attack concerning merit, which was the charge of "Judaizing." He explains that the Fathers were fighting against three errors about faith and justification, all of which originated with the Jews. The first error was the belief that they could be justified by the Law without faith in Jesus. The second was that one should observe the ceremonies of the Law and the Sabbath alongside the teaching of the Gospel, an error Salmerón attributes to the Galatians. The third was that the works of the Law had brought the Jews to the grace of the Gospel, leading some of them to despise Gentile Christians.[64] He counters that the Mosaic Law as such profits no one unto salvation, because everyone must have faith in Christ, who also put an end to most of its observances. Paul opposes works of the law to faith and grace, Salmerón says, but not the works of faith and grace.[65] This counter-argument

---

[61] *CBP*, vol. 3, 40–41.
[62] *CBP*, vol. 3, 33.
[63] *CBP*, vol. 3, 33–34; Council of Trent, Session 6, *Decretum de justificatione*, Ch. 8.
[64] *CBP*, vol. 3, 34–35.
[65] *CBP*, vol. 3, 38–40.

attempts to show that true Catholic teaching comes from the Fathers, who were fighting against Pelagian heresies that, in Salmerón's opinion, had their roots in Jewish errors. He thereby tried to turn the Protestant accusation on its head.

Salmerón thought that disastrous consequences followed from the denial of merit. "As we will demonstrate, those new teachers, who with such great effrontery oppose themselves to merits, are great triflers and sycophants, and they always seek a knot in a bulrush, as is their way."[66] In a lengthy refutation of Bucer's exegesis of Christ's judgment of mankind (Mt 25), Salmerón argues that merit is essential, for apart from it, God is not a just judge as well as a merciful father.[67] He objects to the denigration of human nature that he sees in Protestant teaching. "And we are sharers of his divine nature, as Peter says; how therefore can we be mud, if we are sons of God?"[68] Looking to God as a son does to a father who rewards does not make one a mercenary, at least not in a reprehensible way. "Mercenaries" who work for eternal life are praiseworthy, so long as they look first to God's good pleasure and glory, then to reward.[69]

Salmerón rejected as "insane" the view that works performed under the grace of God are still bad. Even if there are defects in these works, he says, they are not damnable on account of the fact that they do not proceed from fervent charity of God.[70] Contrary to Protestant claims, the good thief (Lk 23:42–43) was not admitted to the kingdom without merits, for he believed, acknowledged his sinfulness, corrected the blaspheming thief, and suffered crucifixion for Christ.[71] The doctrine of merit does not mean that the just can trust and glory in their good works, for all hope is in God, and believers have confidence in their good works as gifts from him. He cites numerous verses from scripture that display this attitude, such as "I know whom I have believed, and I am certain that he is able to keep that which I have committed unto him" (2 Tim 1:12).[72] The merits of the justified man do not derogate from Christ's merits, nor do such merits make a man less humble.[73]

---

[66] *CBP*, vol. 3, 56. This expression means "seeking difficulty where there is none."
[67] *CBP*, vol. 3, 55–56.
[68] *CBP*, vol. 3, 62.
[69] *CBP*, vol. 3, 72.
[70] *CBP*, vol. 3, 64.
[71] *CBP*, vol. 3, 66.
[72] *CBP*, vol. 3, 67.
[73] *CBP*, vol. 3, 65–66.

These arguments from scripture and reason are buttressed by appeals to the Fathers and the Church's worship. An extensive catena of patristic authors, including Dionysius, Gregory Nazianzen, Basil, Cyprian, Ambrose, Gregory the Great, and Augustine, is cited in support of the doctrine of merit.[74] Salmerón also cites numerous liturgical texts, including the Collect of Holy Thursday, which says that "our Lord Jesus Christ gave to each a retribution according to his merits." He claims that the Divine Office contains more than six hundred references to merit, suggesting that he did some careful combing of the Roman Breviary for this section of the *Commentaries*.[75]

The Theological Virtues

The nature of faith was central to the polemics of the sixteenth century, which had consequences for the understanding of the other two theological virtues, especially charity. Catholic theologians generally agreed that justification involves transforming the justified man through the acquisition of faith, hope, and charity, and Salmerón was no exception. He regularly groups these three together when speaking of union with God, as when he says that the peace that is above nature is participation in God, which consists of faith, hope, and charity.[76] Elsewhere he compares faith to the foundation of a house, the walls to hope, and the roof to charity.[77] Salmerón aimed to offer a correct understanding of faith and its relationship to charity in the process of justification against what he regarded as Protestant errors.

Salmerón's characteristic interest in close-readings was especially critical for the question of faith. Although he was quite unambiguous about the correct theological meaning of the term, he acknowledged the complexity of its semantic field. The first meaning is fidelity [*fidelitas*] as opposed to fraudulence [*fraudulentia*], meaning that one acts without deceit or negligence. This is Paul's meaning when he speaks of faith as a fruit of the Spirit (Gal 5:23). Faith can also mean confidence [*fiducia*], which refers to believing someone on account of the trust one has toward him and his promises. A third meaning of faith is equivalent to conscience. As the jurists say, one who possesses something in good faith holds it in good conscience, whereas someone who has something in bad faith has it in bad conscience. The fourth and final meaning

---

[74] *CBP*, vol. 3, 59–61.
[75] *CBP*, vol. 3, 66; *CBP*, vol. 3, 59.
[76] *CEH*, vol. 5, 114.
[77] *CBP*, vol. 4, 175.

concerns belief, namely, firm and certain assent to things that are obscure and not evident.[78]

This final meaning is the one that provides, according to Salmerón, the correct understanding of the theological virtue of faith. "Faith is therefore the firm persuasion of mind, by which we assent to things that are neither seen, nor demonstrated by evident reason or necessary argument."[79] Faith is the middle term between knowledge and opinion. It is akin to knowledge in its stability, but akin to opinion in lacking evidence, for it relies only on authority. This understanding of faith as the assent of the mind, Salmerón says, is consistent with the definition offered in Heb 11:1: "faith is the substance of things to be hoped for, the evidence of things that appear not." Faith in the proper sense concerns the things that God himself speaks, or that his ministers speak in his name.[80]

Salmerón was therefore firmly "intellectualist" in his understanding of faith, a point that is underscored when he differentiates faith [*fides*] from confidence [*fiducia*]. He blames Erasmus for equating the two, which shows that he laid the egg that Luther hatched.[81] Luther and Melanchthon define faith as "confidence in divine mercy," which Salmerón regards as a basic error that leads to other problems in their understanding of justification and the theological virtues.[82] Although he admits that the two are related, he thinks that confidence is closer to hope, which is another virtue altogether, and which pertains to the will rather than the intellect. According to Thomas, confidence is hope strengthened by firm opinion.[83] Salmerón cites instances in Paul's corpus where faith and confidence are distinguished, such as "for they that have ministered well, shall purchase to themselves a good degree, and much confidence in the faith which is in Christ Jesus" (1 Tim 3:13).[84]

Faith and confidence differ as to their objects, subjects, contraries, and etymologies. The opposite of faith is disbelief [*incredulitas*], whereas the opposite of confidence is diffidence [*diffidentia*] or despair [*desperatio*]. Salmerón shows how the Greek and Hebrew equivalents of the Latin terms uphold the same distinctions: *pistis* is also an operation of the intellect, whereas *pepoithēsis*, the

---

[78] *CBP*, vol. 3, 11.
[79] *CBP*, vol. 3, 12.
[80] *CBP*, vol. 3, 12.
[81] *CBP*, vol. 3, 14.
[82] *CBP*, vol. 3, 13.
[83] *CBP*, vol. 3, 13–14. Salmerón's whole teaching on faith and confidence is dependent on Thomas. Cf. *ST*, II–IIae, q. 1–7; *ST*, II–IIae, q. 128.
[84] *CBP*, vol. 3, 13.

equivalent of *fiducia*, is not. Given all this, Salmerón says it would be "really stupid and proximate to insanity" to conflate faith and confidence against the testimony of the whole Church and the Fathers, and submit to Luther and Melanchthon.[85]

With this definition in mind, Salmerón proceeded to explain faith's role in justification. "The first disposition, and from which all others originate toward obtaining the said gift of righteousness, is faith."[86] The *act* of faith (as opposed to its habit) is a gift from God that enlightens the intellect and helps the will to give assent to the articles of Christian belief. This grace allows the natural faculties of the intellect and the will to move freely toward the truth. After surveying various opinions, Salmerón concludes, following Thomas, that the object of faith is God as the one who justifies through Christ, who may be believed in implicitly or explicitly.[87] The act of faith produces many good movements in a person prior to his justification. It shows that God punishes sins, from which a fear of him arises. It also produces repentance, as well as confidence in God as kind and charitable, which in turn gives rise to love for him, or at least the desire of loving him. This is what it means to say that faith justifies: it is the first disposition that leads to justification.[88] Salmerón backs up this claim by citing the Council of Trent as well as a catena of patristic authors.[89]

If the act of faith is the beginning of justification, what else is needed to complete the process? God forgives a person's sins and infuses into him the theological virtues (which are habits) of faith, hope, and charity, which ordinarily takes place at Baptism. Salmerón is insistent on the need for charity, not just faith, to make one righteous. In the justified man, faith works through charity as through its form and perfection.[90] Although he speaks of faith working through charity in the just man, it is also clear that he thinks charity is the more important term, and that the two are separable. When John says that many believed in Jesus because of the signs he performed, but that Jesus did not entrust himself to them (Jn 2:23–24), or that many of the leaders believed in him, but did not confess him for fear of the Pharisees (Jn 12:42), it shows that one may believe without having charity. Paraphrasing the words of James, Salmerón observes that the demons, who are far from charity, believe

---

[85] *CBP*, vol. 3, 15.

[86] *CEH*, vol. 3, 26.

[87] *CBP*, vol. 3, 26–27.

[88] *CBP*, vol. 3, 28.

[89] Council of Trent, Session 6, *Decretum de justificatione*, Ch. 8.

[90] *CBP*, vol. 3, 149.

and tremble (Jas 2:19). He says that the parable of the sheep and the goats (Mt 25:31–46) shows that people are excluded from heaven for having faith but no works of charity.[91]

This priority of charity is a recurrent theme in the *Commentaries*. Salmerón explains that if you take faith without charity, you get the demons and those excluded from heaven for lack of works, whereas if you take charity without faith, you get the angels and the blessed in heaven, because "charity never falleth away" (1 Cor 13:8).[92] He says that the perfection of Christian life consists in charity; the end of every precept and sacrifice is charity; charity is the root of the active life; charity is not ambitious, against those who claim to desire ecclesiastical office out of charity; no one is a student in the school of Christ if he does not love his neighbor.[93] If only, Salmerón sighs, the religious who follow various rules kept charity before their eyes, they would have fewer quarrels.[94] Christ dined with the Pharisees out of charity toward his enemies, and he showed his charity and zeal for the Father when he drove sinners out of the temple.[95] Charity was a theme dear to Salmerón's heart.

Although he tended to lump Protestants and their teachings together, on faith and justification Salmerón was somewhat more discriminating. He reviews at length the different opinions of various leading figures.[96] He observes that in "recent years", Albert of Saxony convened a group of eminent teachers among the heretics to arrive at an agreement about justification. This refers to the meetings that led to the "Formula of Concord" of 1577, which was a key moment for the consolidation of Lutheran teaching.[97] Salmerón's assessment of it, however, was less sanguine.

> They came together and fought bitterly amongst themselves for months, each on behalf of his own opinion, as if contending for home and hearth, and found no basis for coming to agreement. But since the prince urged them with prayers, commands, and threats to arrive at one explanation and teaching within the prescribed time, they produced a fraudulent consensus

[91] *CBP*, vol. 3, 16.
[92] *CBP*, vol. 3, 17.
[93] *CEH*, vol. 8, 404; *CEH*, vol. 4, 246; *CBP*, vol. 3, 219; *CEH*, vol. 4, 576; *CEH*, vol. 5, 188.
[94] *CEH*, vol. 4, 283 (Aa4r).
[95] *CEH*, vol. 4, 285; *CEH*, vol. 6, 47.
[96] *CBP*, vol. 3, 13–25.
[97] See Irene Dingel, "The Culture of Conflict in the Controversies Leading to the Formula of Concord, 1548–1580," in *Lutheran Ecclesiastical Culture, 1550–1675*, ed. Robert Kolb (Boston, MA: Brill, 2008), 15–64.

among themselves, by which they could give the appearance of satisfying their prince. Once the meeting was over, one party returned to its earlier view, and they began to fight amongst themselves again with new and insulting tracts.[98]

As usual, the Jesuit theologian's knowledge of Protestant teachings was deployed primarily for polemical purposes.

The Sacraments

Salmerón usually treated the sacraments as instruments of grace that help souls attain salvation. He describes Christ's humanity as an instrument conjoined to his divinity for performing signs, like making the blind see and the deaf hear. In a like manner, the sacraments are extrinsic instruments that he uses to effect man's salvation.[99] He defended these positions at Trent on a variety of disputed questions, following the general lines of Thomas's thought.[100] Apart from the special case of the Eucharist, he did not typically think of the sacraments as the celebration of mysteries in the wider sense of the term discussed in Chapter 3.[101] According to Salmerón, the sacraments originated in the laying on of hands that Jesus performed in particular Gospel passages.[102] This claim was obviously meant to uphold their divine origin in the face of Protestant attacks. Broadly speaking, this controversy revolved around two issues: the number of the sacraments of the New Testament, and how they communicate grace to their recipients. Although they disagreed among themselves (a point Salmerón was always eager to exploit), all Protestants reduced the number of

---

[98] *CBP*, vol. 3, 13.

[99] *CEH*, vol. 9, 150.

[100] Daniel Iturrioz, *La definición del Concilio de Trento sobre la causalidad de los sacramentos* (Madrid: Ediciones Fax, 1951), 247–51. The council itself sought to avoid favoring any particular school, but the Thomistic perspective prevailed nonetheless. Peter Walter, "Sacraments in the Council of Trent and Sixteenth-Century Catholic Theology," in *The Oxford Handbook of Sacramental Theology*, eds. Hans Boersma and Matthew Levering (New York: Oxford University Press, 2015), 313–328, at 326.

[101] Observing that the Greeks call the sacraments "mysteries," Salmerón says that the Eucharist is rightly called the "sacrament of sacraments" and "mystery of mysteries." *CEH*, vol. 9, 101.

[102] *CEH*, vol. 4, 374. He took this position at Trent, along with the majority of the conciliar fathers. Alfons Knoll, *"Derselbe Geist:" Eine Untersuchung zum Kirchenverständnis in der Theologie der ersten Jesuiten* (Paderborn: Bonifatius, 2007), 667.

sacraments (most often to Baptism and the Eucharist) and downplayed or denied altogether the Roman Church's sacramental realism.

Salmerón's eighth rule on how to interpret Paul within the framework of recognized Catholic teachings (and as counterpoint to the "wiles of the heretics") concerns the sacraments:

> There are seven sacraments of the new law in continuous use from the beginning of the Church's birth up to the present day, which have been known and received. By these God deigns to communicate to us the sanctification of grace, even above our disposition and merits (which means, according to the Scholastic Doctors, conferring grace by the power of the sacraments, that is, *ex opere operato*). They are sensible signs, that is, matter and form, which have come down to us partly from Scripture, and partly from apostolic tradition. They are as follows: Baptism, which was instituted for rebirth and entrance into Christ. Confirmation, which is also called the imposition of hands in the Acts of the Apostles, is for strengthening man for the confession of faith. The Eucharist is for nourishing our spirits with the grace of God, and for feeding the virtues of faith, hope, and charity. Penance is a medicine against sins committed after Baptism and the acknowledgment of Christ. Matrimony is for the propagation of children according to the flesh, and their education and instruction in the faith in a Christian and legitimate manner. Holy Orders, or ordination, which is also called the imposition of hands by the Apostle, is for regenerating, strengthening, and purifying from sin the sons of God according to the Spirit, and for imbuing them with sacred doctrine and holy mysteries. It is also for rightly administering and governing the Church. Finally Anointing is for a safe departure from the present life, and for obtaining a victory over Satan in the final contest of death, and for effacing the remnants of sin, if there are any left over.[103]

In addition to being instruments, the sacraments are also described as certain pacts and covenants of God [*pacta quaedam, ac foedera Dei*] by which through his promise he communicates grace to those who celebrate the ceremonies.[104] For reasons of space, Salmerón's discussion of the seven sacraments is limited here to Baptism, Penance, Eucharist, and Matrimony.

---

[103] *CBP*, vol. 1, 34.
[104] *CEH*, vol. 9, 301.

Baptism

The sacrament of Baptism, in keeping with Salmerón's usual way of proceeding, is dealt with in his commentaries on the relevant passages of the Gospel: the baptism of John and the conversation between Jesus and Nicodemus (Jn 3:1–15). Salmerón offers a brief and rather general theology of Baptism, emphasizing its status as initiation into the Christian life. Baptism is the "door" of the sacraments as well as of the kingdom of God, that is, of the Church Militant and the Church Triumphant.[105] He says that Christ chose water for Baptism so that no one would be lost for defect of matter, and he cites Thales of Miletus for the view that water is the generative principle of all things.[106] He uses another Gospel passage about washing to illustrate the greatness of Baptism:

> If you marvel that Christ washed Peter's feet, you should marvel much more that he washes the flesh, indeed, the sin, of all men in Baptism. As much as the filth of the soul is dirtier than that of the body, so the work by which souls are washed is greater than the work by which bodies are washed.[107]

Salmerón also explains that Baptism illuminates those who receive it, making them able to understand divine teachings. No one is illuminated before Baptism except in unusual cases like Jeremiah, Mary, and John the Baptist.[108]

The central importance of Baptism for initiating Christian life and bringing about the salvation of souls means that everyone is under the obligation to receive it.[109] Although emphatic on this point, Salmerón acknowledges qualifications to this universal obligation when he identifies groups of people who do not incur new sin by not receiving Baptism, such as infants, those who have not heard the Gospel, and those who desire the sacrament, like catechumens, but lack a minister. Since they have the desire for it, they are held as baptized before God, although they do not receive the same abundance of grace as Baptism confers. For this reason, Thomas says that catechumens have to undergo purgation before they can enter heaven.[110]

Salmerón treats the issue of John's baptism at length because numerous "new quack theologians" [*novi theologastri*] like Bucer and Melanchthon teach

---

[105] *CEH*, vol. 8, 30.
[106] *CEH*, vol. 8, 32.
[107] *CEH*, vol. 4, 56.
[108] *CEH*, vol. 2, 177.
[109] *CEH*, vol. 8, 30.
[110] *CEH*, vol. 8, 30; *ST*, III, q. 68, a. 2, ad. 2.

that the baptism of John was equivalent to that of Christ.[111] According to Salmerón, the baptism of John was merely a preparation for the sacramental Baptism offered by Christ. The former was of water only, not of water and the Spirit. Not everyone needed it, nor did it impart a character to the soul, and it involved a general rather than an individual confession.[112]

Another flashpoint of controversy was rebaptism, a question reaching back to the third century that the Anabaptists revived in the sixteenth. Salmerón insisted that Baptism could only be administered once, and his argument relied on a combination of history and tradition. He notes that supporters of Cyprian's heresy of rebaptizing not only brought forth testimony from scripture, but also the support of three councils of Carthage, whereas Pope Stephen relied on the custom of the Roman Church alone to refute it. Turning to the case of the Anabaptists, he continues,

> If indeed the custom of hardly three hundred years prevailed against all the teachings of the councils and the authorities that they brought forth from Scripture, how much more should the custom of the universal Church of more than fifteen hundred years, among those who are strong in faith and prudence, refute these trifles and ravings?[113]

Baptism is therefore received only once in life, and one can be sure of its efficacy and proper administration by looking to the custom of the Church.[114]

Salmerón displayed his habitual interest in the proper ritual and conditions for celebrating the sacraments when discussing Baptism. Any minister, whether priest, lay, faithful, infidel, Jew, pagan, or Saracen who preserves the matter and form celebrates a Baptism efficacious unto salvation.[115] Properly, Baptism is done by immersion, although intinction or aspersion are also legitimate.[116] Triple immersion belongs to the integrity of Baptism but not to its essence, meaning that someone performing a Baptism with correct intent

---

[111] *CEH*, vol. 4, 52.

[112] *CEH*, vol. 4, 16; *CEH*, vol. 4, 35.

[113] *CEH*, vol. 4, 57.

[114] Salmerón's attitude contrasts with that of Erasmus, who expressed conflicting views on this patristic-era controversy in his successive editions of the works of Cyprian. Above all, Erasmus appears to have preferred concord in the Church over arriving at the correct teaching or practice. Jan de Boeft, "Erasmus and the Church Fathers," in *The Reception of the Church Fathers in the West: From the Carolingians to the Maurists*, ed. Irena Backus (New York: Brill, 1997), vol. 2, 537–73, at 558–59.

[115] *CEH*, vol. 8, 34.

[116] *CEH*, vol. 4, 33.

and a single immersion confers a valid one.[117] Salmerón knows of cases where poverty, a lack of understanding, or the shortage of priests leads people to use saliva to baptize on the head, the breast, and between the shoulders, but Innocent III ruled that this was invalid. The church historian Nicephorus tells of a Jew who tried to be baptized with sand while stuck in the desert, and how later the bishop of Alexandria commanded that he be baptized with water, according to the tradition of the Church.[118]

Salmerón deals with issues surrounding the baptismal formula, observing that some, including Ambrose and Peter Lombard, argued from Acts 2:38 that it is not necessary to be baptized in the name of the Father, and of the Son, and of the Holy Spirit, but that it is enough to be baptized in the name of Jesus Christ, or even the Holy Spirit. Others, including Pope Nicholas I, said that since the name of Jesus was hateful to the Jews, Baptism was celebrated in his name alone in the early days of the Church, so as to impress it more fully onto the hearts of believers. Other Fathers, such as Augustine, Basil, and John Damascene, said that scriptural references to Baptism are always to be understood as having been performed according to the proper Trinitarian formula, and that this is necessary for validity. Salmerón's view is that the reference to the name of Christ in Acts 2:38 is to demonstrate that Baptism was instituted by Christ and owes its power to him, but that it was always administered according to the Trinitarian formula.[119]

One curious aspect of Salmerón's theology of Baptism is the connection of this sacrament to circumcision. Salmerón is quite explicit about equating the two: the regeneration of man in the New Testament takes place by means of Baptism, and in the Old Testament by means of circumcision.[120] He says that circumcision was used under the Mosaic Law to remit original sin and confer grace, as well as to restrain concupiscence and keep away carbuncles. Yet Salmerón claims that these effects come from faith, rather than from the rite itself.[121] In other words, circumcision was not efficacious *ex opere operato*. He also takes interest in the details of circumcision. Citing scripture, he says that there is no particular minister for this rite, but that it can be performed by

---

[117] *CEH*, vol. 9, 103.

[118] *CEH*, vol. 8, 33.

[119] *CEH*, vol. 12, 86–87.

[120] *CEH*, vol. 8, 28.

[121] *CEH*, vol. 3, 316–17. The theologians at Trent varied widely in their view of whether and how the sacraments of the Old Testament conferred grace. Iturrioz, *La definición*, 226–27.

anyone. An iron knife may be used if a stone knife is not available. He claims that many think Mary circumcised Jesus, because no one else was worthy.[122]

Other exegetes of the age used scripture as a point of departure for discussing the sacrament of Baptism. Like Salmerón, Barradas clearly distinguishes between the baptism of John and the sacramental Baptism of Christ, rejecting the Protestant equation of the two.[123] Jansen makes this distinction rather succinctly, and in his commentary on the man who was infirm for thirty-eight years (Jn 5), he says that Baptism has its power from the blood of the true sacrifice offered on the cross.[124] Maldonado has more to say about Baptism, using not only the passages about John in the desert, but also Jesus's encounter with Nicodemus and the resurrection accounts to develop his teachings. He underscores the necessity of Baptism for salvation against the Calvinists, insisting that it not be delayed.[125] Marlorat offers a Calvinist theology of Baptism and criticizes Catholic practice, such as the baptism of infants, in numerous places.[126]

Penance

The baptism of John is a major locus for Salmerón's treatment of the sacrament of Penance. He begins with a close-reading of *metanoia/poenitentia*, which can be translated as both "repentance" and "penance." Beginning in the fifteenth century, philological studies had turned the translation of *metanoia* into a theological controversy that threatened to sever the link between the sacrament of Penance and justification.[127] Salmerón sought to meet this philological challenge on its own terms by refuting the explanations of Erasmus and Luther, for which he cites the authority of John Fisher as well as pagan Roman authors.[128] The crux of Luther's error, says Salmerón, is the claim that *metanoia* refers only to new life, not sorrow or satisfaction for sin. The correct understanding is that *metanoia* is like the god Janus: it looks both to the sins

---

[122] *CEH*, vol. 3, 315–16.

[123] Barradas, *Commentaries*, vol. 2, 12–13.

[124] Jansen, *Commentaries*, Prima Pars, 102; Jansen, *Commentaries*, Secunda Pars, 235.

[125] Maldonado, *Commentaries*, vol. 1, cols. 68–70; Maldonado, *Commentaries*, vol. 2, cols. 487–90; Maldonado, *Commentaries*, vol. 1, cols. 806–09.

[126] See Marlorat, *Expositio*, vol. 1, 15; Marlorat, *Expositio*, vol. 1, 17–18; Marlorat, *Expositio*, vol. 2, 676.

[127] McGrath, *Iustitia Dei*, 179–80.

[128] *CEH*, vol. 4, 17.

one has committed and also to new life.¹²⁹ He thus makes a philological case for keeping the link between the act of repentance, the sacrament of Penance, and justification.

The most extensive treatment of Penance is found in the commentary on Jn 20:22–23, when Jesus breathes on the apostles and grants them the power of forgiving sins. According to Salmerón, Christ met with them on this occasion not only to show himself to Thomas, but also to institute the sacrament of Penance, "which is not only magnificent in itself, but also most beneficial to us," and concerning which heretics make war with Catholics after so many centuries of its celebration.¹³⁰ Just as Christ instituted the apostles as priests for offering the Eucharist at the Last Supper, so also he instituted them as priests for the remission of sins at this moment.¹³¹ Salmerón cites scripture and a catena of Fathers, including Jerome, Ambrose, and Chrysostom, on the dual power of priests to bind and loose sins.¹³²

Yet numerous Protestants, especially Calvin in the *Antidote*, denied that Jn 20:22 has anything to do with the sacrament of Penance. According to him, the Holy Spirit is given to the apostles for preaching the word of God. Others, like Luther, thought the verse concerned merely the general obligation to confess sins. An example of this sort of confession is found in the *Confiteor* at the beginning of Mass, which does not entail the enumeration of particular sins. Others said that the ministers of the New Testament do not actually absolve sins, but only proclaim their remission.¹³³ Bullinger and Beza claimed that Catholics trace the rite of confession back to John the Baptist.¹³⁴

Salmerón sought to demonstrate that preaching and the forgiveness of sins were distinct ministries, and that the apostles received the Holy Spirit specifically for the latter. A host of Fathers, including Cyprian, Ambrose, Chrysostom, Augustine, Jerome, and Rupert of Deutz said that in Jn 20:22, Jesus bestowed upon them the power to forgive sins.¹³⁵ Salmerón also cites numerous decrees of the Council of Trent that interpret the verse in the same way, and that anathematize anyone who interprets it otherwise.¹³⁶ Aside from

---

[129] *CEH*, vol. 4, 18.
[130] *CEH*, vol. 11, 134.
[131] *CEH*, vol. 11, 135.
[132] *CEH*, vol. 11, 137.
[133] *CEH*, vol. 11, 130 (M3v).
[134] *CEH*, vol. 4, 36.
[135] *CEH*, vol. 11, 130 (M3v).
[136] *CEH*, vol. 11, 139 (M4r); Council of Trent, Session 6, *Decretum de justificatione*, Ch. 14; Council of Trent, Session 14, *Doctrina de sanctissimis poenitentiae et extremae*

the literal exegesis of this verse, he sees types and allegories of Penance in scripture. Adam and Eve confessed before God that they had eaten from the forbidden tree; God demanded confession of fratricide from Cain; Achan enumerated his particular sins in Josh 7:20; men confessed their sins to John the Baptist.[137] Jesus himself sent the healed lepers to the priests (Mt 8:4) and commended the raised Lazarus to the apostles so they could loosen his burial clothes (Jn 11:44) as signs of the need for sacramental confession. In addition, many Fathers interpreted the power of binding and loosing promised to Peter (Mt 16:19) as meaning the forgiveness of sins.[138]

As noted already, Salmerón treated Penance under the heading of "second justification," which is the way that men who have fallen into sin are restored to grace. This pact of second justification is stricter than the first, since it requires baring one's conscience before a priest and carrying out the penance he assigns.[139] Drawing on a biblical analogy, Salmerón says that Penance is akin to breaking the two tablets of the Decalogue in imitation of Moses (Ex 32:19), because if they were kept whole, everyone would perish.[140] He also uses the language, taken from the Fathers, of Penance as a "second plank" after the shipwreck of sin, a "laborious baptism," and a "baptism of tears."[141]

Salmerón's understanding of the history of Penance was limited, but not altogether absent. He identified two errors in antiquity. The first was that a baptized person could sin again, and if he did, it meant that he never received the Holy Spirit. The other error, which he attributed to the Novatians, is that there is no penance or remission of sin after Baptism (cf. Heb 6:4–6).[142] Salmerón says that this verse from the Letter to the Hebrews is an instance of hyperbole by the sacred author, and he explains that its true meaning is that one cannot return to the fullness of baptismal grace after sin.[143] There is no evidence that Salmerón grasped the difference between the "Mediterranean" and "Irish" models of penance, for example, nor of the way that these came

---

unctionis sacramentis, Ch 1; Council of Trent, Session 14, *Canones de sanctissimo poenitentiae sacramento*, can. 3.

[137] *CEH*, vol. 11, 139–40 (M4r–v).
[138] *CEH*, vol. 11, 137 (M3r).
[139] *CBP*, vol. 3, 42–43.
[140] *CEH*, vol. 4, 301.
[141] *CBP*, vol. 3, 43.
[142] *CEH*, vol. 5, 321–22.
[143] *CEH*, vol. 1, 123; *CEH*, vol. 5, 322.

into conflict on the Continent in the late first millennium.[144] In reply to Erasmus's question about how so few apostles heard so many confessions in the early Church, Salmerón answers that there were seventy-two disciples from the outset, and that the faithful needed to confess less often on account of their greater holiness.[145]

Salmerón offered practical advice to both confessors and penitents. Those who sin through ignorance or weakness of nature more easily obtain forgiveness, but those who willingly sin without desire of the flesh, but out of habit or bad will, are barely worthy of mercy, unless they pay the penalty first.[146] He had critical words for those who do not go to confession, or who fall back into the same sins again and do not repent. No one should flatter himself by saying that he carried out the assigned penance, because priests often give light or arbitrary ones.[147] These words are tempered somewhat by Salmerón's counsel that pastors and confessors should deal gently with penitents.[148] He says that priests should always give absolution, unless there is a good reason for withholding it.[149] They should wait until penitents have restored stolen goods, given up their concubines, burned their heretical books, and so forth.[150] Salmerón's advice is consistent with the new emphases, negotiations, and anxieties concerning this sacrament in the sixteenth century.[151]

One of Salmerón's major preoccupations is the need to confess prior to receiving the Eucharist, "for it is shameful to place the virginal and most pure flesh and body in a heart dirtier than the Augean stables."[152] During the Octave of Corpus Christi, the Church reads 1 Cor 11, he says, as a warning against unworthy reception by those who are in a state of sin.[153] The precept is to confess on a yearly basis, but by divine law Christians are required to go

---

[144] Ladislas Orsy, *The Evolving Church and the Sacrament of Penance* (Denville, NJ: Dimension Books, 1978), 31–48. The Third Council of Toledo in 589 rejected the intrusion of the Irish auricular model, whereas other councils in Gaul were more open to it.

[145] *CEH*, vol. 11, 147.

[146] *CBP*, vol. 3, 42.

[147] *CEH*, vol. 4, 41.

[148] *CEH*, vol. 4, 301.

[149] *CEH*, vol. 4, 552; *CEH*, vol. 7, 69.

[150] *CEH*, vol. 6, 284.

[151] See Patrick O'Banion, *The Sacrament of Penance and Religious Life in Golden Age Spain* (University Park, PA: Pennsylvania State University Press, 2013).

[152] *CEH*, vol. 9, 340.

[153] *CEH*, vol. 7, 140.

as often as they fall into mortal sin or receive the Eucharist; faith alone is not sufficient preparation.[154] He claims that Lateran IV's decree *Omnis utriusque sexus* stipulates that one always goes to confession before Communion, not just at Easter.[155] There has to be a confessor available to comply with this precept, and Salmerón tries to clarify what "available" means when he says that a priest who has already put on his vestments for Mass should not go to the confessional.[156]

Eucharist

Salmerón refers to the Eucharist as the "sacrament of sacraments," because it requires the greatest faith. "We not only believe in the sanctification of grace that is conferred through it upon those who approach worthily, but also that the Body and Blood of Christ are contained in it under the species."[157] He has a great deal to say about this sacrament: its lofty status in the economy of grace, the proper manner of its celebration and administration, its effects on those who receive it, and so forth. Thanks to Steiner's meticulous study of the conciliar debates, it is possible to see the continuity between his interventions at Trent and his Eucharistic teaching in the *Commentaries*.

According to Salmerón, the Eucharist is the greatest manifestation of God's power.[158] Christ looks like an ordinary man, but his light illuminates hearts. In a like manner, the "holy bread" looks like ordinary bread, but it is really the Body of Christ.[159] Salmerón warns against not perceiving the reality beneath the appearances when he says that bad priests take Christ in their hands, like Simeon, but unlike him they do not bless him. "So great and so impudent and temerarious is the audacity of ungrateful priests. Truly they do not see what they take in their hands while they offer sacrifice, for if they did see, they would doubtlessly give thanks."[160]

Salmerón treated the Eucharist as both sacrifice and banquet. He says that the Eucharist is unique among the sacraments in also being a sacrifice for

---

[154] *CEH*, vol. 11, 165; *CEH*, vol. 9, 326.

[155] *CEH*, vol. 9, 329.

[156] *CEH*, vol. 9, 326.

[157] *CEH*, vol. 9, 101. Elsewhere he explains that "sacrament of sacraments" is a Hebrew superlative genitive. *CEH*, vol. 1, 262.

[158] *CEH*, vol. 3, 70.

[159] *CEH*, vol. 3, 297.

[160] *CEH*, vol. 3, 386.

sins.¹⁶¹ One of his preferred biblical passages for this idea is taken from Mal 1:11: "from the rising of the sun even to the going down, my name is great among the Gentiles, and in every place there is sacrifice, and there is offered to my name a clean oblation: for my name is great among the Gentiles, saith the Lord of hosts." He offers a catena of Fathers who interpreted the verse as a prophecy of the Eucharist, ending with the Council of Trent's endorsement of this view.¹⁶² Rabbis Pinchas and Cahanam are cited for the belief that when the Messiah comes, only bread and wine will remain as a sacrificial offering.¹⁶³ Salmerón says the New Testament witnesses the institution of a new sacrifice, a new priesthood, and a new altar: "truly the Eucharist was instituted to proclaim the death of the Lord, and it is the highest cult by which we worship the Lord, and which we offer in a perpetual rite as a sacrifice."¹⁶⁴ Salmerón uses such expressions as "the sacrifice of the Mass," "the sacrifice of the Church of Christ," and "the sacrifice of the New Testament."¹⁶⁵

The Jesuit theologian invites Christians to the banquet of the Eucharist and frequently reflects on its status as spiritual food.¹⁶⁶ It fulfils Isaiah's prophecy of "a feast of fat things, a feast of wine, of fat things full of marrow, of wine purified from the lees" (Is 25:6).¹⁶⁷ Since marrow is not eaten raw, the humanity of Christ had to be cooked by the Spirit in the Incarnation, and in the fire of the Passion.¹⁶⁸ At his death, Christ was in the prime of life, like the fatted calf.¹⁶⁹ Salmerón says he was put in the oven of the Cross and turned from simple bread to hardtack [*panis nauticus*] for those sailing to the heavenly Jerusalem.¹⁷⁰ When, during the siege of Samaria, the king of Israel gave his son to a starving woman to eat (2 Kgs 6:24–30), it was a reminder that the Father

---

[161] *CEH*, vol. 9, 197. As Daly observes, Salmerón locates the essence of the Eucharistic sacrifice in the consecration alone, which became a popular theory in the post-Tridentine period. Robert Daly, "Robert Bellarmine and Post-Tridentine Eucharistic Theology" *Theological Studies* 61 (2000): 239–60, at 249; *CEH*, vol. 9, 222–23.

[162] *CEH*, vol. 9, 198; Council of Trent, Session 22, *Doctrina et canones de sanctissimo missae sacrificio*, Ch 1.

[163] *CEH*, vol. 9, 201.

[164] *CEH*, vol. 9, 208; *CEH*, vol. 9, 211 (Lr).

[165] *CEH*, vol. 2, 18; *CEH*, vol. 9, 125; *CEH*, vol. 9, 201.

[166] *CEH*, vol. 4, 285.

[167] *CEH*, vol. 9, 6.

[168] *CEH*, vol. 9, 9.

[169] *CEH*, vol. 9, 8.

[170] *CEH*, vol. 3, 66.

did the same thing for Christians in the Eucharist.[171] Salmerón recommends gazing upon the Eucharist, as one would gaze upon the dishes at a banquet. "As the forbidden tree stimulated the desire of the first parents unto ruin, so this tree of life inflames our will to eat unto salvation."[172]

The Eucharist, he observes approvingly, is celebrated with more internal reverence and adornment of splendor than any other sacrament. As the Holy of Holies, it needs a church, an altar, vestments, and ornaments, as well as a priesthood set apart for it and faithful to share it.[173] Salmerón attends to the details of these adornments and brings out their symbolic significance. Bells summon the people to the sacrifice and the word of God, "as once silver trumpets in the hands of the priests roused up the faithful to war" (see Num 10:9).[174] Salmerón comments on each of the priest's vestments, which serve to commemorate the reproach Christ suffered in his passion, and encourage the people's devotion. The amice renews the memory of faith and prepares the mind for sacrifice; the alb recalls purity of life; the cincture, chastity; the stole, patience; the maniple, obedience; the chasuble, the operation of charity on behalf of all sins.[175] He counsels priests to learn the rites of the Mass more by observing someone else than by reading books, and he claims that this was how the apostles learned them from Jesus.[176]

The *Commentaries* underscore the importance of attending Mass regularly and making the most of its celebration. The Mass itself is like a compendium of doctrine chosen by Pope Gregory, containing the best of the Old and New Testaments.[177] Salmerón says, however, that it takes effort to enter into the Mass. He complains that people attend it under pretexts, such as carrying out business, showing off, or even doing obscene things.[178] "The Mass, therefore, indeed gives no fruit, if it is only perceived with the senses of the ears and eyes."[179] Seeing and hearing must be accompanied by spiritual understanding, which Salmerón tries to provide with a commentary on the Order of the Mass. Here is one brief excerpt:

[171] *CEH*, vol. 8, 65 (F2r).
[172] *CEH*, vol. 9, 342.
[173] *CEH*, vol. 9, 7.
[174] *CEH*, vol. 9, 251.
[175] *CEH*, vol. 9, 251.
[176] *CEH*, vol. 12, 274.
[177] *CEH*, vol. 9, 367 (Gg6r).
[178] *CEH*, vol. 7, 201.
[179] *CEH*, vol. 9, 367 (Gg6r).

The Epistle that is read represents the teaching of the Old Testament, or the teaching of John the Baptist, the forerunner, which was an introduction or catechism for Christ. The Gradual in turn declares the repentance that the people performed in response to the teaching of John. The Alleluia recited after the Epistle refers to the joy of the interior man at the remission of sins through repentance, which entirely surpasses all the delights of the world, as Blessed Gregory says.[180]

This is akin to Salmerón's explanation of how the whole life of Christ is contained in the Eucharist, only here the emphasis is upon how the liturgical rite itself communicates the same thing. Similar allusions are scattered throughout the *Commentaries*, as when Salmerón compares the washing of the disciples' feet prior to the institution of the Eucharist to the Lavabo during the Offertory.[181]

He insisted that the celebration of this sacrament is meant only for the faithful. Christ, he says, is the brother of all on account of the Incarnation, and the propitiatory offering for all, but in the Eucharist, he is the propitiatory offering for Christians only. He thinks the texts of the Mass themselves indicate this. The expression "for many" [*pro multis*] in the consecration of the chalice is correct, Salmerón says, since only those who receive the offering in faith are worthy of it.[182] The Roman Canon speaks of the pope and "all who are orthodox in belief and who profess the Catholic and apostolic faith," but it includes no prayers for infidels or others outside the Church. He admits, however, that insofar as the Church prays for her expansion, the Eucharist is offered indirectly for pagans.[183]

If he regarded the Eucharist primarily as an act of worship and an entrance into the Christian mysteries, Salmerón also gave attention to the reception of the sacrament. On the one hand, he laments that in his time people receive the Eucharist only once a year because they are compelled to do so by ecclesiastical law, whereas in the early Church this was an everyday occurrence. He offers some strong words for people who receive infrequently.[184] On the other hand, he castigates unworthy reception, calling it the gravest of sins, and compares perpetrators to Uzzah, who died from touching the Ark of the Covenant (2

---

[180] *CEH*, vol. 9, 364 (Gg6v).

[181] *CEH*, vol. 9, 70.

[182] *CEH*, vol. 9, 104.

[183] *CBP*, vol. 4, 203–04.

[184] *CEH*, vol. 7, 140.

Sam 6:6–7).[185] He dedicates about seventeen pages to the subject of appropriate preparation for receiving Communion, saying that unworthy reception is worse than throwing the Lord's body into the sewer.[186] Communion must be preceded by the words "Lord, I am not worthy," and reception should be attended by joyful leaping in one's heart, like David before the Ark.[187]

Although Salmerón's opposition to heresy is a constant feature of the *Commentaries*, it reaches particular vehemence in the case of the Eucharist. He believes that the wickedness of heretics proceeds by stages, the last of which is the denial of the Eucharist, especially the doctrine of transubstantiation.[188] He announces, at the beginning of his treatise on the Lord's Supper, his intent to "slaughter" the opinions of heretics, and he calls them out by name. Luther's denial of transubstantiation opened the way for Karlstadt, Zwingli, Oecolampadius, and others, whom Salmerón likens to "Judas and his fellow traitors."[189] Those who deny transubstantiation are worse than the devil, in his estimation, because even Satan thought that Jesus could change stones into bread.[190]

Yet the Jesuit theologian had more to offer on this subject than verbal attacks. This is where he displayed his greatest interest in, and most accurate knowledge of, Protestant positions.[191] He identifies a dizzying range of sects and their teachings: *Significativi, Figuraturi, Tropistae, Sacramentarii, Impanatores, Ubiquiarii, Energici, Arrhabonarii, Santchariani, Suencfeldiani*. He likens them to the foxes that Samson tied together by their tails (Judg 15:45), because although their faces are different, they are united in their purpose of burning the fields.[192] Their common purpose, however, did not prevent Salmerón from patiently constructing a taxonomy and genealogy of the main Protestant teachings, to which a significant portion of Volume 9 is dedicated. He explains the exegesis of "this is my body" via figures such as Luther, Karlstadt, Calvin,

---

[185] *CEH*, vol. 2, 256 (Y1v).
[186] *CEH*, vol. 9, 351 (Ff5r).
[187] *CEH*, vol. 8, 143; *CEH*, vol. 4, 283 (Aa4r).
[188] *CEH*, vol. 9, 106.
[189] *CEH*, vol. 9, 12; *CEH*, vol. 9, 106.
[190] *CEH*, vol. 9, 110.
[191] Salmerón obtained permission in 1572 to read the works of Protestants. He was mainly interested in their commentaries on the Gospels and Acts, which surely acquainted him with their teachings on the Eucharist. *ES*, vol. 2, no. 354, 282–84.
[192] *CEH*, vol. 9, 107.

Zwingli, Brenz, and numerous others, explaining how their positions and debates gave rise to the great variety of sects listed above.[193]

Much of his information comes out of several important colloquies that took place during the first half of the sixteenth century: Marburg (1529), Wittenberg (1536), and Regensberg (1541). The first two included only Protestants, whereas the third was a meeting of Protestants and Catholics. All three failed to resolve doctrinal differences between the participants.[194] Salmerón was interested in these meetings not just for the information they provided about Protestant teachings, but even more because they served his polemical purpose. In his view, the effort to reach a consensus on the Eucharist, whether among Protestants or between Protestants and Catholics, must end in failure. He saw the truth of the Catholic faith on one side, and the contradictory ravings of heretics on the other. His solution to doctrinal and disciplinary disputes was forsaking the latter and embracing the former.

Salmerón was also on guard against what he regarded as Eucharistic errors among Catholic theologians. The Council of Trent identified three ways of receiving the Eucharist: sacramentally only (without benefit to the soul), spiritually only (in desire, without consumption of the species), and sacramentally and spiritually together.[195] During the conciliar debates, however, Salmerón objected to the idea of spiritual reception alone, claiming that what Christ clearly commanded in Jn 6 was spiritual and sacramental reception together.[196] As he explains in the *Commentaries*, his concern is that the consensus position among "all the more recent heretics" is a purely spiritual reception that excludes the sacrament. Salmerón traces this view back to certain Catholic authors, "who are few and new," who in response to the Hussite controversy in Bohemia had begun to advocate purely spiritual eating of the Eucharist. He includes Gabriel Biel, Nicholas of Cusa, Cajetan, and Ruard Tapper among them.[197] Salmerón saw this "novel" position as a potential threat to the Real Presence, as well as a basis for reception under both species, which he opposed.

---

[193] *CEH*, vol. 9, 106–35. This method of sorting out Eucharistic positions was common in the sixteenth century. Lee Palmer Wandel, *The Eucharist in the Reformation: Incarnation and Liturgy* (New York: Cambridge University Press, 2006).

[194] For early Protestant Eucharistic debates, see Amy Nelson Burnett, *Debating the Sacraments: Print and Authority in the Early Reformation* (New York: Oxford University Press, 2019).

[195] Council of Trent, *Decretum de sanctissimo eucharistiae sacramento*, Session 13, Ch. 8.

[196] Hughes, "Alfonso Salmeron," 157–59. Salmerón was miffed that the conciliar decree did not endorse this specific reading of Jn 6, and he took pains to defend it in the *Commentaries*.

[197] *CEH*, vol. 8, 189–92 (Q5r–v).

The Jesuit theologian was by no means alone in his preoccupation with the Eucharist, for there is an unmistakable emphasis upon it in the works of other exegetes of the period. Maldonado, who generally was more selective in his discussion of sixteenth-century controversies than Salmerón, savages Protestant teachings on the Eucharist at length in his commentary on the Last Supper.[198] He asks rhetorically why, among the four principal mysteries of the faith (Trinity, Incarnation, resurrection of the dead, and Eucharist), Protestants only attack the last.[199] Jansen's exegesis of Jn 6 discusses the Eucharistic meaning of the "bread of life" with ample references to controversies and arguments against Protestants.[200] Barradas expounds on the greatness of the Eucharist and defends it from attacks in numerous places.[201] There is ample evidence that many Catholics exegetes regarded the Eucharist as the crux of their conflict with Protestants.

Matrimony

In his commentary on Eph 5, Salmerón says that Protestants have raised the issue of whether matrimony is one of the seven sacraments of the New Testament. He says that Paul understands it as a sacrament insofar as it is a sign and symbol of the union between Christ and the Church. Salmerón defines marriage as "the joining of male and female that preserves a single custom of life between legitimate persons."[202] This joining, Salmerón explains, does not refer to copulation, because in that case ratified but unconsummated marriages would not be true marriages, thus excluding the union of Joseph and the Blessed Virgin. He then offers a "clearer" definition of matrimony insofar as it is a human contract: "Matrimony is the indissoluble bond between male and female from the mutual exchange of power over their bodies, for the sake of bearing offspring and educating them correctly."[203]

The nature and indissolubility of the marriage bond receives extended treatment in the *Commentaries* in the context of Jesus's disputes with the Pharisees (Mt 19:3–12, Mk 10:2–12, Lk 16:18). Salmerón dedicates to it three

---

[198] Maldonado, *Commentaries*, vol. 1, cols. 560–85.
[199] Maldonado, *Commentaries*, vol. 1, cols. 560–01.
[200] Jansen, *Commentaries*, Secunda Pars, 469–77.
[201] Barradas, *Commentaries*, vol. 2, 647–55; Barradas, *Commentaries*, vol. 3, 211–13; Barradas, *Commentaries*, vol. 4, 62–100.
[202] *CBP*, vol. 3, 260.
[203] *CBP*, vol. 3, 261.

consecutive treatises that run to thirty pages in total. His key claim is that from the beginning God intended man and woman to form an indissoluble bond.[204] He asserts that scripture, tradition, the Fathers, divine law, natural law, civil law, and canon law all agree on the indissoluble nature of the marriage bond, and he cites specific sources from them in support of this claim.[205] Salmerón ridicules the argument of Martin Bucer that secular magistrates can dissolve marriages, on the grounds that this is an instance of God rather than men separating the spouses.[206]

Matthew's codicil about divorce and remarriage "except it be for fornication" (Mt 19:9) does not mean, according to Salmerón, that marriage can be dissolved in the case of fornication, so that the offended party is free to contract a new marriage. Salmerón names prominent Catholic theologians, including Erasmus, Cajetan, and Lefèvre d'Étaples who hold this position "against the Church's definition."[207] This issue is treated at length in Volumes 5 and 8, suggesting that Salmerón thought the error was especially threatening in his times.[208]

> Truly no orthodox Christian, especially among the Latins and the more ancient Greeks, has dared to take another wife after repudiating the first one while the latter lived, or take one who was repudiated after fornication, and the Church has never permitted anyone to attempt this.[209]

This assertion is accompanied by numerous citations from scripture, arguments from reason, and catenas of passages from the Fathers, Scholastic Doctors, and popes, as well as canons from the Councils of Florence and Trent.[210] He

---

[204] *CEH*, vol. 8, 360–61.

[205] *CEH*, vol. 8, 365–68.

[206] *CEH*, vol. 8, 364.

[207] *CEH*, vol. 8, 374–75.

[208] In the decades immediately after Trent, the city of Naples witnessed a significant number of civil and ecclesiastical cases of bigamy, as well as a major transformation of how these cases were conceived and processed. Increasingly, bigamy was treated as a crime against the faith, that is, heresy. See Pierroberto Scaramella, "Controllo e repressione ecclesiastica della poligamia a Napoli in età moderna: dalle cause matrimoniali al crimine di fede (1514–1799)," in *Trasgressioni: Seduzione, concubinato, adulterio, bigamia (XIV–XVIII secolo)*, eds. Silvana Seidel Menchi and Diego Quaglioni (Bologna: Il Mulino, 2004), 443–501.

[209] *CEH*, vol. 5, 227.

[210] *CEH*, vol. 5, 231–35. Salmerón clarifies that fornication is still a most serious sin: it takes away all three goods of marriage, and is a legitimate cause for separation, though not of dismissal. *CEH*, vol. 8, 379.

evidently did not see the Tridentine decree as sparing the Venetians' Greek Orthodox subjects, who allowed divorce on the grounds of adultery, from condemnation.[211] Salmerón saw the issue as critical; as he remarked in a letter concerning the interpretation of Mt 19:9, "you know how many tumults and tragedies have resulted in our age from this verse."[212]

The Faithful Departed

While Salmerón acknowledged the reality of heaven and hell, doing his utmost to encourage his reader to seek the one and avoid the other, he offered no extended treatment of either destination. The *Commentaries* give more attention to another issue concerning the afterlife: the efficacy and importance of prayer for the dead. Although Salmerón appealed to scripture, the centerpiece of his discussion was the Church's public prayer, namely, the Mass for the Dead celebrated on November 2 and at other times during the year. He approves of offering prayers, alms, and fasting to benefit the souls of the departed, and praises the adornment of the Mass of the Dead with particular orations, collects, and sequences that are commonly sung.[213] When defending the thesis that the separated soul has the capacity to see God, Salmerón makes an argument from the Offertory of the Requiem Mass.

> The Church moreover prays that the departed be given eternal rest, and that Michael, the holy standard-bearer, bring them into the holy light which God once promised to Abraham and his descendants. For if this rest were to be postponed until the day of judgment, and indeed given to no one, the Church's prayers would be in vain, since they would obtain nothing for them.[214]

This liturgical appeal reached beyond the Roman Rite. Salmerón observes that the liturgies of Basil, Chrysostom, and James, as well as the Ambrosian and Ethiopian Rites, offer prayer for the dead at Mass. Not everyone may benefit from these prayers, he says, since the Church does not pray for heretics,

---

[211] Council of Trent, Session 24, *Canones de sacramento matrimonii*, can. 7; Walter, "Sacraments in the Council of Trent," 325. For a meticulous treatment of Trent's teaching on marriage, particularly in relation to Greek practice, see E. Christian Brugger, *The Indissolubility of Marriage and the Council of Trent* (Washington, DC: Catholic University of America Press, 2017).

[212] *ES*, vol. 2, no. 359, 296.

[213] *CBP*, vol. 2, 212; *CBP*, vol. 2, 223–24.

[214] *CEH*, vol. 5, 108.

apostates, or the impenitent more generally. Yet if one does not know the state of a person's soul at death, one may pray for him.[215]

Conclusion

In Salmerón's view, the task of saving souls imposes particular responsibilities on the theologian. In addition to possessing righteousness himself, and exhorting others to attain it, he must provide a correct theological account of a host of related issues: God's mercy and grace, human free will, the stages of justification, predestination, and the theological virtues. Although he completed his magnum opus prior to the explosion of the great controversy among Catholic theologians instigated by Molina, Salmerón staked out a position that preserved the characteristically Jesuit emphasis on human freedom, while seeking to avoid the trap of Pelagianism. In so doing, he offered a particular interpretation of the decrees of Trent, which were a touchstone for him. He likewise had to explain and defend the principal means by which the graces unto salvation are communicated, namely, the seven sacraments. Salmerón saw this task as especially urgent in view of the Protestant challenges, which he considered a serious threat to the salvation of souls. He was especially attentive to the sacraments that occasioned the greatest controversy during the Reformation, namely, Baptism, Penance, the Eucharist, and Matrimony. Rather than offer vivid images of heaven and hell to motivate the reader, he encouraged prayer and supplication on behalf of the dead, whose fate is known to God alone.

---

[215] *CBP*, vol. 2, 223.

6 Defending the Church

In his exegesis of the parable of the wicked servant (Mt 18:23–35), Salmerón asks in passing, "Why does anyone dare to go out from this unconquerable fortress of the Church and give himself into the hands of his capital enemies?"[1] This comment illustrates well his view of the Catholic Church: built solidly upon rock and endowed with every gift, yet besieged on every side by foes. This was a common perception in the sixteenth century, when the unity of Western Christendom was rent asunder in a lasting way. Even among Catholics, however, there was a variety of responses to this development. Salmerón's approach to the ecclesiological question was unabashedly defensive, even militant, consisting of three major elements. The first was a positive definition of the Church and a reliance upon the types and images, such as bride, body, and mother, used in scripture, the Fathers, and the Doctors, as well as a few of his own devising. A notable feature of his exegesis is that he interpreted the Gospel theme of the "kingdom of God" as referring to the Church, which provided the opportunity to compare and contrast it with earthly kingdoms.

The "kingdom of God" leads to the second element, which was Salmerón's theory of ecclesiastical polity. Like many Catholic thinkers of his age, he treated this as correlative to the theory of civil polity, such that the two must be taken together if either is to be properly understood. Although he said that the two communities had different origins and ends, he dealt with them as deeply intertwined at both a theoretical and a practical level. Against the widespread conciliarist and royalist ecclesiologies of his time, Salmerón defended a monarchical understanding of the ecclesiastical regime centered on the pope as possessing supreme teaching authority as well as plenitude of jurisdiction.[2]

---

[1] *CEH*, vol. 7, 70.

[2] Papalist ecclesiology conflicted rather strongly with the views of many Spanish churchmen as well as the policy of Charles V. See Xavier Tubau, "Hispanic Conciliarism and the Imperial Politics of Reform on the Eve of Trent," *Renaissance Quarterly* 70, no. 3 (2017): 897–934.

The classification and condemnation of the Church's enemies was the third crucial element of Salmerón's ecclesiology. Although previous chapters have already demonstrated the polemical cast of the *Commentaries*, here his attacks on Jews, heretics, Muslims, pagans, and bad Catholics are dealt with in a more systematic fashion. The unity of the Church is seen through a glass darkly in her enemies: just as the community of believers is a transhistorical community, so also her opponents, in Salmerón's telling, form such a community, whose only principle of unity is precisely this opposition. Not only did he oppose changing any teachings or disciplines to satisfy Protestants, but he also laid emphasis on what separated them from, rather than what united them to, the Catholic Church. His horror of heresy and infidelity, and the corresponding desire to fight against their proponents, indelibly marks the *Commentaries*.

What is the Church?

Although ecclesiological themes appear throughout the *Commentaries*, there are several places where Salmerón treats the subject in a more systematic way. The first appears in his first volume on the letters of Paul, where he dedicates significant space to defining the apostle's use of terms.[3] One of these is "church," which in both biblical and profane usage has the most basic meaning of "meeting" [*coetus*] or "assembly" [*congregatio*].[4] Although the apostles took it from the Septuagint rather than from Athens, Salmerón insists that the term *ecclesia* is no longer to be applied to the Jewish community on account of its denial of Christ.[5] He says that according to scripture and the Fathers, the Church is "the assembly of those called by God through faith and participation in the sacraments, and through these to the grace and blessedness that attains unto God."[6]

He was not quite satisfied with this definition, however, since it did not account for subcategories or parts within the Church: those already in glory, those who are in Purgatory or on earth in a state of grace, and those who have faith and receive the sacraments, but without possessing charity. Salmerón

---

[3] A useful outline of this section of the *Commentaries* may be found in Diego Molina, *La vera sposa de Christo: La primera Eclesiología de la Compañía de Jesús – Los tratados eclesiológicos de los jesuitas anteriores a Belarmino (1540–1586)* (Granada: Facultad de Teología, 2003), 86–87.

[4] *CBP*, vol. 1, 171.

[5] *CBP*, vol. 1, 241; *CBP*, vol. 1, 171.

[6] *CBP*, vol. 1, 172. "Coetus vocatorum a Deo per fidem, et sacramentorum participationem, et per haec ad gratiam, et beatitudinem, quod ad Deum attinet."

uses the analogy of the Jerusalem temple: the first part corresponds to the Holy of Holies, the second to the sanctuary, and the third to the atrium of the sinners.[7] Against the Novatian and Donatist teaching that the Church is made up of only righteous members, Salmerón defends the Catholic idea that it is made up of the good and the bad.[8] He is familiar with numerous schemas for categorizing the Church's members, but the distinction that appears most often is the Church Militant and the Church Triumphant.[9]

The Jesuit theologian claimed a primary role for the Holy Spirit in preserving the Church and her faith and uniting her to Christ. "But you are come to Mount Sion, and to the city of the living God" (Heb 12:22) refers, according to Salmerón, to the first gathering of the Church in Jerusalem, when the Holy Spirit descended.[10] When the Spirit filled the whole house at Pentecost (Act 2:2), it was a type of the Spirit's filling the Church.[11] The Church stands firm even in the face of death because of the Holy Spirit, which is the bond between her and Christ.[12] "That they may be one" (Jn 17:11) is a tacit prayer to the Holy Spirit, since he makes the Mystical Body of Christ one.[13] Madrigal Terrazas calls attention to Salmerón's emphasis on the Church as communion with the Triune God, particularly with the Spirit.[14]

Salmerón made frequent use of images and analogies taken from scripture and the Fathers that are more mystical than polemical in nature. The Church as body, bride, and mother are prominent. He appeals to Rom 12, 1 Cor 12, and Eph 1 for the image of the Church as a body, which is one even though it is partly visible and partly invisible.[15] Salmerón correlates the double power of the Church (orders and jurisdiction) with the true body of Christ [*corpus verum*] and the mystical body [*corpus mysticum*]. These are the Eucharist and

---

[7] *CBP*, vol. 1, 173.

[8] *CEH*, vol. 7, 64; *CBP*, vol. 3, 597.

[9] *CEH*, vol. 3, 92; *CBP*, vol. 3, 737; *CEH*, vol. 7, 37; *CEH*, vol. 5, 100.

[10] *CBP*, vol. 3, 784.

[11] *CEH*, vol. 12, 26 (Fv).

[12] *CEH*, vol. 9, 415.

[13] *CEH*, vol. 9, 572.

[14] Santiago Madrigal Terrazas, "'Nuestra santa madre Iglesia hierárchica' [Ej 353]: La Iglesia de Jesucristo según los *Commentarii* de Salmerón," in *Dogmática ignaciana: "Buscar y hallar la voluntad divina" [Ej 1]*, ed. Gabino Uríbarri Bilbao (Madrid: Comillas, 2018), 468–502, at 495–98. Cf. *CBP*, vol. 4, 164–663 (O4v–O5r); *CBP*, vol. 4, 169.

[15] *CBP*, vol. 1, 269.

the Church, respectively.[16] He uses the head/body metaphor to account for the priority of the community over the individual: the Church is not for men, but men are for the Church.[17] There are five ties that link together head and body: doctrine, life, sacraments, miracles, and the grace of God.[18] One consequence of Salmerón's use of the body analogy is the exclusion of any person or sect not in visible communion with the successor of Peter. Anyone who separates himself from Peter's faith or obedience, like oriental patriarchs, Anglicans, many German bishops, heretics, or schismatics, is separated from the body of Christ.[19] Outside the Church, he says, one finds only shameful deeds [*flagitia*] and no efficacious sacraments or Catholic doctrine, and those who separate themselves from her lose the hope of salvation.[20]

Closely related to the body analogy is the idea that the Church has brought Jews and Gentiles together to form one people.[21] This means that, on the one hand, Gentiles no less than Jews have a place in the Church, and on the other hand, that Christians are the true Jews, in the sense of being a holy people.[22] Whoever receives the faith is a true descendant of Abraham and a true son of Jacob, whether he is a Jew or a Gentile, and there is no distinction between them.[23] The notion of "one flesh" is also apparent in the use of the nuptial metaphor (Eph 5) for the relationship between the Church and Christ, who left his Father as well as his mother to be united to her.[24] The Church is the Lord's spouse, whom he leads and clothes like a naked Ethiopian (Num 12:1).[25] When Christ was pierced on the cross, he spoke the words of the Canticle of Canticles to the Church: "thou has wounded my heart, my sister, my spouse" (Cant 4:9).[26]

Salmerón depicted the Church as both mother and teacher. In the regeneration of Baptism, God is Father and the Church is mother, and she is called

---

[16] *CEH*, vol. 4, 406.
[17] *CEH*, vol. 8, 275.
[18] *CBP*, vol. 1, 226.
[19] *CEH*, vol. 4, 391.
[20] *CEH*, vol. 4, 59; *CEH*, vol. 9, 434.
[21] *CEH*, vol. 8, 432–33.
[22] *CEH*, vol. 12, 209; *CBP*, vol. 4, 71.
[23] *CEH*, vol. 3, 124; *CEH*, vol. 3, 158.
[24] *CEH*, vol. 8. 73; *CBP*, vol. 3, 259.
[25] *CEH*, vol. 2, 217.
[26] *CEH*, vol. 10, 393.

by this name because she gives birth to her children with tears and cries.[27] In his commentary on Jerusalem as mother (Gal 4:26), Salmerón calls the Church the "sterile mother" who gives birth to new children.[28] When Peter speaks of the "rational milk" that Christians should desire, the Jesuit theologian comments that Christians nurse at the breasts of mother Church.[29] It is necessary for salvation to believe all that she teaches, because it comes from God, and neither God nor she can deceive or be deceived. In matters that God and the Church have not defined, Catholics are free to believe what seems to them more probable or consonant with piety. One must verify, by consulting her teachers, that any given person is not speaking against the things that the Church has defined.[30] The teachers are those who have the office of catechizing in any given church. Every cathedral should have at least one teacher of scripture and one of canon law, as the Council of Trent stipulated.[31]

Judging by the space he gave to it and the frequency with which he returned to it, the architectural metaphor was Salmerón's favorite. He calls Jesus the "wise architect" of the Church who lays Peter as the foundation stone [*lapidem in fundamento*].[32] In his analysis of "to build" [*aedificandi*] Salmerón distinguishes Christ as the cornerstone [*lapis angularis*] from Peter and the apostles as foundation stones, offering a lengthy explanation of these two architectural features.[33] The house built upon the rock (Mt 7:24–25) is the Church: Christ is the foundation, the four walls are the cardinal virtues, the length, width, and height are the theological virtues, the floor is humility, the roof is patience, and so forth.[34] Paul called the apostles "pillars" of the Church because they sustained the whole building of it, and Salmerón compares the miracles of the apostles to the wooden scaffolding [*fulcra*] used for building a church.[35]

Although the *Commentaries* provide elements of a *De ecclesia* treatise, the standard motifs found in scripture and tradition are presented somewhat

---

[27] *CEH*, vol. 8, 34; *CBP*, vol. 3, 141.

[28] *CBP*, vol. 3, 145.

[29] *CBP*, vol. 4, 66.

[30] *CBP*, vol. 2, 176. Elsewhere he adds that the Church cannot err in things that pertain to faith and good mores. *CEH*, vol. 12, 542 (Zzv).

[31] *CBP*, vol. 2, 167.

[32] *CEH*, vol. 4, 168. The designation of Christ as architect appears also at *CEH*, vol. 9, 576.

[33] *CBP*, vol. 1, 127–30. He notes that the hymn for the dedication of the Church *Angularis fundamentum* connects the two.

[34] *CEH*, vol. 5, 412.

[35] *CBP*, vol. 3, 96; *CEH*, vol. 6, 12.

haphazardly, without an obvious attempt to integrate or prioritize them. The Church's unity and greatness, as well as the need for all men to enter her, are the predominant ideas, but the Jesuit theologian provided a variety of images and types for the reader to meditate upon, without insisting on the priority of any of them. Even this somewhat haphazard treatment, however, was much more complete than what may be found in the works of other exegetes under consideration. Barradas and Maldonado often cited some of these themes in passing, but not in a systematic way. Jansen briefly discusses the meaning of *ekklesia* and her power to bind and loose, and elsewhere he says that Christians are born sons of God from the virgin mother Church.[36]

Marlorat also comments on the biblical images of the Church as bride of Christ, body of Christ, heavenly Jerusalem, and so forth, and throughout the work he elaborates various elements of ecclesiology.[37] He calls the first three chapters of 1 Tim a "summa of the whole ecclesiastical economy," and he defines the Church in the following terms:

> It is not therefore to be imagined that the Church is an external polity constituted by human traditions, and bound together at certain places; but the Church properly signifies a multitude of the devout who are dispersed throughout the world, who truly believe the Gospel, and who are sanctified by the Holy Spirit, and who have an external mark, that is, the pure Word of God, and the use of the sacraments that agrees with the Gospel.[38]

The Kingdom of God

Salmerón made a key exegetical move that served as a pivot between his properly theological treatment of the Church and his theory of ecclesiastical polity. This is his explanation of a central theme in the preaching of Jesus, namely, the "kingdom of God" or the "kingdom of heaven," which he treats as synonymous. Observing that the history of biblical commentary offers numerous interpretative possibilities, Salmerón states his view that it refers to the Church.[39] His first extended treatment of the issue appears in the commentary on the Beatitudes, where he provides definitions of the term "kingdom."

---

[36] Jansen, *Commentaries*, Tertia Pars, 78–82; Jansen, *Commentaries*, Prima Pars, 24.

[37] Marlorat, *Expositio*, vol. 1, 450; Marlorat, *Expositio*, vol. 1, 196; Marlorat, *Expositio*, vol. 2, 226–27.

[38] Marlorat, *Expositio*, vol. 2, 440.

[39] *CEH*, vol. 5, 305; *CEH*, vol. 12, 295. The other possibilities he cites are Christ, the Gospel, the reward of eternal life, and heavenly glory. *CEH*, vol. 5, 301–03.

But a kingdom is a people subject to the same head and ruled by the same laws for its own benefit, even if it does not have its own proper territory [*locum*], as in the case of the kings of the Vandals or the Goths who invaded the kingdoms of the West, who had no proper territory. Improperly speaking, "kingdom" is used for the place or territory inhabited and possessed by the subjects, which is why we say "the Kingdom of France" or the "Kingdom of Spain"… A kingdom is nothing other than the possession of a king, dependent upon the wealth and honor of its king.[40]

Since according to Salmerón a kingdom is primarily the people subject to the same head and the same laws, God could not be king until a people were subject to him.[41] He specifies that Christ shares kingship over heaven with the Father and the Holy Spirit, but he has another kingship particular to him, namely, the Catholic Church, which is the kingdom that acknowledges him as king. The universal scope of the Church befits the dignity of Christ the King who possesses a multitude of peoples.[42]

Salmerón compares and contrasts the kingdom of God with earthly kingdoms. On the one hand, he emphasizes its spiritual character, saying that Jesus did not want to rule over a temporal kingdom, in accordance with his priesthood.[43] Several times he cites two verses of the Epiphany hymn *Hostis Herodes impie* ["he who gives heavenly kingdoms/takes away no earthly ones"] to express the spiritual character of Christ's kingdom, commenting that priesthood and kingship are distinct.[44] On the other hand, the kingdom of God is like earthly kingdoms in many respects, possessing the following features: law, ministers, punishments, a tribunal, privileges and immunities, a royal table, freedom, and eternal rewards. It also has enemies and rebels opposed to it.[45]

This rule of Christ is both secure and constantly contested. The Jesuit theologian says that the kingdom of God is characterized by both peace (as foreshadowed in Solomon's rule) and conflict (as foreshadowed by the turbulence of David's reign).[46] Christ reigned until the day of his Resurrection, but his kingdom is full of war and contention. His victory will be complete when he has his final triumph over death and hands over his kingdom to his Father,

---

[40] *CEH*, vol. 5, 33.
[41] *CEH*, vol. 5, 301.
[42] *CBP*, vol. 1, 174.
[43] *CBP*, vol. 1, 248.
[44] *CEH*, vol. 3, 359; *CEH*, vol. 4, 413.
[45] *CEH*, vol. 5, 302–03.
[46] *CEH*, vol. 5, 305.

like a Roman emperor handing over conquered provinces to the republic.[47] Salmerón's preference for an ecclesiological understanding of the "kingdom of God" articulates what is only latent in his definition of the Church and the more mystical images and types discussed above. As a kingdom, it must have all the elements of structure, hierarchy, and authority that pertain to a proper polity, which enables the clear demarcation between belonging and not belonging that Salmerón wished to establish. He also meant to indicate the particular regime type of this kingdom. If Jesus is king of the Church, then the Church must be a monarchy with a viceroy on earth.

Ecclesiastical and Civil Polity

Part of Salmerón's systematic treatment of the Church is dedicated to the form of government Christ wanted for it: monarchy, as opposed to democracy or aristocracy. Although using the categories taken from political thought may be counter-intuitive for contemporary ecclesiology, the Jesuit theologian was following a pattern that had been common for centuries. Political theorists, canonists, and theologians readily employed the same concepts and categories for their respective fields of inquiry, meaning that issues of civil and ecclesiastical polity were often treated as correlative.[48] Along with Bellarmine and Suárez, Salmerón adopted the theory of the Dominican Thomists Francisco de Vitoria (1483–1546) and Peter Crockaert (c. 1465–1514), who were highly influential in Paris in the first half of the sixteenth century.[49] Although he cites him rarely in the *Commentaries*, elsewhere Salmerón effusively praised Nicholas Sanders's treatment of ecclesiastical monarchy, "which I devoured like a glutton of books."[50] Sanders therefore ought to be counted as an influence on the Jesuit theologian's ecclesiology.

---

[47] *CEH*, vol. 5, 303–04.

[48] Francis Oakley, *The Watershed of Modern Politics: Law, Virtue, Kingship, and Consent (1300–1650)* (New Haven, CT: Yale University Press, 2015), 140. Salmerón even uses the term *ecclesiastica politia* on one occasion. *CEH*, vol. 12, 411. As Höpfl observes, the Society's "best-stocked armoury" of political concepts was probably its ecclesiology. Harro Höpfl, *Jesuit Political Thought: The Society of Jesus and the State, c. 1540–1630* (New York: Cambridge University Press, 2004), 22.

[49] Paul Oberholzer, "Desafíos y exigencias frente a un nuevo descubrimiento de Diego Laínez," in *Diego Laínez (1512–1565) and his Generalate: Jesuit with Jewish Roots, Close Confidant of Ignatius of Loyola, Preeminent Theologian of the Council of Trent*, ed. Paul Oberholzer (Rome: IHSI, 2015), 45–116, at 93–94.

[50] *ES*, vol. 2, no. 360, 296–99; Nicholas Sanders, *De visibili monarchia ecclesiae* (Louvain: Joannes Foulerus, 1571).

Citing Aristotle, Salmerón says that there are three kinds of good government (monarchy, aristocracy, and democracy) which degenerate into three corresponding kinds of bad government (tyranny, faction, and furor or tumult). Although this is a rather loose reading of Aristotle, Salmerón's purpose is assigning preferred regime types along confessional lines: Protestants or Lutherans think that ecclesial polity is nothing other than an ordered democracy, whereas Calvin regards it as more of an aristocracy. Catholics, by contrast, have a "paternal, benign, and mild monarchy," which is not properly a "dominate" [*dominium*], since the members of the Church are not slaves, but a "principate" [*principatus*] that serves the whole household.[51]

Salmerón first sought to demonstrate why the Protestant ecclesial regimes were false before making his case for the Catholic monarchy. In a popular regime, he says, no one has a magistracy except by the consent of the people, who can also remove officeholders. The fact that no one voted for the apostles or disciples, but that they were instead chosen by Christ, shows that the Church's regime is not democratic. Even during those times in history when bishops were chosen by the people, they only became bishops through the laying on of hands.[52] Since the task of the shepherds is to strengthen the flock, Salmerón says, it would be insane to subject them to the multitude.[53] Democracy itself is a less praiseworthy regime type, which is why the Church does not have it; the wise should rule, which is why Athens turned to Solon to put an end to anarchy.[54]

Salmerón also rejected what he characterized as Calvin's aristocratic theory of Church governance. Although the bishops do form a group of "best men" [*optimates*], there would be need to designate which of them is responsible for resolving important controversies. Since Christ and the apostles did not identify any such figures among their successors, and since no bishops have this power perpetually, the supreme tribunal in the Church is Peter and the popes.[55] Even the frequent calling of councils would not resolve the problem. Who would preside, Salmerón asks, if all bishops were equal, or how could one determine which councils are legitimate? In such an

---

[51] *CBP*, vol. 1, 236.
[52] *CBP*, vol. 1, 236–38.
[53] *CBP*, vol. 1, 139 (V6r).
[54] *CBP*, vol. 1, 241.
[55] *CBP*, vol. 1, 255–56.

arrangement, the external peace of the Church could not be maintained, and heresies and schisms would proliferate.[56]

Having rejected the democratic and aristocratic regimes, Salmerón made his case for ecclesial monarchy, drawing upon both biblical and classical history. The Mosaic Law had a high priest who lived near the temple, a role that Salmerón compares to the office of the pope. Ancient Rome turned to the rule of one man out of necessity, and Paul speaks of his solicitude for all the churches (2 Cor 11:28), indicating the need for a head over them all.[57] Homer wrote in favor of a single king, since many princes struggle amongst themselves for supremacy, and Isocrates preferred monarchy over aristocracy and democracy.[58] Adam's monarchy over the human race was not lost with the Fall, but it was passed along to his descendants, from Seth to Noah, to Melchizedek, Abraham, Isaac, and Jacob. Salmerón claims that Levi and Judah split spiritual and civil matters between them, which prefigured the Christian dispensation. Not only do the law of nations [*ius gentium*] and the civil law prefer monarchy over other forms, but even the founders of heresy aspire to monarchy, as their sects are named after them.[59]

The argument for monarchy was not merely historical, but also metaphysical, since Salmerón thought that monarchy corresponded to the order of the universe. The Trinity is a single principle, and Adam exercised monarchy in paradise. In each family of angels, there is one who stands over it like the head of the household [*paterfamilias*]. All the planets are moved by one prime mover; among the elements, fire holds the first place; herd animals always have a leader; the eagle is the leader of the birds, the lion of terrestrial animals, and man rules over them all. Creatures acknowledge the monarchy of God by recognizing leaders among themselves, whereas Christians recognize the monarchy of Christ in the Church.[60] This notion of cosmic order is closely related to an argument from beauty. The Church's own beauty derives from, at least in part, the beauty of monarchy, whereas democracy and aristocracy are defects from the beauty of order. If the Church had multiple heads, she would not have the image of God and Christ, but of Babel and hell.[61] These passages

---

[56] *CBP*, vol. 1, 256–57. Salmerón cites Calvin's acknowledgment in the *Institutes* that there is no sure way of resolving doctrinal disputes at councils.

[57] *CBP*, vol. 1, 260.

[58] *CBP*, vol. 1, 271.

[59] *CBP*, vol. 1, 265.

[60] *CBP*, vol. 1, 261–63.

[61] *CBP*, vol. 1, 271–72.

also reflect Salmerón's emphasis on the importance of personal governance, a characteristically Jesuit theme.[62]

Refuting the ecclesial regimes of Luther and Calvin required Salmerón to explain why supreme governance of the Church is not in the hands of emperors, kings, or other civil magistrates, which in turn led him to a discussion of the origin and end of the civil power. It is important to note that Salmerón articulated his "political theory" in connection with his ecclesiology, which reflects two realities of his time. First, he inherited a tradition of thought and practice in which the Catholic civil and ecclesiastical powers were closely intertwined. Second, he believed that the principal threat to this arrangement was the encroachment of the civil authorities, a problem that he laid at the feet of Protestant teachers and three of their errors in particular. The first, which he attributes to the Anglicans, is that the royal power of a Christian prince is greater than ecclesiastical power. The second is that royal power extends to judging ecclesiastical cases, and the third is that a Christian prince always has in his kingdom superiority in all civil business over any ecclesiastical magistrate, which not even sin can take away.[63]

On the one hand, Salmerón carefully distinguished the two powers. The civil power, he says, comes mediately from God by way of the law of nations. Despite his words elsewhere about "Adam's monarchy," Salmerón claims that there was no royal power in Paradise, and that it was not established until Nimrod founded Babel (Gen 10:10). Its end is "that we might live a quiet and tranquil life here." By contrast, the ecclesiastical power comes directly from Christ and exists for the sake of eternal life.[64] Kingdoms are established in three ways: by *patria potestas*, as when Adam divided the world among his three sons; by common consent of those who make leaders for themselves; and by violence and tyranny.[65] Christian princes have a civil magistracy, but no part of the Church's governance. Conversely, Christ gave no command concerning civil governance, and there is no civil power in the Church.[66] The king

---

[62] Höpfl, *Jesuit Political Thought*, 190.

[63] *CBP*, vol. 1, 244.

[64] *CBP*, vol. 1, 244. Salmerón does not really explain the nature of Adam's primordial monarchy, but he evidently thinks it was something other than civil power in the proper sense.

[65] *CBP*, vol. 1, 675. Salmerón shares with other early Jesuit political thinkers an emphasis on the importance of consent for the establishment of the political community. Carlos Zeron, "Political Theories and Jesuit Politics," in *The Oxford Handbook of the Jesuits*, ed. Ines Županov (New York: Oxford University Press, 2019), 193–215, at 195.

[66] *CBP*, vol. 1, 139 (V6r).

commands Christians not insofar as they are Christians, but insofar as they are men; God gave kings for ruling the body, but bishops for ruling souls.[67]

On the other hand, Salmerón treats the civil power as deeply related to and transformed by its encounter with the ecclesiastical. He calls the emperor the immediate protector of the Church, and the firm arm of the Apostolic See for punishing heretics and schismatics and pushing back the infidels.[68] It is a teaching of divine law, he says, that Christians only choose Christian kings for themselves, and if a Catholic ruler becomes a heretic or an apostate, the faithful have the right to remove him as king. The reason is that when a king is baptized, and his nation accepts the faith, they agree to do no harm to the Christian faith, an agreement that Salmerón compares to a marriage contract.[69]

Although he seems to tacitly acknowledge the civil community's power to remove a king who violates this contract, Salmerón explicitly places the responsibility in the hands of the bishops, to whom God gave the right to investigate and judge such matters, and if necessary, to depose rulers. This means that while bishops are not properly superior to kings in temporal matters, they are so in matters that concern the faith. Temporal rulers thus have the responsibility to use their power not only for the sake of the temporal end, but also for the sacred and spiritual end, under the direction of the spiritual shepherds.[70] Kings who promote heresies and sins can be warned twice and excommunicated, but if they do not cease their behavior, they can be driven from their office by other princes (presumably at the behest of bishops). It is better, Salmerón says, for the Church to make new kings than dispute spiritual matters before infidel, heretical, or apostate ones.[71]

Salmerón sought to steer a middle course between two extreme positions on the controversial topic of tyrannicide. Some, like Cajetan, said that even private persons may slay a tyrant, whereas Bucer said that all were bound to obey tyrants in everything. According to Salmerón, a tyrant is someone who comes to power by force, rather than someone who turns the government toward his own benefit instead of the public good. He says that bad princes have to be obeyed, even when they come to power through force, in all things that do not offend God. He leans strongly toward the principle of obedience,

---

[67] *CBP*, vol. 1, 245; *CEH*, vol. 12, 337.
[68] *CEH*, vol. 12, 257.
[69] *CBP*, vol. 1, 251.
[70] *CBP*, vol. 1, 251.
[71] *CBP*, vol. 1, 252–53.

seeming to allow only offenses against the faith as legitimate grounds for armed resistance.[72]

Salmerón's theory of civil and ecclesiastical polity followed the same basic lines laid out by more renowned thinkers of his time, and it reflected the mindset, coordinating principles, and much of the social reality of the Catholic world in southern Europe during the sixteenth century. His theory also had two significant problems. First, he moved between analogous understandings of the basic terms of the discussion without acknowledgment. Sometimes "Church" referred to the clergy exclusively, whereas at other times it referred to the clergy and the faithful as distinguished from the civil authorities. Yet when dealing with a Christian polity, he treated rulers as lay members of the Church subject to the bishops, and their kingdoms as provinces within the larger whole of Christendom. When he says that the Church does not execute heretics, but only hands them over to the civil authorities who carry out the sentence by reason of state [*ratione politiae*], Salmerón trades on the ambiguity of his terms.[73] Second, the boundary between temporal and spiritual matters was both murky and the prerogative of the priests to determine, which at least in theory tipped the scales decisively in favor of the spiritual power against the civil power that he also meant to uphold.[74] He implicitly acknowledges that this is the case when he says that before princes enter into the Church, Peter is beneath them in civil matters, but not after. He regards this change of status, however, as the perfecting of the civil power rather than its destruction.[75]

Peter and His Successors

If the Church has a monarchical regime, and if in the final analysis her power is superior to the civil authority's, then a key aspect of ecclesiology is explaining the Church's supreme office. In the words of Diego Molina, the Society of Jesus made an "option for the pope" early in its history.[76] As usual, Salmerón took scripture as his point of departure, using his exegesis of the Gospel passages concerning Peter to develop his position on the papacy. Peter's trials, successes, and failures provided analogies for the behavior of popes across the ages, as well as a template for the duties of the papal office. Like the religious order to which he belonged, Salmerón had a strong view of papal authority,

---

[72] *CBP*, vol. 1, 680–81.
[73] *CBP*, vol. 3, 146.
[74] Höpfl, *Jesuit Political Thought*, 358–63.
[75] *CBP*, vol. 1, 677.
[76] Molina, *La vera sposa*, 22.

though within the limits of the faith and tradition that, in his view, the office exists to protect and preserve.

Salmerón used the earliest encounters between Peter and Jesus in the Gospels to foreshadow the papal office. The use of Peter's name in both Greek and Aramaic (Jn 1:42) shows that he is pastor of Jews and Gentiles alike, which parallels the titles "Messiah" and "Christ." Christ's request of Peter to use his boat to preach (Lk 5:3) shows that the Spirit of Christ is in the Chair of Peter alone, which teaches through the bishops.[77] The most important Petrine passage, however, is Mt 16:15–19, where Jesus entrusts the keys of the kingdom of heaven to Peter. Salmerón comments on these verses at great length, with his usual attention to the lexical, historical, and theological issues at stake. The exegesis of this passage was, of course, a hotly contested issue in the sixteenth century, with Protestants and Catholics quarreling over its significance for the institution of the papacy.

The words "rock" and "keys" are the linchpin of Salmerón's understanding of the passage. Already among the Fathers, there were various opinions about the referent of "rock." After reviewing these, Salmerón states his view: it refers to "Peter of solid faith confessing Christ," which is the foundation of the Church. He regards this as a crucial distinction, for "rock" understood as the person of Peter alone would be inadequate.[78] There are not two foundations of the Church, but Peter is the first one attached to Christ and built up as the foundation for other believers. He is not the foundation in all respects, but only in external things. Salmerón compares the relationship of Christ and Peter to that of a king and his viceroy.[79]

A key is an instrument for opening and closing, and signifies, according to the jurists, the handing on of possession. In the context of Mt 16:19, the keys signify particular powers, the first of which is the power to preach the word of God, which can also be delegated to others. Christ speaks of "keys" in the plural in reference to the two powers of orders and jurisdiction. Here Salmerón relies on a distinction made by the Scholastic Doctors between the sacramental powers conferred through ordination, and the power to rule the Church. The former concerns the true body of Christ (the Eucharist), whereas the second concerns the mystical body (the Church).[80] He interprets the act

---

[77] *CEH*, vol. 4, 170; *CEH*, vol. 4, 222.

[78] *CEH*, vol. 4, 388–91.

[79] *CEH*, vol. 4, 400. In another analogy, he says that Christ is the Good Samaritan, and Peter the innkeeper. *CBP*, vol. 1, 268.

[80] *CEH*, vol. 4, 407.

of "opening and closing" as referring to the power over the faith and the sacraments, whereas "binding and loosing" means the power of jurisdiction.[81]

The fullness of the keys that Peter and his successors possess translates into extensive powers, such that Salmerón does not hesitate to call the pope both "supreme king" and "supreme pontiff." As pontiff, he opens heaven by word and sacrament, and as king, he binds and looses according to justice and merits. Salmerón thinks this is the meaning of Peter's reference to a "kingly priesthood" (1 Pet 2:9).[82] Examples of the exercise of the pope's royal power are excommunicating, punishing and absolving, establishing laws, distributing benefices and bishoprics, convening general councils, and numerous others.[83] The pope can command the death of people, even if the sentence is carried out by others, and he can wage war upon heretics and schismatics.[84] A sign of the pope's authority to speak on behalf of all is found in his use of the "royal we."[85]

Salmerón insisted that this regal power is not given to the pope to be used according to his will and desire, but according to the equity of justice and the merits and good of each. The pope cannot err in determining true doctrine, canonizing saints, reproving heretics, or confirming new religious orders, because the error would extend to the whole Church. General councils do not have authority over such matters except from the pope.[86] Although he calls Rome the "mother and teacher" of all the churches, Salmerón places the accent of the pope's responsibility on governance rather than theology, saying that it is not his job to interpret everything in scripture.[87] Aside from these royal and priestly powers whose end is helping souls to eternal life, the Roman Pontiff has two additional powers. The first is his direct temporal rule

---

[81] *CEH*, vol. 4, 409 (Mmr).

[82] *CEH*, vol. 4, 409 (Mmr). The strong language used by papalist thinkers in this period was, in part, a response to serious challenges and obstacles to the pope's authority and power to act. The successors of Peter in this period were often in the position, practically speaking, of overseeing a commonwealth of national churches. Simon Ditchfield, "Tridentine Catholicism," in *The Ashgate Research Companion to the Counter-Reformation*, eds. Alexandra Bamji, Geert Hansen, and Mary Laven (Burlington: Ashgate, 2013), 15–31.

[83] *CEH*, vol. 4, 409–10 (Mmr–v).

[84] *CBP*, vol. 1, 253.

[85] *CEH*, vol. 12, 112.

[86] *CEH*, vol. 4, 410 (Mmv). In another place, Salmerón says that it is "piously believed" that papal canonizations are infallible, indicating that perhaps he did not view it as certain. *CEH*, vol. 11, 35.

[87] *CEH*, vol. 9, 378; *CEH*, vol. 9, 328.

over the Papal States, thanks to the donations of Constantine, Charlemagne, Matilda, and others. The second is the indirect temporal power that he has over Christian rulers, which he uses as a spiritual father to direct their power to the glory of Christ.[88]

Salmerón understood that the crucial link between Peter and the popes was the former's establishment of his see at Rome. Since this is not attested in scripture, the Jesuit theologian appealed to other historical testimonies to establish it, especially against the challenges of Marsilius of Padua and certain Protestants.[89] He dedicated twenty pages to establishing the fact, circumstances, and chronology of Peter's arrival in Rome from the testimony of the Fathers, the ecclesiastical historians, and the liturgical practice of the Church. He laid emphasis on Peter's alleged pursuit of Simon Magus to the Eternal City, which was discussed in numerous early Christian works. Salmerón also links Peter to Linus and Clement, claiming that the apostle ordained Clement, and appeals to the earliest lists of the succession of bishops at Rome.[90] He uses the following analogy to identify Peter with the popes: "as all the kings of Egypt were called 'Pharaohs,' and all the Roman Emperors 'Caesars,' so all the Roman Pontiffs are 'Peter.'"[91]

Peter's mixed record in the New Testament gave Salmerón the opportunity to both defend papal prerogatives against Protestant attacks and show their limitations. In his exegesis of "the gates of hell shall not prevail against it" (Mt 16:18), he goes against the grain of many commentaries by identifying "it" with Peter the rock, rather than the Church. The "gates of hell" refers to hell's leaders who try to bring souls down there, which includes the demons as well as heretics and schismatics. In response to the claim that Peter's denial of Christ *during* the Passion is an instance of the gates of hell prevailing against him, Salmerón counters that Peter was not *yet* the universal shepherd of the Church: the solidity of his confession was not necessary while Christ lived, but only afterward.[92]

---

[88] *CEH*, vol. 4, 410–410 (Mmv–Mm2r).

[89] He calls Marsilius a "schismatical man" who was trying to please Louis of Bavaria, and he says that his *Defensor pacis* sowed the seeds of war. *CEH*, vol. 12, 387.

[90] *CEH*, vol. 12, 376 (Ii2v); *CEH*, vol. 12, 399–400. Salmerón also uses some manuscript evidence for his life of Peter, saying that he consulted the *Regesta* of Gregory VII in the Vatican Library, and the correspondence of (pseudo)-Ignatius with Maria Cassobolita at the Medici Library in Florence. *CEH*, vol. 12, 398–99.

[91] *CEH*, vol. 12, 482.

[92] *CEH*, vol. 4, 401–02.

While Salmerón was convinced that Peter and his successors never fell away from the faith, the former's failings were real, and they provide instruction for the latter. When Christ called Peter "Satan," this showed that not all the actions he committed as a son of the Church were praiseworthy.[93] According to Salmerón, Peter rejoiced that his denial was written in all four Gospels, because he needed to be humiliated more than others, and this in turn humbles the pride of the Church's shepherds.[94] Even after Pentecost, Peter still had things to learn. When he converted Cornelius the centurion, it showed, as Jerome said, that "he passed from the narrowness of circumcision to the wideness of foreskin."[95] His vision of the sheet full of animals that he was instructed to eat, despite their uncleanness, showed that he was still being weaned from the Mosaic Law (Act 10:10–16).[96]

There are, furthermore, circumstances in which the larger Church is permitted or even obliged to intervene against the pope. If he scandalizes the whole Church, anyone can fraternally correct him, but this task pertains especially to the cardinals.[97] Immoral or scandalous conduct that does not touch upon the faith itself, however, does not give anyone else in the Church authority over the pope. Princes and bishops ought to pray and give him discrete counsel in such instances.[98] If there is doubt about who the pope is, the existence of rival claimants to the office, or a simoniacal election, then the larger Church has the authority to intervene, for anyone not canonically elected is more a demon than the Vicar of Christ, and he wields the keys of hell rather than heaven.[99]

The clearest case where the intervention of the Church is required is papal heresy, which was a standard scholastic question even among the strongest defenders of papal supremacy. Salmerón followed the thought of Juan de Torquemada, the papal apologist of the fifteenth century. Their position rested on several axioms. The papacy is conferred directly by God upon the man whom the cardinals elect, not mediately by the Church's power. A formal heretic is not a member of Christ, and therefore he cannot hold office or exercise any jurisdiction. Someone whose heresy is secret, that is, known to God but not the Church, cannot be elected pope, and if such an election were to take place, it could not stand. Salmerón positioned himself against Cajetan,

---

[93] *CEH*, vol. 4, 400.
[94] *CEH*, vol. 10, 200.
[95] *CEH*, vol. 12, 202.
[96] *CEH*, vol. 12, 208.
[97] *CEH*, vol. 12, 581.
[98] *CEH*, vol. 12, 578.
[99] *CEH*, vol. 12, 569.

who thought that a heretic could be elected, but also that the Church has the power to unmake the pope, just as it has the power to make him. The consequence of the Jesuit theologian's position is that any heretic, even a secret one, who is elected pope is actually an imposter and an antichrist. "One must not keep communion with him or obey him, but contradict him. He must not be received or greeted; he must not be tolerated, but killed, since by the same law he is deprived of any prelacy he has over the faithful."[100] Salmerón says that if a heretic were to be elected pope, eventually his heresy would be exposed, and the Church would be authorized to use necessary means, including force, to drive him out.

Papal heresy, even among the office's strongest defenders, was a subtle question. Bellarmine famously disagreed with an important aspect of this theory (which he attributed to Torquemada rather than to Salmerón) by saying that a pope only becomes a heretic when his heresy becomes public.[101] Although apparently more extreme, Salmerón's explanation separated the papal office from heresy altogether. A heretical pope is a contradiction in terms; even if dressed in the pontifical robes and seated on the chair, he can only be an imposter. Salmerón is careful to note that this has never happened, and he says that unlike the patriarchs of other sees, the popes of Rome have been preserved from heresy, after more than two hundred and thirty of them over the course of nearly sixteen hundred years.[102]

Other exegetes offered theological reflection and defense of the papacy, but not at the same length as Salmerón. In their exegesis of Mt 16, Barradas, Maldonado, and Jansen defend Peter's power of the keys and status as Vicar of Christ against Protestant attacks.[103] Maldonado claims that the Roman Church and the successors of Peter will always keep the faith and must confirm

---

[100] *CEH*, vol. 12, 603–06 (Eee3r–v). Unlike Protestants, Salmerón did not think that the pope was an antichrist, but rather that anyone who was an antichrist, *ipso facto*, could not be pope. The literary elements found in the medieval tradition of the papal antichrist, which were passed on to the Reformation, are also absent. Lawrence Buck, *The Roman Monster: An Icon of the Papal Antichrist in Reformation Polemics* (Kirksville, MO: Truman State University Press, 2014).

[101] Robert Bellarmine, *Controversies of the Christian Faith*, trans. Kenneth Baker (Saddle River, NJ: Keep the Faith Publications, 2016), 836.

[102] *CEH*, vol. 4, 403.

[103] Maldonado, *Commentaries*, vol. 1, cols. 331–43; Barradas, *Commentaries*, vol. 2, 686–93; Jansen, *Commentaries*, Tertia Pars, 26–38. Barradas sees Jn 21 as the fulfilment of the promise made to Peter in Mt 16. Barradas, *Commentaries*, vol. 4, 380–82.

the brethren in it, and that they likewise guarantee the unity of councils.[104] When commenting on the keys of the kingdom of heaven entrusted to Peter in Mt 16, Marlorat thunders against the sacrilege and tyranny of the "Roman Antichrist" who tries to substitute himself as the foundation of the Church in place of Christ.[105] Similar broadsides against the popes may be found throughout his work.

Councils

An account of Church polity requires not only an explanation of the pope's role, but also that of the ecumenical or general council. Salmerón's first priority in this regard was rejecting conciliarism, which had originated in the early fifteenth century and was very much a live issue in the sixteenth and beyond.[106] He relied especially on the anti-conciliarist works of Juan de Torquemada, as well as the ecclesiastical histories composed during the fifteenth century, to show that supreme governance of the Church lies with the pope rather than the council.[107] At the same time, Salmerón endeavored to explain the purpose of councils and how they work in tandem with the pope for the articulation of the faith and the good governance of the Church. In this he was unlike Ignatius, whose orientation toward the papacy did not include a theoretical treatment of the ecclesiological issues of the period.[108]

The word *concilium*, Salmerón says, is synonymous with the Greek *synodos*, which is a gathering together of a multitude of peoples in the same place for the sake of taking counsel. A council can be a civil gathering, in which case it discusses the political good, or it can be ecclesiastical, in which case divine things are discussed for the sake of the common good. Salmerón distinguishes

---

[104] Maldonado, *Commentaries*, vol. 2, cols. 341–42; Maldonado, *Commentaries*, vol. 1, col. 379.

[105] Marlorat, *Expositio*, vol. 1, 133–34.

[106] For an assessment of the historical origins and significance of conciliarism, see Gerald Christianson, Thomas Izbicki, and Christopher Bellitto, eds., *The Church, the Councils, and Reform: The Legacy of the Fifteenth Century* (Washington, DC: Catholic University of America Press, 2008); Francis Oakley, *The Conciliarist Tradition: Constitutionalism in the Catholic Church, 1300–1870* (New York: Oxford University Press, 2003).

[107] He is explicit about his reliance upon Torquemada. *CEH*, vol. 12, 557. For a more thorough treatment of Salmerón's reliance on Torquemada, see Hermann Josef Sieben, "Ein Traktat des Jesuiten Salmerón über in Trient strittige Fragen zur Autorität des Konzils," in *Vom Apostelkonzil zum Ersten Vatikanum: Studien zur Geschichte der Konzilsidee* (Paderborn: Ferdinand Schöningh, 1996), 435–63.

[108] Molina, *La vera sposa*, 52.

three subdivisions of ecclesiastical councils: diocesan, provincial, and ecumenical or universal. The first consists of the bishop and his clergy, the second of a metropolitan bishop and his suffragans, and the third of the greater prelates of the Church, under the authority of the pope.[109]

The first thing to note is Salmerón's initially negative assessment of councils in general. Although provincial councils used to be common in the Church, and the Council of Trent stipulated that they meet every three years, he says there are many good reasons not to hold them. Since often more bad people than good ones attend, and matters have to be put to numerous votes, they are often resolved in a less excellent way. When the wicked gather together, they defend themselves "like the armor of Behemoth" and refuse to be corrected. If learned and holy bishops attend, they help build up the Church, but often the bishops give scandal more than edification, and being together exposes and augments the vices of the participants. For these reasons, Gregory Nazianzen and Basil refused to attend them. National interests and the corrupting influence of heretics (if they are present) are additional problems.[110]

Similar problems affect ecumenical councils, the purpose of which is to define some matter of faith that pertains to the universal Church. Salmerón says that the stipulation of the Councils of Constance and Basel that a council meet every ten years was not received by the Church, and that it is against the custom of the Fathers. Frequent councils would change the Church's divinely given structure, making her into an aristocracy or an oligarchy. Sees would be deprived of their bishops, and everyone would feel put upon by the Apostolic See.[111] This attitude towards councils reflects Salmerón's own experience. Although in the *Commentaries* he speaks almost invariably in positive terms about Trent, his correspondence reveals his weariness with it. In 1562, he wrote Francis Borgia that the council was a "quagmire" [*atolladero*], and in a letter from the following year, he remarked that new prelates were about to arrive from Spain, Scotland, and Flanders, citing the words of the prophet: "thou has multiplied the nation, and hast not increased the joy" (Is 9:3).[112]

This attitude may be explained in part by Salmerón's conviction that councils do not pertain to the divine constitution of the Church. Christ did not explicitly mandate them, since he knew that they would have many problems.[113] Instead, the council came about later by the inspiration of the Holy

---

[109] *CEH*, vol. 12, 546–49.

[110] *CEH*, vol. 12, 547.

[111] *CEH*, vol. 12, 549–50.

[112] *ES*, vol. 1, no. 196, 508; *ES*, vol. 1, no. 201, 516.

[113] *CEH*, vol. 12, 552.

Spirit, who tacitly suggested the idea to Peter.[114] Salmerón seems to be referring to the meeting in Jerusalem (Act 15), but in another place, he says that no councils were called in the first three hundred years of the Church because the successor of Peter sufficed to handle matters.[115] Without saying so explicitly, the Jesuit theologian seems to make councils a matter of apostolic tradition, which serves to clearly subordinate their position in relation to the pope.

His reservations about councils notwithstanding, Salmerón defended their teaching authority. Councils cannot err if confirmed by the pope, and they have sacrosanct and inviolate authority against the heretics of the age.[116] Whoever wants to keep the faith of the Church must have the faith of the councils.[117] At the same time, he at least hints at the possibility that problems may arise when he says that a council should not be like Penelope, sewing and resewing, that is, saying "yes" and "no." Once a council has defined something, it cannot be taken away, for this would open the window to judging the decrees of earlier councils, and confirming the heretics in their errors.[118] The pope is the guarantor of the council's authority, for the Church does not have the plenitude of power from Christ except in her head.[119]

Salmerón raised the issue of who ought to attend councils besides the pope and the bishops, which was a contentious point at the time of Trent. Protestants demanded a "free council in German lands" as a condition for attending, and wrangling among churchmen and princes caused many delays. The question of Protestant attendance became especially acute concerning the second convocation, when some Lutheran envoys came to Trent. No satisfactory agreement was reached, however, on the terms of their participation, and the council's business was conducted effectively without them.[120] Salmerón was vehemently opposed to their participation. He says that those who willfully separate themselves from the Church are not sons or heirs, and therefore they should not be admitted to congresses with Catholics.[121]

---

[114] *CEH*, vol. 12, 550.
[115] *CBP*, vol. 1, 256.
[116] *CEH*, vol. 12, 561.
[117] *CEH*, vol. 12, 562.
[118] *CEH*, vol. 12, 558.
[119] *CEH*, vol. 12, 568.
[120] John O'Malley, *Trent: What Happened at the Council* (Cambridge, MA: Belknap Press, 2013), 149–58.
[121] *CEH*, vol. 1, 373.

Enemies of the Church

The defensive edge already evident in Salmerón's discussion of ecclesiastical polity became considerably sharper with respect to those he identified as the Church's open enemies, namely, Jews, heretics, schismatics, pagans, and Muslims. In his view, the Catholic Church is always beset by enemies, but especially during his time. Although he gave most of his attention to the external enemies, the Jesuit theologian also targeted certain Catholics whom he perceived as dangerous to the faith.

Although he had no shortage of harsh language for the Church's enemies, Salmerón insisted on the principle of charity in dealing with them, while using it to establish a hierarchy among them. The Church prays against her enemies, not to harm them but to maintain her own existence and procure their salvation. He cites verbatim the Collect against persecutors: "Crush, O Lord, we beseech Thee, the pride of our enemies, and prostrate their arrogance by the might of Thy right hand."[122] Citing Paul, Augustine, and Thomas, Salmerón claims that there is a proper order of charity regarding different groups of enemies, according to their degree of love for the Church. Heretics should be loved less than Jews, Jews less than Muslims or pagans, and Muslims or pagans less than sinful Catholics.[123] This "order of charity" is manifest in Salmerón's treatment of each individual group.

Heretics

Those who obstinately denied the articles of the Catholic faith were, in Salmerón's view, the worst of the Church's enemies, and combatting them was a principal motivation behind the *Commentaries*. Although his native land was relatively free of heresy, his time in Italy and Ingolstadt gave him firsthand knowledge of the problem. In addition, some Italian religious circles he considered heterodox made calumnious counter-accusations of heresy against him, including the story that he had absconded to Geneva with a large sum of money.[124] These facts help to explain the sharpness of his polemics.

---

[122] *CEH*, vol. 5, 270–71. "Hostium nostrorum, quaesumus, Domine, elide superbiam, eorumque contumaciam dexterae tuae prosterne."

[123] *CEH*, vol. 5, 84; *CEH*, vol. 8, 497.

[124] Mario Scaduto, *L'epoca di Giacomo Laínez, 1556–1565: Il governo* (Rome: Edizioni La Civiltà Cattolica, 1964), 301. Salmerón's response, as communicated in a letter to a fellow Jesuit, was as follows: "By the grace of God, I will be the Catholic persecutor of heretics I have always been, and as poor and content in my poverty as the pope and the king are content in their palace and realm. And besides, I will laugh at those who accuse me of such things."

In any case, the *Commentaries* are an important witness to Catholic attitudes toward heresy in the sixteenth century.[125] Although Salmerón represented the confrontational approach generally favored in the Society, militant Jesuits in Central Europe sometimes risked alienating local Catholics or earning rebukes from their order's Roman authorities.[126]

Although primarily concerned with Protestants, whom he often calls "the heretics of our age," Salmerón thought of heresy as part of the ongoing conflict between Christ and Satan throughout history. This led him to offer a history of heresy from the Flood onwards. According to him, the dawn of the Christian era witnessed the formation of two major families that gave rise to all subsequent heretics. One was the category of "Judaizers": Nazarenes, Ebionites, and Pharisees. The other took its origin from Simon Magus, and it included Menander, Basilides, Nicholas, the Gnostics, Carpocrates, and others.[127] This genealogy of heresy helped illuminate what Salmerón saw as the deeper affinities and connections between different groups, whatever their quarrels with the Catholic Church and with each other.

Salmerón avers that heretics are guilty of the sin against the Holy Spirit, since they attribute the teaching of the Church, monastic life, and ecclesiastical ceremonies to the spirit of Satan.[128] They raise their heel against the Church who raised them, just as Judas lifted his heel against Jesus at the Last Supper.[129] They follow the way of Balaam, in that they curse the Roman Church for the sake of money, whereas Balaam's ass stands for the humble men of the Church whom they burden and try to lead into error.[130] Here-

---

[125] These attitudes varied widely, from the most zealous champions of persecution to advocates of equal protection under the laws of the realm, like Michel de l'Hopital. There were also many forms of practical toleration in the period. See Benjamin Kaplan, *Divided by Faith: Religious Conflict and the Practice of Toleration in Early Modern Europe* (Cambridge, MA: Belknap Press, 2007).

[126] Markus Friedrich, *The Jesuits: A History*, trans. John Noël Dillon (Princeton, NJ: Princeton University Press, 2022), 248–54. Höpfl complains that militant attitudes developed effortlessly among the early Jesuits, and that among the founders, only Faber was at all generous in this regard. Höpfl, *Jesuit Political Thought*, 64. The image of Peter Canisius as a proto-ecumenist has been challenged. Hilmar Pabel, "Peter Canisius and the Protestants: A Model of Ecumenical Dialogue?" *Journal of Jesuit Studies* 1 (2014): 373–99. Surprisingly, Salmerón himself praised Canisius for his mild approach toward Protestants. *ES*, vol. 2, no. 366, 312–13.

[127] *CBP*, vol. 1, 39.

[128] *CEH*, vol. 8, 123.

[129] *CEH*, vol. 9, 57.

[130] *CBP*, vol. 4, 131.

tics pollute the name of God by their false doctrine, and their sacraments are the bread of demons.[131] Salmerón associates them with darkness, as when he says that they look for shadows at noon, or that they fall into "Cimmerian and beyond-Egyptian gloom, neither understanding the things of which they speak, nor the things they assert."[132]

Near the end of his commentary on the Sermon on the Mount, Salmerón offers an excursus on the ten "garments" that Protestants wear, meaning the characteristics that identify them as enemies. They talk about Christ and the Gospels, but their praise is not in the assembly of the holy ones, but in the assembly of the wicked. They venerate scripture, but they judge everything in it that speaks against them. They teach many true things, but so do demons and all other heretics. They claim to have taste for divine things, but their Christ is fake and their taste comes from the devil. They often suffer persecutions, but not for the sake of righteousness.[133] Generally fond of litanies of this type, Salmerón almost seems to take glee in narrating the alleged offenses of heretics.

In addition to the sin of heresy per se, Salmerón charged Protestants with additional offenses. The rejection of the Church's teaching entails the rejection of all legitimate authority, resulting in the bloody tragedies that have come about under the false pretext of freedom.[134] It is clear, he says, what sort of fruit their new Gospel bears: disobedience, first to the pope, councils, priests, and religious, and then also to kings and princes.[135] The heretics, Salmerón claims, worship Mars in place of Christ, and the Anabaptists in particular attack rulers, the people, and naked virgins.[136] The heretics' putative zeal for Christ is like Judas's zeal for the poor, which led to the destruction of monasteries and the defiling of nuns in Germany.[137]

This charge of licentiousness is prominent in the *Commentaries*. While the pope can dispense from religious vows, Salmerón thinks this is a far cry from the case of heretics who break their vows and take nuns as their wives, which is a sacrilege.[138] He claims that indulgence of the flesh is always part of heresy.

---

[131] *CEH*, vol. 5, 298; *CEH*, vol. 6, 204.
[132] *CEH*, vol. 9, 442; *CBP*, vol. 3, 40.
[133] *CEH*, vol. 5, 401–02.
[134] *CEH*, vol. 3, 100 (M6v).
[135] *CEH*, vol. 3, 407–08.
[136] *CBP*, vol. 1, 226; *CBP*, vol. 1, 232–33.
[137] *CBP*, vol. 1, 234.
[138] *CEH*, vol. 3, 62.

Luther the consecrated monk turned to marriage, and he allowed men to copulate with their servants when their wives were ill. Bucer married thrice and permitted polygamy, and Karlstadt the priest publicly married his wife with a rite that encouraged all priests and monks to follow his example.[139] Despite the exalted names they give themselves, the new heretics are actually lascivious and gluttonous: they drink all the time, take young girls, and fail to follow the evangelical counsels.[140] They grunt like dirty pigs and "new followers of Jovinian" when they commend marriage against the life of chastity, making wide the way of the Lord instead of narrow by taking away the inconvenience of the flesh.[141] Often enough, though, Salmerón is content to hurl insults without specifying the offense, as when he refers to Calvin, Bucer, and others on numerous occasions as "wretches" [*nebulones*].[142] He identifies Luther and "other monsters" as the false prophets of whom Jeremiah speaks (Lam 2:14), whereas Zwingli is called "Absalom" and "traitor Judas."[143]

Language of this kind is too consistent and deliberate to be the product of mere intemperance, and indeed Salmerón defended in principle this way of speaking. In his commentary on the Sermon on the Mount, he explains the meaning of the Lord's words "whoever shall say, Thou Fool, shall be in danger of hell fire" (Mt 5:22). Citing the words of Christ to the scribes and the Pharisees, his rebuke to the disciples on the way to Emmaus, and the *Letter to the Galatians*, Salmerón says that one can use insult for the sake of correction, out of zeal for faith and religion, or for inflicting confusion and infamy on those who offend the faith. "Whence all the Catholic Fathers, otherwise so modest, sharpen their teeth for biting heretics, and reveal their sins, and inveigh against them publicly."[144] He gives examples of such attacks in the writings of Polycarp, Cyprian, Epiphanius, and Jerome, and elsewhere he praises numerous Fathers for narrating the sins and crimes of heretics, adding the name of Cochlaeus, who wrote against Luther.[145] At the same time, he

---

[139] *CBP*, vol. 4, 129.

[140] *CBP*, vol. 1, 227–28.

[141] *CEH*, vol. 6, 67–68; *CEH*, vol. 5, 398. The "Jovinian" insult refers to the fourth-century heretic who said that marriage and virginity were equal states of life. This polemic was revived in the sixteenth century. See Hilmar Pabel, "Reading Jerome in the Renaissance: Erasmus' Reception of the 'Adversus Jovinianum,'" *Renaissance Quarterly* 55, no. 2 (2002): 470–97.

[142] *CBP*, vol. 2, 81; *CBP*, vol. 3, 471; *CBP*, vol. 3, 544; *CBP*, vol. 4, 142; *CBP*, vol. 4, 286.

[143] *CEH*, vol. 4, 215; *CBP*, vol. 1, 266.

[144] *CEH*, vol. 5, 202–03.

[145] *CEH*, vol. 5, 203; *CEH*, vol. 5, 145.

complains against the abusive names that Protestants use for the popes, councils, and saints.[146]

The content and style of Salmerón's treatment of heresy was hardly atypical for the period, for both Catholic and Protestant commentators were apt to hurl such invective at each other. Luther was famous for his insults, and other writers brought out strong language when they thought it was warranted. Salmerón's complaint against Protestant insults reveals too the widespread rejection of moral equivalence. The legitimacy of abusive language in the period's cross-confessional discourse depended less on the content than on the identity of the speaker and his target.[147] Although generally less aggressive in tone or colorful in word choice than Salmerón, all the other exegetes under consideration ridiculed the teachings, and occasionally the members, of other Christian communities.

As a general rule, Salmerón did not agree with the strategy of highlighting common ground between Catholics and Protestants, for he did not believe that they were divided merely by one particular teaching or another. He speaks of the heretics' "new Christ" and "new Gospel," and their "new idolatry of a new god."[148] According to Salmerón, they have only a fake and lying Christ, a new Christ who is not like that of the Church's teaching and worship, but is, rather, opposed to it. He says that this new Christ makes the true Christ a lying prophet, since according to the Protestant account, the latter lied about his promise to the Church. This is the ultimate explanation why the congregations of Luther and Calvin are spurious: if united to a false head, the body is merely imaginary.[149] The new Christ pleases the world by telling people to remain carnal, and he only left behind bread and wine, not the true sacrifice of the priest after the order of Melchizedek.[150]

Although this theme appears rarely in the *Commentaries*, Salmerón defended in principle the use of coercive and repressive measures against heretics. He treats apostates and heretics as "deserters" who remain subject to the

---

[146] *CEH*, vol. 5, 208.

[147] Susan C. Karant-Nunn, "The Wrath of Martin Luther: Anger and Charisma in the Reformer," *Sixteenth Century Journal* 48, vol. 4 (2017): 909–26; Constance Furey, "Invective and Discernment in Martin Luther, D. Erasmus, and Thomas More," *Harvard Theological Review* 98, vol. 4 (2005): 469–88; Peter Maatheson, *The Imaginative World of the Reformation* (Edinburgh: T&T Clark, 2000), 77–92.

[148] *CEH*, vol. 4, 261–62.

[149] *CBP*, vol. 1, 222.

[150] *CBP*, vol. 1, 224 (T4r).

Church, and he expresses gratitude for inquisitors and their activities.[151] He defends the use of capital punishment, saying that heretics are justly executed by Catholic princes as seditious persons.[152] Noting that heretics are sometimes condemned posthumously, even to the point of exhuming their bones, Salmerón says that these actions only affect their reputation and their body.[153]

His vehemence against heresy may have owed something to the protean character of Protestant influence in Italy, where the lines of orthodoxy were rather blurry, and to the fact that heresy was regarded as a serious threat in Naples when he arrived in the 1550s.[154] In any case, he was far from extreme in the context of the sixteenth century. In the 1540s, the first Jesuits were establishing for themselves, in close collaboration with the Dominican Ambrogio Catarino, a reputation for both defending Roman orthodoxy and using persuasion rather than coercion to reconcile heretics to the Church.[155] The prominent cases of Federico Orlandini and Giovan Battista Scotti witnessed a non-inquisitorial approach that, in Scotti's case, even violated the legal norms for dealing with relapsed heretics. Salmerón himself gave Scotti absolution, anticipating the controverted privilege the Society received from Julius III in 1551 to absolve heresy in the forum of conscience.[156]

On rare occasions, Salmerón expressed himself less sharply about heretics. He says all men are to be loved, including heretics, infidels, and criminals,

---

[151] *CEH*, vol. 10, 225; *CEH*, vol. 5, 136; *CEH*, vol. 12, 338. He also mentions the practice of dressing heretics in the *sanbenito*. *CEH*, vol. 3, 319.

[152] *CEH*, vol. 4, 532–33.

[153] *CEH*, vol. 4, 416.

[154] Giorgio Caravale, *Preaching and Inquisition in Renaissance Italy: Words on Trial*, trans. Frank Gordon (Boston, MA: Brill, 2016), 3–4; Emily Michelson, *The Pulpit and the Press in Reformation Italy* (Cambridge, MA: Harvard University Press, 2013), 8, 54. Naples had rebelled in 1547 over Viceroy Toledo's attempt to establish the Spanish Inquisition in the kingdom. See Aurelio Musi, "Political History," in *A Companion to Early Modern Naples*, ed. Tommaso Astarita (Boston, MA: Brill, 2013), 131–51, at 139–40.

[155] Salmerón and Paschase Broët were reconciling heretics in this way in Bologna four years before the papal privilege to do so was granted, apparently with the support of prominent delegates at the Council of Trent. These actions drew the ire of local ecclesiastical authorities. Jessica Dalton, *Between Popes, Inquisitors and Princes: How the First Jesuits Negotiated Religious Crisis in Early Modern Italy* (Boston, MA: Brill, 2020), 42–43.

[156] Giorgio Caravale, *Beyond the Inquisition: Ambrogio Catarino and the Origins of the Counter-Reformation*, trans. Don Weinstein (Notre Dame, IN: University of Notre Dame Press, 2017), 170–73.

because all men are neighbors.[157] When he identifies reasons why people leave the Catholic Church, he acknowledges positive motivations as well as negative ones.[158] In his exegesis of the parable of the sower, he says that mystically the land along the path can stand for the heretic, who is not far from the Church, since he believes many truths.[159] Occasionally he also acknowledges their correct interpretations of scripture, as when he praises the exegesis of Calvin.[160]

The Jews

To use modern theological parlance, Salmerón was firmly "supersessionist" in his understanding of the relationship between the Church and the Jews. He says that the latter lost the dignity of being God's people by denying Christ, a dignity that has passed to Christians.[161] "For we are the true Jews, praising the glory of Christ, and confessing our sins and his righteousness."[162] According to Salmerón, Jesus's intent was not to gather the ten tribes, nor the scattered kingdom of Judah, but to bring together the Church.[163] He says that the Jews sold their inheritance for a bowl of lentils, like Esau, which is why they cannot address God as Father.[164] Salmerón did not see worshipping the same God or keeping the Decalogue as a point of common ground between Jews and Christians. Instead, he says that the Pharisees, along with all the Jews, destroy the commandments. By pertinaciously remaining in their sect and claiming for the Law a power it does not have, they destroy the whole Law.[165]

Salmerón claimed that the Jews had been justly punished in a variety of ways for their sins. He says that the generation that killed Christ was punished not only for this, but for the killing of all the just from the time of Abel.[166] Foremost in his mind is the destruction of Jerusalem by the Romans, which took away their hope of a future Messiah.[167] If Jerusalem were to be rebuilt a

---

[157] *CEH*, vol. 8, 495.
[158] *CEH*, vol. 12, 28. He includes pride and desire for novelty, zeal against abuses, interaction with heretics or their books, and sleeping shepherds.
[159] *CEH*, vol. 7, 25.
[160] *CEH*, vol. 8, 298.
[161] *CEH*, vol. 3, 244.
[162] *CEH*, vol. 5, 177.
[163] *CEH*, vol. 4, 634.
[164] *CEH*, vol. 5, 288.
[165] *CEH*, vol. 5, 181.
[166] *CEH*, vol. 4, 631–32.
[167] *CEH*, vol. 4, 525; *CEH*, vol. 4, 427.

thousand times and given to the Jews, he claims, the Gentiles would still trample it down, at least until the times of the Gentiles are fulfilled.[168] "If the most holy man Zechariah paid the penalty for momentary unbelief, the Jews will pay a much heavier one for their pertinacious and continuing unbelief.".[169]

The Jesuit theologian displayed a skeptical attitude, however, toward more outlandish claims about blood guilt. Some claim that Jewish babies are born with a handful of blood over their heads, he says, or that on Good Friday Jewish men and women suffer a flow of blood that leaves them pale, or that they suffer the same thing during a full moon. "But because these things are not supported with the solid testimonies of historians, we do not dare to assert them, leaving their trustworthiness to the judgment of prudent readers."[170] In other words, Salmerón sought to retain his criterion of historical truth even when dealing with those he regarded as enemies.

In his commentary on the words "his blood be upon us and our children" (Mt 27:25), Salmerón approvingly offers a litany of the social restrictions to which Jews are subject by Christian law. They cannot be lawyers, assessors, doctors, notaries, or procurators to popes or princes. They cannot have Christian servants, or inherit anything from clerics to whom they are related. They cannot build new synagogues or expand existing ones, and Christians should not be familiar with them. Jews must serve Christians on account of the death of Christ, as Constantine said, although they are not in civil servitude. They should wear distinctive dress, as is done at Rome and Venice. They cannot enjoy ecclesiastical immunity or sanctuary, even if they want to become Christian. The Jews, Salmerón concludes, are worse than the Gentiles and the citizens of Sodom, and God wants to treat them this way as a stimulus to conversion.[171] These strictures were almost certainly inspired by the restrictive policies that a series of popes, beginning with Paul IV, imposed upon Jews in the Papal States.[172] Polities of the period often tried to keep Jews and Christians separate, but there were plenty of exceptions to this in practice and in principle.[173]

---

[168] *CEH*, vol. 4, 666.

[169] *CEH*, vol. 2, 265.

[170] *CEH*, vol. 10, 273.

[171] *CEH*, vol. 10, 273–74.

[172] Katherine Aron-Beller, "Ghettoization: The Papal Enclosure and its Jews," in *A Companion to Early Modern Rome*, eds. Pamela Jones, Barbara Wisch, and Simon Ditchfield (Boston, MA: Brill, 2019), 232–46.

[173] Katherine Aron-Beller, "Disciplining Jews: The Papal Inquisition of Modena, 1598–1630," *Sixteenth Century Journal* 41, no. 3 (2010): 713–29; Lisa Kaborycha, "'We do not sell them this tolerance:' Grand Duke Fernando I's Protection of Jews

Salmerón occasionally said things that softened his tone. The Jews should not be oppressed, since this impedes their conversion.[174] Christians should not be proud, even if they have privileges, in relation to Jews and Turks, for Christ died for them too. Perhaps tomorrow they will convert, he says, despite the impediment that the bad life of Christians presents.[175] Salmerón sees the repeated efforts of the great powers of the earth to destroy the Jews as part of the devil's effort to destroy man in general.[176] Once he even gives credit to the Jews as a way of shaming Christians: if there were a quarter of Jewish zeal in Christians, everyone's garments would be rent, given the widespread practice of blasphemy against God and the saints among the faithful.[177]

There is evidence that Salmerón had personal dealings with actual Jews, although not in his native Spain.[178] One of Ignatius's first foundations in Rome was a house of catechumens, which obtained its first convert in 1541. The baptism was celebrated in the presence of men and women of rank, with Salmerón performing the rite and Laínez preaching.[179] In his discussion of Jewish practices of ritual washing, Salmerón says that while he was in Germany, he witnessed the weekly washing of all meal paraphernalia, including tables and benches. Does this mean that he entered a Jewish home?[180] He reports that the city of Salonica (formerly Thessalonica) is now a place where apostates to Judaism go, and that the Jews have a market there.[181] Salmerón's interest in Jewish ritual and ceremony, such as the fastening of scrolls to bodies, is also a consistent feature of the *Commentaries*.[182] Some of his information was

---

in Tuscany and the Case of Jacob Esperiel," *Sixteenth Century Journal* 49, vol. 4 (2018): 987–1018; Debra Kaplan and Magda Teter, "Out of the (Historiographic) Ghetto: European Jews and Reformation Narratives," *Sixteenth Century Journal* 40, no. 2 (2009): 365–94.

[174] *CEH*, vol. 12, 263.
[175] *CBP*, vol. 4, 202.
[176] *CEH*, vol. 3, 392.
[177] *CEH*, vol. 5, 61.
[178] The absence of Jews from the Iberian Peninsula after the expulsions did not prevent a brisk output of anti-Jewish literature. Bruno Feitler, *The Imaginary Synagogue: Anti-Jewish Literature in the Portuguese Early Modern World* (Boston, MA: Brill, 2015).
[179] Robert Maryks, *The Jesuit Order as a Synagogue of Jews: Jesuits of Jewish Ancestry and Purity-of-Blood Laws in the Early Society of Jesus* (Boston, MA: Brill, 2010), 60–61.
[180] *CEH*, vol. 8, 231–32.
[181] *CBP*, vol. 3, 358.
[182] *CEH*, vol. 4, 613–14.

obtained from the work of his contemporary Immanuel Tremellius (1510–80), who first converted from Judaism to Catholicism and then to Calvinism. He taught Hebrew in England and Germany, and he was responsible for translating the Bible.[183]

Salmerón offered a subtle criticism of the Jewish policies of Christian kingdoms. When discussing the salvation of all Israel (Rom 11:25–26), Salmerón observes that in some kingdoms or provinces, princes have forced the Jews to choose between Baptism and expulsion. "Even if this was done out of zeal for God, it did not have a happy outcome, because that conversion did not come from the heart, as experience itself openly demonstrated."[184] This seems to be a thinly veiled criticism of the policy of his native kingdom, which Salmerón avoids mentioning by name. Although he supported all manner of social pressure to encourage Jewish conversion, he stopped short of anything that he regarded as coercion in the strict sense.[185]

Salmerón's anti-Jewish polemic, however reprehensible, was primarily concerned with theology rather than blood or ancestry. This point is underscored by his treatment of converts to Christianity, or *conversos*. This was a vast and complex issue in the sixteenth century, particularly in the Society of Jesus. One accusation against the young order was that it was under the control of *conversos*, especially with the emergence of a "triumvirate" after Ignatius's death: Juan de Polanco, Jerome Nadal, and Salmerón's friend Laínez. After heated controversy over the issue, the Society barred entrance to descendants of Jews and Muslims at General Congregation V (1593–94).[186] Salmerón

---

[183] *CEH*, vol. 9, 22.

[184] *CBP*, vol. 1, 655.

[185] To be sure, the *Commentaries* are hardly vocal on this point, and Salmerón clearly saw the Jews as recalcitrant, saying they are harder to convert than Gentiles. *CEH*, vol. 12, 90.

[186] The issue of *conversos* in the Society has generated abundant literature, of which only a sampling is offered here. James Reites, *St. Ignatius and the People of the Book: An Historical-Theological Study of St. Ignatius of Loyola's Spiritual Motivation in His Dealings with the Jews and Muslims* (Rome: Pontifical Gregorian University, 1977); Marc Rastoin, *Du même sang que Notre Seigneur: Juifs et jésuites aux débuts de la Compagnie* (Paris: Bayard, 2011); Mariano Delgado, "…todos los males y perturbaciones de la Compañía han venido de ellos:" Reflexiones acerca del giro anti-converso en la Compañía de Jesús," in *Diego Laínez (1512–1565) and his Generalate: Jesuit with Jewish Roots, Close Confidant of Ignatius of Loyola, Preeminent Theologian of the Council of Trent*, ed. Paul Oberholzer (Rome: IHSI, 2015), 191–213; Robert John Clines, "How to Become a Jesuit Crypto-Jew: The Self-Confessionalization of Giovanni Battista Eliano through the Textual Artifice of Conversion," *Sixteenth Century Journal* 48, vol. 1 (2017): 3–26; Claude Stuczynski, "Jesuits and Conversos

attacks "false Christians" who persecute men of Jewish ancestry and try to take away from them all offices and honors, whether civil or ecclesiastical. Such people forget that Christ died for everyone.[187] In another place, he includes descendants of Muslim ancestry as victims of this behavior, complaining that it is a grave sin against the peace of the Church.[188] His emphasis on the Church as a spiritual community that brings together Jew and Gentile into one body was incompatible with the contemporary vogue for "purity of blood," which is why he opposed discriminatory measures against *conversos* in the Society of Jesus.[189]

Other exegetes also treated the Jews as enemies, but not in the same way. Maldonado says that the Jews of recent times have fallen far from the holiness of their ancestors, he criticizes them for giving Mary abuse rather than praise, and he accuses them of perfidy and contumacy more generally.[190] Jansen occasionally repeats standard tropes of Jewish rejection of Jesus, unbelief, and blasphemy.[191] Barradas's treatment of the Jews is closer to Salmerón's steady drumbeat of accusations and criticism, including their eternal condition of exile, although his perspective is overall more apocalyptic.[192] Marlorat offers a fairly standard litany of accusations against Jewish carnality, unbelief,

---

as a 'Tragic Couple': Introductory Remarks," *Journal of Jesuit Studies* 8 (2021): 159–72; David Martín López, "Jesuits and Conversos in Sixteenth-Century Toledo," *Journal of Jesuit Studies* 8 (2021): 173–94.

[187] *CBP*, vol. 4, 218. The marginal note even calls this a certain way of "Judaizing." Sicily and Naples had large, highly integrated *converso* populations in the sixteenth century, which may have influenced Salmerón's perspective. See Fabrizio D'Avenia, "From Spain to Sicily after the Expulsion: *Conversos* between Economic Networks and the Aristocratic Elite," *Journal of Early Modern History* 22 (2018): 421–45.

[188] *CBP*, vol. 3, 204. As David Graizbord observes, the expression of sympathy for New Christians or even expelled Jews did not necessarily make one a "Judeophile" in Spain. David Graizbord, "Philosemitism in Late Sixteenth- and Seventeenth-Century Iberia: Refracted Judeophobia?" *Sixteenth Century Journal* 38, no. 3 (2007): 657–82.

[189] Maryks, *Jesuit Order*, 141. On the basis of his defense of *conversos*, García de Castro concludes that Salmerón was "very probably" of *converso* descent himself, but stronger proofs are lacking. José García de Castro Valdés, *Polanco: El humanismo de los jesuitas (Burgos 1517–Roma 1576)* (Madrid: Comillas, 2012), 189–90.

[190] Maldonado, *Commentaries*, vol. 2, col. 28; Maldonado, *Commentaries*, vol. 2, col. 62; Maldonado, *Commentaries*, vol. 2, cols. 151–52.

[191] Jansen, *Commentaries*, Prima Pars, 45; Jansen, *Commentaries*, Secunda Pars, 354; Jansen, *Commentaries*, Secunda Pars, 313.

[192] Barradas, *Commentaries*, vol. 3, 546–48; Barradas, *Commentaries*, vol. 3, 551–59; Barradas, *Commentaries*, vol. 1, 16–17; Barradas, *Commentaries*, vol. 1, 50.

blindness, and blasphemy, while also consistently highlighting the "Jewish prerogative," that is, their place of priority in the Church with respect to the calling of the Gentiles.[193]

Pagans

Although he was also critical of ancient philosophers, Salmerón's main "pagan" target was the Muslims.[194] He usually refers to them as "Mohammedans" [*mahometani*], although he says that the proper term is "Hagarenes," [*agareni*], since they descend from Ishmael.[195] The *Commentaries* do not evince detailed knowledge of Islam, and its placement in the category of paganism indicates that Salmerón regarded it as further removed from Christianity than Judaism, even if Muslims rank higher in the order of charity than the Jews.

Regarding its origin, Salmerón claims that the "sect of Mohammed" was formed out of other sects, like pagans, idolaters, Samaritans, and others who were cut off from the Jews, along with Arian heretics like Sergius and Paul the Monk.[196] The presence of the last two figures suggests that perhaps Salmerón also thought of Islam as a Christian heresy. He includes Mohammed among the deniers of the Trinity and the Incarnation (with a citation from Sura 11 of the Qur'an), saying that he learned his denial of Christ's divinity from heretical groups that are now extinct.[197] He disputes the Muslim claim that Jesus's actual words to his disciples were, "When Mohammed comes, whom I will send from the Father" (see Jn 15:26).[198] This evidence suggests that Salmerón was uncertain about the status of Islam, which in some places he treated as paganism, but in others as heresy. In any case, he gave little attention to the endeavor of converting Muslims to Christianity.[199]

---

[193] For the Jewish prerogative, see Marlorat, *Expositio*, vol. 1, 58; Marlorat, *Expositio*, vol. 1, 314.

[194] He groups Muslim attacks on the Gospels together with the teaching of other pagans. *CEH*, vol. 1, 435–36.

[195] *CEH*, vol. 4, 192. The term "Saracens" appears occasionally as well.

[196] *CBP*, vol. 1, 200. Salmerón claims that Islam will end after a thousand years, and attributes this view to Muslim teaching as well.

[197] *CEH*, vol. 1, 98; *CEH*, vol. 1, 101; *CEH*, vol. 4, 430.

[198] *CEH*, vol. 1, 436.

[199] This is perhaps surprising given the contemporary efforts to do so, particularly in Naples, which had a large Islamic slave population that churchmen of the sixteenth and seventeenth centuries sought to Christianize. Peter Mazur, "Combating 'Mohammedan Indecency': The Baptism of Muslim Slaves in Spanish Naples, 1563–1667," *Journal of Early Modern History* 13 (2009): 25–48.

It is clear that Salmerón had a low estimation of Mohammed and his teaching, which he places in the category of false law.[200] He thought that the Qur'an was more suited to beasts than to man's reason, like the work of a drunk or demented man.[201] "Impurity" is a term he frequently associates with Islam, principally because Mohammed allegedly taught that happiness (including the life of heaven) consisted in carnal delights, which makes Aristotle's teaching better than his.[202] Bellicosity and cruelty are themes that appear now and again in connection with Islam, as when Salmerón claims that Islam was spread primarily by the sword, and that Mohammed was a promoter of unjust war.[203] This waging of war against Christ's followers, says the Jesuit theologian, makes Mohammed and the Turks types of the Antichrist, and the beast with seven heads and ten horns refers to the coming of Mohammed.[204]

Bad Catholics

The *Commentaries* are peppered with general laments about the bad behavior of Catholics, both for the risk it poses to their salvation and the scandal that it gives to others. Since such people, in Salmerón's view, do not deviate from the faith, they are the least wicked of those who oppose Christ, and therefore the most deserving of charity. There were two coreligionists, however, whom Salmerón consistently associated with bad exegesis and doctrine, and therefore regarded as a serious threat: the Dutch humanist Desiderius Erasmus and the Dominican cardinal Tommaso de Vio, better known as Cajetan. After formal heretics, they appear most frequently as foils for the Jesuit theologian's exposition of scripture and the Catholic faith.

Although Salmerón did not say as much, it seems likely that he learned his distaste for them at a relatively young age. The University of Alcalá had Erasmian sympathizers, but Salmerón would have begun his education right around the time that the Dutchman's teachings were condemned at Valladolid in 1527. More significantly, Salmerón arrived in Paris amidst heated anti-Erasmian polemics, led by Noël Beda, syndic of the College of Montaigu. The Paris faculty's official condemnation of Erasmus's works appeared in print

---

[200] *CEH*, vol. 5, 2.
[201] *CEH*, vol. 5, 4.
[202] *CEH*, vol. 1, 231; *CEH*, vol. 1, 414.
[203] *CEH*, vol. 1, 414; *CEH*, vol. 12, 263.
[204] *CBP*, vol. 3, 388–89; *CBP*, vol. 4, 365. At the same time, he denies that Mohammed was personally the Antichrist.

in 1531.²⁰⁵ As for Cajetan, Salmerón may have been inspired by his friend Ambrogio Catarino. In 1542, he wrote a polemical work against his fellow Dominican, *Annotations against Cajetan's Commentaries on Sacred Scripture*, which identified Erasmus as the source of some of Cajetan's opinions.²⁰⁶

Erasmus, whom Salmerón derides as a "manufacturer of novelties" and "the censor of heaven and earth," is his principal target.²⁰⁷ Salmerón accuses him of two major errors in biblical exegesis: rejecting the spiritual sense, and imputing lapses of memory to the sacred authors.²⁰⁸ In addition, he attacked the Dutchman's editions of the New Testament on two principal grounds. First, it was impertinent of him to reject the Vulgate and replace it with his own version.²⁰⁹ Second, Salmerón considered many of his editorial choices to be erroneous. Sometimes his objections are merely textual, as when Salmerón says that Erasmus should not have translated *tektōn* as "carpenter" instead of the more general term "artisan."²¹⁰

Often, however, Salmerón linked the editorial choices to doctrinal error, especially Arianism. He found evidence for this charge in Erasmus's substitution of *sermo* for *verbum* in Jn 1:1, in his rejection of the "Johannine comma," and in his denial of Peter's explicit knowledge of the divinity of Christ when he made his confession at Caesarea Philippi.²¹¹ In addition, Erasmus is accused of resurrecting the Pelagian error in his translation of Rom 5:12, of doubting the perfection of Christ's soul from the moment of his conception, of wrongly

---

²⁰⁵ Erika Rummel, *Erasmus and his Catholic Critics* (Nieuwkoop: De Graaf, 1989), vol. 2, 49.

²⁰⁶ Ambrogio Catarino, *Annotationes in commentaria Cajetani super sacram Scripturam* (Lyons: Matthias Bonhomme, 1542); Rummel, *Erasmus*, vol. 2, 129. Rummel incorrectly identifies the publication year of this work as 1532. For the polemic between Catarino and Cajetan about the interpretation of scripture, see Allan Jenkins and Patrick Preston, *Biblical Scholarship and the Church: A Sixteenth-Century Crisis of Authority* (Aldershot: Ashgate, 2007), 149–72.

²⁰⁷ *CEH*, vol. 3, 311; *CEH*, vol. 6, 295.

²⁰⁸ *CEH*, vol. 1, 69; *CEH*, vol. 1, 106.

²⁰⁹ Salmerón includes Erasmus in a list with Lorenzo Valla, Lefèvre d'Étaples, and Cajetan who sing this "lullaby" (*cantilena*) against the Vulgate. *CEH*, vol. 1, 416. For the importance of Erasmus's editions of the New Testament, see Riemer Faber, "Erasmus' *Novum Instrumentum* (1516): Reforming the Bible into the Bible of the Reformation," in *Renaissance und Bibelhumanismus*, eds. J. Marius J. Lange van Ravenswaay and Herman Selderhuis (Göttingen: Vandenhoeck & Ruprecht, 2020), 294–312.

²¹⁰ *CEH*, vol. 4, 323.

²¹¹ *CEH*, vol. 2, 16–18; *CEH*, vol. 2, 49–50; *CEH*, vol. 4, 387.

interpreting the Lord's teaching on oaths, and even of claiming that the parable of the steward praises theft.²¹² The *Commentaries* are filled with such jabs against the Dutch humanist, which sets Salmerón apart from the other exegetes under consideration. Jansen consistently shows Erasmus respect, whereas Barradas cites him sparingly on textual issues, but without animus. Marlorat also cites him on textual matters, but in one instance excoriates him concerning the corruption of the human race in Adam (Rom 5:12).²¹³

Like other critics of the period, Salmerón made a connection between Erasmus and the heretical movements of the sixteenth century.²¹⁴ The ambiguity of his teaching led Salmerón to wonder whether he should be numbered among Catholics or heretics, and he repeats the trope that Erasmus laid the egg that Luther hatched.²¹⁵ Erasmus wanted to find a middle term between the Church of Peter and the synagogue of Luther, which Salmerón compares to finding a middle term between Noah's ark and the waters of the Flood.²¹⁶ When works of Erasmus were burned at Naples in 1560, it is hard to imagine that Salmerón shed any tears.²¹⁷

The Jesuit theologian made Cajetan, whose name was often mentioned together with Erasmus's, guilty by association. In his exegetical work, Cajetan used Erasmus's New Testament, which not only Catholics, but even some heretics, refused to use. Cajetan agreed with Jerome on the biblical canon, which entailed rejecting certain books that the Church approved, and he questioned the canonicity of the Letter to the Hebrews, James, 2 Peter, and 2 and 3 John. Salmerón was especially critical of the fact that Cajetan "worked out in the gym of the Scholastic Doctors" to the neglect of the Fathers, only making use of the latter when he thought it really necessary.²¹⁸ As in the case of Erasmus, disparaging comments about him are frequently found in the *Commentaries*,

---

[212] *CBP*, vol. 1, 436 (Mm4v); *CEH*, vol. 3, 441; *CEH*, vol. 5, 241; *CEH*, vol. 7, 180.

[213] Marlorat, *Expositio*, vol. 2, 34.

[214] The reception of Erasmus among Catholics and Protestants alike was mixed. Peter Canisius, sometimes claimed as a sympathizer of Erasmus, was rather ambivalent toward him. See Hilmar Pabel, "Praise and Blame: Peter Canisius's Ambivalent Assessment of Erasmus," in *The Reception of Erasmus in the Early Modern Period*, ed. Karl Enenkel (Boston, MA: Brill, 2013), 129–51.

[215] *CBP*, vol. 1, 57. Scholarship has shown that Luther had a complex relationship to Erasmus. Arnoud Visser, "Irreverent Reading: Martin Luther as Annotator of Erasmus," *Sixteenth Century Journal* 48, no. 1 (2017): 87–109.

[216] *CBP*, vol. 1, 194.

[217] *ES*, vol. 1, no. 159, 415. But he reports that Jesuit teachers wish to have copies of Erasmus's *Adages*.

[218] *CBP*, vol. 1, 57.

along with occasional words of praise. There is little reason to think that his attitude flowed out of a sense of rivalry with Dominicans in general, as Salmerón made no mention of the conflicts the early Jesuits had with certain members of the Order of Preachers.[219]

Conclusion

Salmerón thought of the Church as a wondrous kingdom of grace under attack, a perfectly ordered city under siege. He provided a consistent yet relatively unsystematic treatment of its theological-mystical dimension, reflecting his thorough knowledge of the Fathers and Doctors. He offered a definition of the Church as an assembly, while also emphasizing the analogies of Christ's body and the architecture of a building. Salmerón gave proportionately more attention to polemical matters, however, defending papal monarchy against conciliarists and royalists, and the whole Church against her external enemies and certain allegedly dangerous Catholics, such as Erasmus and Cajetan. His political theory was correlative with his ecclesiology, and it was consistent with the ideas of his more illustrious confreres, although he was more restrictive on the question of tyrannicide than some of them. His steady polemic against any and all opponents of Catholicism, or of his particular ecclesiological positions, confirms an aspect of Salmerón's self-image that has already manifested itself: he thought of himself as a combatant. In the battle for the Church of his time, he wished to be found on the ramparts.

---

[219] See Terence O'Reilly, "The Spiritual Exercises and Illuminism in Spain: Dominican Critics of the Early Society of Jesus," in *Ite Inflammate Omnia: Selected Historical Papers from Conferences Held at Loyola and Rome in 2006*, ed. Thomas McCoog (Rome: IHSI, 2006), 199–228; Terence O'Reilly, "Melchor Cano and the Spirituality of St. Ignatius Loyola: The *Censura y parecer contra el Instituto de los Padres Jesuitas*," *Journal of Jesuit Studies* 4 (2017): 365–94; A.D. Wright, "The Jesuits and the Older Religious Orders in Spain," in *The Mercurian Project: Forming Jesuit Culture, 1573–1580*, ed. Thomas McCoog (St. Louis, MO: Institute of Jesuit Sources, 2004), 913–44.

7 Promoting Good Mores

"And when ye pray, you shall not be like the hypocrites, that love to stand and pray in the synagogues and corners of the streets, that they may be seen by men" (Matt 6:5). In his commentary on this verse, Salmerón makes the following observation about the posture of prayer:

> The publican and the Pharisee prayed standing. Wherever therefore this custom is maintained, as among the Greeks, it is not an offense. The Latin Church's custom of kneeling, however, seems more commendable and more universal, and more consonant with devotion. This is the manner of prayer that Christ observed in the garden, where first he prayed on his knees, and then prostrate on the ground. Hence laziness or lack of devotion makes us often sit or stand during the sacrifice of the Mass (except at the Gospel). But the way to correct these practices, or the scandal that results from them, is uncertain.[1]

This passage demonstrates Salmerón's concern for the *mos Ecclesiae*, or custom of the Church. This means, first and foremost, the liturgy, but it also includes her ascetical and penitential discipline, for Salmerón looked not only to what Catholics believe and teach, but also what they do.[2] According to him, the customs [*consuetudines*] of the Church manifest the will of God not less than scripture does, and so they are to be observed.[3] They form the overarching matrix of the social and moral order that makes good Christian conduct possible. Salmerón also used the custom of the Church as a weapon against Protestants, whom he excoriated for deviating from it.[4]

---

[1] *CEH*, vol. 5, 279.
[2] "For Salmeron, the praxis of the Roman Church was a norm and guide: for him, orthodoxy showed itself in orthopraxis." Niccolo Steiner, *Diego Laínez und Alfonso Salmerón auf dem Konzil von Trient: Ihr Beitrag zur Eucharistie-und Messopferthematik* (Stuttgart: Kohlhammer, 2019), 124.
[3] *CEH*, vol. 3, 385.
[4] *CBP*, vol. 2, 146.

The discussion of these customs led Salmerón in turn to comment on another fundamental set of mores, namely, the relations between the sexes. Although he affirmed the subordination of women, the Jesuit theologian also thought that the sexes were equal in certain respects, and manifested esteem for women's spiritual capacities. His characteristic interest in historical context and change, however, faded away on this topic; he regarded right order between the sexes primarily as a matter of unchanging principle, upon which the health of both the civil and ecclesial communities depends.

Salmerón also dealt with mores in the more specific sense of morality, that is, the standards that govern human conduct. The primary locus for the development of his moral theology is scripture, particularly the Beatitudes. Partly in response to contemporary controversies about the Law and the Gospel, Salmerón developed a theory of the relationship between the natural law, the Mosaic Law, the Christian observance of the Ten Commandments, and the Beatitudes. He presented Jesus as the supreme lawgiver who bestowed upon the human race the highest law, which presupposes, fulfils, and supersedes previous stages of legislation. The "Gospel law" moves between the two polarities of a purified Decalogue and the Beatitudes, which are meant to keep Christian behavior above a certain lower limit and summon it to a higher standard that anticipates the life of heaven. His emphasis, however, on the role that concupiscence and weakness play in men's actual behavior had a sobering effect on his moral thought.

The Liturgy

Whereas other chapters of the present volume discuss Salmerón's use of liturgical sources on particular topics, here the goal is to explain his understanding of liturgy in general. Salmerón offers a theory *in nuce* of religious ceremonial, which he says has three aims: to bring Christians into one people and make "men of one manner to dwell in a house" (Ps 67:7), to adorn and protect divine worship, and to recall the Lord's teaching.[5] Worship and ceremony must be done in determinate ways and places. In his commentary on worship "in spirit and in truth" in Christ's encounter with the Samaritan woman (Jn 4:23), Salmerón rejects the claim, which he attributes to "heretics," that there is no need for churches or altars, or external cult, rites, or chant. He counters that Christ would not make a promise to his true worshipers and then take away

---

[5] *CEH*, vol. 8, 237–38.

the means of worship, for the removal of rites, cult, and penance would weaken the Church.⁶

The Eucharist, according to Salmerón, has its own cult, and he explains the significance of such gestures as the bowing of the head, the joining of hands, prostration, the striking of the breast, and the sign of the cross. The physical building of the church declares that Christians are temples of the Holy Spirit; the altar of immolation for the Eucharist reminds them to offer themselves as victims; images place the examples of the saints before their eyes; holy water is a reminder of the water that flowed from Christ's side; priestly vestments represent the sufferings of Christ.⁷ The weak in particular, Salmerón says, need the Church's ceremonies, images, and songs to ascend the mountain of God. ⁸

The relationship between stability and change in the liturgy was an issue at Trent. Catholic theologians generally accepted that there was a distinction between essential and accidental parts, as well as a historical process of addition, but they reached no consensus about the particulars. The Carmelite Anthony Riccius de Novarella, for example, thought that the rite of the Mass was already well developed in apostolic times, whereas Diego Laínez explicitly said that Christ did not institute the non-essential elements of the Mass.⁹ This lack of agreement explains in some measure the vagueness of the council's canon on apostolic traditions.¹⁰ It was commonly accepted that there were traditions, including liturgical ones, that could be traced back to the apostles, and that Protestants were wrong to reject them, but pinning down what exactly these were was a more difficult matter.

This ambivalence is evident in the *Commentaries*. On the one hand, Salmerón was wont to treat some of the Christian practices of his day as reaching back to apostolic times. He attributes to apostolic tradition the Greek custom of the priest elevating his eyes and showing the chalice to the people, and the Latin practice of making the sign of cross over the chalice, during the

---

⁶ *CEH*, vol. 4, 198–99.

⁷ *CEH*, vol. 4, 199. Araldo reported the donations of rich vestments to the collegiate church in Naples. Perhaps such things were important to Salmerón. Francesco Divenuto, *Napoli l'Europa e la Compagnia di Gesu nella "Cronica" di Giovan Francesco Araldo* (Naples: Edizioni Scientifiche Italiane, 1998), 110–11.

⁸ *CEH*, vol. 9, 519.

⁹ Reinold Theisen, *Mass Liturgy and the Council of Trent* (Collegeville, MN: St. John's University Press, 1965), 31–42.

¹⁰ John O'Malley, *Trent: What Happened at the Council* (Cambridge, MA: Belknap Press, 2013), 92–98.

Eucharistic prayer.[11] Salmerón says that the "outline" [*lineas*] of the Canon of the Mass can be found already in Paul's letters, and he claims the status of apostolic tradition for holding funeral banquets in memory of the dead.[12] When commenting on the words of institution at Mass, he calls it a crime [*nefas*] to change rites that have been handed down, and a sacrilege to manipulate the covenant of the Eucharist or try to fashion a new one.[13] He defends the principle of repetition along with stability, saying that no one should loathe the weekly recitation of the same Psalter, or the repetition of the litanies and the Rosary. "The Jews without cause disdained eating manna, but Christians should find greater spirit and savor in the same prayers, rather than seek a new text or teaching."[14]

On the other hand, Salmerón showed awareness of liturgical development over time. Although he generally defended the Church's ceremonies, he says that even if they are ancient and from apostolic tradition, this does not mean they are necessary for the essence of the sacrament.[15] Ceremonies are subject to variation, and particular religious orders have their own.[16] He observes that the Roman Canon was formed as apostles and apostolic men gradually added to it.[17] In commenting on Paul's instructions to the Corinthians concerning Church discipline, Salmerón says that at this early date public worship did not yet include such things as antiphonal chanting in choir, or specific ministers assigned to the Gospel and the Epistle.[18] He speaks approvingly of how Gregory VII and Pius V returned the Divine Office to its pristine form, indicating his awareness that the liturgy may sometimes need renewal.[19]

Salmerón was imprecise about the authority of the liturgy as a theological source, saying that by itself it is insufficient to prove a dogma. He opposes the

---

[11] *CEH*, vol. 9, 101; *CBP*, vol. 1, 155.

[12] *CEH*, vol. 9, 255; *CBP*, vol. 2, 221.

[13] *CEH*, vol. 9, 131.

[14] *CEH*, vol. 10, 125.

[15] *CEH*, vol. 9, 223–24.

[16] *CEH*, vol. 4, 101.

[17] *CEH*, vol. 9, 254.

[18] *CBP*, vol. 2, 142.

[19] *CBP*, vol. 2, 260. The liturgical celebrations in Rome underwent significant elaboration, especially regarding their expense, under Paul IV. See Margaret Kuntz, "Liturgical, Ritual, and Diplomatic Spaces at St. Peter's and the Vatican Palace: The Innovations of Paul IV, Urban VIII, and Alexander VII," in *A Companion to Early Modern Rome*, eds. Pamela Jones, Barbara Wisch, and Simon Ditchfield (Boston, MA: Brill, 2019), 75–98.

attempt to abolish old rites and establish new ones, because this leads people to believe that the Church once erred in her faith.[20] At the same time, he admits that the Divine Office may contain falsehoods "like tares among the wheat," and he gives specific examples, such as the story that the Apostle Thomas asked not to be sent to India.[21] Salmerón cites Augustine and Thomas for the view that any rite for worshiping God that does not come from him or from the Holy Spirit through the Church, but that is the product of human will, is superstitious.[22]

Although he was not an expert on the subject, the correlation between texts and musical forms in the liturgy attracted Salmerón's attention. Observing that music is used to arouse various emotions, he says that the Church can use it to arouse piety and devotion, and increase prayer in the spirit.[23] He defends the Church's music not only against Protestants, but also against Cajetan, who said that it would be better for the Church to celebrate the Mass and the Office without music, so that the words could be better understood. Salmerón says that this strategy does not apply to the Office or other public prayers.[24] He upholds the use of the organ in church, reminding the reader that Pliny the Younger wrote to the Emperor Trajan that the Christians sang to Christ.[25] Aware that music moves the hearer in different ways, Salmerón distinguishes the movement of the Holy Spirit from the "pythonical" movement people experience in their gut [*venter*].[26]

His most extensive commentary on musical forms in the liturgy is found in the treatment of Luke's infancy narrative, specifically the three canticles sung during the Divine Office. A canticle, Salmerón explains, is the consonance of different voices in a single melody. The Old Testament contains many examples of these canticles sung after the reception of certain goods or benefits. The temporal benefits commemorated in them prefigure the spiritual benefits that the Messiah was to bestow.[27]

To take one example, the Church stands for the *Magnificat* (Lk 1:46–55) that is sung at Vespers because Mary was standing at the moment when she

[20] *CEH*, vol. 9, 181; *CEH*, vol. 9, 250.
[21] *CEH*, vol. 4, 295.
[22] *CBP*, vol. 3, 347.
[23] *CEH*, vol. 6, 108.
[24] *CBP*, vol. 2, 183.
[25] *CBP*, vol. 2, 188.
[26] *CEH*, vol. 3, 134. This may be a reference to Lev 20:27, which prescribes stoning for anyone with a "pythonical or divining spirit."
[27] *CEH*, vol. 3, 97.

first recited it. Salmerón identifies it with the "new song" of which Psalms 145 and 32 speak, saying that its novelty consists in the renewal of the mind that singing it brings about.[28] Canticles are also called "decachords," a name that has numerical significance for him, for he observes that the *Magnificat* has ten verses. Just as the sacrifices of the Old Testament represented the one sacrifice of Christ on the cross and in the Eucharist, so the Old Testament canticles represent the New Testament canticles. There are a total of ten of the former, which correspond to the ten principal mysteries of the Messiah. The principle of ten relates also to the Decalogue, as well as to the nine choirs of angels, to which the human race was added in the order of sanctification to praise God.[29]

Salmerón sometimes compared the liturgical traditions of different parts of the Church. The Latin Church, he says, is much more certain in her celebrations than the Eastern Church, so the former is a standard for the latter.[30] Despite this conviction, he showed respect for other rites as well. The liturgies of James, Chrysostom, and Basil provide support for his teaching on the form of Eucharistic consecration.[31] The Ethiopians commemorate 14,000 holy innocents, a figure that Salmerón treats as reliable.[32] He was aware that Christians of Ethiopia and India practiced circumcision, despite the fact that Baptism had replaced it as a rite of initiation. He did not favor the practice, but he did not consider it sinful either, since according to Salmerón these Christians put no theological hope in circumcision. These groups believe they are descended from David according to the flesh and therefore they continue this rite. By contrast, being circumcised out of devotion, which some do so that they can suffer with Christ, is not consistent with scripture or the practice of the Catholic Church.[33]

The treatment of liturgy includes a defense of it against Protestant attacks. The heretics, Salmerón observes, mock hymns, sequences, graduals, and tracts, saying that the Catholic Church has substituted them in place of Paul's psalms, doctrines, revelations, tongues, and interpretations in worship (1 Cor 14:26). They also criticize the use of lessons from the Fathers and the lives of the saints in the liturgy, saying that they contain many fables. Salmerón replies that the Psalms sung in Church come from David, the hymns are from scripture or the

[28] *CEH*, vol. 3, 98.
[29] *CEH*, vol. 3, 98–99.
[30] *CBP*, vol. 3, 88.
[31] *CEH*, vol. 9, 80–89.
[32] *CEH*, vol. 3, 415.
[33] *CEH*, vol. 3, 318.

Fathers, and the graduals and tracts also come from scripture, especially the Psalms.[34] He comments that if Paul used the ecclesiastical custom of his own time as a strong argument, fifteen hundred years of custom should be much stronger against the heretics of the age.[35]

The other exegetes under consideration showed less interest in liturgical questions than Salmerón. Maldonado observes that, since prayer is central to religion, heresies of all periods always invent their own forms of prayer, abusing the example of Christ.[36] Barradas's lengthy excursus on the Jerusalem temple contains numerous references to the reverence and adornment that befits Christian worship, but his tone is less defensive and he does not enter into the same level of detail as Salmerón.[37] Marlorat regularly pillories Catholic worship, especially the Mass and the Divine Office, but he does not propose a mandatory alternative. After objecting to the selling of "that temple chant they call Gregorian," he says that "the holy rite in the vernacular of some churches, which is done free of charge by a common harmony singing psalms and pious hymns in churches, is not to be condemned, nor are those churches that do not sing to be condemned. For it is enough that in them there be holy and righteous prayer."[38]

It seems fitting to treat under the heading of liturgy Salmerón's discussion of the gift of tongues, which arises in his commentary on the Letter to the Corinthians. Paul had to correct this community's preference for tongues over charity and other gifts, and recall them to the pristine condition of their faith.[39] Although Salmerón acknowledges that those who spoke in tongues used exotic languages, he thinks that the gift of tongues was principally given in Hebrew, Greek and Latin, because at that time they were the most widely used.[40] He does not reject the gift of tongues, but he observes that there is need for interpreting them, while rejecting tongues for private and public prayer if no one understands them.[41] The Jesuit theologian says that the Church can do fine without tongues, except as an aid to explaining prophecies.[42]

---

[34] *CBP*, vol. 2, 193.
[35] *CBP*, vol. 1, 15.
[36] Maldonado, *Commentaries*, vol. 2, cols. 205–06.
[37] See, for example, Barradas, *Commentaries*, vol. 2, 164.
[38] Marlorat, *Expositio*, vol. 2, 328.
[39] *CBP*, vol. 2, 159–60.
[40] *CBP*, vol. 2, 162–63.
[41] *CBP*, vol. 2, 186–87.
[42] *CBP*, vol. 2, 194.

The Latin Language

The discussion of tongues in the Letter to the Corinthians led Salmerón to offer his lengthiest defense of the use of Latin in the liturgy. He began by summarizing the arguments in favor of translating the Bible, Mass, Office, and other prayers into the vernacular. Since scripture is the food, healing, and law for Christians, and since there is no longer Jew or Greek, slave or free, it should be understood by all. The apostles used the many languages of the places they went, and many Christian peoples, such as the Armenians and Ethiopians, use their native language in worship.[43] Salmerón reports the argument of Marlorat, who claimed that the Church in Europe had erred ever since Latin ceased to be the common tongue, and that now men attend church without fruit to hear scripture in Latin, a language they do not understand. Salmerón's rejoinder leans heavily on the principle of tradition.

> The Church has observed, and still observes, the things that her ancestors handed down for observance. For indeed the holy mystery of the Mass and the Divine Office were celebrated only in Hebrew among the Hebrews, in Greek among the Greeks, and in Latin among the Latins, but never in the vernacular or the mother tongue at all.[44]

He continues that the chants and prayers are not totally unknown even among the unlearned, and that preachers use the vernacular when preaching to the people. Against Calvin's argument that no one can gain fruit from prayers they do not understand, Salmerón says that the dead benefit from prayers they do not hear, that the Lord prayed for the deaf and the ill, and that he also praised the children who cried out on Palm Sunday (Mt 21:15–16), even though these prayers were above their understanding.[45]

The use of Latin was another aspect of the larger linguistic question in the sixteenth century. Many Protestants preferred the biblical and vernacular languages to the Church's official tongue and especially criticized its use in worship. Salmerón expresses his clear preference for the three "universal languages" in which both the scriptures and intellectual disciplines have been written. These three languages, he says, give glory to the Trinity and owe their status to the inscription above Christ on the cross.[46]

The argument on behalf of the three universal languages, particularly Latin, was partly a historical one. Salmerón explains that after the Babylonian

---

[43] *CBP*, vol. 2, 255–56.
[44] *CBP*, vol. 2, 183.
[45] *CBP*, vol. 2, 183.
[46] *CBP*, vol. 2, 257.

captivity, the Jews stopped speaking Hebrew, but they continued to worship in this tongue. To this day, they speak the vernacular of the provinces where they live, but they read scripture in Hebrew. Although the apostles used many languages, they never wrote scripture in anything other than Hebrew, Greek, and Latin.[47] The custom of the Church for a thousand years was to read scripture and worship in Greek and Latin, even in those places where it was not the common tongue. When Spain was invaded by Goths and Vandals, their vernacular was not adopted, nor did the English, French, or Germans use anything other than Latin. Salmerón cites copiously from late antique and early medieval sources, including commentaries on the liturgy, to demonstrate that Latin was not the vernacular tongue of the regions that adopted it for worship. Even among the Gentiles a non-vernacular language is sometimes used for sacrifice: the Romans used Etruscan, and the Druids, who lived in Gaul in the time of Julius Caesar, used the language of their native Britain.[48]

Latin was closely connected in Salmerón's mind to the unity of the Church, which is expressed in faith, worship, charity, and customs, "and what is greater, in the very sacrament of charity, which is the Eucharist."[49] He believed that all these manifestations of unity would be lost with the move from Latin to the vernacular. The different languages in the Mass and Divine Office among various regions would lead to misunderstanding between them about their faith, so that "he who moved from one province to another would be going to a people of another faith and worship, and they would be like barbarians to each other."[50] This in turn, Salmerón predicts, would soon lead to the change of the rites and ceremonies themselves, as has already happened among Protestants, and it would open the window to errors and heresies. Experience also shows that a common language promotes love and mutual benevolence among people; changing the language of worship would take away its unity, and thereby dissolve the community itself.[51] Take away Latin, Salmerón asks, and who will be able to read the Fathers, councils, and canons of the Church? When the urgent necessity of something is removed, its usefulness goes away with it. People would only produce their own thoughts and dreams, and even if the ancient sources were translated into the vernacular, eventually knowledge

---

[47] *CBP*, vol. 2, 258. Salmerón notes that some authors think Mark wrote his Gospel in Latin. Against the objection that Matthew may have written in Aramaic, Salmerón replies that this was no longer a vernacular language, but a literary one.

[48] *CBP*, vol. 2, 258–60.

[49] *CBP*, vol. 2, 260.

[50] *CBP*, vol. 2, 260.

[51] *CBP*, vol. 2, 261.

of Latin would be lost altogether, with the consequent reign of simplicity [*rusticitas*] and ignorance [*idiotismus*].[52]

In his defense of Latin, Salmerón also appealed to the need for mystery in divine worship, citing the works of Basil the Great, Dionysius the Areopagite, and Gregory Nazianzen, who all said that holy things are not to be divulged to all. In a like manner, the Council of Trent defended the whispered Canon, "which we call the secret within the secret" [*secreta in secretis*]. This need for mystery is why the catechumens used to be sent away prior to the consecration, as Dionysius and Chrysostom testified.[53] Salmerón observes that when divine mysteries are divulged everywhere, they cease to be mysteries, and since there is nothing more sacrosanct than the mystery of the Eucharist, it should never be celebrated in the vernacular.[54] He brings forth examples from both the Old and New Testaments to support this notion of mystery. The Passover lamb was eaten at night in silence within the walls of each household; Moses ascended the mountain alone, and the people were forbidden to approach it on punishment of death; the Bread of the Presence was placed within the tabernacle, and only the priests were allowed to eat of it.[55] The Lord remained hidden at home from age twelve to thirty; he celebrated the Eucharist only in the presence of the Twelve; he appeared to the disciples after the resurrection behind closed doors, and not to all of them, but only to those chosen by God.[56]

Vernacular celebration of the Mass would also, Salmerón thought, play directly into the hands of Protestants. Since the root of their demand was heresy and the desire to create schism within the Church, they would certainly take permission for it as a victory for themselves. "To concede this to them would be nothing else than confirming them in their error or heresy."[57] He says that the Fathers, general councils, and the Church as a whole have never conceded anything that smacked of heresy, but instead they have issued constitutions and decrees to heal heretics of their disease. The Jesuit theologian feared that allowing the vernacular in worship would lead to even worse things, "like the marriage of priests and monks, Communion under both species, and religious liberty, or what they call 'neutrality.'"[58]

---

[52] *CBP*, vol. 2, 262.

[53] *CBP*, vol. 2, 265; cf. Council of Trent, Session 22, *Canones de sanctissimo missae sacrificio*, can. 9.

[54] *CBP*, vol. 2, 266.

[55] *CBP*, vol. 2, 265.

[56] *CBP*, vol. 2, 266.

[57] *CBP*, vol. 2, 269.

[58] *CBP*, vol. 2, 269.

Lent and Fasting

Salmerón wished to promote and defend not only the Catholic liturgy in the Latin language, but also the Church's ascetical practices. The primary locus is his commentary on Christ's fast in the desert, which in turn is closely tied to his explanation and justification of Lent. He shows his usual polemical edge: the Lord's first reason for not eating in the desert was to show that the true Gospel includes fasting and abstinence, contrary to the "new Gospel" proposed by heretics in Germany.[59]

Salmerón grounds the obligation to fast not only in scripture, but also in the natural law, while conceding that the natural law provides no specification for its fulfilment. Jews, Christians, and Saracens fulfill the obligation in different ways.[60] This leads him to the thorny question of the status of the forty days of the Lenten fast: is it a divine precept, or a precept of the Church/apostolic tradition? He produces catenas of patristic citations in favor of both positions, seeking to mediate between them. All the Fathers agreed that Lent is "most ancient," and that those who fail to observe it are justly punished. In Salmerón's opinion, the Lenten fast is a precept of the Church, but a very ancient one based on apostolic tradition, and it fulfills Christ's prediction that his followers would fast after his departure (Mt 9:15).[61]

Whatever the historical origins of the season, Salmerón underscores this point: the faithful should embrace the Church as a mother by following her norms of fasting during Lent and at other times of the year, for the rites and ceremonies that have been handed down by tradition, scripture, and ecclesiastical law need to be obeyed.[62] He produces evidence from Fathers, popes, synods, and councils that all are bound under sin to observe Lent.[63] In addition to the formal issue of obedience to the Church's norms, the Jesuit

---

[59] *CEH*, vol. 4, 91. Salmerón observes, however, that Jesus did not observe strict fasting and abstinence throughout his life so as not to scare people away. *CEH*, vol. 4, 282. Early Jesuits engaged in polemics with Protestants on fasting and abstinence. See Sylvio Hermann de Franceschi, "La morale catholique posttridentine et la controverse interconfessionnelle. Jeûne et abstinence dans la confrontation entre protestants et jésuites: privations alimentaires et confessionnalisation," in *Jésuites et protestantisme: XVIe–XXIe siècles*, eds. Yves Krumenacker and Philippe Martin (Lyons: LARHRA, 2019), 69–93.

[60] *CEH*, vol. 4, 98–99.

[61] *CEH*, vol. 4, 102–03; *CEH*, vol. 4, 99.

[62] *CEH*, vol. 4, 91; *CEH*, vol. 4, 99–100. Those who prefer their own judgment on fasting to that of the Church sin mortally in so doing. *CEH*, vol. 4, 98.

[63] *CEH*, vol. 4, 104–06.

theologian is specific about the content of the penitential observances. He says that the Church fasts at Lent, on Ember Days, and feasts of the Blessed Virgin, the Apostles, and some others. This means eating just once a day, with no meat, eggs, or dairy products allowed.[64] It is the custom of the Church not to break the fast until after the ninth hour, when Christ died.[65]

Salmerón identified numerous benefits of fasting. It helps for conquering the flesh, the world, and the devil, and angels come to assist the faithful when they fast, as they did Jesus. Daniel and the three youths who fasted in Babylon were more robust and beautiful than the others (Dan 1). Not only does fasting please God in various ways, but the variation brought about by fasting and abstinence makes life happier.[66] The excellence of the monastic life rests in part upon such practices, and Salmerón catalogs the observances of various monastic orders, singling out the Carthusians for their austerity.[67] He promises that if the faithful overcome temptation during Lent by fasting, then the priests, who represent the angels, will give them the bread of life on Easter.[68]

In his commentary on Jesus's foretelling of his Passion and death on the way to Jerusalem (Lk 18:31–33), Salmerón notes approvingly that the Church reads this Gospel on the final days of Carnival [*Bacchanales*], in which the devil triumphs through men's vices. On these days of Satan's institution, men go crazy, jump around, and put on masks in commemoration of his victory over Adam. Salmerón did not see Carnival as a necessary release, but rather he thought that Christian behavior on this occasion made a mockery of the Lenten fast. He compares it to handing Christ over again to pagans, Jews, and heretics, or to a man who goes to prostitutes before his wedding, or to someone who vomits so that he can eat more.[69] The fact that Naples was known for the extravagance of its public festivals, and that social tensions and

---

[64] *CEH*, vol. 4, 100. The Western fasting regimen, particularly the prohibition of dairy products, was progressively loosened during the modern period, beginning with Pope Benedict XIV (1740–58).

[65] *CEH*, vol. 5, 45. Formerly Mass was celebrated at particular hours depending on the liturgical day. On penitential days, it took place after the hour of None.

[66] *CEH*, vol. 4, 110–11.

[67] *CEH*, vol. 4, 108.

[68] *CEH*, vol. 4, 142.

[69] *CEH*, vol. 4, 573–74. In a later period, ecclesiastics tried to prevent people from going to Mass on Ash Wednesday in masks and costumes. Perhaps Salmerón was acquainted with similar behaviors. Laura Barletta, "Un esempio di festa: il Carnevale," in *Capolavori in Festa: Effimero barocco a Largo di Palazzo (1683–1759)*, ed. Giuseppe Zampino (Naples: Electa Napoli, 1997), 91–104, at 92.

disturbances manifested themselves during Carnival in particular, may provide additional context for Salmerón's consternation.[70]

Veiling and the Sexes

Among the many customs of the Church that Salmerón mentioned, one recurred with frequency: the covering of the head. A number of issues converge here: the interpretation of Paul, the levels of authority and obligation attaching to Church praxis, the differentiation between the sexes, and the authority of women to teach.

The most basic meaning of the veiling of women, according to Salmerón, is their subjection to men.[71] He explains that Paul's instructions reverse the Jewish and Gentile way of praying, according to which men covered their heads and women uncovered them. The Jewish high priest used to pray with his feet bare and his head covered, whereas now the Catholic priest prays shod and with his head uncovered, because "Christ the head" has come. It dishonors the man to cover his head, because it should signify the glory of God.[72] Women, by contrast, should cover their heads in accordance with the order of nature when they are praying or prophesying, showing that they have a man who has power over them.[73] Salmerón also cites Paul's explanation for veiling that it is done out of respect for the angels (1 Cor 11:10). Admitting that there is more than one possible explanation of this verse, he thinks that it refers to the presence of the good angels during the celebration of the Mass, who may be offended by a woman's facial expressions, gestures, or movements of the body.[74]

---

[70] Gabriel Guarino, "Spanish Celebrations in Seventeenth-Century Naples," *Sixteenth Century Journal* 37, no. 1 (2006): 25–41; Gabriel Guarino, "Public Rituals and Festivals in Naples, 1503–1799," in *A Companion to Early Modern Naples*, ed. Tommaso Astarita (Boston, MA: Brill, 2013), 257–79. In two letters sent from Rome in 1560 and 1561, Salmerón complains that the distractions of Carnival prevent serious business from getting done. *ES*, vol. 1, no. 130a, 359; *ES*, vol. 1, no. 168b, 444.

[71] *CEH*, vol. 12, 425; *CBP*, vol. 2, 143–44.

[72] *CBP*, vol. 2, 143–44. Salmerón cites the testimony of Plutarch for the Jewish practice. Sometimes priests in the north have to wear a hat, which Salmerón calls *pileolus*, on account of the cold.

[73] *CBP*, vol. 2, 144. Salmerón does not explain why this agrees with the order of nature, nor why the Jewish and Gentile practice is, by implication, against nature.

[74] *CBP*, vol. 2, 145–46.

Another relevant biblical passage is the Pauline prohibition against women speaking in church (1 Cor 14:34–35), which Salmerón qualified in a number of ways. First, he explicitly contradicts those who claim this is a matter of divine law that admits of no dispensation.[75] He points to Catherine of Siena as a woman of great sanctity who spoke multiple times before the pope and cardinals in consistory.[76] In scripture, some women have the gift of prophecy, like Miriam, Hannah, the Blessed Virgin, and Anna.[77] Salmerón also acknowledges this gift in a secondary sense when he says that, although women cannot preach the word of God to the people, they prophesy when they sing God's praise in public, as nuns do in Church, or tell the future, as did the Sibyls and certain holy virgins and matrons.[78] Salmerón observes that although women were not to have the office of preaching, they perceived the risen Christ more quickly than men did. Paul and Luke did not mention the women's testimonies of the Resurrection because of the generally weak status of women in antiquity, but the Church regards their testimony as no less solid than the apostles'.[79] "Truly women have not been left behind in Christ, as they were in Moses, but they are often found ahead of and more faithful than men, for the sake of confounding pride."[80]

The term "little women" [*mulierculae*] occasionally appears in the *Commentaries*, normally with a disparaging connotation. Salmerón says that John's words about testing spirits (1 Jn 4:1) are meant for pastors and teachers, not "country bumpkins and little women" who can barely count the fingers on their hands.[81] He is exceedingly skeptical of the "little women" of his own time who go into ecstasy and claim to see visions and wonders.[82] Such women also help spread heresies by going into feminine spaces that are inaccessible to men, and even among the heretics of antiquity, such as the Donatists and the Circumcellions, they practiced free love in their gatherings.[83] He cites Virgil's verse: "*Woman's a various and a changeful thing. And women desire now this,*

---

[75] *CEH*, vol. 12, 425.
[76] *CBP*, vol. 2, 196.
[77] *CBP*, vol. 2, 144.
[78] *CBP*, vol. 1, 143.
[79] *CEH*, vol. 11, 85.
[80] *CEH*, vol. 3, 402.
[81] *CBP*, vol. 4, 276.
[82] *CBP*, vol. 4, 278.
[83] *CBP*, vol. 3, 602 (Eeev).

now that, and now they loathe the thing they have, and take delight in other new things."[84]

Other exegetes occasionally made asides about women, often in a deprecatory way. Jansen observes that Mary's keeping all things in her heart shows that she did not have "womanish loquaciousness," and he claims that libido is especially blind and impotent in women. Elsewhere, however, he eagerly enumerates the virtues of the Syrophoenician woman.[85] Maldonado remarks that women weep more than men in accordance with their nature, and that not every single "little woman" performs miracles.[86] Barradas praises holy and faithful women, citing Sirach 26, but explains how "deceived little women" follow their heretical teachers like cows follow bulls.[87] When explaining Jesus's injunction to "turn the other cheek," Marlorat observes that "a slap is usually delivered as a sign of contempt to women, boys, or otherwise effeminate or feeble persons."[88]

Salmerón's view of women was characterized by tension. On the one hand, he took their subordination to men in external, public matters very much for granted, and he wrote disparagingly about their supposed weaknesses. On the other hand, he insisted on their spiritual equality with men, at least in certain respects, and he acknowledged the gifts of some women, particularly of those in the Bible and in the register of the saints.[89] This tension, however, betrayed no interest in the historical conditioning of relations between the sexes. For Salmerón, men and women, and the right relations between them, were quite stable across time and place, and this stability is key to promoting good mores. Behavior that did not conform to these expectations was treated as deviant.[90]

---

[84] *CBP*, vol. 3, 603; Virgil, *Aeneid* 4.569–70. "Varium et mutabile semper foemina."

[85] Jansen, *Commentaries*, Prima Pars, 96; Jansen, *Commentaries*, Secunda Pars, 451; Jansen, *Commentaries*, Tertia Pars, 13.

[86] Maldonado, *Commentaries*, vol. 1, cols. 628–29; Maldonado, *Commentaries*, vol. 1, col. 809.

[87] Barradas, *Commentaries*, vol. 2, 149; Barradas, *Commentaries*, vol. 1, 128.

[88] Marlorat, *Expositio*, vol. 1, 38.

[89] Salmerón does not acknowledge in the *Commentaries* the crucial role that aristocratic women, like Roberta Carafa and Isabella della Rovere, played in the establishment and growth of the Jesuit presence in Naples, particularly the building of the Church of the Gesù Nuovo or the community's collection of relics. Elisa Novi Chavarria, "The Space of Women," in *A Companion to Early Modern Naples*, ed. Tommaso Astarita (Boston, MA: Brill, 2013), 177–96, at 182.

[90] This is despite the vigorous debate about the relations between the sexes in literary and religious circles during the sixteenth and seventeenth centuries, as well as evidence that standards of masculinity were neither uniform nor always reassuring

When commenting on Plato's *Republic*, he criticizes the view that men and women should both practice horseback riding and gymnastics, "when nature has yet distinguished the duties and gifts of men and women."[91]

The Law of Christ

Salmerón did not treat morals in an abstract way, or even really as a distinct branch of theology. Just as scripture was the framework and inspiration of his thought as a whole, so also his treatment of morals was embedded in both scripture and the custom of the Church. Although he discusses moral issues throughout the *Commentaries*, the most important locus for them is Volume 5, which is dedicated to the Sermon on the Mount. The choice to deal with these short texts at such length, in imitation of Augustine, speaks to the great importance of this biblical source in Salmerón's understanding of Christian morality. Here he dealt with the crucial matter of the relationship between law and Gospel, as well as the particular content of Christian teaching as communicated in the Decalogue and the Beatitudes.

The question of law was central to sixteenth-century polemics in a number of respects. In the first place, it pertained to the interpretation of Paul's teaching on justification, as explained in Chapter 5. In the view of Protestants, the Catholic Church had corrupted the original Christian message by binding believers to the observance of ecclesiastical law, which amounted to a revival of Judaism. In the second place, Luther placed the opposition between law and Gospel at the center of his theological vision. Although other Protestant leaders eschewed this approach, Luther's prominence, especially for the earliest Catholic polemicists, ensured that Salmerón would need to argue for the harmony of law and Gospel. In the third place, Protestant rejection of the

---

for men. See Merry Wiesner-Hanks, *Women and Gender in Early Modern Europe*, 3rd ed. (New York: Cambridge University Press, 2008), 24–34; Androniki Dialeti, "From Women's Oppression to Male Anxiety: The Concept of 'Patriarchy' in the Historiography of Early Modern Europe," in *Gender in Late Medieval and Early Modern Europe*, eds. Marianna Muravyeva and Raisa Maria Toivo (New York: Routledge, 2013), 19–36; Katherine Crawford, "Catherine de Médicis and the Performance of Political Motherhood," *Sixteenth Century Journal* 31, no. 3 (2000): 643–73; Grace Coolidge, "'Neither Dumb, Deaf, nor Destitute of Understanding': Women as Guardians in Early Modern Spain," *Sixteenth Century Journal* 36, no. 3 (2005): 673–93. Naples in particular had notable participation of women in intellectual, political, and commercial life during the late sixteenth century. See Chavarria, "Space of Women."

[91] *CEH*, vol. 5, 3.

Church's law raised the specter of the overturning of all law. Luther himself felt compelled to disown the uprisings associated with the German Peasants' War, which was by no means an isolated disturbance in the tumultuous 1520s and 1530s.[92] Catholic authors frequently pointed to these incidents as evidence of the anarchic character of Protestantism, and Salmerón was no exception to this pattern. That still left to defenders of the Catholic faith the task of explaining the relationship of different kinds of law to each other, which was complicated by the perceived encroachment of the civil authorities, Catholic and Protestant alike, into the ecclesiastical sphere.

The centerpiece of Salmerón's solutions to all of these issues was the presentation of Christ as the supreme lawgiver of the most excellent and sublime law. When the first set of tablets of the Law was broken at the foot of the mountain, and a new set obtained (Ex 34:1–4), "the wisest Moses wished to show clearly that the first law declared by him was to be abolished and abrogated by another, later law."[93] Indeed, Salmerón saw the whole of Matthew's Gospel as structured around the idea of Christ as lawgiver. In the first four chapters of this Gospel, Jesus drew the people to himself by means of words, signs, and the inspiration of interior impulses; in chapters five, six, and seven, he gave the law; from the eighth through the twenty-third chapter he confirmed its truth through innumerable signs and miracles. Chapters twenty-four and twenty-five demonstrated the execution of Christ's law with respect to the distribution of rewards and punishments, and the final part of the Gospel narrated the legislator's death, his return to immortal life, and his sending of the apostles to preach his message.[94] As Willis observes, Salmerón took his cue from the Council of Trent, which explicitly condemned the proposition that Christ came only as a redeemer, not as a lawgiver.[95]

In Salmerón's telling, Moses was not the only lawgiver whom Christ surpassed. In antiquity, many legislators claimed to have received their law from the gods. Osiris, who gave laws to Egypt, said they came from Mercury; Zoroaster taught the Bactrians and Persians the laws of their god Ahura Mazda [*Oromasis*]; Solon gave to the Athenians what he received from Minerva, Lycurgus taught the laws of Apollo to the Spartans, and Numa learned the

---

[92] Carlos Eire, *Reformations: The Early Modern World, 1450–1650* (New Haven, CT: Yale University Press, 2016), 185–285.

[93] *CEH*, vol. 5, 1.

[94] *CEH*, vol. 5, 1.

[95] John Willis, "Love Your Enemies: Sixteenth Century Interpretations," (PhD dissertation: University of Chicago, 1989), 485 fn3; Council of Trent, Session 6, *Canones de justificatione*, can. 21.

laws he gave to the Romans from the nymph Egeria. According to Salmerón, Mohammed lied when he claimed to teach the Arabs by the authority of the Angel Gabriel. In contrast to all these figures, Jesus, full of divine majesty and power, came to give the true law, and despoiled all the false gods of the Gentiles. Salmerón observes that none of the false gods ever claimed to possess the fullness of divinity, only seeking to exercise part of it over some particular domain of life: Minerva over learning, Mars over war, Apollo over music, Neptune over the sea, and so forth. But the one Jesus Christ, like the most splendid light of the world, expelled all shadows, imposed silence on all the oracles of the gods, and cast them all down from their places.[96]

Salmerón saw the whole of human history as awaiting the revelation of the Gospel law, with two other kinds of law corresponding to stages of preparation for it. The first of these is the natural law [*lex naturae*], which corresponds to the nature, powers, and wisdom that man possesses as man. Although man is able to perceive many right things according to the natural law, on account of original sin he cannot see all of them, nor is he able to fulfil all of this law's precepts by his own powers, or attain to the happiness for which he was created. The second is the Mosaic Law, which gave greater light, along with signs and evidence for God's providence toward man, so that the followers of this law could see their true end and the way that leads toward it. Since, however, men could not fulfil this law by their own powers, the Messiah was promised to them, who would lead them out of captivity to the devil and sin, and make them able to fulfil the law. For this purpose, the third and final law was given, the Gospel law, together with the sacraments, to make men holy and capable of entering into eternal life.[97]

The culmination of all law in the Gospel law represents the fulfilment of the laws corresponding to the previous stages of history. As Willis explains, Salmerón thought in terms of hierarchical, graded forms of human life to which each subsystem of law, whether natural, civil, canonical, and so forth, applies.[98] In his commentary on the Sermon on the Mount, he is especially concerned with the status of the Mosaic Law. If Jesus came not to abolish the Law but to fulfil it (Mt 5:17), in what sense has it been surpassed, and in what sense is it still in force? The Jesuit theologian carefully navigated this question, with the aim of showing that the Christian dispensation does not do away with precepts altogether, but rather it demands a higher level of fulfilment that is only possible through true charity.

---

[96] *CEH*, vol. 5, 2.

[97] *CEH*, vol. 5, 5.

[98] Willis, "Love Your Enemies," 483.

According to Salmerón, the aim of the Sermon on the Mount was to show that true righteousness consisted not in external ceremonies, but in worship of God and trust in him, in love of one's neighbor and one's enemies, and in a more perfect and holy life.[99] All of these things are ordered toward the end of beatitude. Salmerón carries out a close-reading of the term. "Beatitude" signifies plenitude or abundance of all goods, and the Greek adjective *makarios* adds the notion of an immortal beatitude, that is, one not subject to corruption. Beatitude is therefore proper to God, and applies also to anyone who participates in the divine nature, which man does by way of his intellect rather than his body, for in the former he is made in the image and likeness of God. True beatitude consists of knowing God, not by the light of nature or even of faith, but by the light of glory in heaven, since this is permanent and perfect.[100] "They are therefore called blessed in this passage who have the right and the merit to obtain eternal life."[101]

Salmerón introduced a crucial distinction between the imperfectly and the perfectly blessed. The former have a right to glory through grace and their good works, whereas the latter, as the Letter to the Hebrews says, "have moreover tasted the good word of God, and the powers of the world to come" (Heb 6:5). The Beatitudes concern the acts of the perfectly blessed people, meaning that they are characteristic of heroic rather than common virtue, and they flow from the gifts of the Holy Spirit.[102] The fact that the Beatitudes go against all the world's assumptions helps explain their heroic character, and Christ offers the greatest rewards for those who exercise them.[103]

This explanation of beatitude is important for understanding the overarching trajectory of God's stages of lawgiving, as well as the status of the Mosaic Law in the Christian dispensation. According to Salmerón, the term "Torah" means rule, instruction, or teaching, and it contains both interior and exterior norms [*cultus*]. The former pertain to faith, hope, and charity, whereas the latter concern rites and fasts, which are not strictly necessary. The Law also gives instruction for the formation of the people's mores.

> The Law is truly nothing other than instruction for worshiping God, not only by faith, hope, and charity, but also with external honors. But the force

---

[99] *CEH*, vol. 5, 18.

[100] *CEH*, vol. 5, 19.

[101] *CEH*, vol. 5, 20.

[102] *CEH*, vol. 5, 20. Elsewhere Salmerón says it is sinful to refuse to do a heroic deed that is asked of one, suggesting that heroic virtue is not always optional. *CEH*, vol. 4, 152.

[103] *CEH*, vol. 5, 37; *CEH*, vol. 5, 91.

[*nervus*] and essence of the Law is both to show the essential worship of God that pleases him per se, which consists of withdrawing from sin and drawing near to God through the righteousness of faith and love of neighbor, and to foreshadow Christ, by whose grace this worship can be offered.[104]

Salmerón thus saw the Mosaic Law as already containing, at least in its interior dimension, the worship that God wants from mankind.

Christ therefore did not come to abolish the Law, which would mean taking away its power, but to fulfil it, because in terms of the essentials, Christians and Jews share the same faith. They both confess the one true God, creator of heaven and earth, who led Israel out of Egypt, and who gave the Law and the prophets. They likewise share hope in God as the giver of all good things, and teach love of God and neighbor. Fulfilling the Law means, however, bringing its external cult, which was a type of greater things to come, to an end.[105] One can therefore say that the Mosaic Law was abrogated with respect to ceremonies and punishments [*iudicia*]. The core of the Law, that is, love and grace, remain, as do the moral commandments, which were not merely given by Moses, but by God.[106] The problem with the Mosaic Law, says Salmerón, is that in practice it lost sight of the intrinsic end of law, which is to make men good.[107]

He explains in more detail how Christ fulfilled the Law, which is crucial for understanding the relationship between Judaism and Christianity as well as his moral theology. As a master painter corrects the work of his student, Christ perfects and gives color to the Mosaic Law.[108] First, he fulfilled the Law by showing love of neighbor, as Rom 13:8–10 stipulates. Second, he showed that its promises were being fulfilled, as scripture testifies: "that all things must needs be fulfilled, which are written in the law of Moses, and in the prophets, and in the psalms, concerning me" (Lk 24:44). Third, he perfected the Law, which meant taking away its imperfections and adding things that would better bring about the end for which its precepts had been established. As

---

[104] *CEH*, vol. 5, 173.

[105] *CEH*, vol. 5, 174.

[106] *CEH*, vol. 5, 175.

[107] *CEH*, vol. 5, 177.

[108] *CEH*, vol. 5, 255. Although the original source for this image is Theophylact, Willis believes that Salmerón's proximate source was his fellow Jesuit Juan de Maldonado. The problem with this idea is that the latter's unfinished commentaries on the four Gospels were not submitted to General Acquaviva until 1583, and were not first published until 1596–97. Willis, "Love Your Enemies," 483–84.

examples of the imperfections, Salmerón cites the permissions to exact usury in transactions with Gentiles and to issue bills of divorce. Christ added to the Law new articles of faith on the Trinity, the Incarnation, the Eucharist, and the other mysteries. Through Baptism, he extended the promises of the Law to all mankind, and offered the evangelical counsels as a way to the love of God, making clear the inferiority of temporal goods to eternal ones. He greatly increased the punishment of transgression of the moral commandments, no longer threatening the consequences contained in the Mosaic Law, but rather eternal damnation.[109]

Salmerón saw both continuity and discontinuity between the Mosaic Law and the Gospel. In his commentary on the Sermon on the Mount, he shows how the Decalogue not only remains in force, but also how it has been purified and elevated in the Christian dispensation. This standard of conduct, which surpasses the demands of the Mosaic Law, is only a lower limit for Christians, since violating it merits damnation. The Beatitudes, however, point to a higher level of conduct still, one that is perfect, heroic, and that already anticipates the life of heaven. Far from positing an opposition between law and Gospel, Salmerón sought to show that the Gospel was the highest law, coming from Jesus the perfect and supreme lawgiver, and leading to the end to which previous stages of law pointed but could not attain: eternal blessedness. It is significant that Salmerón's treatment of Christian conduct begins with the Beatitudes and interprets the Decalogue in light of them. This is surely dictated by the fact that Matthew begins the Sermon on the Mount with the Beatitudes, but it also indicates the Jesuit theologian's preference for the more perfect standard of conduct.

The Beatitudes and the Decalogue

Following the texts of Matthew and Luke, Salmerón's treatment of the Beatitudes is more complete than his treatment of the Decalogue. A sampling of texts shows how he understood the relationship between these two standards of Christian conduct. Citing Euthymius, Salmerón observes that after teaching the Beatitudes, the Lord brought forth the greater commandments to show how the righteousness of Christians should surpass that of the scribes and Pharisees.[110] Keeping the Ten Commandments is obligatory for Christians, and they occupy an intermediate position between, on the one hand, the higher standard of the Beatitudes, and on the other hand, the imperfect

---

[109] *CEH*, vol. 5, 175–76.
[110] *CEH*, vol. 5, 190.

observance of the Mosaic Law. Salmerón moves readily up and down this scale to show his reader the heights to which he may aspire, as well as the depths into which he dares not fall, if he wishes to honor God and attain salvation.

Blessed Are the Poor in Spirit

Salmerón explains that Jesus begins his legislation with this Beatitude because riches are the first obstacle to salvation, as the story of the rich young man demonstrates (Mt 19:16–24).[111] Exegetes generally choose to emphasize either "poor" or "in spirit" when commenting on this verse, and Salmerón was no exception. According to him, Christ is speaking primarily of those who lack the goods of fortune, like money and other belongings. Salmerón considers at length the meanings of "in spirit," and while he accepts multiple possibilities, he is opposed to any attempt to mitigate the emphasis on poverty in favor of humility.

He also provides a taxonomy of the "poor." Although this Beatitude includes those who are merely willing to forfeit all goods rather than offend God, it speaks more properly of those who voluntarily abandon both the desire of possessing and the actual possession of goods, as Christ did. Beggars are a borderline case, for being a beggar is not the same thing as being poor. Salmerón defends the legitimacy of begging according to the Lord's example, as Benedict, Bernard, Francis, and Dominic did. These considerations lead to a definition: the poor are those who embrace actual poverty, whether under the impulse of the Holy Spirit, or by their own spiritual will. This may be done with or without vows, or with or without actual begging, but it entails either living by alms or from the common possessions of a religious order.[112]

Salmerón excludes from the category of "poor in spirit" the worldly poor who unwillingly enter into this condition, and who would gladly steal in order to become rich. Unwilling religious, or those who are more religious in name than in actual condition, are also excluded, as are those who enter the life for the sake of rising to ecclesiastical office, so they can enjoy its riches. Finally, those who renounce riches for merely human reasons do not belong to this category. As examples, Salmerón cites numerous ancient philosophers, like Socrates, who became poor for the sake of wisdom, or Diogenes the Cynic, who wanted to be admired by others. Only those who keep Christ before their eyes are blessed, that is, poor in spirit.[113]

---

[111] *CEH*, vol. 5, 26.

[112] *CEH*, vol. 5, 25.

[113] *CEH*, vol. 5, 25–26.

Aware that relatively few people even acknowledge the blessedness of poverty, much less embrace it for themselves, Salmerón sought to both answer worldly objections to it and demonstrate that it is not without some foundation in the natural order. Some people wrongly say that one should not tempt God by throwing away goods, or that it benefits the commonwealth for men to be wealthy, so that they can provide in emergencies. Salmerón scoffs at this reasoning, for he says it is ridiculous to worry that everyone will become poor in spirit or in reality.[114] In response to the argument of a hypothetical Jew who opposes poverty on the grounds that the patriarchs were wealthy, the Jesuit theologian retorts that this esteem of wealth corresponded to the younger age of the people at that time, who needed different laws. With Christ, maturity has come, with the understanding that spiritual goods are greater than temporal ones.[115]

Even some philosophers saw the wisdom of rejecting wealth, which was a good preparation for the Gospel, even if their motives were inadequate. Aristotle, following only the light of nature, knew that happiness lay not in external goods, although he was only partially correct to say that at least some earthly goods were necessary for happiness. Salmerón says this is true of civil and human happiness, but not of the happiness of the next life.[116] It is typical of his approach to Christian morality that, no matter how high its standards ascend, or how much it is mocked or opposed by the world, he never decoupled it from the natural order and its intelligibility to natural reason.

Blessed Are They That Mourn

According to Salmerón, "mourning is nothing other than pain, expressed with external tears, over a lost good that is loved, or over a present evil that is hated."[117] There are three kinds of mourning: natural, deliberate bad, and deliberate good. The first is morally indifferent, whereas the second proceeds from excessive love of self and is found in the weeping of the damned in hell. Salmerón finds fault with exaggerated mourning of the dead among Christians, which he compares to Augustine's tears over Aeneas and Dido in the *Confessions*.[118] He reasons against crying over the dead in the following way. If the deceased is in hell, then tears can do nothing to save him, whereas if he

---

[114] *CEH*, vol. 5, 30.

[115] *CEH*, vol. 5, 31.

[116] *CEH*, vol. 5, 28–29; *CEH*, vol. 5, 30.

[117] *CEH*, vol. 5, 37.

[118] *CEH*, vol. 5, 38.

is in heaven, this is not something to cry over. If he is in Purgatory, there are ways to help him besides immoderate weeping, and it is a cause of rejoicing that he is on the way to salvation.[119]

There is, by contrast, a good kind of mourning, which Salmerón calls "Christian and blessed." This consists principally in mourning over sin, as in the case of Adam and other figures in scripture. Some sins, even if forgiven, are worthy of tears for the rest of one's life, as in the case of Peter's denial of Jesus, or Paul's persecution of the Church. It is worth mourning over the sins of one's neighbors, over heresies and schisms, the abuses of priests, the perfidy of the Jews, and the suffering of the faithful among pagans, Turks, and even fellow Christians. He produces a catena of biblical verses that encourage this good kind of weeping, as when David "beheld the transgressors, and pined away" (Ps 118:158), or when Jesus wept over Jerusalem (Lk 19:41).[120]

Salmerón says that interior mourning must be matched by exterior mourning, which he identifies with avoiding the enjoyment of food and splendid clothing.[121] He begins a mini-treatise on these topics, which one might have expected under the heading of poverty. The rationale for placing it here is that he associates "blessed are they that mourn" with repressing the concupiscence of the flesh more generally. Clothing is necessary, as indicated by Adam's nakedness in the Garden, so Salmerón rejects the nudism of the ancient Cynics as well as contemporary "Adamites" in Bohemia and Holland. Going about naked makes for the erroneous claim that one's nature is whole and innocent.[122]

Wearing fine clothing, however, proceeds from pride and gives a bad example. Salmerón says that the rich man who wore purple and fine linen (Lk 16:19) was a precursor of the Antichrist, and he cites Augustine's practice of selling off gifts of clothing. The Jesuit theologian complains against the excesses of dress in his own time, especially among ecclesiastics and women. The latter wear things that promote lasciviousness, while their husbands permit this and

---

[119] *CEH*, vol. 5, 39.

[120] *CEH*, vol. 5, 41–43.

[121] *CEH*, vol. 5, 44–45.

[122] *CEH*, vol. 5, 45. There were various nudist sects in the Middle Ages. The ones from the Netherlands emerged in the thirteenth century as an offshoot of the Brethren of the Free Spirit, whereas the Bohemian version, under the leadership of the priest Peter Kanis, splintered from the radical wing of the Hussite movement. Salmerón notes approvingly that princes repressed the Adamites in Holland. *CBP*, vol. 4, 92.

priests absolve them without scruple. Such people not only refuse to weep, but they also provoke the wrath of God.[123]

Salmerón included other behaviors in the category of external mourning. One must sleep, but those who do so excessively become soft, effeminate, and too delicate to bear their cross. One should get up early and avoid a nocturnal existence. Although there is need for recreation, jokes and laughter should be short and restrained, for men need little laughter and much weeping. As Tertullian says, all spectacles are forbidden to Christians, along with shows of women, dice and other forms of gambling, and many other things.[124] In Salmerón's view, the injunction to mourn covers a wide array of behaviors. All Christians are obliged to do some weeping, and the best are eager to do more of it.

Clearly the Beatitudes present a demanding standard of conduct, but Salmerón was also attentive to the rewards that accompany it, as the codicil to this Beatitude ("for they will be comforted") shows. One of the rewards is consolation, which he defines as "a certain conversation with God in us from the presence of the Holy Spirit" [*quoddam colloquium Dei in nobis ex praesentia Spiritus sancti*], and which he says is equivalent to joy. Those who live the Beatitudes discover the truth that the pleasures of the soul are higher than those of the body, so much so that some men enjoy greater consolation even than the angels. The consolation that mourning merits is twofold, for it is experienced in this life and in the next.[125]

Thou Shalt not Kill

After preaching the Beatitudes, Jesus in Matthew's Gospel moved to the "greater commandments," beginning with the Fifth: "thou shalt not kill." According to Salmerón, this was not only a precept of the Mosaic Law, but also of the natural law, and the prohibition against murder is already present in the biblical accounts of Cain and Noah. The prohibition applies to taking away human life, not the life of plants or animals, as the most foolish Manichaeans and Pythagoras taught.[126] Salmerón grounded this commandment in the dig-

---

[123] *CEH*, vol. 5, 46. While in Venice in 1564, he persuaded some women to wear a style of dress that went up all the way to the neck, which was dubbed "the Salmerón." This may be the earliest Jesuit contribution to women's fashion. Mario Scaduto, *L'epoca di Giacomo Laínez, 1556–1565: L'azione* (Rome: Edizioni La Civiltà Cattolica, 1974), 580.

[124] *CEH*, vol. 5, 47–48.

[125] *CEH*, vol. 5, 53–54.

[126] *CEH*, vol. 5, 190–91.

nity of man. "It is therefore to be understood as being about man, whom it is not permitted to kill for any reason, because man exists for himself [*propter se est*], and he answers only to God."¹²⁷ Even when man, who is free by nature, becomes the slave of those who have greater natural capacity or intelligence, he remains human in dignity and he cannot be killed by his masters.¹²⁸

Having stated the principle, however, Salmerón lists exceptions to it. As the true Prince and Lord of life and death, God may command someone to kill, as he did in the cases of Abraham, Samson, and Saul. The Jesuit theologian explains that not everything that is prohibited to some particular person is prohibited simpliciter to everyone. Since God has true and proper dominion over all men, he can command them as he pleases, which includes dispensing from the Fifth Commandment in certain cases. Princes, judges, and magistrates licitly kill by the authority given to them by God, when they do so under the law, with right intention, and with zeal for justice. In support of this claim, Salmerón cites multiple verses from both testaments of scripture. Anyone whose actions depart from justice and disturb the peace of the commonwealth may be killed. He specifically mentions witches as people whom the civil authorities may justly execute. One may also licitly kill in the act of self-defense, or when an intruder comes into the home, and such acts carry with them no divine, civil, or ecclesiastical punishment.¹²⁹ Human law permits killing a wife or daughter caught in adultery, but this is still a sin before God. This illustrates the principle that human law permits certain evils for the sake of avoiding greater ones, as also in the case of usury and prostitution.¹³⁰

Salmerón lists additional sins that fall under the prohibition against murder. Citing multiple figures from classical antiquity and scripture, such as Cato, Lucretia, and Razis (2 Mac 14:41–46), he explains that suicide is forbidden. Although Thomas, following Augustine, excused the Roman virgins who threw themselves into the Tiber, the Jesuit theologian did not think such an action was licit; as Agatha said, being deflowered does not cause one to lose the crown of martyrdom, but rather doubles it.¹³¹ But Salmerón does

---

[127] *CEH*, vol. 5, 191.

[128] *CEH*, vol. 5, 191.

[129] *CEH*, vol. 5, 191–92. One may not, however, kill an intruder who is too weak to do harm, or who steals out of necessity rather than malice.

[130] *CEH*, vol. 5, 193. Only in the sixteenth century did the civil authorities take over from the husband the right to punish his wife for adultery, and his vengeance was still permitted as long as he killed both her and her lover. Wiesner-Hanks, *Women and Gender*, 47.

[131] *CEH*, vol. 5, 194–95.

say that if God ordered someone to kill himself, as in the case of Samson, that command would have to be obeyed.[132] One may not maim oneself, as Origen is reported to have done, or Democritus, who took out his own eyes.[133] The precept against killing applies to anything that puts someone in danger of death, as well as procuring sterilization or abortion. He calls abortion a "more than bestial crime."[134]

The Fifth Commandment, however, is not merely about the prohibition of killing and the external deeds annexed to it, as the additional words of Jesus make clear: "but I say to you, that whosoever is angry with his brother, shall be in danger of the judgment" (Mt 5:22). It is also a matter of overcoming wrath, for which Salmerón provided a taxonomy. Anger [*ira*] is the desire for vengeance. When it is a virtue, it is called zeal; when it is a vice, wrath [*iracundia*].[135] Zeal means desiring revenge (understood as the punishment of evil) according to the order of reason and charity.[136] Wrath results from desiring vengeance beyond charity, which can make for venial or mortal sin, and it is categorized as a capital sin because of all the crimes that flow from it.[137]

Salmerón denied that Jesus's words about turning the other cheek (Mt 5:39) made protecting oneself from attack illicit for Christians, for the law of grace perfects rather than destroys the law of nature. The Lord brought to an end the *lex talionis*, which was never a moral precept, but a way of regulating punishments, because the Jews had difficulty observing moderation in this regard.[138] "Turning the other cheek" means the prohibition of private vengeance, but not the legitimate coercive and punitive measures of the civil

---

[132] *CEH*, vol. 5, 195. He says that without the certainty that it has come from God, the command to kill oneself must be understood as coming from Satan. Salmerón does not explain, however, how one arrives at such certitude.

[133] *CEH*, vol. 5, 194.

[134] *CEH*, vol. 5, 195. Salmerón adds, however, that if quickening has not yet occurred, killing the fetus is not homicide, nor does it incur ecclesiastical irregularity. In another place, he speaks of abortion simply as homicide. *CEH*, vol. 3, 52. The exact status of the sin of abortion was debated in the sixteenth century, which Sixtus V sought to resolve when in 1588 he issued a bull mandating that anyone who tried to terminate a pregnancy was to be tried as a murderer and excommunicated. John Christopoulos, "Papal Authority, Episcopal Reservation, and Abortion in Sixteenth-Century Italy," in *Episcopal Reform and Politics in Early Modern Europe*, ed. Jennifer DeSilva (Kirksville, MO: Truman State University Press, 2012), 110–27.

[135] *CEH*, vol. 5, 195.

[136] *CEH*, vol. 5, 198.

[137] *CEH*, vol. 5, 198–99.

[138] *CEH*, vol. 5, 247–48.

authorities, or of self-defense against attacks on one's person or one's goods.[139] Yet Salmerón's understanding of self-defense and its legitimacy only becomes complete in light of the higher standard of the Beatitudes.

The meek are blessed (Mt 5:4) because they restrain the desire for vengeance, which places them not only above the law of the flesh, but also above the Law of Moses and above those who conquered the promised land by the sword.[140] The perfect man prefers to lose his goods than kill his neighbor or expose his brother to danger. The law of grace teaches men to despise the lower goods, and self-defense should ultimately be evaluated according to the preservation of man's end of beatitude.[141] While acknowledging the continuing vigor of the natural law, Salmerón did not leave it untouched by grace and the law of Christ.

Even his defense of just war is colored by the Beatitudes. The glory of war flourished, he says, until Christ came and taught to overcome with patience and meekness.[142] Even if princes can, and sometimes must, wage war, this is not a license for bloodlust, least of all when Christians fight Christians. Commenting on Christ's presence wherever two or three are gathered in his name (Mt 18:20), Salmerón laments,

> But woe to us, who have forgotten such a teaching and make the cross of Christ fight with the cross, and who make the symbol of peace, which should call us back from all dissension, into a symbol of war. What will we say of those who put the names of the apostles onto cannons, and carve their images into them? Or of what is deplorable, that they place in churches, among the statues of the apostles and the martyrs, trophies soaked in the blood of men for whom Christ died, whom they in the meantime avenged for private injuries in a deceitful and treacherous manner? As if it were equally devout to make a martyr as to be one.[143]

Although he was no pacifist, the Jesuit theologian objected to exalting "the glory of war" over the strictures of a purified Decalogue and the still higher way of the Beatitudes.[144]

---

[139] *CEH*, vol. 5, 248–50.
[140] *CEH*, vol. 5, 63.
[141] *CEH*, vol. 5, 250–51.
[142] *CEH*, vol. 5, 63.
[143] *CEH*, vol. 5, 123.
[144] Although not engaged in ministry to soldiers himself, Salmerón's concerns dovetail in many respects with the catechetical and pastoral endeavors of some Jesuit contemporaries toward soldiers and sailors. See Vincenzo Lavenia, "Missiones

Thou Shalt not Commit Adultery

After the prohibition against killing comes the prohibition against adultery, because it is a most grievous injury against the person, and one that men who desire honor avenge. Salmerón defines adultery [*moechia*] as coitus with someone else's wife, but he says that into this category fall all sexual acts outside of legitimate matrimony, which requires respecting the end of generating children and minimizing the ardor of concupiscence. The forbidden acts include simple fornication, concubinage, adultery, incest, sacrilege, rape, "the sin against nature," and effeminacy.[145]

According to the Jesuit theologian, adultery is the gravest kind of sin. It violates the sacrament of matrimony, which is a sign of Christ and the Church, and it is more harmful to the commonwealth than other sins, because it gives greater offense to the citizenry, as the case of Paris and Helen demonstrates. It undermines the education of children, frequently leads to murder *in flagrante*, and often gives rise to hatred and blasphemy. For this reason, it was a capital offense in the Mosaic Law, and it is punished by Christian princes as well. Men and women alike should flee adultery even when enticed, as Joseph the patriarch did (Gen 39:7–10).[146]

Although he gives several reasons for forbidding prostitution, Salmerón also discusses the parameters that should be set for it as a tolerated evil. Citing the Law of Moses, Aristotle, and Augustine, he says that if prostitutes are allowed in the city, then they should be confined to their own district apart from other women. Otherwise, good people will be inclined to visit them, even priests and religious. Salmerón complains that in Italy, prostitutes are allowed in the middle of the city and even inside churches.[147] He commends

---

Castrenses: Jesuits and Soldiers between Pastoral Care and Violence," *Journal of Jesuit Studies* 4 (2017): 545–58.

[145] *CEH*, vol. 5, 214.

[146] *CEH*, vol. 5, 215–17. Salmerón's words reflect post-Tridentine concern for the sanctity of marriage, without touching upon the economic issues at stake. See Mauro Carboni, "The Economics of Marriage: Dotal Strategies in Bologna in the Age of Catholic Reform," *Sixteenth Century Journal* 39, no. 2 (2008): 371–87. For the legal and juridical complexities surrounding adultery in this period in Italy, see Laura Turchi, "Adulterio, onere della prova e testimonianza. In margine a un processo correggese di età tridentina," in *Trasgressioni: Seduzione, concubinato, adulterio, bigamia (XIV–XVIII secolo)*, eds. Silvana Seidel Menchi and Diego Quaglioni (Bologna: Il Mulino, 2004), 305–50.

[147] Although he took a clear moral stance against prostitution, Salmerón's refusal to say that it ought simply to be outlawed reflects ambiguity found throughout Christian history, including his own age. Some cities, like Venice, implemented

the practice of establishing houses for their reform, while refuting objections against these institutions. Some ask, if God punishes prostitution with the "French disease," why should we stand in his way? Salmerón replies that one should not add affliction to those who are already afflicted, but rather console them with words and alms, lest they fall into greater sadness.[148]

Another sin that captured his attention was sodomy. In commenting on Rom 1, Salmerón explains how God punished the Gentiles' sins of fornication, particularly sodomy. He used fire and brimstone on Sodom and Gomorrah (Gen 19:24–25), and Rome burned in the time of Nero as punishment for the marriages with men that he had contracted in Greece and in the Senate. He cites Catherine of Siena for the view that not even the demons can tolerate being present while such acts are committed.[149] Salmerón rejects the theory, which he attributes to Nicholas of Lyra, that avarice or denial of hospitality, rather than lust, was the real sin of Sodom.[150] According to the Jesuit theologian, sodomy is the terminus of vice: flesh satiated by gluttony moves to fornication, and from there, to the vice of Sodom.[151] He also complains about the failure of the civil authorities to punish it more severely, without explaining what the punishment ought to be.[152]

Arguably more important than the specific sins and their corresponding punishments, however, was the larger question of the integration of the Mosaic Law, the Decalogue, and the Beatitudes. What did Christ add to the Sixth Commandment? In the first place, he made it clear that simple fornication is a sin, something that both Gentiles and the authors of the Talmud often disregarded, even though in certain places (Ecclus 9:1–13, Tob 3:16–18) scripture forbids all concupiscence in men and women.[153] Salmerón says that those who dare to ask why simple fornication is a sin might as well ask why

---

regulations of the kind he recommends, but the social separation was usually not achieved, both because the laws were not enforced and because prostitutes often found favor in their communities. See Paula Clarke, "The Business of Prostitution in Early Renaissance Venice," *Renaissance Quarterly* 68, no. 2 (2015): 419–64; Tessa Storey, *Carnal Commerce in Counter-Reformation Rome* (Cambridge: Cambridge University Press, 2008).

[148] *CEH*, vol. 4, 287–88. He may have been thinking of the house of Santa Marta that Ignatius established in Rome for this purpose.

[149] *CBP*, vol. 1, 328.

[150] *CEH*, vol. 4, 353; *CEH*, vol. 4, 496.

[151] *CEH*, vol. 5, 342.

[152] *CEH*, vol. 8, 287. The bull *Horrendum illud scelus*, which Pius V issued in 1568, may provide some clues.

[153] *CEH*, vol. 5, 218.

it is forbidden to prostitute one's wife or daughters.[154] In the second place, Christ showed the difference between the external Law of Moses and the spiritual law of Christ. The latter is more excellent, not only because it is concerned with the good of man simply, and therefore forbids anything against it, but also because it assigns determinate punishments for such transgressions. Christ forbids deliberately looking at a woman with lust, which is adultery of the heart, and Salmerón cites scripture and Augustine to explain how such sins are committed interiorly.[155]

There is an unexpected correlation between the Beatitudes and the Sixth Commandment. In his commentary on "blessed are they that mourn", Salmerón says that the Church [*Christiana respublica*] has two states of life:

> the first and superior of them, which observes perfect mourning, belongs to those who profess virginity and chastity, by which someone deprives and despoils himself of all faculty of marrying. The other is a little inferior and belongs indeed to those who devote themselves to marriage for the preservation of the world. They nevertheless do not lack some mourning now and again.[156]

Salmerón explains that marriage is good and the enjoyment of sex is not a sin, but celibacy or virginity is clearly better; denying this is like preferring earth to heaven.[157] In addition to being monogamous and permanent, marriage knows periods of abstinence for the sake of prayer and fasting, menstruation, and the weakness of one of the spouses. This abstinence, along with the prohibition of divorce, the necessity of tolerating each other, the burdens of caring for the family and educating the children, and the avoidance of lust, constitute the mourning of married life.[158]

Salmerón offers a few words on the greatness and spiritual fecundity of celibacy. "Celibacy truly has its own lofty and spiritual progeny which is worthier of heaven than of earth."[159] Aristotle was wrong to say that the solitary man, without a wife, children, friends, a splendid table and clothing, could not be happy, as he did not know Christ. God's commandment to be fruitful and multiply only remained in vigor until the earth was full. After that, God himself preached that those who mourned and became eunuchs for the kingdom

---

[154] *CEH*, vol. 5, 55.
[155] *CEH*, vol. 5, 218–20.
[156] *CEH*, vol. 5, 49.
[157] *CEH*, vol. 5, 50.
[158] *CEH*, vol. 5, 49.
[159] *CEH*, vol. 5, 50.

of heaven were blessed, a way of life that Christ, John the Baptist, and the apostles undertook as an example to others. It is most absurd, Salmerón says, to claim that marriage is equal to or better than virginity, because the latter imitates the life of heaven, where "they shall neither marry nor be married, but shall be as the angels of God in heaven" (Mt. 22:30). Salmerón had no sympathy for Protestant objections to celibacy, and he attacked the failure of those who violated their promises so they could marry, like Luther and Bucer, as well as the hypocrisy of those who embraced the state of life without accepting the gift of continence. He ridicules the objection that the world would die if everyone chose this path. "O singular solicitude of charity for the world! You go and get married, and let us be celibates."[160]

The Misery of Life

The *Commentaries* often refer to the heavy burden of concupiscence to which all men are subject, which Salmerón regards as one of the principal miseries of the human condition. In a lengthy catalog of the consequences of the Fall of Adam, he says that,

> man was stripped of that good spirit that inclines toward God, but the feeble power of becoming angry remained, along with the power of desiring, which is prone to delights and pleasures of the flesh…He was despoiled of the dominion over all things that he possessed, so that everything fights and plots against him, and the rebellion by which he fell from God in a certain way punishes him. Howsoever everything, as I said, rises up against man, nothing does so more than man himself.[161]

In another commentary on the "fourfold misery" of the human condition after the Fall, Salmerón says that the lusting of the flesh against the spirit is a great unhappiness, but worse still is that man does not think this lusting is an evil. He willingly gives in to it and lends a hand to sin. Even when he is in Christ and possesses knowledge of the divine law and charity in his heart, he still has concupiscence fighting against him.[162] "Yes indeed, if you look at man's nature, mores, and character, you would call him the cruelest tyrant. He indulges his

---

[160] *CEH*, vol. 5, 51. It has been suggested that a key aspect of Jesuit masculinity is the notion of "chastity made easy" found in Ignatius's *Autobiography*. Ulrike Strasser, *Missionary Men in the Early Modern World: German Jesuits and Pacific Journeys* (Amsterdam: Amsterdam University Press, 2020), 56.

[161] *CEH*, vol. 3, 142–43.

[162] *CBP*, vol. 1, 527–28.

life with pleasures, spares the life of no creature, and the rest fear him, hate him, and flee from him."[163]

The technical theological term for this aspect of man's condition is the "tinder of sin" [*fomes peccati*], which refers to a bad kind of ardent desire or concupiscence.[164] The *fomes* is not itself actual sin, because it is not a voluntary act, nor even original sin, but it is an effect of original sin.[165] It remains in man permanently even after Baptism.[166] Salmerón likens the *fomes* to an "internal Jebusite" (see Josh 15:63), or to the tail of a snake that still moves even after its head has been cut off.[167] Life is certainly much harder on account of it, but Salmerón suggests that God has left the *fomes* even in the justified man for a good reason. "Like a skilled doctor, God left a scar in wounded man, so that he would remember his woundedness and his wounds, and the doctor who healed him, and be grateful to him and love him."[168] Although Christians will not be free of the *fomes* until they get to heaven, Salmerón recommends devout reception of the Eucharist as a means for repressing it.[169] The permanence of the tinder of sin, which was a common teaching among the theologians, was crucial to Salmerón's moral theology, insofar as it helped explain why man falls so far short of the Gospel law's standards.

---

[163] *CBP*, vol. 3, 683.

[164] *CBP*, vol. 1, 166. Marlorat attacks the Catholic teaching that concupiscence requires consent to be sin, saying that the Lord condemns as adulterers those who admit *quasvis punctiones* of lust. Marlorat, *Expositio*, vol. 1, 35.

[165] *CBP*, vol. 1, 441.

[166] *CBP*, vol. 4, 14; *CBP*, vol. 4, 179.

[167] *CEH*, vol. 4, 91; *CBP*, vol. 4, 182. It is unclear from these texts if Salmerón is closer to Thomas or to the Jesuit tradition on the *fomes*. McAleer identifies the latter with Francisco de Toledo and Diego Laínez in the sixteenth century, and with Karl Rahner and Gaston Fessard in the twentieth. In the Jesuit tradition, he claims, sensuality is in a relationship of violence with reason at a metaphysical level, whereas Thomas sees the *fomes* as merely a disorder of sensuality. Salmerón's emphasis on the *fomes* as a postlapsarian condition leaves the Thomistic option open. Graham McAleer, "Jesuit Sensuality and Feminist Bodies," *Modern Theology* 18, no. 3 (2002): 395–405.

[168] *CBP*, vol. 4, 182.

[169] *CEH*, vol. 9, 11; *CEH*, vol. 9, 189.

Conclusion

Salmerón intended not only to provide instruction about good mores, but also to assist the reader in acquiring them. This entailed, first of all, an immersion into the *mos Ecclesiae*, or the organic whole of Catholic liturgical and ascetical praxis. Social in nature, it rests not merely on the ingenuity and consent of the community, but on the divine guidance of the Holy Spirit throughout the Church's history. It requires, according to Salmerón, the maintaining of an asymmetrical relationship between the sexes as the basis of the social order, while simultaneously acknowledging the spiritual aptitude of women. He also provided the theoretical foundation of Christian morality, which is characteristically biblical in inspiration, and consists of the careful integration of the Beatitudes and the Decalogue into an understanding of the "Gospel law." This understanding of Christ as lawgiver was indebted to Salmerón's experience and interpretation of the Council of Trent. He relied heavily on the theological tradition he had received for the articulation of it, but he also sought to present it anew in light of the Protestant challenges of the sixteenth century, especially regarding the excellence of virginity and continence. The Gospel law may have a lower limit, but it has no upper limit, and the best way to draw men upward is through participation in public worship, ascetical practice, and prayerful meditation on the Sermon on the Mount.

8 The *Commentaries* and the Jesuits

When commenting on the great fruit that the apostles bore in the primitive Church, despite their small numbers, Salmerón makes an analogy with the religious orders.

> For behold, the Carthusian Order took its beginning from seven pious men, the head of which was blessed Bruno. The congregation of blessed Francis began from thirteen brothers, as the congregation of blessed Dominic was propagated from sixteen. Our Society of Jesus, which certainly came later than all the others, started from ten men.[1]

This is one of very few references in the *Commentaries* to their author's religious order. In contrast with his usual prolixity, Salmerón was abrupt on this subject, yet this should not be confused with lack of interest. The aforementioned passage captures well his desire to present, in few words, the Jesuit order as faithfully continuing the teaching and work of the Catholic Church for the salvation of souls in the larger tradition of religious life. If some observers past and present have sought to highlight what distinguishes the Society of Jesus from the mainstream of the Church, Salmerón's approach was exactly the opposite.

This chapter has a twofold purpose: to explain and evaluate the presentation of the Jesuits in the *Commentaries*, and to situate Salmerón's theological vision within early Jesuit history. The latter task is more challenging and must remain provisional, for several reasons. First, the *Commentaries* were a unique source among the first Jesuits; no other founder provided comparable data with which to compare them. Second, the material that the other companions left behind usually had an immediate practical purpose, and in many cases, it was only published by later editors. This makes it more difficult to know how they would have presented a theological vision to the world, rather than amongst themselves. Third, a complete comparative study of all the available sources lies beyond the scope of the present volume, which limits itself to comparing Salmerón with his close friend Diego Laínez. In many ways their

---

[1] *CEH*, vol. 12, 39.

perspectives were similar, but there were also key differences between the two Jesuit founders.

The Jesuits in the *Commentaries*

The Society of Jesus is far more notable in Salmerón's work by its absence than by its presence. In his lengthy commentary on the name of Jesus, there is no mention of the order that bears this name.[2] When discussing the relationship between the active and contemplative life, there is no use of Nadal's expression "contemplatives in action," or any other mention of the Society.[3] When speaking about pilgrimage to the Holy Land, Salmerón makes no reference to Ignatius's time in Jerusalem, or to the first companions' plan to establish themselves there after their departure from Paris.[4] The various models of governance in religious orders, or even the mention of founders who journeyed to Rome to obtain approval for their communities, elicit not a word about Jesuits.[5] When discussing apostasy from religious life, Salmerón mentions the traditions and institutes established by Augustine, Benedict, Dominic, and Francis, but not Ignatius.[6] When he gives examples of saints who begged, he includes Benedict, Bernard, Francis, and Dominic, but not Ignatius.[7] Peter Canisius is a glaring omission from the catalog of contemporary theologians, given their personal friendship and Salmerón's effusive praise of his writings elsewhere.[8]

Salmerón was singled out by Ignatius for his abilities in giving the Spiritual Exercises.[9] It is curious, then, that Salmerón appears to have mentioned them only once, and that he also passed over obvious opportunities to connect them to various topics. One of Salmerón's criteria for distinguishing between true and false prophets is that they are approved or disapproved by those who have

---

[2] *CEH*, vol. 3, 323–36.

[3] *CEH*, vol. 4, 517–20.

[4] *CEH*, vol. 1, 505–20.

[5] *CEH*, vol. 4, 425; *CEH*, vol. 4, 427.

[6] *CBP*, vol. 3, 522.

[7] *CEH*, vol. 5, 25.

[8] *ES*, vol. 2, no. 366, 311–18.

[9] MHSI. MI. *Fontes Narrativi de S. Ignatio de Loyola et de Societatis Iesu initiis* (hereafter *FN*), vol. 1, *Narrationes scriptae ante annum 1557*, eds. Dionisio Fernández Zapico and Cándido de Dalmases (Rome: MHSI, 1943), 658. Ignatius places him after Faber, and ahead of Francisco de Villanueva and Jerome Domenech.

the gift of the discernment of spirits, but he says nothing about the *Exercises*.[10] His words about the behavior of angels resonate with the "Rules for the Discernment of Spirits:" the good ones frighten at first but then console, whereas Satan first consoles but then frightens or terrorizes. Yet the *Spiritual Exercises* are not identified as the source for this idea.[11] The "degrees of humility" that Salmerón identifies do not correspond to the ones found in Ignatius's meditation on this subject.[12]

How can this silence be explained? One possibility may be immediately discarded: that Salmerón was indifferent to, or ignorant of, the Society's documents and affairs. He was very much in the thick of the order's history, whether as a preacher, professor, conciliar theologian, ambassador, provincial, or vicar-general. His theological expertise was sought on important matters; while at the final convocation of Trent, for example, he helped Peter Canisius revise his catechism.[13] His correspondence reveals detailed knowledge of, and meticulous attention to, internal issues and relations to the wider Church and world.[14] Another, more likely explanation is that early Jesuits were often less inclined than contemporary Jesuits to highlight their distinctiveness, as John O'Malley and Timothy O'Brien have shown.[15] To take other exegetes of the period for comparison, Maldonado says nothing in his *Commentaries* about the Society, whereas Barradas says that its purpose is "to conquer heresies, idolatry, and sins throughout the whole world." He highlights the indispensability of "soldiers prompt to obedience" for this purpose, praising Ignatius's famous letter on obedience, which said that the Society distinguished itself

---

[10] *CEH*, vol. 1, 170.

[11] *CEH*, vol. 2, 257 (Y3r); Cf. *MHSI. MI. Series Secunda: Exercitia Spiritualia S. Ignatii de Loyola et eorum directoria*, vol. 1, *Exercitia Spiritualia* (hereafter *SpEx*), eds. Joseph Calaveras and Cándido de Dalmases (Rome: IHSI, 1969), §314–15, 374.

[12] *CEH*, vol. 4, 67; Cf. *SpEx*, §165–68, 260–62.

[13] Carlos Sommervogel, *Bibliothèque de la Compagnie de Jésus*, new edition (Brussels: Oscar Schepens, 1896), vol. 7, cols. 482–83.

[14] Esther Jiménez Pablo, "El P. Alfonso Salmerón S.I. y el gobierno de los colegios de Nápoles," *Magallánica* 2, vol. 4 (2016), 57–79; Mark Lewis and Jennifer Selwyn, "Jesuit Activity in Southern Italy during the Generalate of Everard Mercurian," in *The Mercurian Project: Forming Jesuit Culture 1573–1580*, ed. Thomas McCoog (St. Louis, MO: Institute of Jesuit Sources, 2004), 532–57.

[15] John O'Malley and Timothy O'Brien, "The Twentieth-Century Construction of Ignatian Spirituality: A Sketch," *Studies in the Spirituality of Jesuits* 52, no. 3 (2020): 1–40; John O'Malley, "The Distinctiveness of the Society of Jesus," *Journal of Jesuit Studies* 3, no. 1 (2016): 1–16.

from other orders in the observance of it.¹⁶ He also manifests the order's characteristic pride in its missionary endeavors when he compares the Society to the four rivers flowing forth from Paradise, making innumerable Christians and fighting heresies across the globe.¹⁷

Salmerón's presentation of the Society, however terse, was nevertheless carefully crafted. His portrayal of the order focuses on men rather than on an institution, and more specifically, on his friends.¹⁸ The first words about a fellow Jesuit appear in the general preface.

> I am fully aware that I owe much to some of my contemporaries and also to men who have already died. There are still others of whom I should perhaps make appreciative mention, but one above all whom I cannot pass over in silence. This is Father Diego Laínez, of happy memory, former general of the Society of Jesus, a man who was as religious as he was learned. He was endowed with a singular, almost divine, intellect, well-nigh miraculously informed in the subtleties of various branches of learning, and particularly acute in his knowledge of the sacred scriptures and in the writings of the ancient Fathers…
>
> By a singular favor of God there existed between Father Laínez and myself, even before the beginnings of the Society, a certain intimate, mutual understanding and comradeship in life, religion, and studies. I do not think I could escape the charge of ingratitude unless I pointed out in this Preface that I have been tremendously inspired and encouraged by the studies and labors of this great man of God.¹⁹

He is elsewhere called the "most erudite and most religious Father Diego Laínez of happy memory" when Salmerón praises his position at Trent against granting the chalice to the laity.²⁰ Salmerón wanted his memory to abide and, above all, to be historically accurate. In 1584, he sent a letter to Rome with a

---

[16] Barradas, *Commentaries*, vol. 3, 342.

[17] Barradas, *Commentaries*, vol. 3, 534.

[18] Strasser thinks that the Society exercised a strong appeal as an all-male community, in response to the Protestant attack on clerical masculinity. "The masculine self that emerged from the Exercises was emotionally oriented both toward other Jesuits ('one in desire and will') and also the larger world." Ulrike Strasser, *Missionary Men in the Early Modern World: German Jesuits and Pacific Journeys* (Amsterdam: Amsterdam University Press, 2020), 46, 70–71.

[19] *CEH*, vol. 1, Preface, 5r. English translation (slightly modified) in Joseph Fichter, *James Laynez: Jesuit* (St. Louis, MO: Herder, 1944), Appendix III, 271.

[20] *CEH*, vol. 9, 307.

list of nineteen corrections to Ribadeneyra's *Life of Laínez*.²¹ Salmerón's reverence for the man is captured in a vignette related by the same Ribadeneyra. After hearing Salmerón preach, a lay nobleman asked him if it was really possible that Laínez (whom the nobleman had never met) was equally as learned. Salmerón replied, "I promise that the difference between Father Laínez and me is as great as the difference between me and you."²²

The second Jesuit whom Salmerón discusses makes his appearance near the beginning of Volume 6, which is about Jesus's miracles. He explains that miracles are rare now because the testimony of the Gospel and the power of prayer and the sacraments are sufficient to bring people to faith. Yet he maintains that "the hand of the Lord is not shortened" (Is 59:1), and that God sometimes continues to work miracles through the living or the dead to confirm their sanctity.²³

> Truly I would show myself ungrateful to the great servant of God and my very close friend bound to me in Christ, and not lightly failing toward God himself, if in this passage which is first for elucidating the name of Christ Jesus, and then for celebrating his magnificent works, I did not bring forth the things that the divine goodness deigned to accomplish through Father Francis Xavier of happy memory, one of the first professed in our Society of the name of Jesus.²⁴

Salmerón proceeds to list a number of these miracles, including raising someone from the dead, giving sight to a blind man, and restoring speech to a mute man. In a single year of his preaching, Xavier baptized with his own hands over one hundred thousand people "like a sort of new apostle," so that he no longer had the strength to raise his hands to touch the water, pronounce the baptismal formula, or intone the Litany of the Saints. According to Salmerón, Xavier had the apostolic gift of preaching in a single language and being understood by his diverse hearers, and his body was found incorrupt after being unearthed three months after his death. Salmerón insists that this testimony does not rest merely on his own authority, but that John III of Portugal

---

[21] *ES*, vol. 2, no. 532, 733–38.

[22] Miguel Lop Sebastià, *Alfonso Salmerón, SJ (1515–1585): Una biografía epistolar* (Madrid: Comillas, 2015), Appendix, 359–372, at 370.

[23] *CEH*, vol. 6, 11–12.

[24] *CEH*, vol. 6, 13.

ordered his ministers to collect authentic accounts of Xavier's life and death and send them back to Portugal.[25]

This brief treatment of the life, death, and miracles of Xavier emphasizes two points. First, God performed great works in him that were equivalent (or at least nearly so) to what Christ and the apostles themselves had done. Second, Xavier's activity of baptizing, that is, administering the sacraments, is narrated with a particular flair for the dramatic. Salmerón returns to this theme later in the *Commentaries* when he discusses the baptism of one hundred and twenty people at Pentecost, claiming that Xavier performed a total of four hundred thousand baptisms in the Indies.[26]

The third and final Jesuit whom the *Commentaries* name and discuss is the founder of the order, Ignatius of Loyola. Salmerón's words appear in his treatment of the sacrament of Penance.

> But, nevertheless, in this place I will freely expound upon this matter: our father of happy memory Ignatius of Loyola, the principal founder of our Society, a man of remarkable holiness and adorned with extraordinary prudence. He brought companions into his fellowship and called them from the waves of life by which they were tossed into the serene port of his religious order by nothing more than the frequent and regular reception of the sacraments, and by certain pious and spiritual exercises for a holy life ordered towards general confession, a method of meditating on the life of Christ, and zeal for adapted prayers. He himself also used this plan of frequently confessing and receiving the Eucharist, and of occasionally making general confessions, and by both his example and word, he established and recommended it for all his students and sons. But while his men try to excel in this same matter, his Society has ascended with the favor of God to its present stature, which is now so great, from its most humble beginnings. By no other stronger weapons or more potent defenses does the Society of Jesus, wherever it exists, bring forth some spiritual fruit for its neighbors than by this diligent recommendation and exhortation of the reception of the sacraments. If we wish to tell the truth, these are nearly all of the goods of our Society that she brings forth in herself and in others, the fruit of those seeds that that most holy and religious man sowed. Since the Spirit of God, who appointed that man as founder of this Society, also sent him to the Church as a planter, so to speak, then he did so because he was

---

[25] *CEH*, vol. 6, 13–14. In 1556, John III ordered his viceroy in India to collect testimonies of Xavier's life and virtues. Georg Schurhammer, *Francis Xavier: His Life, His Times*, trans. M. Joseph Costelloe (Rome: The Jesuit Historical Institute, 1982), vol. 4, 648.

[26] *CEH*, vol. 12, 89.

foreseeing, with the rise of Luther's and Calvin's heresies, that no more opportune and at-hand remedy could be brought forth to extinguish that conflagration than this recourse to frequent confession and communion, so that they might completely overthrow and shatter their heresies, which to a large extent strive to topple these two sacraments. Blessed be God who in his marvelous wisdom knows to send, on account of the time, suitable and useful workers into his vineyard, so that they might purge the Church of vices and defend her from heresies, and urge her, by words and example of life, to fulfill the holy commands of Christ.[27]

"Spiritual exercises" almost certainly refers to Ignatius's retreat manual, and Salmerón apparently thought that its initial purpose was preparing someone to make a general confession.[28]

Even more so than in the cases of Laínez and Xavier, here the emphasis is on the reception of the sacraments. Salmerón brings up Ignatius in the context of Penance, links Penance to the reception of Communion, and explains the order's genesis and growth in terms of the promotion of these two sacraments. This is an important point, because the relationship between and relative priority of the "ministries of the word" and the administration of the sacraments is an issue in Jesuit historiography. No less an authority than Francisco Suárez gave primacy of place to the ministries of the word as the distinctive feature of Jesuit priesthood, a point that John O'Malley and others have reinforced.[29] As an exegete and a preacher, Salmerón by no means neglected these ministries, nor are they absent from his presentation of Xavier and Ignatius. Yet his unmistakable accent upon the administration of the sacraments is consistent with the idea of the Jesuits as "reformed priests."[30]

Salmerón's presentation of the Society of Jesus had several features. Men were highlighted more than the institution, which received hardly any treatment at all. These men were united, above all, by their faithful defense and administration of the sacraments, and the holiness of their lives gave witness to God's inspiration of their work. They met distinctive challenges of the age: the clamoring for the chalice in the north, the new mission fields in the east,

---

[27] *CEH*, vol. 11, 167.

[28] The Latin text is *piisque quibusdam, ac sanctae vitae spiritualibus exercitiis ad confessionem generalem, ac meditandae vitae Christi rationem, precationisque studium accommodatis*.

[29] Paul Murphy, "God's Porters: The Jesuit Vocation According to Francisco Suárez," *AHSI* 70, fasc. 139 (2001): 3–28; John O'Malley, *The First Jesuits* (Cambridge, MA: Harvard University Press), 91–162; Emily Michelson, *The Pulpit and the Press in Reformation Italy* (Cambridge, MA: Harvard University Press, 2013), 141–42.

[30] See Mark Lewis, "The First Jesuits as 'Reformed Priests,'" *AHSI* 65 (1996): 111–27.

and the war with heresy throughout the world. Salmerón's picture of the order was not a random sketch, but designed on the basis of carefully chosen figures and ideas, and its coherence with the overall theological vision of the *Commentaries* is apparent. Salmerón saw himself as presenting the truth of scripture in accordance with the Fathers and Doctors, and defending the Church's faith and practice against heresies and novelties. He fits the Jesuits seamlessly into this constant tradition, while showing how they were responding to the particular circumstances of the sixteenth century.

One of the subtlest issues in discussing the self-perception of early Jesuits is accounting for the shift that occurred after the death of Ignatius. Scholars have identified a trend, visible especially in the works of Nadal and Ribadeneyra, towards reinterpreting the establishment of the Society in terms of combating the Protestant threat.[31] Salmerón's emphasis on the Society's administration of the sacraments in his words about Ignatius is clearly united to an anti-Protestant polemic. Since Salmerón was part of the original circle of companions, the question of when he formulated this view of the Society is critical. The evidence is not altogether conclusive, but at the very least Salmerón had a consistent record of opposition to heresy dating back to the 1540s. His troubles with Cardinal Morone over preaching against Lutheran teaching on justification in Modena have already been mentioned. His sermon at Trent in 1546, although mostly focused on the failures of Catholic bishops, gave a dire warning about the Protestant danger. His correspondence throughout the 1550s and 1560s is peppered with reports on the progress of heresy and his efforts to thwart it.[32]

Absent from these earlier writings, however, is any explicit connection between the fight against heresy and the foundation of the Society of Jesus. While Salmerón may have been zealous against Protestantism from his youth, it is only in the *Commentaries* that he explains, if briefly, the purpose of the order and its founder in these terms. Even so, Salmerón is the founding Jesuit who best bridged the decades between 1540 and 1580 with a consistent focus on heresy, suggesting that while Nadal, Ribadeneyra, and others may have reinterpreted the Society's origins in terms of later concerns, this reinterpretation nevertheless had a foundation in the earlier period.

---

[31] O'Malley, *First Jesuits*, 278; Terence O'Reilly, *The* Spiritual Exercises *of Saint Ignatius of Loyola: Contexts, Sources, Reception* (Boston, MA: Brill, 2021), 3–55; Jorge Cañizares-Esguerra, Robert Maryks, and R.P. Hsia, eds., *Encounters between Jesuits and Protestants in Asia and the Americas* (Boston, MA: Brill, 2018), 1–8.

[32] *ES*, vol. 1, no. 24, 63; *ES*, vol. 1, no. 53, 126; *ES*, vol. 1, no. 55, 131; *ES*, vol. 1, no. 56, 132–33; *ES*, vol. 1, no. 81, 214–15; *ES*, vol. 1, no. 192, 501; *ES*, vol. 1, no. 220a, 547; *ES*, vol. 2, no. 289, 107.

It is fair to say, however, that Salmerón's presentation of the origin and progress of the order overlooked much of the evidence: early accusations of heresy and *alumbradismo* against Ignatius; attacks on the first companions in Rome at the time of the founding; conflicts with civil and ecclesiastical rulers; disputes with other theologians and religious orders, who accused Jesuits of error and novelty; internal battles within the Society over prayer, membership, distribution of authority, and so forth. The order's break with choir, missionary orientation, and lack of obligatory penances or religious habit really were features that set it apart from other institutes. As an important player in the founding and growth of the Jesuits for forty years, Salmerón could not have been ignorant of these matters or the controversy they occasioned. It seems fair to conclude that, while Salmerón believed in the image of the Society he presented, he also avoided anything that would make his order a target of criticism.

The *Commentaries* and Early Jesuit thought

The *Commentaries* are a unique source among the first Jesuits with respect to their genesis, genre, and purpose. Although from the 1570s numerous Jesuits embarked on writing careers, Salmerón was the only founding member granted this opportunity. Situating his magnum opus within early Jesuit thought is a prodigious task to which the present chapter can make only a modest twofold contribution. The first is evaluating the *Commentaries* according to general criteria provided by other scholars of the early Society. It will be demonstrated that Salmerón hews closely to the general features of a recent formulation of "Ignatian dogmatics," but with some nuances. The second contribution is comparing the *Commentaries* with the work of his friend and model Diego Laínez.

Ignatian Dogmatics

Even if the early Jesuits were less self-conscious than later generations, disputes about the Society's theological vision go back to its earliest days. Accusations of heresy that had dogged Ignatius continued to be a problem for the young order, and there was considerable debate within its ranks about the range of legitimate opinion, fueled especially by controversies with the Dominicans. The emergence of prominent and influential minds like Bellarmine, Suárez, and Molina led to the development of a Jesuit "school" broadly conceived. With the volume *Dogmática ignaciana*, a team of Spanish Jesuits has offered an updated perspective on the issue. These scholars identify in the writings of

Ignatius (and those of a few others, including Salmerón) distinctive elements that constitute, in their view, "Ignatian dogmatics."

Following Michel Fédou, Gabino Uríbarri Bilbao offers a list of the key features of Ignatian dogmatics:

- The concern for accounting for the faith in each moment, paying attention to the diversity of times and places
- The principal concern for helping souls, which manifests itself in the following elements:
- moral issues like cases of conscience, confession, and spiritual direction
- the importance of concrete human beings and their growth in their vocation
- attention to ecclesial praxis (the sacraments) and spiritual life (devotions)
- Elements taken more directly from the *Exercises*:
- appreciation for human freedom, inspired by the Principle and Foundation
- a pure Christocentrism, manifest especially in the exercises of the Second Week
- a constant interest in a theology with and in the Church and at its service, taken from the Rules for Thinking with the Church[33]

How well do the *Commentaries* match this template? Accounting for the faith in each moment according to the "diversity of times and places" received world-historical treatment at the hands of Salmerón. He was intent on showing that God's providence, as well as man's positive response to God's initiative, are manifest at all times and places. The concrete expression "helping souls" is not very prominent in the *Commentaries*, but it is one of the principal concerns of the work, insofar as the study of scripture is ordered toward this end. Whereas cases of conscience and spiritual direction are not much in evidence, the sacraments, devotions, and ecclesial praxis receive considerable attention. The concrete people and the growth in their vocation that Salmerón has most in mind are biblical figures, such as Mary, John the Baptist, and Peter.

The *Commentaries* never indicate a direct reliance upon the *Spiritual Exercises*, but this does not mean that they had no influence on Salmerón's way of thinking. Appreciation for human freedom is a coordinating idea in his thought, especially in his discussions of God's providence in history and justification. One may certainly question whether, and in what sense, Salmerón's Christocentrism is "pure," but Jesus Christ is at the center of his exegesis and indeed his whole theology. Without attributing to him this specific intent,

---

[33] Gabino Uríbarri Bilbao, "Del 'sentir y gustar' [Ej 2] a las 'materias teólogas' [*FN* II, 198]: El sentido de una 'dogmática ignaciana,'" in *Dogmática ignaciana: "Buscar y hallar la voluntad divina" [Ej 1]*, ed. Gabino Uríbarri Bilbao (Madrid: Comillas, 2018), 23–41, at 30.

the *Commentaries* may be seen as an exegetical-theological companion to the *Spiritual Exercises*.[34] The chronological journey through the life of Christ in prayer finds an analogue in the chronological journey through the life of Christ in Salmerón's arrangement of the Gospel history, which is enriched with historical, dogmatic, and spiritual commentary.

A constant interest in theology at the service of the Church is an apt description of the mindset behind Salmerón's work, and it correlates with the brief propositions of the "Rules for Thinking with the Church" contained in the *Spiritual Exercises*. These rules are at least as concerned with defending the traditions, practices, and ceremonies of the Catholic Church as they are with dogmas proper.[35] The *Commentaries* are not merely a defense of all these things, but also an extended explanation of their intrinsic worth and rationale. It is often said, on the basis of *Spiritual Exercises* §15, that Jesuit spirituality manifests a high level of trust in the way that God works with the individual soul in prayer. This is undoubtedly true, and one may reasonably suppose that Salmerón shared this trust, which was consistent with his refrain that God cares for and desires to save every member of the human race. Following a trend among early Jesuits that is only now receiving due attention, however, he normally presented man's encounter with God more in terms of its mediation than its directness.[36] Scripture and tradition, the counsels of the saints, the hierarchical Church and her praxis, and the liturgy never fade into the background, but always serve as the rich, dense, and regulative matrix within which the soul's encounter with God takes place. Materially and formally, Salmerón's thought is very much in keeping with the broad features of "Ignatian dogmatics."

The authors of *Dogmática ignaciana* do not mention, however, two additional tendencies associated with the Society: voluntarism and pragmatism. Often enough, these terms are used imprecisely, or with the intent of indicting

---

[34] It has been observed that Salmerón's approach to the "mysteries" corresponds to the theological depth of the *Exercises*. Santiago Madrigal Terrazas, "'Nuestra santa madre Iglesia hieráchica' [Ej 353]: La Iglesia de Jesucristo según los *Commentarii* de Salmerón" in *Dogmática ignaciana: "Buscar y hallar la voluntad divina" [Ej 1]*, ed. Gabino Uríbarri Bilbao (Madrid: Comillas, 2018), 468–502, at 475.

[35] Rules 2–3 say that Jesuits should praise sacramental confession, yearly and more frequent reception of Communion, the frequent hearing of Mass, the Divine Office, and other long prayers and singing. Other rules praise various devotions and ecclesiastical traditions, though without using the latter term. *SpEx*, §352–70, 404–14.

[36] Aaron Pidel, "Ignatius Loyola's 'Hierarchical Church' as Dionysian Reform Program," *Theological Studies* 83, no. 4 (2022): 554–78.

the order's spiritual tradition, but that does not mean that they are altogether inaccurate.[37] In the present context, "voluntarism" refers to giving the will relative priority in its relationship to the intellect, an issue that has particular importance for the Jesuit understanding of obedience. The expectation that subjects not only carry out the commands of superiors, but also conform their will and judgment to them, has been identified as a mark of voluntarism.[38] The evidence for Salmerón's view of this issue is mixed.

On the one hand, Salmerón had a strong sense of the importance of obedience to civil and ecclesiastical authorities. This comes across in his restrictive understanding of tyrannicide, as well as his lament that heretics refuse obedience to the Church and her ministers. He explains that his writing of the *Commentaries* entailed submitting his intellect, like a neck, to obedience, and he praises Joseph for practicing "blind" obedience toward God.[39] In a catena on the vestiges of the Trinity found in the virtues, he says, "Obedience is not to be given in deeds only, but also in will and in judgment."[40] These references to blindness and conformity of will and judgment are trademarks of the Jesuit position on obedience.

On the other hand, the *Commentaries*, as well as Salmerón's correspondence, gave scant attention overall to any theoretical questions surrounding

---

[37] Lawlor notes that some Catholic writers have called Ignatius a voluntarist and a pragmatist. Francis Lawlor, "The Doctrine of Grace in the *Spiritual Exercises*," *Theological Studies* 3, no. 4 (1942): 513–42. In his classic work, De Guibert observes that although voluntarism is not the core of Ignatian spirituality and can be easily caricatured, it is nevertheless present. Joseph de Guibert, *The Jesuits: Their Spiritual Doctrine and Practice*, ed. George Ganss, trans. William Young (St. Louis, MO: Institute of Jesuit Sources, 1986), 170–72. The order's "spiritual" faction of the late sixteenth century, which included a number of prominent Italian Jesuits, thought the Society was too pragmatic and ordered toward service, at the expense of the interior life. Esther Jiménez Pablo, *La forja de una identidad: La Compañía de Jesús (1540–1640)* (Madrid: Ediciones Polifemo, 2014), 133.

[38] This is in contrast to the Thomistic view that commands must be reasonable, and that the scope of obedience is limited. See Sam Zeno Conedera, "Leading the Blind: Aquinas, Ignatius, and other Jesuits on Obedience," in *Ignatius of Loyola and Thomas Aquinas: A Jesuit Ressourcement*, eds. Justin Anderson, Matthew Levering, and Aaron Pidel (Washington, DC: Catholic University of America Press, 2024), 217–45.

[39] *CEH*, vol. 1, Preface, 4r; *CEH*, vol. 3, 235.

[40] "Obedientia non tantum opera praestanda, sed et voluntate, et iudicio." *CEH*, vol. 9, 508.

obedience, in contrast to some other early Jesuits.⁴¹ The paucity and brevity of his references is notable, and the aforementioned ones that have a distinctively "Jesuit" tone appear quite randomly. Overall his thought, following Thomas, has an intellectualist rather than a voluntarist bent, which is confirmed by a striking statement. "When the will dominates the intellect, it easily follows that it believes white things to be black."⁴² Salmerón clearly intended to be critical of the will's domination by the intellect, and his statement stands in contrast to one of the "Rules for Thinking with the Church."

> If we wish to proceed securely in all things, we must hold fast to the following principle: what seems to me white, I will believe black if the hierarchical Church so defines. For I must be convinced that in Christ our Lord, the bridegroom, and in his spouse the Church, only one Spirit holds sway, which governs and rules for the salvation of souls.⁴³

Salmerón does not mention this text, which has been variously interpreted, and it seems unlikely that he would have deliberately uttered criticism of the "Rules." His words nevertheless testify to a more intellectualist outlook.⁴⁴

The issue of pragmatism in this context does not concern so much attention to practical tasks, as it does their relationship to other goods and to the observance of forms and rules in pursuing an objective. The Society's pragmatism in this sense has long been associated with the abandonment of the Divine Office in choir, along with a general preference for flexibility and apostolic

---

⁴¹ Salmerón's correspondence contains occasional references to his doing something under obedience, or telling someone else to observe obedience. He says in a letter of 1557, for example, that he goes to visit Philip II in the company of Cardinal Caraffa as a son of obedience, despite the fact that he does not like courts. *ES*, vol. 1, no. 78, 207. He also complains about one Fr. Escobar who is not disposed to obediently go where he is sent. Salmerón says that Escobar thinks that being a religious means shutting oneself in a room with books all day without bending to the words of the superior or showing any humility. *ES*, vol. 1, no. 148, 386–87. He apparently had no objection, however, to the proposal of releasing Jesuits from obedience to the superior general so that they could run the Portuguese Inquisition under royal authority. Jessica Dalton, *Between Popes, Inquisitors and Princes: How the First Jesuits Negotiated Religious Crisis in Early Modern Italy* (Boston, MA: Brill, 2020), 130.

⁴² *CEH*, vol. 4, 573 (Bbb4r).

⁴³ *SpEx*, §364, 410–12; English trans. Louis Puhl, *The Spiritual Exercises of St. Ignatius: Based on Studies in the Language of the Autograph* (Chicago, IL: Loyola Press, 1952), §365, 160.

⁴⁴ Curiously, Salmerón appears to agree with Erasmus, who ridiculed the idea that the pope can make white things black. Santiago Madrigal Terrazas, *Eclesialidad, reforma, y misión: El legado teológico de Ignacio de Loyola, Pedro Fabro y Francisco de Javier* (Madrid: San Pablo, 2008), 132.

labors over ceremonies, obligatory penances, and other traditional features of religious life.[45] Although he was inflexible in certain respects, Ignatius often gave wide discretionary powers to his immediate subordinates, with the expectation that they would be used for the greater glory of God and the good of souls in any given situation. How would this priority intersect with the Church's customary way of doing things, particularly liturgical celebration?

Ignatius himself was ambiguous on this point. On the one hand, the singular place of the Mass and the Divine Office in his prayer is well known, and he even obtained a dispensation from the latter, lest the copious tears he shed while praying cause damage to his health.[46] As general, he often ordered Jesuits to say Masses for various intentions.[47] On the other hand, the *Constitutions* that he authored sometimes display an instrumental approach to corporate worship. They say, for example, that Jesuits should not gather for the canonical hours or sung Masses unless they would be more effective in bringing people to hear a sermon or lecture.[48] In response to Andrés de Oviedo's request to say two or three Masses a day out of devotion, Ignatius replied that

---

[45] One scholar sees the idea of the Jesuit as an "instrument" as crucial to the Society's spirituality, apostolate, and structures of governance. Christopher van Ginhoven Rey, *Instruments of the Divinity: Providence and Praxis in the Foundation of the Society of Jesus* (Boston, MA: Brill, 2014).

[46] Ignatius himself provides terse but repeated documentation of these tears in his *Spiritual Diary*. *MHSI. MI. Sancti Ignatii de Loyola Constitutiones Societatis Jesu*, vol. 1, *Monumenta Constitutionum Praevia*, (Rome: Pontifical Gregorian University, 1934), 86–158. Nadal reports that Ignatius shed so many tears that he nearly went blind and had to pause over almost every word of the Office, so that he spent the greater part of the day saying it, and Ribadeneyra says the same about his praying of the Mass and the Office. *FN*, vol. 2, *Narrationes scriptae annis 1557–1574* (Rome: MHSI, 1951), 126, 157; *FN*, vol. 4, *Vita Ignatii Loyolae* (Rome: MHSI, 1965), 736–37. The text of the dispensation, granted in January 1539, can be found in *FN*, vol. 1, 552–53. See Ángel Suquía Goicoechea, *La santa misa en la espiritualidad de San Ignacio de Loyola* (Madrid: Dirección General de Relaciones Culturales, 1950).

[47] *MHSI. MI. Sancti Ignatii de Loyola Epistolae et Instructiones* (hereafter *MI Epp*) (Madrid: Gabriel López del Horno, 1903–11), vol. 1, no. 31, 177; *MI Epp*, vol. 1, no. 153, 466; *MI Epp*, vol. 1, no. 209, 621; *MI Epp*, vol. 2, no. 353, 123.

[48] *MHSI. MI. Sancti Ignatii de Loyola Constitutiones Societatis Jesu*, vol. 3, *Textus Latinus* (Rome: Pontifical Gregorian University, 1938), 189; *The Constitutions of the Society of Jesus and Their Complementary Norms*, ed. John Padberg (St. Louis, MO: Institute of Jesuit Sources, 1996), §586–87, 256. Yet Salmerón reported in 1561 that Ignatius granted a dispensation for chanting in Rome, where the abundance of personnel meant there was no harm to studies or hearing confessions. *ES*, vol. 1, no. 168b, 445.

such a request did not accord with the Society's way of proceeding, as saying two Masses a day would be better for a hermit who had nothing else to do.[49]

Salmerón may well have agreed with Ignatius's judgment in Oviedo's case, but it is more difficult to see him taking an instrumental attitude toward liturgical celebration. In a letter of 1574, he communicated his desire to retain the use of Gregorian chant in the Jesuit church in Naples, although he entrusted the final decision to Mercurian.[50] Although he says that direct work for the salvation of souls ought to be prioritized over chanting or fasting of devotion, liturgical sources and praxis influence his thought and priorities scarcely less than scripture or the Fathers and Doctors. Salmerón did not evince a willingness to dispense with forms and approved usages in the pursuit of apostolic endeavors. More so than other extant sources from the first Jesuits, the *Commentaries* manifest a notable reliance upon the Church's public prayer.

The *Commentaries* and Laínez

This chapter makes one major contribution to situating the *Commentaries* within early Jesuit thought by investigating the relationship between Salmerón and Laínez. They went to school together, they collaborated at the Council of Trent, they shared the burden of governance in the Society, and Laínez even dictated to Salmerón his memories of Ignatius, which are regarded as the first biographical account of the order's founder.[51] Salmerón and Ribadeneyra both reported that the former greatly admired Laínez and sought to imitate him in all things. Do their extant writings show the two friends, who represent "the intellectual summit of the first Jesuits," to be of one mind theologically?[52]

The first point to note is that Salmerón's admiration for Laínez did not prevent him from providing critical feedback. In a letter to Polanco of 1554, Salmerón gave his opinion on a draft of Laínez's "compendium of theology," a project that was never brought to completion. On the whole, he considered

---

[49] *MI Epp*, vol. 2, no. 260, 11–12.

[50] *ES*, vol. 2, no. 385, 352–53. Mercurian replied that Salmerón could make use of the dispensation that had already been granted, but that he should follow the Jesuit *Constitutions* on this issue. *ES*, vol. 2, no. 385a, 353.

[51] See Antonio Alburquerque, *Diego Laínez, SJ: First Biographer of Saint Ignatius of Loyola*, trans. John Montag (St. Louis, MO: Institute of Jesuit Sources, 2010).

[52] Santiago Madrigal Terrazas, "La participación del Maestro Diego Laínez en el Concilio de Trento (1545–1563)," in *Diego Laínez (1512–1565): Jesuita y teólogo del Concilio*, ed. José García de Castro Valdés (Madrid: Comillas, 2013), 101–57, at 114.

the book learned and useful, but he thought that it could be improved in several respects. The citations from the Fathers and Doctors ought to be reduced in number and length, and the arguments, objections, and solutions stated clearly in each chapter. Laínez also ought to provide definitions of terms, which Salmerón says he knows how to do very well. The citations of scripture ought to be embellished and given "a little life," so that the reader could understand better how they support the arguments. Finally, Salmerón wanted to see a chapter on the understanding of the mysteries of the Trinity and the Incarnation among the Gentiles.[53] These criticisms are consistent with the theological interests and priorities found throughout the *Commentaries* (perhaps apart from the request for brevity), and demonstrate that Salmerón did not limit himself to simply repeating the ideas of Laínez.

The theological oeuvre of the second Jesuit general is somewhat elusive. Unlike his friend, he never had the opportunity to dedicate himself to writing on a full-time basis. Despite this, Laínez left to posterity a considerable body of work, but apparently none of it was intended for publication. Some of his writings have been lost and leave a trace only in older catalogs, and a number of other texts are extant only in manuscripts in his nearly illegible handwriting, which has driven numerous would-be editors to despair.[54] Aside from his interventions at Trent, which may be found in the conciliar acts, the available printed sources consist of two volumes of treatises on various topics edited by Grisar (misleadingly entitled "Tridentine disputations," as not all of them are taken from Trent) and eight volumes of his correspondence and other writings compiled for the *MHSI*.

For several reasons, the Trent material is excluded from consideration here. First, the texts consist of what the secretaries rather than Laínez wrote down. Second, it is certain that Salmerón and Laínez worked very closely during the council, so much so that it is not always possible to neatly distinguish what may be attributed to each of them.[55] Third, considerations of space make it

[53] *ES*, vol. 1, no. 45, 111–13.

[54] Even Salmerón had a hard time deciphering his friend's handwriting. *ES*, vol. 1, no. 121, 325–26; *ES*, vol. 1, no. 136, 368. Grisar's complaint is more forceful still. *Jacobi Laínez secundi praepositi generalis Societatis Jesu Disputationes tridentinae* (hereafter *DT*), ed. Hermann Grisar (Innsbruck: Felicianus Rauch, 1886), vol. 1, *22.

[55] Numerous authors have confirmed that the two Jesuits used each other's material. See Paul Dudon, "Sur un texte inédit de Salmeron (1562)," *Gregorianum* 11 (1930): 410–17; Jesús Olzarán, "En el IV centenario de un voto tridentino del jesuita Alfonso Salmerón sobre la doble justicia," *Estudios Eclesiásticos* 20 (1946): 211–40. As Hughes observes, there was a significant dispute over the authorship of the opinion on the residency of bishops that Laínez delivered at Trent, with

impossible to deal adequately with the great abundance of conciliar sources. The sources from Laínez's own hand are sufficient to draw some preliminary conclusions about the minds of the two friends.

The categories of comparison are selected from the present volume's exploration of the *Commentaries*, although they are not all equally relevant. Laínez's extant works mention the Blessed Virgin only rarely and give no evidence of the highly developed Mariology that Salmerón offered.[56] He rarely used the term "mystery," which appears most often when he cites scripture or the Fathers verbatim, and he did not define it or organize any of his works around the exposition of the Christian mysteries.

History represents a special case for the comparison of the two Jesuits. On the one hand, Laínez had no concept of the "Gospel history," and the discipline in general did not play the coordinating role in his thought that it did in Salmerón's. On the other hand, he deployed historical erudition where he thought it appropriate, usually relying on ecclesiastical sources rather than profane ones. His hope for the reconciliation of Protestants at Trent rested on his knowledge of the Council of Ferrara-Florence, where the Greek and Latin churches came to an agreement despite the fact that the former did not have equal voting rights.[57] When counseling Catherine de Médici against allowing Huguenots to have their own churches, Laínez appealed to a series of historical examples. The empire of Constantinople, he says, lost the favor of God through heresies and by withdrawing obedience from the Roman Church, until at last, God punished it by means of the Turks.[58] Laínez's parting counsel to the queen mother was that she ought to do as Emperor Louis the Pious did during the iconoclast controversy, and leave judgment of religious questions to the pope.[59]

---

the editors of Salmerón's *MHSI* volumes arguing that the work can be attributed largely to Salmerón. John Hughes, "Alfonso Salmeron: His Work at the Council of Trent" (PhD dissertation: University of Kentucky, 1974), 25–29.

[56] One important exception is his assertion, which Salmerón also makes, that the soul of Christ is first in illuminating the whole celestial hierarchy, followed by the soul of Mary. *DT*, vol. 1, 145 (cf. *CEH*, vol. 12, 455).

[57] *MHSI. Lainii Monumenta* (hereafter *LM*) (Madrid: Gabriel López del Horno, 1912–17), vol. 8, Appendix, no. 52, 787.

[58] *LM*, vol. 8, Appendix, no. 51, 782.

[59] *LM*, vol. 8, Appendix, no. 51, 785.

Integrating Scripture and Tradition

Laínez wrote nothing like the *Commentaries*, yet his extant works articulate some of the same ideas about scripture, tradition, and education as Salmerón's. His most relevant works are three treatises on the interpretation of scripture, on preaching, and on the Christian student. Although far less detailed in his discussion of the interpretation of scripture, Laínez shared a basic emphasis on explaining the literal sense from close study of the text and the commentaries of theologians, with a secondary place for spiritual meanings. Like Salmerón, he sought to integrate scripture, the Fathers, and the Doctors, as well as emphasize the importance of leading a holy life. Both men were outstanding preachers, but Laínez had more to say about the methods and techniques of preaching, manifesting a greater esteem for the art of rhetoric.

The use of rhetoric points to an important difference between the *Commentaries* and the writings of Laínez: the latter assume that the exposition of scripture is done orally, that is, through preaching or lecturing. Given their fame as sacred orators, it is likely that the two Jesuits shared this assumption throughout most of their lives. Once Salmerón was instructed to compose the *Commentaries*, however, he had to make the transition to a literary mode.[60] This may help explain Laínez's greater attention to the art of preaching, as well as the absence of the organizational frameworks for understanding scripture that are essential to Salmerón's work.[61]

According to Laínez, the most important thing for the interpreter of scripture is that he be rightly disposed toward God. He must have rectitude of faith in the intellect, purity of conscience in the affect, and the submission of humility in both. He must pray before and after reading, offering everything to God, and asking for the grace of understanding. The priority must always be on what works more toward salvation and progress in the good, rather than the progress of knowledge that is characteristic of the natural sciences.[62] Anyone who takes up preaching for money or to win a name for himself through eloquence errs greatly.[63] He must also be prepared to resist the difficulties preachers encounter. Worldly men react negatively to being corrected, and without love for God, the preacher will succumb to

---

[60] See Giorgio Caravale, *Preaching and Inquisition in Renaissance Italy: Words on Trial*, trans. Frank Gordon (Boston, MA: Brill, 2016), 23–26.

[61] Students at the University of Ingolstadt perceived a difference between Laínez and Salmerón: both served "fine banquets" in their lectures, but Salmerón's were more of an acquired taste. Bangert, *Jay and Salmerón*, 201–2.

[62] *DT*, vol. 2, 501–02.

[63] *DT*, vol. 2, 506.

fear, and become like a mute dog unable to bark.⁶⁴ All these ideas, broadly speaking, dovetail with Salmerón's.

Natural talent is also essential to becoming a preacher, according to Laínez. God may have once spoken through an ass (Num 22:28–30), but this was miraculous, and one does not tempt God by presuming on miracles. Laínez says bluntly, "if you lack natural talent, it is evident that God did not choose you as a herald of his word; if he had chosen you, he would also have supplied the means."⁶⁵ Proper training goes along with talent. Most of what Laínez says to students and preachers alike about this concerns the acquisition of virtues and the need for prayer, but there is also advice about the content of their studies. A preacher must be well trained in scholastic theology and other disciplines, or he will easily fall into error, and he needs to know scripture and the Fathers as well.⁶⁶ Scripture should be read alongside "select interpreters," and the preacher should adhere to "severe and solid doctrine."⁶⁷ Laínez shared with Salmerón a basic vision of the intellectual training of preachers.

Given the context, it is not surprising that his reading list inclined more toward the practical than the speculative. As a general rule, Laínez thought that old books ought to be preferred to new ones, and he put together a basic curriculum for the preacher.⁶⁸ The interpreter of scripture needs to know what the holy doctors say about the virtues and Christian life, so he should read thoroughly the *Prima Secundae* and *Secunda Secundae* of Thomas Aquinas's *Summa theologiae* and the *Summa virtutum et vitiorum*, whose unnamed author was William Perault (c. 1190–1271). Laínez praises Chrysostom and Gregory the Great, saying that the latter is the best at explaining the New Testament. He seems to assume, however, that his readers will rely on florilegia for the Fathers, and he recommends several examples.⁶⁹ He was well aware that few would attain his own level of knowledge and erudition.

Laínez defended the use of scholastic teachers against those who refuse to listen to anyone after the time of Bernard on the grounds that they were not ancient. In the time of the early councils, men like Athanasius, Gregory of Nazianzen, and others were not yet ancient, but they were still cited

---

64   *DT*, vol. 2, 508.
65   *DT*, vol. 2, 511.
66   *DT*, vol. 2, 510.
67   *DT*, vol. 2, 502; *DT*, vol. 2, 503.
68   *DT*, vol. 2, 463.
69   *DT*, vol. 2, 522.

as authorities. "It is not so much time, as what they say, that ought to give authority."[70] He extols the four hundred years of scholasticism, and expresses his view that the Church will have such Doctors until the end of time, so that she will not fall into error.[71] In their mastery of so much material and their defense of positive and scholastic theology, the two Jesuits thought in tandem.

Their methods of commenting on scripture were much alike as well. According to Laínez, the text itself should first be explained, with attention to anything that can be gleaned from knowledge of the original languages. Next the interpreter should look to the primary literal sense, that is, the one that best accords with the plain meaning of the text, before bringing forth additional literal senses. This shows that the two Jesuits agreed on the multiplicity of the literal sense. Then comes the doctrinal implications of the literal sense, followed by further recourse to the Doctors for resolving any controversial points or bringing out anything else that is important or beautiful. Then any errors about the literal sense or doctrine should be attacked again. Finally, the exegete brings out the mystical senses, which can be dealt with more briefly in lectures, but at greater length in preaching.[72] Clearly Laínez shared with Salmerón a stated preference for the literal sense, especially where making doctrinal arguments was concerned, and at least in theory, he wanted to limit the use of the mystical senses.

Their respective treatments of rhetoric were different, although they both objected to its abuse. Laínez complains that often eloquence and style are esteemed over wisdom and understanding, which is an error of those who disdain scholasticism.[73] Like Salmerón, he offers a disparaging remark about the "pigments of oratory," and he is quite censorious about the effort to entertain one's hearers.[74] The interpreter of scripture must conduct himself in a serious manner, avoiding anything that could occasion laughter in his hearers, since it is better to elicit tears. It is a sacrilege, Laínez says, to include worldly trifles in sacred oratory.[75] Likewise the preacher must avoid yelling, waiving his hands, or other undignified means of moving the audience.[76]

---

[70] *DT*, vol. 1, 139–40. He thinks that, other things being equal, what is older has greater authority.
[71] *DT*, vol. 1, 141.
[72] *DT*, vol. 2, 503–04.
[73] *DT*, vol. 1, 140.
[74] *DT*, vol. 2, 510.
[75] *DT*, vol. 2, 519–20.
[76] *DT*, vol. 2, 517–18.

These similarities notwithstanding, Laínez offered much more instruction for preachers than Salmerón. His strictures against laughter did not prevent him from saying that hearts ought to take delight in what they hear. The best way to achieve this is by proposing what is unknown or not easily seen, or by using rhetorical figures to present what is already known in a new way. This is because people prefer new and beautiful ideas, whereas the same old figures annoy them.[77] Laínez provides numerous concrete examples to show the reader how to construct figures properly. To take an example, the verse "he entered into a certain town" (Lk 10:38) is a point of departure for constructing a sermon. Laínez plays on the double meaning of the Latin term *castellum*, which can mean "town" or "fortress."

> For this reason, all evil things come upon us, hearers, because without question we are not at all like a fortress, and this is also why Jesus does not come to us either. Strive, I beg you, to understand this rightly. Do you desire that God dwell in your souls? Then be firm and solid in virtues like a fortress.[78]

Laínez proceeds to elaborate his hypothetical text, which takes the form of an imaginary address by God to the believer, exhorting him to be strong and castigating him for being weak.

Further on, however, Laínez shifts his imagery and biblical allusions somewhat to give the sermon additional texture. The aforementioned verse from Luke is accompanied by this one taken from the Canticle of Canticles: "behold threescore valiant ones of the most valiant of Israel surrounded the bed of Solomon" (Cant. 3:7). Laínez continues,

> The breast which would wish to be a bridechamber for God must be powerful in fortitude. Threescore valiant ones of the most valiant of Israel must surround it. Let its counsels not be of just any kind, but tenacious. God indeed gladly uses these hearts for his dwelling and for taking rest. Is this surprising? Do not men also, if they have enemies, choose a secure abode?[79]

While pursuing the same idea of the soul as a fortress, in this section Laínez uses the imagery of the king's guard protecting his bridechamber. Here God appears less as the demanding judge of a soul's worthiness and more as someone in need of protection, which is heightened by the nuptial context of the Canticle of Canticles and the presence of the bride in the background.

---

[77] *DT*, vol. 2, 521–22.
[78] *DT*, vol. 2, 527.
[79] *DT*, vol. 2, 532.

Laínez wanted preachers to have concrete examples of how to capture the hearer's imagination and prevent exhortation from the pulpit from becoming too pedestrian. In his extant works, scripture, the Fathers, and the Doctors come together for the edification of the *hearer*, whereas in Salmerón's *Commentaries* they come together for the edification of the *reader*. This difference of audience, as well as the greater leisure that Salmerón enjoyed, may help explain the greater sophistication of his magnum opus regarding the integration of scripture and tradition. Both men saw the importance and the dangers of rhetoric, but Laínez provided more concrete instruction on how to use it.

Saving Souls

The salvation of souls was a priority for Laínez in his pastoral and theological labors no less than for Salmerón, as his correspondence clearly testifies.[80] Like his friend, he also dealt with some of the relevant theological issues in his writings. He shared the emphasis on the reality of human freedom and its cooperation with grace, such that Cerceda did not hesitate to identify his position as "Molinist."[81] In his *Disputation on Imputed Righteousness*, Laínez expresses himself on a key point in the same way as Salmerón: justification only takes place with the coming of charity into the heart of the believer.[82]

Unlike Salmerón, however, who swiftly dismissed the concept of imputed righteousness, Laínez carefully considered multiple possible meanings of the term and their compatibility with Catholic theology. To take one example, he discussed the idea that the term refers to someone whose inhering righteousness was lacking during his life and who gratuitously receives the gift of eternal life anyway when he stands before the tribunal of Christ. He makes an analogy between this situation and that of Abraham, whose faith was meritorious in view of the future grace of Christ.[83] Laínez rejects this theory, however, and he replies that there is no need for a new imputation of the grace of Christ in such a circumstance, but only the application of Christ's righteousness by way of merit or retribution. Those who are perfect will enter heaven; those who have venial sins still merit eternal life, but they will have to be purified in Purgatory; those guilty of unrepented mortal sin are *ipso facto* not justified, and

---

[80] Laínez's letters to Ignatius in particular are filled with reports of the edification brought about by his preaching, confessions, and giving of the Exercises. For examples, see *LM*, vol. 1, no. 3, 4; *LM*, vol. 1, no. 8, 17.

[81] Feliciano Cerceda, *Diego Laínez en la Europea religiosa de su tiempo* (Madrid: Ediciones Cultura Hispánica, 1946), vol. 2, 468.

[82] *DT*, vol. 2, 153.

[83] *DT*, vol. 2, 157.

they go to hell. His treatment of this aspect of justification was more careful and detailed than Salmerón's.

The explanation and defense of the Church's sacramental system was part and parcel of both Jesuits' labors for the salvation of souls, and both made significant contributions to the definitions of the Council of Trent. As noted above, Salmerón singled out his friend's intervention on the concession of the chalice. Laínez's treatise on this subject runs to fifty pages in Grisar's edition, giving significant space to explaining the debate that unfolded at Trent. He highlights two main issues: whether the chalice should be granted to all, or only to some, of the faithful, and whether it ought to be granted by the council or the pope.[84]

Given his strong opposition to granting the chalice, Laínez's treatment is surprisingly careful and nuanced. He says that if it is to be granted to all, then it should be the decision of the whole council, but if only to some, then the decision of the pope.[85] Like Salmerón, he thought that both usages (distribution of the species of bread alone and the distribution of both species) were licit and holy according to divine and natural law, and that any community following either usage did not sin, assuming they had permission under positive law to do so. This is because Christ and the apostles, as well as the Greek Church, distributed Communion under both species.[86] At the same time, Laínez thought it was unwise to go against the custom of the Roman Church and abrogate the law of the Council of Constance against offering the chalice. Like Salmerón, he did not think that the Church ought to change her laws just because some break them, and doing so would threaten the consciences of those Catholics who regarded reception under both species as illicit.[87] He explains that the Church keeps her positive laws so long as the reason for them remains, not least because positive law is a determination of divine law, and disregard of the former easily leads to disregard of the latter.[88] In other words, Laínez shared Salmerón's vision of an interlocking hierarchy of types of law, wherein rash or unnecessary changes at the lower level could easily lead to disruptions at the higher level.

Like Salmerón, Laínez identified a host of additional objections to the introduction of the chalice. There is the risk of spillage, as well as the apparent succor that administration of the chalice would give to those who deny

---

[84] *DT*, vol. 2, 27.
[85] *DT*, vol. 2, 27–28.
[86] *DT*, vol. 2, 29–30.
[87] *DT*, vol. 2, 33–34.
[88] *DT*, vol. 2, 35.

the liceity of Communion under one species. He also objected to the fact that allowing both rites would leave the matter to "popular choice," which he thought would lead to a situation of maximum confusion, as well as undermine the legitimate authority of princes and bishops in their particular places. Since most Catholics follow the ancient rite, which has been confirmed by the custom of the Church, granting the chalice would risk a sure danger to their faith for the sake of an uncertain benefit on behalf of the few who ask for it.[89]

Even when the desire for both species is not motivated by heresy, it is still reprehensible as proceeding from childishness, "as children tend to prefer what is small, childish, and fun [*ludicra*] to what is great and precious, and if they don't get what they want, they wail and yell like those who are being injured or oppressed."[90] Laínez claims that the first one to assert that Western Christians were obliged to receive under both species was the devil, who then told Luther to spread this idea.[91] The concession of the chalice confirms rather than destroys errors surrounding the Eucharist and would mean the deformation of the Church and the relaxation of her discipline.[92] Laínez observes that previous limited concessions of the chalice in Bohemia and some German lands was of no profit, meaning the experiment should not be repeated.[93]

Laínez's behavior as the Jesuit general was consistent with the views he expressed in this treatise. When Pius IV granted the use of the chalice to certain territories in 1564, Laínez opposed its introduction in Jesuit churches, without denying the pope's authority to grant it. He supported the Vienna community's refusal to allow the chalice, even though it gave offense to the emperor, saying "we are altogether zealous to hold onto the old rite, although we assert that the new one is licit, if the proper conditions are kept."[94] He explained that since the Jesuits were not pastors of souls, they were not, strictly speaking, obliged to administer the Eucharist. Their custom and devotion was to offer it to those who confessed in their churches. If princes should compel Jesuits to do otherwise, they were only to permit those whom they personally knew as Catholics to receive under both species.[95]

The records of other ecclesiastical affairs also bear witness to Laínez's Eucharistic thought. The queen mother of France, Catherine de Médici, convened a

[89] *DT*, vol. 2, 36–37.
[90] *DT*, vol. 2, 42.
[91] *DT*, vol. 2, 45.
[92] *DT*, vol. 2, 48.
[93] *DT*, vol. 2, 50.
[94] *LM*, vol. 8, no. 2138, 174.
[95] *LM*, vol. 8, no. 2136, 167.

colloquy at Poissy in 1562 as an effort to resolve the confessional conflicts then afflicting the kingdom.[96] The Jesuit general attended with two aims in mind: first, to convince the French to participate in the Council of Trent rather than leave the cause of doctrine and discipline in the hands of princes; second, to debate Huguenot leaders like Theodore Beza and Peter "Martyr" Vermigli. One of the central topics was the Real Presence, which Laínez vigorously defended against their arguments, and records of his speeches have been preserved in the *MHSI*.[97] He deals with the issue of locomotion, explaining how Jesus can be present in the species without having to descend from heaven, and he defends a Catholic reading of Augustine, explaining that this Father's description of the Eucharist as a sign or figure of the body of Christ was not intended as a denial of the Real Presence.[98]

Laínez was generally no less taciturn than Salmerón regarding personal information or motives, but he was capable of making an exception where topics of particular devotion were concerned. He addressed the queen mother at Poissy with resounding words about the Eucharist.

> And since Fra Peter Martyr exhorted those present to confess their faith, I also confess, madam, that what I have said to you concerning the Real Presence of Christ in the Eucharist, in memory of his passion, is a Catholic truth, for which I, with the grace of the Lord, am prepared to die. And I implore Your Majesty to always defend and confess Catholic truth, as the Church does, and to fear God more than men, because in this way God will provide protection for you and your son, the Most Christian King.[99]

Although the *Commentaries* provide far more extensive theological discussion of the Eucharist, Salmerón and Laínez were agreed upon its central importance from a doctrinal and disciplinary standpoint, and they directly confronted the Protestant challenges of their age. They opposed the introduction of the chalice while accepting its liceity, although each did so in a way in keeping with his respective character: Laínez more carefully and subtly, Salmerón more bluntly and aggressively.[100]

---

[96] See Christopher Nugent, *Ecumenism in the Age of the Reformation: The Colloquy of Poissy* (Cambridge, MA: Harvard University Press, 1974).

[97] On the centrality of the Eucharist at Poissy and in French confessional conflict more generally, see Jeanne Harrie, "The Guises, the Body of Christ, and the Body Politic," *Sixteenth Century Journal* 37, no. 1 (2006): 43–57.

[98] *LM*, vol. 8, Appendix, no. 49, 764–66.

[99] *LM*, vol. 8, Appendix, no. 49, 767.

[100] This difference between them was also manifest in their respective views of the catechism of Archbishop Carranza, who was charged with heresy. See Feliciano

Defending the Church

Ecclesiology provides the best field in which to compare the thought of the two Jesuits, for Laínez's most substantial extant treatise is entitled *A Disputation on the Origin of the Bishops' Jurisdiction and on the Primacy of the Roman Pontiff*. Although a complete study of this work, which runs to over three hundred and fifty pages in Grisar's modern edition, lies beyond the scope of this chapter, even a cursory engagement allows for a comparison with Salmerón's thought. Both Jesuits were ardent defenders of the pope as the source of all jurisdiction in the Church, and both thought of the civil and ecclesiastical powers in correlative terms, developing their theories of each in tandem. The *Disputation* is also a good showcase of Laínez's theological method, which was similar to his friend's.

Laínez places his argument about the jurisdiction of bishops within a wide theological framework. In the loose sense of the term found in many of the Fathers, divine law can include things established by the Church's own power, but in the strict sense it means something immediately established by God.[101] Laínez then turns to the ecclesiastical power, which is one of the two powers that govern the lives of men. Like Salmerón, he thought of the sacral or ecclesiastical power as correlative with the civil, although they differed slightly in the explanation of the genesis of each. Laínez thought that even among the Gentiles, there was always a division between priestly and civil offices, whereas Salmerón did not.[102]

Like Salmerón, Laínez asserts that both powers come from God, but that the ecclesiastical power, which is superior, descends immediately from Christ to Peter. The civil power comes mediately from God, because it lies first in the hands of the people, who choose their own rulers.[103] The ecclesiastical power is superior to the civil, meaning that the latter should serve the former, although neither should usurp the other's legitimate domain. Laínez does not follow Salmerón in explaining how the two became intertwined historically with the baptism of rulers, although he does mention in passing that the pope may deprive them of their office for the good of the Church.[104] He appears to have had less interest in particular questions of civil polity than his friend.

Cerceda, "Laínez y Salmerón y el proceso del catecismo de Carranza," *Razón y Fe* 100 (1932): 212–66.

[101] *DT*, vol. 1, 2. Salmerón used the exact same distinction in his discussion of Lent.

[102] *DT*, vol. 1, 57–58.

[103] *DT*, vol. 1, 58–61.

[104] *DT*, vol. 1, 155.

Ecclesiastical power is subdivided into the power of orders and the power of jurisdiction, which are the same basic categories found in the *Commentaries*. Laínez then seeks to demonstrate the origin of the apostles' jurisdiction in the apostle Peter, which in turn is a template for explaining how episcopal jurisdiction is derived from the pope's. He provides extensive catenas from scripture, the Fathers, and the Doctors in support of this position, while also providing the arguments and sources used by opponents. Like Salmerón, Laínez also argues from the excellence of a particular regime type.

> But among temporal regimes, the best is the monarchical, in which the king has all the power of the commonwealth, and distributes it to other judges and princes. In the Church therefore, which is the kingdom of Christ, the vicar has from Christ the plenitude of power, and through him it was distributed to the other apostles.[105]

He also rejects the thesis that the primitive Church had a democratic or an aristocratic regime, patiently and carefully presenting his arguments and refuting his opponents'.

Laínez also defended the successors of Peter while acknowledging their problems. Ecumenical councils have no jurisdiction over the pope, and if he needs to be reformed, it should be accomplished by other means, such as the intervention of the legates of princes, or private conversation by the council fathers, or anything else that preserves the pope's dignity.[106] In an address at Paris, however, the Jesuit general sounded a more critical note about the papacy, saying that the scandal given by the head of the Church is responsible for the loss of so many people to heresy, such that not even Spain or Italy are guaranteed to remain Catholic. The abuses include the popes' efforts to increase their earthly kingdoms, granting to princes privileges that do not belong to them, and appointing unworthy men as cardinals.[107]

If the pope does not see to his own reform, Laínez warns, a situation could arise where even the teachers who most defend his authority acknowledge that the only way to deal with the universal disturbance of the Church is for the council to meet without his permission and determine the means to resist him. Even more seriously, the pope's failure to reform himself could be interpreted as a sign that he lacks true faith [*que le falta la fe recta*], in which case he would be judged as no longer fit for the office [*que no es capaz del papado*].[108]

---

[105] *DT*, vol. 1, 86.
[106] *DT*, vol. 2, 75; *DT*, vol. 2, 84–85.
[107] *LM*, vol. 8, Appendix, no. 57, 801.
[108] *LM*, vol. 8, Appendix, no. 57, 804.

For someone who argued so vigorously on behalf of papal primacy, these are surprising words. In any case, it is evident that even stalwart defenders of the papacy like Laínez and Salmerón thought there were limits to its authority, and they proposed various means for resisting a pope who fell into heresy or otherwise seriously compromised the Church's life and discipline.

As evident already in his discussion of the Eucharist, Laínez believed in facing the challenges of heretics directly. His interventions at Poissy include some general statements about dealing with them, as well as vigorous counsel to the queen mother about why they should not have their own churches in France.

> From what I have always read and seen from experience, it is a very dangerous thing to deal with or listen to people who leave the Church because, as Ecclesiasticus says, "who will pity an enchanter struck by a serpent, or any that come near wild beasts?" (Ecclus 12:13). For those who leave the Church are called in scripture serpents, and wolves in sheep's clothing, and foxes.[109]

Laínez proceeds to explain the artifices that various sects have long used, beginning with the Pelagians, to conceal the heretical nature of their teaching, giving it instead the name of orthodoxy. As a remedy, he proposes two measures, one that he calls good, and the other a lesser evil. The first is to leave the resolution of matters of faith to the clergy, especially the general council. The second is that, if the queen mother insists on holding disputations with heretics, she do so only in the presence of learned and experienced people, so as to maintain mercy and charity.[110] Like Salmerón, Laínez deeply mistrusted Protestants and did not refrain from verbally attacking them.

The Jesuit general opposed the proposal of allowing French Protestants the right to their own churches for several reasons. Since France had accepted the faith of Christ for centuries, a new religion would cause great harm, and it would entail the view that the kings and people of past ages had not been on the path to salvation.[111] Granting heretics churches would be an act of public favor towards them and would lead infinite souls away from salvation, be a cause of scandal, and cause injury to the kingdom's bishops.[112] The concession would be an instance of *lèse majesté* against God and against the most Christian king, and it would lead to the weakening of the kingdom and of the

---

[109] *LM*, vol. 8, Appendix, no. 49, 760.

[110] *LM*, vol. 8, Appendix, no. 49, 760–61.

[111] *LM*, vol. 8, Appendix, no. 51, 776.

[112] *LM*, vol. 8, Appendix, no. 51, 779; *LM*, vol. 8, Appendix, no. 51, 783–84.

love and obedience of subjects toward their ruler.[113] Laínez explicitly argued against the idea that the "way of tolerance" would help keep peace and allow a lesser evil to avoid a greater one. "In this way of appeasing the party that is lesser in numbers and goodness, the queen would make herself hateful to the greater and better part of her kingdom."[114] He adds that the adherents of the new religion, despite their small numbers, have become so insolent as to occupy whole cities in France, throw out the Catholics, deprive religious of their houses, burn and loot churches, and desecrate the Most Holy Sacrament. Granting them churches would only embolden them further, and lead to the seditions and civil wars that have been experienced elsewhere.[115]

Despite all they had in common, there were also important differences in the way that Laínez and Salmerón treated heresy, and those whom they regarded as the Church's enemies more generally. In his addresses in France on reform, Laínez clearly states that the cause of heresy is the bad behavior of the clergy, and that the way to resolve the former problem is through correction of the latter.[116] While Salmerón wrote often of the sins of the clergy, and occasionally admitted their role in driving people away, he laid far more emphasis on the wickedness of the heretics themselves. This was consistent with his understanding of history: just as God is always at work for the salvation of the human race and inspiring men in every age to serve him, so also Satan is at work seeking to destroy mankind in the same way. Salmerón treated heretics as part of a loose transhistorical federation of Satan's servants, internally at war with each other, but united by their common opposition to Christ and his Church. This idea is not articulated in Laínez's work.

Another related difference is that the author of the *Commentaries*, while intent upon their conversion, treated heretics more like enemies to be fought, whereas Laínez saw them as in need of conversion. The most striking example of this attitude is found in his position on inviting heretics to councils, which is articulated in a brief treatise entitled *Whether and How Heretics Are to be Heard at a Council, and How to Debate Them*. Citing Paul and Irenaeus, he claims that obstinate and hopeless heretics are not to be debated, but that those who are not obstinate can and must be heard, even when they are opposed to doctrine that has already been defined.[117] His basis for this claim is the experience of previous councils, including Carthage IX, Chalcedon, Lateran IV, Lyons, and

---

[113] *LM*, vol. 8, Appendix, no. 51, 782.
[114] *LM*, vol. 8, Appendix, no. 51, 780.
[115] *LM*, vol. 8, Appendix, no. 51, 782.
[116] *LM*, vol. 8, Appendix, no. 52, 785; *LM*, vol. 8, Appendix, no. 55, 792.
[117] *DT*, vol. 2, 17.

numerous others, where figures who denied defined teaching were allowed to attend and speak. He offers the following rationale for this practice.

> As often as it is necessary, Mother Church ought to open her mouth to teach and instruct. The Holy Spirit does not illuminate everyone at the same time, but he blows where and when he wills. Those who do not receive illumination in one council will perhaps receive it in another. It is therefore necessary to attend councils often, so that the heresy that cannot be destroyed in one may be destroyed in another.[118]

This bespeaks a different attitude, and the martial language and imagery that is so prevalent in Salmerón's *Commentaries* is more muted in Laínez's writings. None of this is to say that he countenanced any compromises. He asserts that a council never changes the matters of faith defined by the holy Fathers on account of the cunning or sophistries of heretics, for such definitions are immutable.[119]

Vigilance concerning the Church's "enemies" is evident in Laínez's words about the Jews, which come in the context of his advice to bishops about visiting their dioceses. Like Salmerón, he stipulates numerous restrictive measures, saying that Jews should not be allowed to build up their synagogues, lest their error and obstinacy increase, and that Christians are forbidden from listening to their teachings. Laínez insists that Jews be compelled to listen periodically to Christian preaching ordered to their conversion. He wants Jewish books prohibited, except for the Bible. He also says that Jews cannot be allowed to exact usury beyond the legal limit, men must wear their yellow hat and women their veil, and they must be prohibited from blaspheming.[120] Laínez instructs bishops to establish congregations for converts from Judaism and Islam, so that they may attend the Mass and Divine Office, receive the sacraments, and undergo instruction in a particular church designated for this purpose.[121] What is missing from these repressive measures is the *odium theologicum* so prevalent in the *Commentaries*.

---

[118] *DT*, vol. 2, 18–19.

[119] *DT*, vol. 2, 20.

[120] *DT*, vol. 2, 434.

[121] *DT*, vol. 2, 435.

Promoting Good Mores

Unlike Salmerón, Laínez appeals to liturgical sources sparingly in his theological works, although his early teaching career demonstrates familiarity with them.[122] Appeals to the custom of the Church in general appear more frequently, and he saw the proper celebration of Mass and the Divine Office as important to the cause of reform.[123] He says that Latins who ask for the chalice are breaking with the custom they have received from the Roman Church, and that heretics of ages past also altered the rites as part of their deviation from the faith.[124] In an address given at Paris in 1562 on the restoration of divine worship, Laínez observes that abuses of the Mass, such as celebrating it for financial gain, or indecency and ignorance regarding the manner of its celebration, have rendered it contemptible in the eyes of men. As a remedy, he called for cleaning the churches and putting their altars, vestments, chalices, corporals, and missals in good order.[125]

These concerns were backed up by his actions as superior general. He ordered the provincials to ensure a greater uniformity in the celebration of the Divine Office, at least within the same province. He comments that while this lack of uniformity is not a great offense, nor the Society's greatest concern, the Office should still be celebrated with decorum.[126] When Emperor Ferdinand I died in 1564, Laínez ordered all Jesuit priests to say twelve Masses for his repose, and all non-priests to offer prayers for the same end.[127] A letter to Laínez from France observes with satisfaction that more than forty thousand

---

[122] When he taught at La Sapienza in Rome in 1537, Laínez lectured on Gabriel Biel's exposition of the Canon of the Mass. Paul Grendler, "Laínez and the Schools in Europe," in *Diego Laínez (1512–1565) and his Generalate: Jesuit with Jewish Roots, Close Confidant of Ignatius of Loyola, Preeminent Theologian of the Council of Trent*, ed. Paul Oberholzer (Rome: IHSI, 2015), 639–68. In addition, he appears to have written his own commentary on the Canon around the time of the Colloquy of Poissy. Cerceda, *Diego Laínez*, vol. 2, 468.

[123] At Trent, he argued that the rite of the Mass must be retained because its parts are good, not contrary to scripture, and help increase devotion. Reinold Theisen, *Mass Liturgy and the Council of Trent* (Collegeville, MN: St. John's University Press, 1965), 42.

[124] *DT*, vol. 2, 39; *DT*, vol. 2, 49.

[125] *LM*, vol. 8, Appendix, no. 55, 792–93.

[126] *LM*, vol. 8, no. 2082, 51.

[127] *LM*, vol. 8, no. 2126, 144.

people participated in a Palm Sunday procession, indicating that the author thought the superior general would approve of this outcome.[128]

Like Salmerón, Laínez took an interest in the relations between the sexes and their consequences for social mores. This is most apparent in his treatise *On Makeup and the Adornment of Women*.[129] Although in general outline his position on this issue was similar to Aquinas's, Laínez dealt with particular cases in significantly greater detail.[130] He argues that in principle the adornment of women is licit, based on the example of biblical women like Judith, Esther, and the queen of Ps 44, who arrayed themselves for the sake of glorifying God.[131] Reason leads to the same conclusion, as he explains:

> Woman is conjoined to man, and she soberly adorns herself without any perverse intention, but rather with the purpose of pleasing her husband. She judges that it is probably necessary for eliciting her husband's love and initiating conjugal relations, and for keeping him away from other women. If she does this in charity, she not only does not sin, but she does well to modestly paint and adorn herself, so that her husband does not forbid it, but rather rejoices (as often happens).[132]

In practice, however, such conditions are rarely met, leading Laínez to an explanation of when the use of makeup and adornment is a venial sin, and when a mortal sin. All told, he identifies twelve circumstances that make for the latter.

Laínez explains that when a woman spends too much money on adorning herself, or does it to entice someone into sin, or becomes enamored of her appearance, she violates charity toward God and men, and she can even become guilty of idolatry. Laínez undertakes a sustained diatribe against these practices, explicitly rejecting the argument that the words of scripture and the Fathers against excessive adornment are counsels rather than precepts, or that they apply only to past times. He laments that in his times men as well as women wear perfumes, soft clothing, jewelry and precious metals,

---

[128] *LM*, vol. 8, no. 2059, 3.

[129] Cerceda thinks this treatise was made on the basis of Laínez's preaching to Spanish expatriate communities in southern Italy in 1549–50, possibly in response to the concerns of the viceroy and his wife. Cerceda, *Diego Laínez*, vol. 2, 471.

[130] Cf. *ST*, II–IIae, q. 169, a. 2.

[131] *DT*, vol. 2, 465–66.

[132] *DT*, vol. 2, 467. He also acknowledges notable deformity or ugliness as a legitimate cause. *DT*, vol. 2, 468.

and many other superfluous things, which is far more deplorable in men.[133] Like Salmerón, he was concerned that what he considered the proper lines of demarcation between the sexes were not being respected.

Certain moral issues received lengthy treatment at Laínez's hands. The most notable difference between the two Jesuits here is that Salmerón's friend dove deeply into technical questions. His *Disputation on Usury and Various Business Affairs of Merchants*, addressed to the Genoese, runs to nearly a hundred pages. He acknowledges the difficulty of the subject matter, saying that theologians, jurists, and merchants each claim competence to judge these matters, and he advises the Christian teacher to take a middle path between extremes, neither scrupulously imputing sin where none exists, nor opening the way to injustice.[134] What follows is a thorough treatment of the relevant issues: what usury is, why it is gravely sinful according to divine and natural law, and what specific behaviors count as such. Laínez relies upon scripture, the Fathers and Doctors, the jurists, along with his own abilities to calculate complex exchanges.[135] There is nothing like this in the *Commentaries*, and it demonstrates the Jesuit general's capacity for painstaking, technical work. In a similar vein, his work on simony addressed to Paul IV displays his thorough knowledge of the relevant canon law, as well as scripture and the theologians, about why simony is sinful and the conditions that determine it.

It may reasonably be asked why a theologian of such stature descended to the minutiae of particular moral questions—there is something incongruous about the luminary of Trent and future superior general of the Jesuit order opining on how much makeup counts as a mortal sin, or exactly what sort of profit margins are formally usurious. In part, this is testimony to the contours of his own mind, which had a tremendous capacity for detail along with a high level of confidence in the reliability of its judgments. Yet it may also be explained in terms of his extensive contact with ordinary people and his pastoral solicitude for the problems and obstacles they faced. The demanding standards that both Jesuits put before their audiences, and Laínez's juridical mindset in particular, probably seemed excessive to many of their hearers. At the same time, they were in high demand everywhere they went, and the extant

---

[133] *DT*, vol. 2, 474–75.

[134] *DT*, vol. 2, 229–31.

[135] The issue of usurious contracts was hotly debated among early Jesuit moral theologians, but the order's hierarchy refrained from taking a clear stand on the finer points. Stefania Tutino, "Jesuit Accommodation, Dissimulation, Mental Reservation," in *The Oxford Handbook of the Jesuits*, ed. Ines Županov (New York: Oxford University Press, 2019), 216–40; Paola Vismara, "Moral Economy and the Jesuits," *Journal of Jesuit Studies* 5 (2018): 610–30.

evidence indicates they were largely successful in persuading their audiences to lead more devout lives.

Conclusion

Did Salmerón seek to imitate his friend in all things? The two men clearly had much in common in terms of their training, vision, and priorities, and on a wide range of questions, they held identical positions. The sources they used, and their methods of argumentation, had much in common; they were obviously men of notable erudition in scripture, the Fathers, and the Doctors. Given that they did their schooling together, joined the Society together, and worked closely at Trent together, this is unsurprising. The *Commentaries* pay respect to Laínez for all that Salmerón learned from him.

At the same time, there were differences between the two Jesuits. Laínez used the works of historians, but he did not incorporate a theory of history into his work. Both men were accomplished speakers, but Laínez took much greater care to explain the importance and technique of rhetoric, while tying it to virtue and holiness. Salmerón took a more aggressive posture in their common defense of the faith against heresy, and Laínez displayed greater subtlety of mind. Whatever his indebtedness to his friend, Salmerón clearly developed lines of thought that are not evident in the extant works of Laínez. His unusual organization of the *Commentaries*, his theory of history, his attempt to integrate the sources of Christian revelation into a coherent account, his labors in Mariology, and his deep interest in the liturgy, seem to have been his own work. While there are limits to what the sources reveal about the relationship between them, Laínez and Salmerón were of similar, but not identical, minds. If, as Ribadeneyra claimed, Salmerón was a son and almost a disciple of Laínez, it must be admitted that in certain areas of inquiry, the disciple was greater than his master.

Salmerón's presentation of his fellow Jesuits in the *Commentaries* is terse but carefully crafted. Laínez, Xavier, and Ignatius were, first and foremost, faithful ministers of the sacraments in an age of expanding mission fields and the onslaught of heresy. God confirmed his work in them through the great signs and miracles that Xavier performed in the east. This profile of the order's origin and purpose may be surprising to contemporary scholars and Jesuits, who are accustomed to a greater emphasis on the order's distinctiveness. For Salmerón, by contrast, the priority was demonstrating that in the Society there was nothing new under the sun, but only a continuation of the Church's perennial concern for the salvation of souls and the increase of holiness among her members.

Conclusion:
The Wisdom of Salmerón

By now the theological vision of Alfonso Salmerón's *Commentaries* ought to be discernible. His magnum opus combines verse-by-verse exegesis of the New Testament with lengthy dogmatic codicils to provide a biblical theology that he regarded as both perennially true and suited for the circumstances of the sixteenth century. An emphasis on history and God's saving activity within it runs like a thread through his efforts to integrate scripture and tradition, lead the reader to contemplation, honor Mary, advance the salvation of souls, defend the Church, and promote good mores. Salmerón's brief discussion of the Society of Jesus shows how he wished to present his brethren to the world: as faithful ministers of the sacraments within the tradition of religious life whom God chose and blessed in a time of upheaval. His reverence for Diego Laínez did not prevent Salmerón from making significant intellectual advances, especially regarding history, beyond the thought of his friend.

The comparison of Salmerón with other exegetes sheds light on his place in the intellectual history of the period. His learning, while impressive and very much on display in the *Commentaries*, was consistent with that of other leading scholars of the late sixteenth century: biblical languages, culture and history of the ancient world, and the Fathers and Doctors. The overall structure and method of Salmerón's work is indebted to Jansen, and he accomplished his stated intent to provide a compendium of Catholic commentary to counter Marlorat. If it was commonplace for Catholic exegetes to assert the priority of the literal sense of scripture, there were nevertheless various ways of portraying its relationship to the spiritual senses. Jansen, Salmerón, and especially Barradas gave significant place to the spiritual senses, whereas Maldonado focused almost exclusively on the literal sense.

Three things, however, set Salmerón apart from the other writers under consideration: his insertion of major dogmatic treatises into the text, his well-articulated account of scripture's relationship to history, and his interest in liturgy. If authors in this period did not separate exegesis from dogmatic theology, Salmerón was unusually thorough in trying to demonstrate their coherence. While the other four writers dealt with historical issues, none of them theorized about it in the way that Salmerón did, and none of them treated worship as a topic of great intrinsic interest or as critical to interconfessional polemics.

There is much about Salmerón, however, that remains concealed or paradoxical even after a careful perusal of the *Commentaries*. His apparent reluctance to write, supposedly overcome only by the command of his superior general, did not prevent him from completing a massive work. While offering sustained access to the working of his mind, Salmerón remained persistently stingy with personal information. Not the least bit shy about putting forth his opinions, he nevertheless insisted that the reader draw his own conclusions. His pugilistic tone belies a lifetime dedicated to spiritual direction and the care of souls, as well as relative optimism about men's prospects of salvation. Almost fanatically opposed to novelty and the heresies of the age, the Jesuit theologian made extensive use of the latest sources and methods of the sixteenth century, including those that originated among authors he considered suspect. A man thoroughly enmeshed in the affairs of his order for more than forty years, Salmerón said very little about it, yet his words were carefully chosen. The renown he enjoyed in his time, and the prodigiousness of his posthumous output, have not prevented him from being largely forgotten, even among Jesuits.

Although the present work aims to be comprehensive, the *Commentaries* have much more to offer scholars of early modern Catholicism, especially its flourishing of biblical studies. Salmerón's exegetical methods and use of the Fathers in particular warrant closer attention, as does his treatment of the sacraments, above all the Eucharist. More thorough comparative approaches will be helpful in more accurately situating him within the manifold intellectual endeavors and debates of the sixteenth century. In a like manner, further research into Salmerón's place in the early Society of Jesus may provide better understanding of the order's intellectual history and development. The present work, in other words, may be the first major study of the *Commentaries*, but it should not be the last.

One unmistakable trend in Jesuit historiography of recent decades is the explosion of research carried out by laymen, such that Jesuits no longer have the primary role, much less an exclusive one, in driving the scholarly discussion of their order's history.[1] Yet religious communities have an ineradicable stake in their own history, especially their founding era, because it remains

---

[1] Thomas Worcester, "Jesuit Studies in the Age of a Jesuit Pope," *Renaissance Quarterly* 69, no. 4 (2016): 1401–12; John O'Malley, "Past, Present, and Future of Jesuit Studies: Historiographical Thoughts," *Journal of Jesuit Studies* 5 (2018): 501–10.

Conclusion: The Wisdom of Salmerón

a point of reference for how they live and move and have their being in the present, as well as how they envision their future. Does the study of Salmerón have anything to offer the contemporary Society of Jesus?

On the one hand, Salmerón took positions that may be identified as characteristically Jesuit, not only for his times, but even across the ages. Although he warned against the danger of damnation, his view of justification and salvation aligned with the relative optimism and emphasis on human freedom found in early Jesuit thought. A vigorous Mariology, especially the defense of the Immaculate Conception, has been characteristic of the order, along with Eucharistic devotion and advocacy for frequent Communion. His theory of civil and ecclesiastical polity was in keeping with the early patterns of Jesuit political thought, and "loose Thomism" in theology and philosophy has always been common. Even his reticence about the Society and its activities, which goes against the grain of much current thought and practice, may have been more typical among his original confreres than is usually acknowledged.

On the other hand, much of the content and tone of the *Commentaries* can be of only historical interest to contemporary Jesuits, thanks to the watershed of the Second Vatican Council and the general congregations the order has held in its wake.[2] Mainstream Catholic discourse since then has changed so significantly on so many questions, such as the Church's relationship to the Jews and to other Christians, the relations between the sexes, religious liberty, and liturgy (to name just a few), that many of Salmerón's positions and methods have been rendered objectionable, if not opaque, to today's readers. The same is perforce true of the work of the other Jesuit founders, as well as of prominent thinkers like Canisius, Bellarmine, and Suárez, who also thought within the parameters of the mainstream discourse of their times.

Given this state of affairs, it may be helpful to identify some features of the *Commentaries* that are more pertinent to the Society and its theological endeavors in the present. In the first place, Salmerón's theology is grounded: in scripture, in the Fathers and Doctors, and in the prayer and praxis of the Church. He thought that the theologian must first master and internalize what has been passed down to him before he could make any contribution of his own. Although capable of dealing with matters abstractly, Salmerón did not prefer to theologize in this way. He did not possess the speculative power of some of his more illustrious confreres, but there was rarely any danger that, even in his more adventurous moments, he would stray from tradition.

---

[2] Patrick Howell, *Great Risks Had to be Taken: The Jesuit Response to the Second Vatican Council, 1958–2018* (Eugene, OR: Cascade Books, 2019).

Sensitivity to historical issues dovetails with the concerns of multiple trends in theology of the last hundred years. Salmerón lived prior to important philosophical developments that shape contemporary intellectual life, as well as the discovery of new evidence and paradigms for biblical and ecclesiastical history, but his Augustinian emphasis on God's initiative across the ages is crucial to any effort to think theologically about history, or historically about theology. A moral theology that accounts for the relationship between the Beatitudes and the Decalogue, and that combines high demands with richness in mercy, may strike a chord in the present moment. Surely Salmerón's zeal for the Christian mysteries and the holy things, and his desire to share them with others, finds an echo in the hearts of his descendants.

In saying this, however, I stray beyond my bailiwick, for I am a historian rather than a theologian. The present work contributes to the preliminary task of making Salmerón's thought better known and understood among scholars and Jesuits alike. The assessment of his wisdom awaits someone else.

Bibliography

Primary sources

Alburquerque, Antonio, ed. *Diego Laínez, SJ: First Biographer of Saint Ignatius of Loyola.* Translated by John Montag. St. Louis: Institute of Jesuit Sources, 2010.
Baronius, Caesar. *Annales Ecclesiastici.* 10 vols. Rome: Congregation of the Oratory, 1593.
Barradas, Sebastião. *Commentaria in Concordiam et Historiam Evangelicam.* 4 vols. Mainz: Hermann Mylius, 1600–1609.
Bellarmine, Robert. *The Autobiography of St. Robert Bellarmine.* Translated by Ryan Grant. Post Falls, ID: Mediatrix Press, 2016.
———. *Controversies of the Christian Faith.* Translated by Kenneth Baker. Saddle River, NJ: Keep the Faith Publications, 2016.
Betuleius, Xystus. *Sibyllinorum Oraculorum.* Basel: Johannes Oporin, 1545.
Bolland, Jean, ed. *Imago Primi Saeculi Societatis Jesu.* Antwerp: Balthasar Moretus, 1640.
Calvin, John. *Harmonia ex Evangelistis tribus composita.* Geneva: Etienne Vignon, 1582.
———. *A Harmony of the Gospels: Matthew, Mark, and Luke.* Translated by A.W.N. Morrison. 3 vols. Grand Rapids, MI: Eerdmans, 1994–95.
Canisius, Peter. *De Maria Virgine Incomparabili, et Dei Genitrice Sacrosancta.* Ingolstadt: David Sartorius, 1573.
Cano, Melchor. *De locis theologicis.* Louvain: Servatius Saffenus, 1569.
Castellio, Sebastian. *Sibyllina Oracula: De Graeco in Latinum conversa, et in eadem annotationes.* Basel: Johannes Oporin, 1546.
Catarino, Ambrogio. *Annotationes in commentaria Cajetani super sacram Scripturam.* Lyons: Matthias Bonhomme, 1542.
Concilium Tridentinum: Diariorum, actorum, epistularum, tractatuum nova collection. Edited by Societas Goerresiana. 13 vols. Freiburg im Breisgau: Herder, 1901–2001.
Costerus, Franciscus. *Vyftich meditation van de gantsche historie der Passie en des lijdens Ons Heeren Jesu Christi.* Antwerp: Jan Mourentorf, 1597.
Driedo, John. *De ecclesiasticis scripturis et dogmatibus.* Louvain: Bartholomaeus Gravius, 1535.
Erasmus, Desiderius. *Collected Works of Erasmus: Paraphrase on Luke 11–24.* Translated by Jane Phillips. Toronto: University of Toronto Press, 2003.

Firpo, Massimo and Dario Marcatto, eds. *Il processo inquisitoriale del Cardinal Giovanni Morone: Edizione critica*. Rome: Istituto Storico Italiano per L'età Moderna e Contemporanea, 1981–1995.

Ignatius of Loyola. *The Spiritual Exercises of St. Ignatius: Based on Studies in the Language of the Autograph*. Edited by Louis Puhl. Chicago, IL: Loyola Press, 1952.

Illyricus, Matthias Flacius. *Ecclesiastica historia congesta per aliquot iuros in urbe Magdeburgica*. 13 vols. Basel: Johannes Oporin, 1559–74.

Jansen, Cornelius. *Commentariorum in suam concordiam, ac totam historiam evangelicam*. Louvain: Petrus Zangrius Tiletanus, 1571.

Lapide, Cornelius a. *Commentarii in quatuor Evangelia*. Antwerp: Martin Nutius, 1639.

Laínez, Diego. *Jacobi Laínez secondi praepositi generalis Societatis Jesu Disputationes tridentinae*. Edited by Hermann Grisar. 2 vols. Innsbruck: Felicianus Rauch, 1886.

Lightfoot, J.L. *The Sibylline Oracles: With Introduction, Translation, and Commentary on the First and Second Books*. New York: Oxford University Press, 2007.

Maldonado, Juan de. *Commentarii in quatuor evangelistas*. Mainz: Arnoldus Mylius, 1602.

Marlorat, Augustin. *Novi Testamenti catholica expositio ecclesiastica, id est, ex universis probatis theologis (quos Dominus diversis suis ecclesiis dedit) excerpta, a quodam verbi Dei ministro, diu multumque in theologia versato, sive bibliotheca expositionum Novi Testamenti, id est, expositio ex probatis omnibus theologis collecta, et in unum corpus singulari artificio conflate, quae instar bibliothecae multis expositrobus refertae esse possit*. 2 vols. Geneva: Henricus Stephanus, 1561.

———. *Novi Testamenti catholica expositio ecclesiastica, id est, ex universis probatis theologis (quos Dominus diversis suis ecclesiis dedit) excerpta, a quodam verbi Dei ministro, diu multumque in theologia versato, sive bibliotheca expositionum Novi Testamenti, id est, expositio ex probatis omnibus theologis collecta, et in unum corpus singulari artificio conflate, quae instar bibliothecae multis expositrobus refertae esse possit*. 2nd ed. 2 vols. Geneva: Henricus Stephanus, 1564.

MHSI. *Epistolae P. Alphonsi Salmeronis*. 2 vols. Madrid: Gabriel López del Horno, 1906–1907.

———. *Lainii Monumenta*. 8 vols. Madrid: Gabriel López del Horno, 1912–17.

MHSI. MI. *Fontes Narrativi de S. Ignatio de Loyola et de Societatis Iesu initiis*, vol. 1, *Narrationes scriptae ante annum 1557*. Edited by Dionisio Fernández Zapico and Cándido de Dalmases. Rome: MHSI, 1943.

———. *Sancti Ignatii de Loyola Constitutiones Societatis Jesu*, vol. 1, *Monumenta Constitutionum Praevia*. Rome: Pontifical Gregorian University, 1934.

---. *Sancti Ignatii de Loyola epistolae et instructiones.* 12 vols. Madrid: Gabriel López del Horno, 1903–1911.

---. *Series Secunda: Exercitia Spiritualia S. Ignatii de Loyola et eorum directoria,* vol. 1, *Exercitia Spiritualia.* Edited by Joseph Calaveras and Cándido de Dalmases. Rome: IHSI, 1969.

Montano, Benito Arias. *Prefacios de Benito Arias Montano a la Biblia Regia de Felipe II.* Edited and translated by María Asunción Sánchez Manzano. León: University of León, 2006.

Morales, Pedro. *In Caput Primum Matthaei.* Lyons: Horatius Cardon, 1614.

Nadal, Jerome. *Evangelicae Historiae Imagines ex ordine Evangeliorum, quae toto anno in Missae sacrificio recitantur, in ordine temporis vitae Christi digestae.* Antwerp: Martin Nuyts, 1593.

Pérez de Ayala, Martín. *De divinis, apostolicis, et ecclsiasticis traditionibus.* Cologne: Jaspar Gennepaeus, 1549.

Pérez de Valdivia, Diego. *Tratado de la Inmaculada Concepción de nuestra Señora* (1582). Edited by Juan Cruz Cruz. Pamplona: University of Navarre, 2004.

Salmerón, Alfonso. *Commentarii in Evangelicam Historiam et in Acta Apostolorum.* 12 vols. Madrid: Luis Sánchez, 1597–1601.

---. *Commentarii in Evangelicam Historiam et in Acta Apostolorum.* Vol. 1, *De Prolegomenis in Sacrosancta Evangelia.* Brescia: Matthias Colosinus and Baretius Baretius, 1601.

---. *Commentarii in Evangelicam Historiam et in Acta Apostolorum.* 12 vols. Cologne: Antonius Hierat and Johannes Gynmnicus, 1602–1604.

---. *Commentarii in Evangelicam Historiam et in Acta Apostolorum.* 12 vols. Cologne: Antonius Hierat and Johannes Gynmnicus, 1612–1614.

---. *Commentarii in Omnes Epistolas B. Pauli et Canonicas.* 4 vols. Madrid: Luis Sánchez, 1602.

---. *Commentarii in Omnes Epistolas B. Pauli et Canonicas.* 4 vols. Cologne: Antonius Hierat and Johannes Gynmnicus, 1604.

---. *Commentarii in Omnes Epistolas B. Pauli et Canonicas.* 4 vols. Cologne: Antonius Hierat and Johannes Gynmnicus, 1614–15.

---. *Oratio Reverendi Patris Magistri Alphonsi Salmeronis de Societate Iesu Theologi, nuper in Concilio Tridentino habita, in qua ad exemplar Divi Ioannis Evangelistae vera Praelatorum forma describitur.* Rome: Stephanus Nicolinus, 1547.

Sanders, Nicholas. *De visibili monarchia ecclesiae.* Louvain: Joannes Foulerus, 1571.

Tanner, Matthias, ed. *Societatis Jesu Apostolorum Imitatrix.* Prague: Charles University, 1694.

Tejada y Ramiro, Juan. *Colección de cánones y de todos los concilios de la iglesia de España y de América.* Vol. 4. Madrid: P. Montero, 1859.

Titelmans, Francis. *Elucidatio in omnes epistolas apostolicas.* Antwerp: Johannes Steelsius, 1540.
Wright, Benjamin. *The Letter of Aristeas.* Boston, MA: De Gruyter, 2015.

Secondary sources

Alvar Ezquerra, Antonio. "El Colegio de San Jerónimo o Colegio Trilingüe." In *Historia de la Universidad de Alcalá*, edited by Antonio Alvar Ezquerra, 215–22. Alcalá de Henares: University of Alcalá de Henares, 2010.
Andrés, Melquíades. "La compasión de la Virgen al pie de la cruz, deducida de su triple gracia, según Salmerón." *Estudios Marianos* 5 (1946): 359–88.
Aron-Beller, Katherine. "Disciplining Jews: The Papal Inquisition of Modena, 1598–1630." *Sixteenth Century Journal* 41, no. 3 (2010): 713–29.
Aron-Beller, Katherine. "Ghettoization: The Papal Enclosure and its Jews." In *A Companion to Early Modern Rome*, edited by Pamela Jones, Barbara Wisch, and Simon Ditchfield, 232–46. Boston, MA: Brill, 2019.
Backus, Irena. *Historical Method and Confessional Identity in the Era of the Reformation (1378–1615).* Boston, MA: Brill, 2003.
Bangert, William. *Claude Jay and Alfonso Salmerón: Two Early Jesuits.* Chicago, IL: Loyola University Press, 1985.
Barletta, Laura. "Un esempio di festa: il Carnevale." In *Capolavori in Festa: Effimero barocco a Largo di Palazzo (1683–1759)*, edited by Giuseppe Zampino, 91–104. Naples: Electa Napoli, 1997.
Baroni, Victor. *La Contre-Réforme devant la Bible.* Lausanne: La Concorde, 1943.
Bastero, Juan Luis. *Mary, Mother of the Redeemer.* Translated by Michael Adams and Philip Griffin. Dublin: Four Courts Press, 2006.
Beaver, Adam. "Scholarly Pilgrims: Antiquarian Visions of the Holy Land." In *Sacred History: Uses of the Christian Past in the Renaissance World*, edited by Katherine van Liere, Simon Ditchfield, and Howard Louthan, 267–84. New York: Oxford University Press, 2012.
Bertrand, Dominique. "The Society of Jesus and the Church Fathers." In *The Reception of the Church Fathers in the West: From the Carolingians to the Maurists*, edited by Irena Backus, vol. 2, 889–950. New York: Brill, 1997.
Black, Charlene Villaseñor. "Love and Marriage in the Spanish Empire: Depictions of Holy Matrimony and Gender Discourses in the Seventeenth Century." *Sixteenth Century Journal* 32, no. 3 (2001): 637–67.
Boeft, Jan de. "Erasmus and the Church Fathers." In *The Reception of the Church Fathers in the West: From the Carolingians to the Maurists*, edited by Irena Backus, vol. 2, 537–73. New York: Brill, 1997.

Boero, Giuseppe. *Vie du Père Jacques Lainez...suivie de la biographie du Père Alphonse Salmerón*. Translated by Victor de Coppier. Paris: Descleé de Brouwer, 1894.

Boon, Jessica. "The Agony of the Virgin: The Swoons and Crucifixion of Mary in Sixteenth Century Castilian Passion Treatises." *Sixteenth Century Journal* 38, no. 1 (2007): 3–25.

Boss, Sarah Jane. "The Development of the Doctrine of Mary's Immaculate Conception." In *Mary: The Complete Resource*, edited by Sarah Jane Boss, 207–35. New York: Oxford University Press, 2007.

Bouvier, Claire. *Être écrivain et religieux au Siècle d'or: Pedro de Ribadeneyra S.I. et le ministère de l'écriture dans la Compagnie de Jésus*. Madrid: Casa de Velázquez, 2023.

Bravo Lozano, Cristina. "La Concepción Inmaculada de María en el contexto de la *pietas hispánica*." In *Intacta María: Política y religiosidad en la España barroca*, edited by Pablo González Tornel, 109–19. Valencia: Generalitat Valenciana, 2017.

Brugger, E. Christian. *The Indissolubility of Marriage and the Council of Trent*. Washington, DC: Catholic University of America Press, 2017.

Buck, Lawrence. *The Roman Monster: An Icon of the Papal Antichrist in Reformation Polemics*. Kirksville, MO: Truman State University Press, 2014.

Burnett, Amy Nelson. *Debating the Sacraments: Print and Authority in the Early Reformation*. New York: Oxford University Press, 2019.

Burrieza Sánchez, Javier. "Diego Laínez: La Compañía de Jesús más allá de Ignacio de Loyola." In *Diego Laínez (1512–1565): Jesuita y teólogo del Concilio*, edited by José Garcia de Castro Valdés, 55–99. Madrid: Comillas, 2013.

Cameron, Euan. "Angels, Demons, and Everything in Between: Spiritual Beings in Early Modern Europe." In *Angels of Light? Sanctity and the Discernment of Spirits in the Early Modern Period*, edited by Clare Copeland and Jan Machielsen, 17–52. Boston, MA: Brill, 2013.

Cañizares-Esguerra, Jorge, Robert Maryks, and R.P. Hsia, eds. *Encounters between Jesuits and Protestants in Asia and the Americas*. Boston, MA: Brill, 2018.

Caravale, Giorgio. *Beyond the Inquisition: Ambrogio Catarino and the Origins of the Counter-Reformation*. Translated by Don Weinstein. Notre Dame, IN: University of Notre Dame Press, 2017.

Carboni, Mauro. "The Economics of Marriage: Dotal Strategies in Bologna in the Age of Catholic Reform." *Sixteenth Century Journal* 39, no. 2 (2008): 371–87.

———. *Preaching and Inquisition in Renaissance Italy: Words on Trial*. Translated by Frank Gordon. Boston, MA: Brill, 2016.

Cerceda, Feliciano. *Diego Laínez en la Europea religiosa de su tiempo*. 2 vols. Madrid: Ediciones Cultura Hispánica, 1946.

———. "Laínez y Salmerón y el proceso del catecismo de Carranza." *Razón y Fe* 100 (1932): 212–66.

Chalk, Casey. *The Obscurity of Scripture: Disputing Sola Scriptura and the Protestant Notion of Biblical Perspicuity*. Steubenville, OH: Emmaus Road Publishing, 2023.

Chau, Wai-Shing. *The Letter and the Spirit: A History of Interpretation from Origen to Luther*. New York: Peter Lang, 1995.

Chavarria, Elisa Novi. "The Space of Women." In *A Companion to Early Modern Naples*, edited by Tommaso Astarita, 177–96. Boston, MA: Brill, 2013.

Christianson, Gerald, Thomas Izbicki, and Christopher Bellitto, eds. *The Church, the Councils, and Reform: The Legacy of the Fifteenth Century*. Washington, DC: Catholic University of America Press, 2008.

Christopoulos, John. "Papal Authority, Episcopal Reservation, and Abortion in Sixteenth-Century Italy." In *Episcopal Reform and Politics in Early Modern Europe*, edited by Jennifer DeSilva, 110–27. Kirksville, MO: Truman State University Press, 2012.

Chung-Kim, Esther. *Inventing Authority: The Use of the Church Fathers in Reformation Debates over the Eucharist*. Waco, TX: Baylor University Press, 2011.

Clark, Frederic. "The Varieties of *Historia* in Early Modern Europe." In *New Horizons for Early Modern European Scholarship*, edited by Ann Blair and Nicholas Popper, 111–30. Baltimore, MD: Johns Hopkins University Press, 2021.

Clarke, Paula. "The Business of Prostitution in Early Renaissance Venice." *Renaissance Quarterly* 68, no. 2 (2015): 419–64.

Clines, Robert John. "How to Become a Jesuit Crypto-Jew: The Self-Confessionalization of Giovanni Battista Eliano through the Textual Artifice of Conversion." *Sixteenth Century Journal* 48, no. 1 (2017): 3–26.

Conedera, Sam Zeno. "Forgotten Saint: The Life and Writings of Alfonso Salmerón, SJ." *Studies in the Spirituality of Jesuits* 52, no. 4 (2020): 1–34.

———. "Leading the Blind: Aquinas, Ignatius, and other Jesuits on Obedience." In *Ignatius of Loyola and Thomas Aquinas: A Jesuit Ressourcement*, edited by Justin Anderson, Matthew Levering, and Aaron Pidel, 217–45. Washington, DC: Catholic University of America Press, 2024.

Coolidge, Grace. "'Neither Dumb, Deaf, nor Destitute of Understanding': Women as Guardians in Early Modern Spain." *Sixteenth Century Journal* 36, no. 3 (2005): 673–93.

Copenhaver, Brian, and Daniel Stein Kokin. "Egidio da Viterbo's *Book on Hebrew Letters*: Christian Kabbalah in Papal Rome." *Renaissance Quarterly* 67, no. 1 (2014): 1–42.

Crawford, Katherine. "Catherine de Médicis and the Performance of Political Motherhood." *Sixteenth Century Journal* 31, no. 3 (2000): 643–73.
Dalton, Jessica. *Between Popes, Inquisitors and Princes: How the First Jesuits Negotiated Religious Crisis in Early Modern Italy*. Boston, MA: Brill, 2020.
Daly, Robert. "Robert Bellarmine and Post-Tridentine Eucharistic Theology." *Theological Studies* 61 (2000): 239–60.
D'Avenia, Fabrizio. "From Spain to Sicily after the Expulsion: *Conversos* between Economic Networks and the Aristocratic Elite." *Journal of Early Modern History* 22 (2018): 421–45.
De las Heras, José Luis. "Indultos concedidos por la Cámara de Castilla en tiempos de los Austria." *Studia Histórica: Historia moderna* 103 (1983): 115–40.
De Lanversin, F. "Salmerón, Alphonse." In *Dictionnaire de théologie catholique*, vol. 14, pt. 1, cols. 1040–47. Paris: Letouzey et Ané, 1898–1950.
Delgado, Mariano. "…todos los males y perturbaciones de la Compañía han venido de ellos:" Reflexiones acerca del giro anti-converso en la Compañía de Jesús." In *Diego Laínez (1512–1565) and his Generalate: Jesuit with Jewish Roots, Close Confidant of Ignatius of Loyola, Preeminent Theologian of the Council of Trent*, edited by Paul Oberholzer, 191–213. Rome: IHSI, 2015.
De Maio, Romeo. *Alfonso Carafa: Cardinale di Napoli (1540–1565)*. Vatican City: Biblioteca Apostolica Vaticana, 1961.
Del Páramo, Severiano. "María, Madre de la Iglesia y su influjo en el Cuerpo místico de Cristo, según el P. Alfonso Salmerón, S.J." In *Temas Bíblicos*, vol. 3, *Temas mariológicos y josefinos*, 115–35. Santander: Comillas, 1967.
Delville, Jean-Paul. "Jansenius de Gand (1510–1576) et l'exégèse des paraboles." *Revue d'Histoire Ecclesiastique* 92, no. 1 (1997): 38–69.
Delville, Jean-Pierre. *L'Europe de l'exégèse au XVIe siècle: Interprétations de la parabole des ouvriers a la vigne (Mt 20:1–16)*. Leuven: Leuven University Press, 2004.
Dialeti, Androniki. "From Women's Oppression to Male Anxiety: The Concept of 'Patriarchy' in the Historiography of Early Modern Europe." In *Gender in Late Medieval and Early Modern Europe*, edited by Marianna Muravyeva and Raisa Maria Toivo, 19–36. New York: Routledge, 2013.
Dingel, Irene. "The Culture of Conflict in the Controversies Leading to the Formula of Concord, 1548–1580." In *Lutheran Ecclesiastical Culture, 1550–1675*, edited by Robert Kolb, 15–64. Boston, MA: Brill, 2008.
Ditchfield, Simon. *Liturgy, Sanctity and History in Tridentine Italy: Pietro Maria Campi and the Preservation of the Particular*. New York: Cambridge University Press, 1995.
———. "Tridentine Catholicism." In *The Ashgate Research Companion to the Counter-Reformation*, edited by Alexandra Bamji, Geert Hansen, and Mary Laven, 15–31. Burlington, VT: Ashgate, 2013.

Divenuto, Francesco. *Napoli, l'Europa e la Compagnia di Gesù nella "Cronica" di Giovan Francesco Araldo*. Naples: Edizioni Scientifiche Italiane, 1998.
Domínguez Reboiras, Fernando. "Biblical Criticism." In *A Companion to the Spanish Scholastics*, edited by Harald Braun, Erik de Bom and Paolo Astorri, 165–98. Boston, MA: Brill, 2022.
Dudon, Paul. "Sur un texte inédit de Salmeron (1562)." *Gregorianum* 11 (1930): 410–17.
Duerloo, Luc. *Dynasty and Piety: Archduke Albert (1598–1621) and Habsburg Political Culture in an Age of Religious Wars*. New York: Routledge, 2016.
Eire, Carlos. *Reformations: The Early Modern World, 1450–1650*. New Haven, CT: Yale University Press, 2016.
Ellington, Donna Spivey. *From Sacred Body to Angelic Soul: Understanding Mary in Late Medieval and Early Modern Europe*. Washington, DC: Catholic University of America Press, 2001.
Faber, Riemer. "Erasmus' *Novum Instrumentum* (1516): Reforming the Bible into the Bible of the Reformation." In *Renaissance und Bibelhumanismus*, edited by J. Marius J. Lange van Ravenswaay and Herman Selderhuis, 294–312. Göttingen: Vandenhoeck & Ruprecht, 2020.
Fastiggi, Robert. "Mary in the Work of Redemption." In *The Oxford Handbook of Mary*, edited by Chris Maunder, 303–19. New York: Oxford University Press, 2019.
Feitler, Bruno. *The Imaginary Synagogue: Anti-Jewish Literature in the Portuguese Early Modern World*. Boston, MA: Brill, 2015.
Fernández López, Sergio. *Lectura y prohibición de la Biblia en lengua vulgar: Defensores y detractores*. León: Universidad de León, 2003.
Fichter, Joseph. *James Laynez: Jesuit*. St. Louis, MO: Herder, 1944.
Fischer, Benedict, Wim François, Antonio Gerace, and Luke Murray, "The 'Golden Age' of Catholic Biblical Scholarship (1550–1650) and its Relation to Biblical Humanism." In *Renaissance und Bibelhumanismus*, edited by J. Marius, J. Lange van Ravenswaay, and Herman Selderhuis, 217–74. Göttingen: Vandenhoeck and Ruprecht, 2020.
François, Wim. "Augustine and the Golden Age of Biblical Scholarship in Louvain (1550–1650)." In *Shaping the Bible in the Reformation: Books, Scholars, and Their Readers in the Sixteenth Century*, edited by Bruce Gordon and Matthew McLean, 235–89. Boston, MA: Brill, 2012.
———. "John Driedo's *De ecclesiasticis scripturis et dogmatibus* (1533): A Controversy on the Sources of the Truth." In *Orthodoxy, Process, and Product*, edited by Mathijs Lamberigts, Lieven Boeve, and Terrence Merrigan, 85–118. Walpole, MA: Uitgeverij Peeters, 2009.
Frieder, Braden. *Chivalry and the Perfect Prince. Tournaments, Art, and Armor at the Spanish Habsburg Court*. Kirksville, MO: Truman State University Press, 2008.

Friedrich, Markus. *The Jesuits: A History*. Translated by John Noël Dillon. Princeton, NJ: Princeton University Press, 2022.
Furey, Constance. "Invective and Discernment in Martin Luther, D. Erasmus, and Thomas More." *Harvard Theological Review* 98, vol. 4 (2005): 469–88.
Galtier, Paolo. "La compagnia di Gesù e la teologia dommatica." In *La Compagnia di Gesù e le scienze sacre: conferenze commemorative del quarto centenario dalla fondazione della Compagnia di Gesù tenute alla Pontificia università gregoriana, 5–11 novembre 1941*, 45–81. Rome: Gregorian University, 1942.
Gambero. Luigi. *Mary and the Fathers of the Church: The Blessed Virgin Mary in Patristic Thought*. Translated by Thomas Buffer. San Francisco, CA: Ignatius Press, 1999.
García de Castro Valdés, José. *Polanco: El humanismo de los jesuitas (Burgos 1517–Roma 1576)*. Madrid: Comillas, 2012.
Gerace, Antonio. *Biblical Scholarship in Louvain in the 'Golden' Sixteenth Century*. Gottingen: Vandenhoeck and Ruprecht, 2019.
Gilmont, Jean-François. *Les écrits sprituels des premiers jésuites: Inventaire commenté*. Rome: IHSI, 1961.
Ginhoven Rey, Christopher van. *Instruments of the Divinity: Providence and Praxis in the Foundation of the Society of Jesus*. Boston, MA: Brill, 2014.
Graef, Hilda. *Mary: A History of Doctrine and Devotion*. Notre Dame, IN: Ave Maria Press, 2009.
Grafton, Anthony. "Church History in Early Modern Europe: Tradition and Innovation." In *Sacred History: Uses of the Christian Past in the Renaissance World*, edited by Katherine van Liere, Simon Ditchfield, and Howard Louthan, 3–26. New York: Oxford University Press, 2012.
———. *What Was History? The Art of History in Early Modern Europe*. New York: Cambridge, 2007.
Graizbord, David. "Philosemitism in Late Sixteenth- and Seventeenth-Century Iberia: Refracted Judeophobia?" *Sixteenth Century Journal* 38, no. 3 (2007): 657–82.
Grendler, Paul. "Laínez and the Schools in Europe." In *Diego Laínez (1512–1565) and his Generalate: Jesuit with Jewish Roots, Close Confidant of Ignatius of Loyola, Preeminent Theologian of the Council of Trent*, edited by Paul Oberholzer, 639–68. Rome: IHSI, 2015.
———. "The Universities of the Renaissance and Reformation." *Renaissance Quarterly* 57, no. 1 (2004): 1–42.
Guarino, Gabriel. "Public Rituals and Festivals in Naples, 1503–1799." In *A Companion to Early Modern Naples*, edited by Tommaso Astarita, 257–79. Boston, MA: Brill, 2013.
———. "Spanish Celebrations in Seventeenth-Century Naples." *Sixteenth Century Journal* 37, no. 1 (2006): 25–41.

Guibert, Joseph de. *The Jesuits: Their Spiritual Doctrine and Practice*. Edited by George Ganss, translated by William Young. St. Louis, MO: Institute of Jesuit Sources, 1986.

Hall, Linda. *Mary, Mother and Warrior: The Virgin in Spain and the Americas*. Austin, TX: University of Texas, 2004.

Harrie, Jeanne. "The Guises, the Body of Christ, and the Body Politic." *Sixteenth Century Journal* 37, no. 1 (2006): 43–57.

Heal, Bridget. *The Cult of the Virgin Mary in Early Modern Germany: Protestant and Catholic Piety, 1500–1648*. New York: Cambridge University Press, 2007.

Hermann de Franceschi, Sylvio. "La morale catholique posttridentine et la controverse interconfessionnelle. Jeûne et abstinence dans la confrontation entre protestants et jésuites: privations alimentaires et confessionnalisation." In *Jésuites et protestantisme: XVIe–XXIe siècles*, edited by Yves Krumenacker and Philippe Martin, 69–93. Lyons: LARHRA, 2019.

Hernández, Rosilie. *Immaculate Conceptions: The Power of the Religious Imagination in Early Modern Spain*. Toronto: University of Toronto Press, 2019.

Homza, Lu Ann. *Religious Authority in the Spanish Renaissance*. Baltimore, MD: Johns Hopkins University Press, 2000.

Höpfl, Harro. *Jesuit Political Thought: The Society of Jesus and the State, c. 1540–1630*. New York: Cambridge University Press, 2004.

Horbury, William. "Petrus Galatinus and Jean Thenaud on the Talmud and the *Toledot Yeshu*." In *Jewish Books and their Readers: Aspects of the Intellectual Life of Christians and Jews in Early Modern Europe*, edited by Scott Mandelbrote and Joanna Weinberg, 125–50. Boston, MA: Brill, 2016.

Howell, Patrick. *Great Risks Had to be Taken: The Jesuit Response to the Second Vatican Council, 1958–2018*. Eugene, OR: Cascade Books, 2019.

Hughes, John. "Alfonso Salmeron: His Work at the Council of Trent." PhD diss., University of Kentucky, 1974.

Iturrioz, Daniel. *La definición del Concilio de Trento sobre la causalidad de los sacramentos*. Madrid: Ediciones Fax, 1951.

Izbicki, Thomas. "The Immaculate Conception and Ecclesiastical Politics from the Council of Basel to the Council of Trent: The Dominicans and Their Foes." *Archiv für Reformationgeschichte* 96 (2005): 145–70.

Jenkins, Allan, and Patrick Preston. *Biblical Scholarship and the Church: A Sixteenth-Century Crisis of Authority*. Aldershot: Ashgate, 2007.

Jiménez Pablo, Esther. *La forja de una identidad: La Compañía de Jesús (1540–1640)*. Madrid: Ediciones Polifemo, 2014.

———. "El P. Alfonso Salmerón S.I. y el gobierno de los colegios de Nápoles." *Magallánica* 2, no. 4 (2016): 57–79.

Kaborycha, Lisa. "'We do not sell them this tolerance:' Grand Duke Fernando I's Protection of Jews in Tuscany and the Case of Jacob Esperiel." *Sixteenth Century Journal* 49, no. 4 (2018): 987–1018.

Kainulainen, Jaska. "Virtue and Civic Values in Early Modern Jesuit Education." *Journal of Jesuit Studies* 5, no. 4 (2018): 530–48.
Kaplan, Benjamin. *Divided by Faith: Religious Conflict and the Practice of Toleration in Early Modern Europe.* Cambridge, MA: Belknap Press, 2007.
Kaplan, Debra and Magda Teter. "Out of the (Historiographic) Ghetto: European Jews and Reformation Narratives." *Sixteenth Century Journal* 40, no. 2 (2009): 365–94.
Karant-Nunn, Susan C. "The Wrath of Martin Luther: Anger and Charisma in the Reformer." *Sixteenth Century Journal* 48, no. 4 (2017): 909–26.
Kiecker, James. *The Postilla of Nicholas of Lyra on the Song of Songs.* Milwaukee, WI: Marquette University Press, 1998.
Klepper, Deanna. *The Insight of Unbelievers: Nicholas of Lyra and the Christian Reading of Jewish Text in the Later Middle Ages.* Philadelphia, PA: University of Pennsylvania Press, 2007.
Knoll, Alfons. *"Derselbe Geist:" Eine Untersuchung zum Kirchenverständnis in der Theologie der ersten Jesuiten.* Paderborn: Bonifatius, 2007.
Koivisto, Jussi. "Martin Luther's Conception of the Serpent Possessed by the Devil (Gen 3) and the Antecedent Tradition." In *"Wading Lambs and Swimming Elephants:" The Bible for the Laity and Theologians in the Late Medieval and Early Modern Era,* edited by Wim François and August den Hollander, 111–51. Walpole, MA: Peeters, 2012.
Kramp, Igna. "Der Jesuit Alfonso Salmerón (1515–1585) als humanistischer Theologe: Ähnlichkeiten und Unterschiede zu Erasmus von Rotterdam." *Theologie und Philosophie* 90 (2015): 504–27.
Kreitzer, Beth. *Reforming Mary: Changing Images of the Virgin Mary in Lutheran Sermons of the Sixteenth Century.* New York: Oxford, 2004.
Krey, Philip, and Lesley Smith, eds. *Nicholas of Lyra: The Senses of Scripture.* Boston, MA: Brill, 2000.
Kuntz, Margaret. "Liturgical, Ritual, and Diplomatic Spaces at St. Peter's and the Vatican Palace: The Innovations of Paul IV, Urban VIII, and Alexander VII." In *A Companion to Early Modern Rome,* edited by Pamela Jones, Barbara Wisch, and Simon Ditchfield, 75–98. Boston, MA: Brill, 2019.
Lavenia, Vincenzo. "Missiones Castrenses: Jesuits and Soldiers between Pastoral Care and Violence." *Journal of Jesuit Studies* 4, no. 4 (2017): 545–58.
Lawlor, Francis. "The Doctrine of Grace in the *Spiritual Exercises.*" *Theological Studies* 3, no. 4 (1942): 513–42.
Lécrivain, Philippe. *Paris in the Time of Ignatius of Loyola (1528–1535).* Translated by Ralph Renner. St. Louis, MO: Institute of Jesuit Sources, 2011.
Leturia, Pietro. "Il contributo della Compagnia di Gesù alla formazione delle scienze storiche." In *La Compagnia di Gesù e le scienze sacre: conferenze commemorative del quarto centenario dalla fondazione della Compagnia di Gesù*

tenute alla Pontificia università gregoriana, 5–11 novembre 1941, 161–202. Rome: Gregorian University, 1942.

Levy, Ian Christopher. *Introducing Medieval Biblical Interpretation: The Senses of Scripture in Premodern Exegesis.* Grand Rapids, MI: Baker Academic, 2018.

Lewis, Mark. "The First Jesuits as 'Reformed Priests,'" *AHSI* 65 (1996): 111–27.

Lewis, Mark and Jennifer Selwyn. "Jesuit Activity in Southern Italy during the Generalate of Everard Mercurian." In *The Mercurian Project: Forming Jesuit Culture 1573–1580*, edited by Thomas McCoog, 532–57. St. Louis, MO: Institute of Jesuit Sources, 2004.

Liere, Katherine van. "Humanism and Scholasticism in Sixteenth-Century Academe: Five Student Orations from the University of Salamanca." *Renaissance Quarterly* 53, no. 1 (2000): 57–107.

Llorca, Bernardino. "Los escritores jesuitas españoles y la Inmaculada Concepción en el primer período de la Compañía de Jesús." *Estudios Marianos* 16 (1955): 233–44.

Lop Sebastià, Miguel. *Alfonso Salmerón, SJ (1515–1585): Una biografía epistolar.* Madrid: Comillas, 2015.

Maatheson, Peter. *The Imaginative World of the Reformation.* Edinburgh: T&T Clark, 2000.

MacFarlane, Kirsten. "Gospel Harmonies and the Genres of Biblical Scholarship in Early Modern Europe." *Renaissance Quarterly* 76 (2023): 1027–67.

MacGregor, Kirk. *Luis de Molina: The Life and Theology of the Founder of Middle Knowledge.* Grand Rapids, MI: Zondervan, 2015.

Madrigal Terrazas, Santiago. *Eclesialidad, reforma, y misión: El legado teológico de Ignacio de Loyola, Pedro Fabro y Francisco de Javier.* Madrid: San Pablo, 2008.

———. "'Nuestra santa madre Iglesia hierárchica' [Ej 353]: La Iglesia de Jesucristo según los *Commentarii* de Salmerón." In *Dogmática ignaciana: "Buscar y hallar la voluntad divina" [Ej 1]*, edited by Gabino Uríbarri Bilbao, 468–502. Madrid: Comillas, 2018.

———. "La participación del Maestro Diego Laínez en el Concilio de Trento (1545–1563)." In *Diego Laínez (1512–1565): Jesuita y teólogo del Concilio*, edited by José García de Castro Valdés, 101–57. Madrid: Comillas, 2013.

Maréchal, Joseph. "Application des sens." In *Dictionnaire de spiritualité ascétique et mystique*, vol. 1, 810–28. Paris: Beauchesne, 1937–75.

Martín López, David. "Claroscuros de la vida de Alfonso Salmerón Díaz, un jesuita ejemplar de primera generación." *Magallánica* 2, no. 4 (2016): 29–56.

———. "Jesuits and Conversos in Sixteenth-Century Toledo." *Journal of Jesuit Studies* 8, no. 2 (2021): 173–94.

Maryks, Robert. *The Jesuit Order as a Synagogue of Jews: Jesuits of Jewish Ancestry and Purity-of-Blood Laws in the Early Society of Jesus*. Boston, MA: Brill, 2010.
Matava, Robert. *Divine Causality and Human Free Choice: Domingo Báñez, Physical Premotion, and the Controversy* De Auxiliis *Revisited*. Boston, MA: Brill, 2016.
Mazur, Peter. "Combating 'Mohammedan Indecency': The Baptism of Muslim Slaves in Spanish Naples, 1563–1667." *Journal of Early Modern History* 13 (2009): 25–48.
McAleer, Graham. "Jesuit Sensuality and Feminist Bodies." *Modern Theology* 18, no. 3 (2002): 395–405.
McDonald, Grantley. *Biblical Criticism in Early Modern Europe: Erasmus, the Johannine Comma, and Trinitarian Debate*. New York: Cambridge University Press, 2016.
McGrath, Alister. Iustitia Dei: *A History of the Christian Doctrine of Justification*. 4th ed. New York: Cambridge University Press, 2020.
McNutt, Jennifer Powell, and David Lauber, eds. *The People's Book: The Reformation and the Bible*. Downer's Grove, IL: IVP Academic, 2016.
Meconi, David and Carl Olson, eds. *Called to Be the Children of God: The Catholic Theology of Human Deification*. San Francisco, CA: Ignatius Press, 2016.
Medina, F.B. "Pérez de Nueros y Maynar, Bartolomé." In *Diccionario histórico de la Compañía de Jesús*, edited by Charles O'Neill, vol. 3, 3092–93. Madrid: Comillas, 2001.
Michelson, Emily. *The Pulpit and the Press in Reformation Italy*. Cambridge, MA: Harvard University Press, 2013.
Miola, Robert. "Stabat Mater Dolorosa: Mary at the Foot of the Cross." *Sixteenth Century Journal* 48, no. 3 (2017): 653–79.
Miralles, Antonio. *El concepto de tradición en Martín Pérez de Ayala*. Pamplona: University of Navarre, 1980.
Mitchell, Nathan. *The Mystery of the Rosary: Marian Devotion and the Reinvention of Catholicism*. New York: New York University Press, 2009.
Molina. Diego. *La vera sposa de Christo: La primera Eclesiología de la Compañía de Jesús – Los tratados eclesiológicos de los jesuitas anteriores a Belarmino (1540–1586)*. Granada: Facultad de Teología, 2003.
Motta, Franco. "Jesuit Theology, Politics, and Identity: The Generalate of Acquaviva and the Years of Formation." In *The Acquaviva Project: Claudio Acquaviva's Generalate (1581–1615) and the Emergence of Modern Catholicism*, edited by Pierre-Antoine Fabre and Flavio Rurale, 349–370. Boston, MA: Institute of Jesuit Sources, 2017.
Murphy, John. *The Notion of Tradition in John Driedo*. Milwaukee, WI: Seraphic, 1959.

Murphy, Paul. "God's Porters: The Jesuit Vocation According to Francisco Suárez." *AHSI* 70, fasc. 139 (2001): 3–28.
Murray, Luke. *Jesuit Biblical Studies after Trent: Franciscus Toletus and Cornelius a Lapide*. Göttingen: Vandenhoeck and Ruprecht, 2019.
———. "Jesuit Hebrew Studies after Trent: Cornelius a Lapide (1567–1637)." *Journal of Jesuit Studies* 4, no. 1 (2017): 76–97.
Musi, Aurelio. "Political History." In *A Companion to Early Modern Naples*, edited by Tommaso Astarita, 131–51. Boston, MA: Brill, 2013.
Mütel, Mathias. *Mit den Kirchenvatern gegen Martin Luther? Die Debatten um Tradition und auctoritas patrum auf dem Konzil von Trient*. Paderborn: Ferdinand Schöningh, 2017.
Nichols, Aidan. *The Shape of Catholic Theology: An Introduction to Its Sources, Principles, and History*. Collegeville, MN: Liturgical Press, 1991.
Nugent, Christopher. *Ecumenism in the Age of the Reformation: The Colloquy of Poissy*. Cambridge, MA: Harvard University Press, 1974.
Oakley, Francis. *The Conciliarist Tradition: Constitutionalism in the Catholic Church, 1300–1870*. New York: Oxford University Press, 2003.
———. *The Watershed of Modern Politics: Law, Virtue, Kingship, and Consent (1300–1650)*. New Haven, CT: Yale University Press, 2015.
O'Banion, Patrick. *The Sacrament of Penance and Religious Life in Golden Age Spain*. University Park, Pennsylvania, PA: Pennsylvania State University Press, 2013.
Oberholzer, Paul. "Desafíos y exigencias frente a un nuevo descubrimiento de Diego Laínez." In *Diego Laínez (1512–1565) and his Generalate: Jesuit with Jewish Roots, Close Confidant of Ignatius of Loyola, Preeminent Theologian of the Council of Trent*, edited by Paul Oberholzer, 45–116. Rome: IHSI, 2015.
———. "El círculo de los primeros compañeros y las competencias en el establecimiento de la nueva Orden." In *Diego Lainez (1512–1565) and his Generalate: Jesuit with Jewish Roots, Close Confidant of Ignatius of Loyola, Preeminent Theologian of the Council of Trent*, edited by Paul Oberholzer, 15–34. Rome: IHSI, 2015.
Olds, Katrina. *Forging the Past: Invented Histories in Counter-Reformation Spain*. New Haven, CT: Yale University Press, 2015.
Olzarán, Jesús. "En el IV centenario de un voto tridentino del jesuita Alfonso Salmerón sobre la doble justicia." *Estudios Eclesiásticos* 20 (1946): 211–40.
O'Malley, John. "The Distinctiveness of the Society of Jesus." *Journal of Jesuit Studies* 3, no. 1 (2016): 1–16.
———. *The First Jesuits*. Cambridge, MA: Harvard University Press, 1993.
———. "Past, Present, and Future of Jesuit Studies: Historiographical Thoughts." *Journal of Jesuit Studies* 5, no. 4 (2018): 501–10.
———. *Trent: What Happened at the Council*. Cambridge, MA: Belknap Press, 2013.

O'Malley, John and Timothy O'Brien. "The Twentieth-Century Construction of Ignatian Spirituality: A Sketch." *Studies in the Spirituality of Jesuits* 52, no. 3 (2020).

Orella y Unzue, José L. de. *Respuestas católicas a las Centurias de Magdeburgo (1559–1588)*. Madrid: Fundación Universitaria Española, 1976.

Orsy, Ladislas. *The Evolving Church and the Sacrament of Penance*. Denville, NJ: Dimension Books, 1978.

O'Reilly, Terence. "Melchor Cano and the Spirituality of St. Ignatius Loyola: The *Censura y parecer contra el Instituto de los Padres Jesuitas*." *Journal of Jesuit Studies* 4, no. 3 (2017): 365–94.

———. "The Spiritual Exercises and Illuminism in Spain: Dominican Critics of the Early Society of Jesus." In *Ite Inflammate Omnia: Selected Historical Papers from Conferences Held at Loyola and Rome in 2006*, edited by Thomas McCoog, 199–228. Rome: IHSI, 2006.

———. *The Spiritual Exercises of Saint Ignatius of Loyola: Contexts, Sources, Reception*. Boston, MA: Brill, 2021.

O'Sullivan, Orlaith, ed. *The Bible as Book: The Reformation*. London: British Library, 2000.

Pabel, Hilmar. "Peter Canisius and the Protestants: A Model of Ecumenical Dialogue?" *Journal of Jesuit Studies* 1, no. 3 (2014): 373–99.

———. "Praise and Blame: Peter Canisius's Ambivalent Assessment of Erasmus." In *The Reception of Erasmus in the Early Modern Period*, edited by Karl Enenkel, 129–51. Boston, MA: Brill, 2013.

———. "Reading Jerome in the Renaissance: Erasmus' Reception of the 'Adversus Jovinianum.'" *Renaissance Quarterly* 55, no. 2 (2002): 470–97.

Parente, Ulderico. "Alfonso Salmerón 1515–1585." *AHSI* 59 (1990): 279–93.

Parigi, Paolo. *The Rationalization of Miracles*. New York: Cambridge University Press, 2012.

Parker, Geoffrey. *Emperor: A New Life of Charles V*. New Haven, CT: Yale University Press, 2019.

Pereda, Felipe. "*Vox Populi*: Carnal Blood, Spiritual Milk, and the Debate Surrounding the Immaculate Conception, ca. 1600." In *Interreligious Encounters in Polemics Between Christians, Jews, and Muslims in Iberia and Beyond*, ed. Mercedes García-Arenal, Gerard Wiegers, and Ryan Szpiech, 286–334. Boston, MA: Brill, 2019.

Pidel, Aaron. "Ignatius Loyola's 'Hierarchical Church' as Dionysian Reform Program." *Theological Studies* 83, no. 4 (2022): 554–78.

Pinto Cardoso, Arnaldo. *Da Antiga à Nova Aliança: Relações entre o Antigo e o Novo Testamento em Sebsatião Barradas (1543–1615)*. Lisbon: Instituto Nacional de Investigação Científica, 1987.

Porrer, Sheila. *Jacques Lefèvre d'Étaples and the Three Maries Debate*. Geneva: Librairie Droz, 2009.

Quantin, Jean-Louis. "The Fathers in Seventeenth Century Roman Catholic Theology." In *The Reception of the Church Fathers in the West: From the Carolingians to the Maurists*, edited by Irena Backus, vol. 2, 951–86. New York: Brill, 1997.

Ramos Riera, Ignacio. "¡He aquí a nuestro Padre teólogo! [*FN* II, 202]. ¿Qué es lo 'ignaciano' y lo teológico ignaciano?" In *Dogmática ignaciana: "Buscar y hallar la voluntad divina" [Ej 1]*, edited by Gabino Uríbarri Bilbao, 44–69. Madrid: Comillas, 2018.

Ransom, Emily. "St. Ignatius in the Affective School of Ludolph of Saxony." *Studies in the Spirituality of Jesuits* 53, no. 3 (2021): 1–41.

Rastoin, Marc. *Du même sang que Notre Seigneur: Juifs et jésuites aux débuts de la Compagnie*. Paris: Bayard, 2011.

Reiser, Marius. "The History of Catholic Exegesis, 1600–1800." In *The Oxford Handbook of Early Modern Theology, 1600–1800*, edited by Ulrich Lehner, Richard Muller, and A.G. Roeber, 75–88. New York: Oxford University Press, 2016.

Reites, James. *St. Ignatius and the People of the Book: An Historical-Theological Study of St. Ignatius of Loyola's Spiritual Motivation in His Dealings with the Jews and Muslims*. Rome: Pontifical Gregorian University, 1977.

Remensnyder, Amy. *La Conquistadora: The Virgin Mary at War and Peace in the Old and New Worlds*. New York: Oxford University Press, 2014.

Riudor, Ignacio. "Influencia de San Bernardo en la mariología de Salmerón y Suárez." *Estudios Marianos* 14 (1954): 329–53.

Rose, Stewart. *St. Ignatius and the Early Jesuits*. London: Burns and Oates, 1891.

Ruiz, Teofilo. *A King Travels: Festive Traditions in Late Medieval and Early Modern Spain*. Princeton, NJ: Princeton University Press, 2012.

Rummel, Erika. *Erasmus and his Catholic Critics*. 2 vols. Nieuwkoop: De Graaf, 1989.

Sánchez, Magdalena. *The Empress, the Queen, and the Nun: Women and Power at the Court of Philip III of Spain*. Baltimore, MD: Johns Hopkins University Press, 1998.

Sander, Christoph. "Alfonso Salmerón über weltliche Wissenschaften im Dienste der Bibelexegese." *Freiburger Zeitschrift für Philosophie und Theologie* 64, no. 2 (2017): 344–60.

Scaduto, Mario. *L'epoca di Giacomo Laínez, 1556–1565: Il governo*. Rome: Edizioni La Civiltà Cattolica, 1964.

———. *L'epoca di Giacomo Laínez, 1556–1565: L'azione*. Rome: Edizioni La Civiltà Cattolica, 1974.

Scaramella, Pierroberto. "Controllo e repressione ecclesiastica della poligamia a Napoli in età moderna: dalle cause matrimoniali al crimine di fede (1514–1799)." In *Trasgressioni: Seduzione, concubinato, adulterio, bigamia*

(XIV–XVIII secolo), edited by Silvana Seidel Menchi and Diego Quaglioni, 443–501. Bologna: Il Mulino, 2004.

Scheeben, Matthias. *Handbook of Catholic Dogmatics*. Bk. 1, *Theological Epistemology*, pt. 2, *Theological Knowledge Considered in Itself*. Translated by Michael Miller. Steubenville, OH: Emmaus Academic, 2019.

Schloesser, Stephen. "Accommodation as a Rhetorical Principle: Twenty Years after John O'Malley's *The First Jesuits* (1993)." *Journal of Jesuit Studies* 1, no. 3 (2014): 347–72.

Schurhammer, Georg. *Francis Xavier: His Life, His Times*. 4 vols. Translated by M. Joseph Costelloe. Rome: The Jesuit Historical Institute, 1982.

Shea, Henry. "The Beloved Disciple and the *Spiritual Exercises*." *Studies in the Spirituality of Jesuits* 49, no. 2 (2017): 1–35.

Sieben, Hermann Josef. "Ein Traktat des Jesuiten Salmerón über in Trient strittige Fragen zur Autorität des Konzils." In *Vom Apostelkonzil zum Ersten Vatikanum: Studien zur Geschichte der Konzilsidee*, 435–63. Paderborn: Ferdinand Schöningh, 1996.

Sommervogel, Carlos. *Bibliothèque de la Compagnie de Jésus*. New edition. 12 vols. Brussels: Oscar Schepens, 1896.

Soyer, François. *Antisemitic Conspiracy Theories in the Early Modern Iberian World: Narratives of Fear and Hatred*. Boston, MA: Brill, 2019.

Steiner, Niccolo. *Diego Laínez und Alfonso Salmerón auf dem Konzil von Trient: Ihr Beitrag zur Eucharistie-und Messopferthematik*. Stuttgart: Kohlhammer, 2019.

Storey, Tessa. *Carnal Commerce in Counter-Reformation Rome*. Cambridge: Cambridge University Press, 2008.

Strasser, Ulrike. *Missionary Men in the Early Modern World: German Jesuits and Pacific Journeys*. Amsterdam: Amsterdam University Press, 2020.

Stuczynski, Claude. "Jesuits and Conversos as a 'Tragic Couple': Introductory Remarks." *Journal of Jesuit Studies* 8, no. 2 (2021): 159–72.

Taylor, Scott. *Honor and Violence in Golden Age Spain*. New Haven, CT: Yale University Press, 2008.

Terrien, Jean-Baptiste. *La Mère de Dieu et la mère des hommes: D'après les pères et la théologie*. 4 vols. Paris: P. Lethielleux, 1900–2.

Theisen, Reinold. *Mass Liturgy and the Council of Trent*. Collegeville, MN: St. John's University Press, 1965.

Tubau, Xavier. "Hispanic Conciliarism and the Imperial Politics of Reform on the Eve of Trent." *Renaissance Quarterly* 70, no. 3 (2017): 897–934.

Turchi, Laura. "Adulterio, onere della prova e testimonianza. In margine a un processo correggese di età tridentina." In *Trasgressioni: Seduzione, concubinato, adulterio, bigamia (XIV–XVIII secolo)*, edited by Silvana Seidel Menchi and Diego Quaglioni, 305–50. Bologna: Il Mulino, 2004.

Tutino, Stefania. "Jesuit Accommodation, Dissimulation, Mental Reservation." In *The Oxford Handbook of the Jesuits*, edited by Ines Županov, 216–40. New York: Oxford University Press, 2019.

———. *Uncertainty in Post-Reformation Catholicism: A History of Probabilism*. Oxford: Oxford University Press, 2018.

Tvrtković, Rita. "Our Lady of Victory or Our Lady of Beauty?: The Virgin Mary in Early Modern Dominican and Jesuit Approaches to Islam." *Journal of Jesuit Studies* 7, no. 3 (2020): 403–16.

Twomey, Leslie. *The Serpent and the Rose: The Immaculate Conception and Hispanic Poetry in the Late Medieval* Period. Boston, MA: Brill, 2008.

Uríbarri Bilbao, Gabino. "Del 'sentir y gustar' [Ej 2] a las 'materias teólogas' [*FN* II, 198]: El sentido de una 'dogmática ignaciana.'" In *Dogmática ignaciana: "Buscar y hallar la voluntad divina" [Ej 1]*, edited by Gabino Uríbarri Bilbao, 23–41. Madrid: Comillas, 2018.

Vismara, Paola. "Moral Economy and the Jesuits." *Journal of Jesuit Studies* 5, no. 4 (2018): 610–30.

Visscher, Eva de. "Marian Devotion in the Latin West in the Later Middle Ages." In *Mary: The Complete Resource*, edited by Sarah Jane Boss, 177–201. New York: Oxford University Press, 2007.

Visser, Arnoud. "Irreverent Reading: Martin Luther as Annotator of Erasmus." *Sixteenth Century Journal* 48, no. 1 (2017): 87–109.

Wandel, Palmer. *The Eucharist in the Reformation: Incarnation and Liturgy*. New York: Cambridge University Press, 2006.

Walter, Peter. "Sacraments in the Council of Trent and Sixteenth-Century Catholic Theology." In *The Oxford Handbook of Sacramental Theology*, edited by Hans Boersma and Matthew Levering, 313–328. New York: Oxford University Press, 2015.

White, L. Michael, and G. Anthony Keddie. *Jewish Fictional Letters from Hellenistic Egypt: The Epistle of Aristeas and Related Literature*. Atlanta, GA: SBL Press, 2018.

Wiesner-Hanks, Merry. *Women and Gender in Early Modern Europe*. 3rd ed. New York: Cambridge University Press, 2008.

Wilkinson, Robert. *The Kabbalistic Scholars of the Antwerp Polyglot Bible*. Boston, MA: Brill, 2007.

———. *Orientalism, Aramaic and Kabbalah in the Catholic Reformation: The First Printing of the Syriac New Testament*. Boston, MA: Brill, 2007.

Willis, John. "A Case Study in Early Jesuit Scholarship: Alfonso Salmerón, S.J., and the Study of Sacred Scripture." In *The Jesuit Tradition in Education and Missions: A 450-Year Perspective*, edited by Christopher Chapple, 52–68. Scranton, PA: University of Scranton Press, 1993.

———. "Love Your Enemies: Sixteenth Century Interpretations." PhD diss, University of Chicago, 1989.

Worcester, Thomas. "Jesuit Studies in the Age of a Jesuit Pope." *Renaissance Quarterly* 69, no. 4 (2016): 1401–12.

Wright, A.D. "The Jesuits and the Older Religious Orders in Spain." In *The Mercurian Project: Forming Jesuit Culture, 1573–1580*, edited by Thomas McCoog, 913–44. St. Louis, MO: Institute of Jesuit Sources, 2004.

Zeron, Carlos. "Political Theories and Jesuit Politics." In *The Oxford Handbook of the Jesuits*, edited by Ines Županov, 193–215. New York: Oxford University Press, 2019.

Index

abortion, 249
Acquaviva, Claudio, 7, 12 n.50, 19 n.18, 77 n.140, 78, 242 n.108
Adamites, 246
adultery, 184, 248, 251, 253
Alcalá de Henares, University of, 4, 74, 83, 219
Ambrose, St, 34, 36, 73, 128, 132, 147, 157, 163, 171, 173
Anabaptists, 23 n.35, 33, 170, 209
angels, 36, 49, 62, 94, 101, 103, 130, 134, 137, 143, 149 n.185, 159, 166, 195, 228, 234, 235, 247, 254, 259
anger, 249
Annunciation, 97, 122, 133, 145
Antwerp Bible, 66
Apollonius of Tyana, 22
Aquinas, Thomas, 36, 50, 55, 59, 76, 77–9, 84, 93, 98, 111, 114, 127, 137, 138–9, 154, 157, 159, 164, 165, 167, 169, 173, 207, 227, 248, 255 n.167, 268 n.38, 269, 275, 288
Araldo, Giovan Francesco, 18–19, 225 n.7
Arianism, 95, 220
Arias Montano, Benito, 44, 63, 82
Aristotle, 74, 154, 194, 219, 245, 253
aristocracy, 193, 194, 195, 205, 283
art, 122, 125, 127
assumption, 71, 133, 134, 142–4, 149
Athanasius, St, 28, 73, 275
Augustine, St, 16, 24, 28, 38, 55, 58, 63, 72, 73, 120, 125, 127, 138, 143, 147, 151, 154, 155, 157–8, 159, 163, 171, 173, 207, 227, 238, 245, 246, 248, 251, 253, 258, 281
Augustus, 28, 42, 44, 103
Avignon, 42

banquets, 46–7, 110, 176–77, 226
baptism, 27, 28, 72, 90, 111, 155, 159 n.54, 165, 168, 169–72, 174, 185, 189, 215, 216, 228, 243, 255, 262, 282
Baronius, Caesar, 41, 43

Barradas, Sebastião, 12, 20, 29, 40, 45, 61, 73, 85, 95, 114, 117, 142, 160, 172, 182, 191, 203, 217, 221, 229, 237, 259, 291
Basel, Council of, 139, 205
Beatitudes, 191, 224, 238, 241, 243–7, 250, 252–3, 256
Beda, Noël, 219
Bellarmine, Robert, 1, 8, 77, 158, 193, 203, 265, 293
Benedict, St, 244, 258
Benedict XIV, Pope, 234 n.64
Bernard, St, 73, 100, 105, 123, 130 n.87, 132, 137, 138, 244, 258, 275
Beza, Theodore, 20, 80, 173, 281
Biel, Gabriel, 181, 287 n.122
Bobadilla, Nicholas, 7
Bohemia, 43, 181, 246, 280
Borgia, Francis, 1, 18, 205
Bridget of Sweden, 130, 132, 138
Broët, Paschase, 4, 212 n.155
Bucer, Martin, 21, 80, 111, 155, 162, 169, 183, 197, 210, 254
Bullinger, Heinrich, 21, 148, 173

Caesar, Julius, 39, 112
Cajetan, a.k.a. Tommaso de Vio, 23, 28, 34, 80 n.155, 113, 138, 140, 152, 181, 183, 197, 202–3, 219–22, 227
Calvin, John, 18 n.12, 21, 56, 95, 111, 147, 173, 180, 194–6, 210, 211, 213, 230, 263
Canisius, Peter, 6, 7, 41 n.118, 106 n.94, 117, 123 n.46, 135 n.115, 208 n.126, 221 n.214, 258, 259, 293
Cano, Melchor, 49, 66 n.85, 67, 69, 75 n.131, 80, 81, 222 n.219
Canticle of Canticles, 56–7, 60, 189, 277
canticles, 104, 126, 227–8
capital punishment, 212, 248, 251
Carthusians, 109 n.111, 234, 257
carnival, 234–5

Index

Catarino, Ambrogio, 81, 98, 139 n.136, 158 n.45, 212, 220
Catherine of Siena, 138, 236, 252
Catholic Church, 14, 23, 24, 25, 34, 43, 49, 50, 51, 56, 63, 64 n.75, 186, 228, 238, 257, 267
  as body, 188–9
  as bride, 189
  as building, 190
  as kingdom of God, 191–3
  as mother, 189–90
  as teacher, 189–90
  authority of, 31, 50, 69
  definition of, 187–8
  enemies of, 207–22
  feasts of, 28
  history of, 40–3, 47
  regime of, 13, 193–206
  rites of, 8, 88, 96, 133, 141, 142, 155, 163, 178, 184, 224–8, 231, 233, 241, 279–80, 287
Catholics, 16, 18, 20, 21, 41, 60, 67, 71, 72–3, 80, 83, 96, 110, 114, 142, 145–6, 148, 150, 152, 153, 155, 160, 163, 173, 181–2, 183, 185, 186, 187, 190, 194, 199, 206, 207, 208, 211, 219–22, 223, 225, 238, 239, 264, 279–80, 285
Celibacy, 253–4
Centuries of Magdeburg, 41, 147
Charles V, Holy Roman Emperor, 83, 123 n.44, 186 n.2
charity
  as gift, 229
  as theological virtue, 40 n.115, 51, 57, 68, 92, 94, 100, 129, 131, 150, 153, 154, 161, 162, 165–6, 168, 187, 231, 240, 241, 249, 254, 278, 284, 288
  order of, 207, 218, 219
  sacrament of, 231
chastity, 124, 125, 210, 253, 254 n.160
Chrysostom, John, St 28, 39, 51, 73, 120, 127, 138, 141, 173, 184, 228, 232, 275
Cicero, 22, 24, 30, 39, 43, 46
circumcision, 108, 111, 171–2, 202, 228
civil polity, 13, 186, 193–8, 282, 293
clothing, 4, 113, 246–7, 253, 284, 288

Communion *see* Eucharist
Complutensian Bible, 67
confession *see* Penance
conciliarism, 186, 204, 222
Congruism, 158
consolation, 94, 247
Constance, Council of, 205, 279
Constantine, 42, 201, 214
contemplation, 76, 87–9, 93, 114, 117, 133, 134
contemplative life, 87, 88, 104, 149, 258
Conversos, 216–17
Coster, Francis, 20
Councils, 5, 6 n.23, 9, 10, 13, 49, 50, 61, 64, 71 n.115, 76, 95, 99, 100, 122, 130, 141, 150, 152, 154–5, 156, 161, 165, 167, 170, 171 n.121, 173, 175, 176, 177, 181, 183–4, 185, 190, 200, 204–6, 209, 225, 231, 232, 233, 239, 256, 259, 260, 264, 271, 272, 273, 275, 279, 281, 284, 285–6, 287 n.23, 289, 290, 293
  authority of, 57, 68–9, 81, 139–40, 194–5, 200, 206, 211, 283
  definition of, 204–5
Crockaert, Peter, 193
Cusa, Nicholas of, 54, 80, 111, 181
custom, 45–7, 67, 70, 125, 133, 134, 148, 152, 170, 182, 205, 223–4, 225, 229, 231, 234, 235, 238, 279, 280, 287

Damascene, John, St, 34, 39, 73, 143, 171
David, King, 56, 98, 107, 112, 121, 122, 123, 129, 145, 155, 180, 192, 228, 246
De auxiliis controversy, 156, 158
Decalogue, 34, 174, 213, 224, 228, 238, 243–54, 256, 294
Degen, Jakob (Schegkius), 95
democracy, 193–5
Divine Office, 112 n.128, 163, 226, 227, 229–31, 267 n.35, 269, 270, 286, 287
Dominic, St, 144, 244, 257, 258
Dominicans, 6, 69, 78–9, 135, 139, 156, 158 n.45, 193, 212, 219–20, 222, 265
Doumoulin, Charles, 148
Driedo, John, 49, 63, 66–9, 74 n.128, 80
Druids, 231

Index

ecclesiastical polity, 13, 186, 191, 193–198, 207, 293
Eck, Johann, 67, 138
election, 156–8
Elijah, 47, 113, 119, 143
Erasmus, Desiderius, 11–12, 34, 72, 73, 80, 81, 96, 110, 122, 123, 123, 128, 144, 148, 148, 164, 170 n.114, 172, 175, 183, 219–21, 222, 269 n.44
Étaples, Lefèvre d', 28, 80, 81, 111, 183, 220 n.209
Ethiopia
  language of, 62, 230
  people of, 31, 189
  rites of, 45, 184, 228
Etruscan, 231
Eucharist, 80, 158, 281, 293
  as banquet, 177–8
  as Body of Christ, 188, 199
  as mystery, 89–90, 99–101, 115, 167, 230–2, 243
  as sacrament, 168, 173, 176–82, 185, 231, 292
  as sacrifice, 81, 176–7, 228
  celebration of, 38, 87–8, 108, 132, 133, 134, 173, 178, 179, 184–5, 223, 227, 229, 234 n.65, 235, 270–1, 286, 287
  enemies of, 180–2
  reception of, 143, 145–6, 175–6, 179–80, 232, 255, 262–3, 267 n.35, 279–280, 293
  ritual adornment of, 178, 225–6
Eusebius of Caesarea, 24, 27, 34, 38, 43, 44, 62, 103
Evangelists, 5, 16, 26, 27, 29–35, 43, 44, 65, 99, 119, 128, 132, 143
exegesis, 9, 10, 16, 50, 52, 55, 61, 73, 291

faith
  as virtue, 36, 41, 52, 57, 60, 75, 77–8, 86, 89, 100, 103, 111, 116, 128, 129, 134, 144, 145, 146, 147–8, 155, 159, 163–6, 168, 176, 178, 179, 187, 199, 229, 231, 241–2, 261, 274, 278, 280, 281
  Catholic, 13, 24, 25–6, 48, 49, 53, 68, 77–78, 84, 89, 90, 93, 99, 101, 114, 136, 137, 143, 179, 181, 182, 183 n.208, 188, 189, 190 n.30, 197–8, 199–200, 202, 203, 204, 205, 206, 207, 210, 219, 227, 231, 239, 242, 243, 264, 266, 284, 286, 287, 290
  contrasted with *fiducia*, 164–5
  definition of, 163–5
  mystery of, 100
  role in justification of, 150, 160–1, 163–6
fasting, 68, 161, 184, 233–4, 253, 271
Fathers and Doctors, 32, 231, 260, 272, 291
  as historians, 43, 64, 201
  as mystagogues, 91, 273
  as theological sources, 28, 40, 84, 85, 93, 95, 113, 115, 221, 271, 282, 290
  as witnesses to tradition, 49–50, 62, 67–79, 83, 205, 274, 293
  authority of, 13, 24, 57, 100, 140, 232, 233, 264, 286
  ecclesiology of, 186, 187, 188, 199, 222, 283
  exegesis of, 23, 36, 51, 53, 55, 56, 59, 66, 80, 87, 98, 99, 123, 275, 278, 292
  in the liturgy, 228–9
  Mariology of, 117, 119, 122, 124, 129, 132–3, 136, 137–8, 141, 142–4, 147, 148
  on heretics, 210
  on justification, 153, 154
  on merit, 161–3
  on morals, 288, 289
  on predestination, 157, 159
  on the sacraments, 165, 170–1, 173–4, 177, 183
Ferrara-Florence, Council of, 183, 273
Fisher, John, 67, 80, 138, 172
Fogliani, Francesco, 1
Fomes peccati, 255
Formula of Concord, 166
fornication, 152, 183, 251–3
Francis, St, 244, 257, 258
Franciscans, 84, 111, 125, 155

Gabriel, Angel, 97, 120, 122, 123, 129, 146, 147, 148, 240
General Congregation III, 8
General Congregation V, 19, 216

Gentiles, 25, 34, 35–40, 42, 47, 52, 60, 95, 97, 107, 109, 110, 112, 151 n.4, 177, 179, 187, 189, 199, 207, 214, 216 n.185, 218–19, 231, 234, 240, 243, 246, 252, 272, 282
Gonçalves, Luis, 7
Good Friday, 109–10, 152, 214
"Gospel history," 2, 12, 13, 15, 17, 18, 20, 21–9, 32, 35, 39, 43, 44, 47, 59, 69, 267, 273
grace, 8, 75, 86, 94, 100, 106, 116, 121, 123–4, 127, 129, 130, 131, 133, 134–5, 145, 147, 149, 150–1, 154–5, 156–9, 160–2, 165, 167–8, 169, 171, 174, 176, 185, 187, 189, 207 n.124, 222, 241, 242, 249, 250, 274, 278, 281
Greek
  Church, 93, 160, 183, 184, 223, 225, 273, 279
  language, 4 n.17, 39, 61–4, 65, 144, 161, 164, 199, 204, 229, 230–1, 241
  rites, 45, 133, 141, 184, 228, 232
  text of scripture, 24, 66–7, 81, 96
Gregorian chant, 229, 271
Gregory of Nazianzen, St, 34, 73, 131, 163, 205, 232, 275
Gregory the Great, Pope St, 73, 123, 163, 178–9, 275
Gregory VII, Pope, 201 n.90, 226

Hebrew language, 4 n.17, 36, 61–7, 79, 82–3, 117–18, 144, 161, 164, 176 n.157, 216, 229, 230–1
heresy, 11, 61, 83, 95, 111, 146, 156, 170, 180, 183 n.208, 187, 195, 202–3, 207–13, 218, 232, 264–5, 280, 281 n.100, 283, 284–6, 290
heretics, 23 n.35, 28 n.56, 40, 60, 64 n.75, 76, 77, 80, 142, 149, 175, 187
  attendance at councils of, 205–6, 285–6
  characteristics of, 61, 202–3, 207–213
  disagreements of, 33, 166–7
  influence on Salmerón of, 20–1
  offenses and errors of, 25, 26, 31, 52, 56, 59, 70, 72, 74 n.126, 75 n.133, 78, 81, 95, 100, 105, 107 n.98, 123, 126, 147–8, 153 n.13, 161–2, 173, 180–2, 189, 201, 205, 208–213, 224, 228–9, 232, 233, 234, 236–7, 268, 284–5, 287
  prayers for, 184–5
  punishment of, 197, 198, 200, 211–12
  reconciliation of, 212, 273
  taxonomy of, 208, 218–19, 221
  toleration of, 203, 208, 285
Herod the Great, King, 44, 102, 192
history, 13, 15–16, 21–6, 28, 29–32, 35–7, 40–5, 47–8, 52, 53, 54, 63–5, 67, 69, 75, 84, 86, 95, 103, 105, 111–12, 142, 170, 174, 191, 194, 195, 198, 208, 240, 251 n.147, 256, 257, 259, 266, 273, 285, 290, 291–2
Holy Land, 44–5, 258
Holy Sepulcher, 45
Holy Spirit, 24, 50, 52–3, 56, 58–9, 64–5, 67, 86, 87, 90, 91–2, 95, 96, 104, 119, 126, 144, 160, 171, 173, 174, 188, 191, 192, 208, 225, 227, 241, 244, 247, 256, 286
Homer, 29, 195
hope, 39, 60, 145, 148, 162, 163–5, 168, 189, 213, 228, 241–2
Huguenots, 12, 273, 281
Hussites, 43, 181, 246 n.122

idolatry, 92, 141, 146, 211, 259, 288
"Ignatian Dogmatics," 265–7
Immaculate Conception, 71, 79, 117, 133, 135–42, 149, 293
infidelity, 103, 151, 159, 187
Ingolstadt, University of, 6, 274 n.61
Inquisition, 82, 158 n.45, 212 n.154, 269 n.41
intellect, 51, 91, 92, 115, 164–5, 241, 268–9, 274
Islam, 218–19, 286
Italy, 7, 207, 212, 251, 283, 288 n.129

Jansen (the Elder), Cornelius, 12, 18–20, 27, 29, 40, 50, 61, 72, 73, 80, 85, 94, 114, 117, 141, 160, 172, 182, 191, 203, 217, 221, 237, 291
Jay, Claude, 6

Jerome, St, 24, 27, 33 n.78, 43, 51, 55, 57, 61, 62, 63, 64–6, 73, 102, 118, 123, 173, 202, 210, 221
Jerusalem, 16, 27, 34, 45, 73, 90, 102, 105–6, 177, 188, 190, 191, 206, 213, 229, 234, 246, 258
Jesuits
  as exegetes, 9, 12, 242 n.108
  ecclesiology of, 193 n.48, 198
  education of, 26 n.46, 76 n.138
  enemies of, 81, 222
  history of, 10, 18, 19, 45, 83, 237 n.89, 247 n.123, 250 n.144
  Mariology of, 123 n.46, 135–6, 139 n.138
  masculinity of, 254 n.160
  on *conversos*, 216–17
  on heretics, 208, 212, 233 n.59
  on justification, 156, 158 n.45, 185
  on politics, 196
  prayer of, 88–9, 106 n.94
  Salmerón as, 1, 3–8, 292, 293–94
  Salmerón's view of, 13, 257–64, 290, 291
  theology of, 14, 16, 20, 50, 63, 73 n.125, 76 n.137, 77–9, 84, 255 n.167, 265–90
Jesus Christ, 16–17, 24 n.36, 69, 225, 228, 273 n.56
  as architect, 190
  as bridegroom, 57, 60, 182, 188, 189, 191, 269
  as judge, 163
  as king, 192–96, 283
  as lawgiver, 224, 229, 233, 238–45, 247–54, 256
  as savior, 150, 151–2, 159–60, 161
  as teacher, 51–2, 70, 75, 79
  body of, 56, 100, 112, 113, 145, 175, 176, 180, 186, 188–9, 191, 199, 217, 222, 281
  charity of, 166
  divinity of, 82, 91, 93, 95
  enemies of, 140 n.141, 187, 208–11, 213–15, 217–20, 285
  faith in, 164–65
  historians of, 29, 31, 32–4
  incarnation of, 15, 16, 23, 28, 32, 35–6, 62, 78, 86, 89–90, 96–9, 101, 105, 107, 113, 115, 121, 124, 177, 179, 182, 218, 243, 272
  in history, 15, 35–40, 43
  in the sacraments, 99–101, 167–72, 173–81, 279, 281
  life of, 21–2, 27–8, 44, 45–7, 101–114, 115, 266–7
  merits of, 162, 278
  miracles of, 261–62
  name of, 258
  on tradition, 68, 69
  power of, 205–6, 282
  prayer of, 223
  prophecies of, 25, 42, 54 n.23, 55, 58–60, 65, 234
  relation to Mary, 116–21, 122, 123–4, 125–35, 137, 142, 143, 144–5, 146, 147–8, 149
  relation to Peter, 199, 201–4, 246
  Salmerón's conversations about, 85
  worship of, 225, 227
Jews, 14, 33, 36, 37–8, 44–5, 47, 108, 119, 123, 170–1, 231, 233, 235, 242, 249, 293
  as enemies of the Church, 112, 187, 207, 213–18
  as members of the Church, 189, 199, 230
  carnality of, 104, 105, 217
  exegesis of, 53, 56, 62, 117
  offenses and errors of, 59, 64, 65–6, 82–3, 95, 100, 105, 107, 110, 113, 129, 148, 160–2, 226, 234, 245
  prerogative of, 218
  punishment of, 106, 109, 151 n.4, 213–14, 286
  Salmerón's dealings with, 215–16
  unbelief of, 29, 35, 39, 52, 97, 102, 187, 246
Joan, Pope, 42
Johannine comma, 95–6, 220
John the Baptist, St, 27, 31, 119, 126, 156, 159, 169–70, 172, 173, 174, 179, 254, 266
John the Evangelist, St, 5, 27, 31, 32–3, 35, 43, 90, 91–2, 94–5, 99, 113, 119, 128, 130–1, 143, 165, 221, 236
John III, King of Portugal, 261–2
John VIII, Pope, 42

Joseph, St, 34, 78, 80, 102, 119, 121 n.37, 124–5, 127–8, 131, 182, 268
Josephus, 22, 30, 34, 37, 44, 64, 119
Judas, 31, 60, 100, 109, 159, 180, 208, 209, 210
Julius III, Pope, 212
justification, 13, 150, 152–56, 160–61, 163–66, 172–74, 238, 264, 266, 278–79, 293
Justin Martyr, 34, 38, 39, 65, 119, 120

Kabbalah, 64, 82–3
"Kingdom of God," 169, 186, 191–3
kneeling, 223
Kramp, Igna, 11–12

La Sapienza, University of, 287 n.122
Lactantius, 37, 38
Laínez, Diego, 3, 4, 5–7, 13, 63 n.72, 215, 216, 225, 255 n.167, 257, 260–1, 263, 265, 271–90, 291
Lapide, Cornelius a, 9
Lateran IV, 76, 96, 176, 285
Latin
  Church, 45, 142, 183, 223, 225, 228, 229, 230–2, 233, 273, 287
  language, 3 n.12, 4 n.17, 6, 18, 30, 38, 39, 61–5, 67, 118, 129 n.83, 144, 148, 164, 277
law, 125, 137, 140, 154–5, 192, 203, 214, 219, 230, 238–43, 245, 279
  civil, 183, 195, 208 n.125, 248
  divine, 68, 72, 175, 183, 197, 236, 238–43, 254, 279, 282, 289
  ecclesiastical, 42, 76, 160, 179, 183, 190, 200, 233, 238–43, 279, 289
  gospel, 168, 224, 238–43, 249, 250, 253, 255, 256
  natural, 159, 183, 224, 233, 238–43, 249, 250, 279, 289
  of history, 22
  of Moses, 34–5, 39, 64, 75, 86, 87, 104, 126, 128, 161, 171, 195, 202, 213, 224, 238–43, 244, 247, 250, 251, 252, 253
  of nations, 195, 196
  Roman, 111

Lent, 5, 6, 70, 72, 134 n.111, 233–5, 282 n.101
Letter of Aristeas, 64
liturgy, 13, 118, 133–5, 141, 144, 149, 223, 224–32, 233, 267, 290, 292, 293; *see also* rites
Louis the Pious, Emperor, 273
Loyola, St Ignatius of, 3, 139 n.138, 153 n.14, 262–3
Luther, Martin, 11, 21, 57 n.42, 75, 80, 96, 110, 120 n.28, 122 n.42, 123, 146–8, 152, 160, 164–5, 172, 173, 180, 196, 210–11, 221, 238–9, 254, 263, 280
Lutherans, 33, 41, 56, 95, 110, 153, 166, 194, 206, 264
Lyra, Nicholas of, 28, 34, 53–4, 55, 56, 58–9, 252

Madrid, 2, 19
Magnificat, 126, 132 n.101, 227–8
makeup, 26, 288–9
Maldonado, Juan de, 12, 20, 29, 31, 40, 58, 60, 61, 72, 73, 80, 85, 94, 114, 117, 120, 121 n.29, 141, 160, 172, 182, 191, 203–4, 217, 229, 237, 242 n.108, 259, 291
Marburg Colloquy, 181
Marlorat, Augustin, 12–13, 20–1, 29, 60–1, 72, 73, 85, 95, 114, 118, 160, 172, 191, 204, 217–18, 221, 229, 230, 237, 255 n.164, 291
marriage *see* matrimony
Marsilius of Padua, 201
Mary, Blessed Virgin, 5, 13, 31, 34, 57, 60, 80, 98, 102, 116–49, 156, 169, 172, 236, 266, 273, 291
  Annunciation of, 97, 122–4, 133, 145
  as *coredemptrix*, 117, 129–30
  as "full of grace," 116, 123–4, 129, 134–5, 147
  as model of contemplation, 87, 91, 104, 116, 237
  as "neck," 135, 145
  as "New Eve," 119–21, 129–30
  Assumption of, 71, 133, 134, 142–4, 149
  at the Passion, 128–31
  at the Resurrection, 132
  enemies of, 146–9, 217

Index

Immaculate Conception of, 71, 79, 117, 133, 135–42, 149, 293
 in Islam, 148–9
 in the liturgy, 133–5, 140–1, 227–8, 234
 marriage of, 124–5, 182
 martyrdom of, 127
 motherhood of, 33, 55, 129, 130–1, 132–3
 name of, 144
 on Saturday, 134
 purification of, 104, 126–7
 Salmerón's devotion to, 116, 135
 titles of, 144–5
 types of, 119–22, 130
 virginity of, 36, 78, 118–19
Mary Magdalene, 113, 132
Mass *see* Eucharist
matrimony, 33, 47, 55, 56, 75, 79, 97, 101, 119, 120, 125, 168, 182–4, 197, 210, 232, 251–4
Médici, Catherine de, 273, 280–1
Melanchthon, Philip, 21, 107 n.98, 147, 148, 161, 164, 165, 169
mercenaries, 162
Mercurian, Everard, 7, 82 n.165, 89, 271
mercy, 96, 121, 125, 145, 150, 151–2, 157, 160, 164, 175, 185, 284, 294
merit, 59, 87, 113, 131, 134, 148 n.183, 157–63, 168, 200, 241, 278
method, 12, 16, 17, 25, 26, 28, 31, 49, 50, 69, 73–4, 76, 79–80, 83, 84, 88, 90, 91, 99, 107, 116–17, 122, 136–7, 142, 149, 262, 274, 276, 282, 290, 291–3
Mirandola, Pico della, 82
misery, 111, 254–5
Mohammed, 33, 53, 218–19, 240
monarchy, 35, 42, 83, 104, 107, 111, 123, 191–97, 199–200, 222, 281, 283, 284
Montano, Benito Arias, 44, 63, 82
Morales, Pedro, 9
Morone, Cardinal, 153, 264
Moses, 30, 35, 58, 64, 75, 86, 87, 94, 112, 121, 174, 232, 236, 239, 242, 250, 251, 253
mourning, 110 n.117, 111, 130, 245–7, 253
music, 46, 227, 240
Muslims, 26, 33, 95, 218–19
mystery, 85–115, 167 n.101, 273
 definition of, 85–6
 in the life of Christ, 32, 36, 90, 96–114
 in the life of Mary, 124, 125–33
 in worship, 230–2
 of faith, 100

Nadal, Jerome, 20, 216, 258, 264, 270 n.46
Naples, 3, 6–7, 12 n.50, 13, 18, 19 n.18, 67 n.92, 76 n.138, 88, 123, 183 n.208, 212, 217 n.187, 218 n.199, 221, 225 n.7, 234, 237 n.89, 237 n.90, 271
Nativity, 87, 90, 101–4
Nero, Emperor, 252

obedience, 62, 106, 125, 178, 189, 197–8, 233, 259–60, 268–9, 273, 285
O'Malley, John, 9–10, 26 n.46, 259, 263
Oviedo, Andrés de, 270–1

Paez, Diego, 1
pagans *see* Gentiles
Pagninus, Santes, 34, 62, 63
papacy, 6, 13, 41, 42, 79, 80–1, 136, 138, 139, 141, 156, 179, 186, 194–5, 198–206, 209, 214, 236, 269, 273, 279–80, 282–4
parables, 17, 56, 59, 79–80
Paris, 4, 28 n.57, 65, 74, 83, 96, 110, 138, 139, 193, 219, 258, 283, 287
Passion, 17, 20, 26 n.48, 32, 90, 102, 105, 107–111, 113, 127, 128–31, 134, 148, 177, 178, 201, 234, 281
Passover, 232
Paul, St 2, 17, 32, 43, 51, 56, 59, 68, 69, 71, 75, 78, 81, 86, 91, 105, 119, 120, 137, 147, 148, 154, 161, 163, 164, 168, 182, 187, 190, 195, 207, 226, 228, 229, 235–6, 238, 246, 285
Paul III, Pope, 5
Paul IV, Pope, 5, 214, 226 n.19, 289
Peasants' War, 239
Pelagianism, 138, 150, 156–8, 160–2, 185, 220, 284
Penance, 155, 168, 170, 172–6, 185, 225, 262–3, 265, 266, 267, 270, 278 n.80
Perault, William, 275
Pérez de Ayala, Martín, 49, 71

Pérez de Nueros, Bartolomé, 2, 3 n.11, 19, 25, 87 n.11, 88
Peter, St, 32, 43, 60, 70, 78, 108, 113, 143, 155, 162, 169, 174, 189, 190, 194, 198–204, 206, 220, 221, 246, 266, 282–3
Pharisees, 46, 75, 102, 140, 165, 166, 182, 208, 210, 213, 223, 243
Philip II, King of Spain, 7, 269 n.41
Pigge, Albert, 80, 155
Pius IV, Pope, 280
Pius V, Pope St, 5, 88, 141, 226, 252 n.152
Plato, 36, 75, 238
Poissy, Colloquy of, 281, 284, 287 n.122
Polanco, Juan de, 13, 216, 271
Postel, Guillaume, 54, 83
poverty, 102–3, 171, 207 n.124, 244–5, 246
prayer, 13, 52, 85, 87–9, 107, 114–15, 122, 133–5, 146–7, 148, 158, 166, 179, 184–5, 188, 223, 226–32, 253, 256, 261, 262, 265, 267, 270–1, 275, 287, 293
preaching, 5, 14, 24, 26, 37, 43, 70, 71, 88, 95, 109, 148, 173, 191, 230, 236, 247, 261, 264, 274–8, 286, 288 n.129
presentation, 90, 104–5, 126–7, 133
Protestants, 14, 15 n.2, 16, 21, 41, 47, 48 n.164, 53, 61, 63 n.73, 67–8, 72, 73, 96, 119, 122, 142, 144, 146–9, 150, 153, 155, 160–2, 163, 166–7, 172–3, 180–2, 185, 187, 194, 196, 199, 201, 203, 206, 208–12, 221, 223, 225, 227, 228, 230, 232, 233, 238–9, 254, 256, 260 n.18, 264, 273, 280, 284
predestination, 75, 144, 153, 156–60, 185
prostitution, 248, 251–2
Psalms, 45, 56, 60, 88 n.13, 226, 228–9, 242
Purgatory, 81, 110, 111, 187, 246, 278

Qur'an, 148, 219

Realino, Bernardino, 7–8, 67 n.92
Regensburg Colloquy, 181
religious liberty, 232, 293
Resurrection, 17, 32, 38, 39, 51, 55, 71, 75, 90, 105, 107, 111–14, 132–3, 134, 142–3, 172, 182, 192, 232, 236
Reuchlin, Johann, 82

rhetoric, 25–6, 274, 276–8, 290
Ribadeneyra, Pedro de, 3, 7, 8, 20, 85, 87–8, 116 n.2, 261, 264, 270 n.46, 271, 290
Riccius de Novarella, Anthony, 225
rites, 8, 88, 96, 133, 141, 142, 155, 163, 178, 184, 224–8, 231, 233, 241, 279–80, 287; *see also* liturgy
Roman Canon, 100, 179, 226, 287 n.122
Roman Church, 88, 93, 132, 140–1, 168, 170, 203, 208, 223 n.2, 273, 279, 287
Roman Empire, 28, 37, 42, 44, 111–12, 131, 193, 201
Roman Pontiff, 57, 68, 140, 200, 201, 282
Rome, 4, 5, 6, 19, 30, 42, 43, 60, 70, 103, 105, 107 n.99, 112, 113, 123, 136, 143, 146, 195, 200–1, 203, 214, 215, 226 n.19, 235 n.70, 252, 258, 260, 265, 270 n.48, 287 n.122
Rosary, 226
"Rules for Thinking with the Church," 153, 266, 267, 269
Rupert of Deutz, 73, 93, 132, 173

Sacramentarians, 33
sacraments, 42, 99–101, 150–1, 155, 167–85, 187, 189, 191, 199, 200, 209, 226, 231, 240, 251, 261, 262–4, 266–7, 279–81, 285, 286, 290, 291, 292
  definition of, 168
  number of, 70, 86, 168
salvation, 36, 39, 69, 70, 97, 110, 119, 120, 130, 144, 150, 151, 155, 156–62, 167, 169, 170, 172, 178, 185, 189, 190, 207, 216, 219, 244, 246, 257, 269, 271, 274, 278–81, 284–5, 290, 291–3
Sánchez, Luis, 2
Sanders, Nicholas, 193
Sasbout, Adam, 81
Satan, 22–3, 60, 86, 168, 180, 202, 208, 234, 249 n.132, 259, 285
Scheeben, Matthias, 9, 50 n.2
scholasticism, 11, 63, 72–8, 81, 90, 153, 154–5, 199, 202, 275–6
Senses of Scripture, 49, 51, 53–61, 79–80, 84, 117–18, 119, 142, 220, 274, 276, 291
Sensus fidelium, 140

Septuagint, 36, 63–6, 70, 102 n.77, 117, 187
Sermon on the Mount, 17, 210, 238, 240–1, 243–54, 256
Sibyls, 37–40, 112, 236
Simeon, 104–5, 176
Simon Magus, 201, 208
sin, 34, 60, 86, 98–9, 100, 104, 105, 106, 108, 109, 111, 113, 118, 124, 126, 129, 130, 137–9, 141–2, 147, 151, 152, 154–5, 157, 159, 162, 165, 166, 168, 169, 171, 172–6, 177, 178, 179, 183 n.210, 188, 196, 197, 207, 208–9, 210, 213, 217, 228, 233, 240, 241 n.102, 242, 246, 248–9, 251–3, 254–5, 259, 278, 279, 285, 288–9
Sitz im Leben, 43–6, 47
Society of Jesus *see* Jesuits
Sodomy, 252
Solomon, 56, 192, 277
"Solomon of Naples," 13–14
Soto, Domingo de, 80, 81
Spain, 19, 71 n.115, 73, 123, 125 n.59, 136, 139, 140, 192, 205, 215, 231, 283
Spiritual Exercises, 4, 17 n.9, 108, 109, 132, 258–9, 262–3, 266–7
Suárez, Francisco, 77, 117, 158, 193, 263, 265, 293
suicide, 248–9
Syriac, 24 n.36, 83, 123, 144

Tapper, Ruard, 80, 181
Ten Commandments *see* Decalogue
Tatian, 16
Thales of Miletus, 169
Thomism, 77–9, 84, 155, 167 n.100, 255 n.167, 268 n.38, 293
Titelmans, Francis, 81
Toledo, 4
 Third Council of, 175
Tongues, gift of, 92, 228, 229–31
Torah, 241
Torquemada, Juan de, 80, 139, 202–3, 204
Tostado, Alonso, 58, 60, 80
Tradition, 11, 13, 17, 24, 32, 41, 43, 49–50, 55, 57, 61, 62, 64, 67–72, 73, 77, 84, 85, 114, 122, 144, 168, 170, 171, 183, 190, 191, 199, 206, 225–6, 228, 230, 233, 267, 274–8, 291, 293

Transubstantiation, 100, 180
Tremellius, Immanuel, 216
Trent, Council of, 5, 6 n.23, 9, 10, 50, 61, 64, 68 n.97, 71 n.115, 76, 81, 100, 122, 130, 139, 141, 150, 152, 154–5, 156, 161, 165, 167, 171 n.121, 173, 176, 177, 181, 183–4, 185, 190, 205–6, 212 n.155, 225, 232, 239, 256, 259, 260, 264, 271, 272, 273, 279, 281, 287 n.123, 289, 290
Trinity, 36, 38, 62, 87, 89–90, 91–6, 99, 115, 126, 144, 182, 195, 218, 230, 243, 268, 272
Turks, 215, 219, 246, 273
Tyrannicide, 197–8, 222, 268

Universities, 61, 117, 136, 139–40, 149
Usury, 243, 248, 286, 289

Vatican II, 293
veiling, 108, 235
Vermigli, Peter "Martyr," 281
Vestments, 108, 176, 178, 225, 287
Vienna, 139, 280
Vienne, Council of, 61
Virgil, 25, 236
virginity, 36, 38, 118–19, 122, 124, 145, 210 n.141, 253–4, 256
virtues, 8, 13, 28, 112, 121, 131, 134, 145, 154, 163–7, 168, 185, 190, 237, 268, 275, 277
Vitoria, Francisco de, 66 n.85, 75 n.131, 193
Vulgate, 11, 17, 24 n.36, 61, 63–7, 70, 79, 81, 84, 86, 95, 102, 123, 124, 220

war, 43, 60, 103, 111–12, 136, 200, 250, 285
will, 75, 150, 156, 157, 164–5, 185, 268–9
Wittenberg Colloquy, 181
women, 26, 34, 37–8, 46, 106, 113, 119, 121, 127, 134, 148, 224, 235–8, 246–7, 251, 256, 288
wrath, 109, 247, 249

Xavier, St Francis, 261–2, 263, 290

zeal, 249
Zurkinden, Nikolaus, 56 n.38
Zwingli, Ulrich, 21, 180, 181, 210

www.ingramcontent.com/pod-product-compliance
Lightning Source LLC
Chambersburg PA
CBHW060845090425
24824CB00005B/1207